Home & Garden Television's

COMPLETE
FIX-IT

Home & Garden Television's
COMPLETE
FIX-IT

TIME
LIFE
BOOKS

Alexandria, Virginia

Table of Contents

Introduction

YOUR HOUSE IS AN INTRICATE WEB OF SYSTEMS—plumbing, wiring, heating, appliances. When they're working properly, they work together to make your home a comfortable place to live. When they're not working together, life can get pretty uncomfortable. Think of yourself with no water, no power, and no air conditioning on the hottest day of the year.

Fortunately, things don't all break down at the same time. When your dishwasher stops working, it's not the electrical system that's wrecked, it's not the plumbing system, and it certainly isn't the entire web of systems conspiring against you. It's a leaky fitting, a loose wire, a water pump that's given up the ghost. That's why this book is organized the way it is—system-by-system, project-by-project, and step-by-step.

In fact, the pages of this book are organized pretty much the same way the yellow pages are. If you needed to call a repairman, for example, you'd look to see if the water dripping from the ceiling was from a leaky pipe or a leaky roof. Depending on the answer, you'd call the plumber or the roofer.

But you don't want to call someone to do the repair. You want to do it yourself, and you want to do it right. So instead of calling the plumber or the roofer, you'd flip through this book to the plumbing section or the section on gutters, roofs, and siding. And instead of looking over the plumber's shoulder once he starts working, you get to look over his shoulder before the work starts, before you do it yourself. Read the introduction first—it explains the basics, like how to turn the water off and the tools you need. Look at the troubleshooting chart to get to the heart of the problem. And if you'd like to know more about how things work, read the overview of the entire system, explaining how drains, vents, and supply lines work.

Once you're ready, a table of contents in each section gets you to the right page for the repair

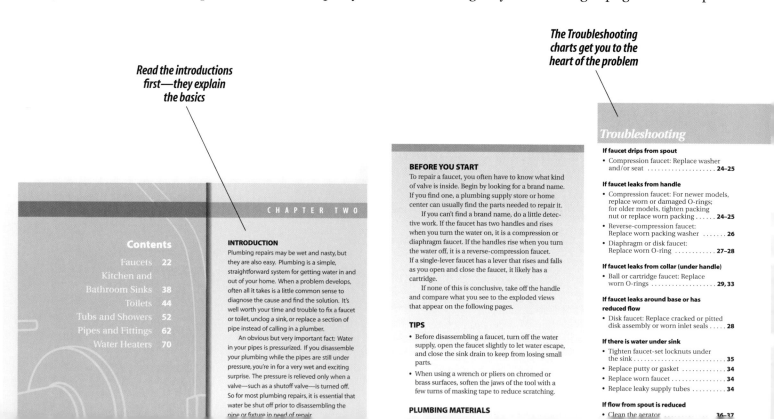

Read the introductions first—they explain the basics

The Troubleshooting charts get you to the heart of the problem

CHAPTER TWO

Contents

INTRODUCTION

Plumbing repairs may be wet and nasty, but they are also easy. Plumbing is a simple, straightforward system for getting water in and out of your home. When a problem develops, often all it takes is a little common sense to diagnose the cause and find the solution. It's well worth your time and trouble to fix a faucet or toilet, unclog a sink, or replace a section of pipe instead of calling in a plumber.

An obvious but very important fact: Water in your pipes is pressurized. If you disassemble your plumbing while the pipes are still under pressure, you're in for a very wet and exciting surprise. The pressure is relieved only when a valve—such as a shutoff valve—is turned off. So for most plumbing repairs, it is essential that water be shut off prior to disassembling the pipe or fixture in need of repair.

BEFORE YOU START

To repair a faucet, you often have to know what kind of valve is inside. Begin by looking for a brand name. If you find one, a plumbing supply store or home center can usually find the parts needed to repair it.

If you can't find a brand name, do a little detective work. If the faucet has two handles and rises when you turn the water on, it is a compression or diaphragm faucet. If the handles rise when you turn the water off, it is a reverse-compression faucet. If a single-lever faucet has a lever that rises and falls as you open and close the faucet, it likely has a cartridge.

If none of this is conclusive, take off the handle and compare what you see to the exploded views that appear on the following pages.

TIPS

- Before disassembling a faucet, turn off the water supply, open the faucet slightly to let water escape, and close the sink drain to keep from losing small parts.
- When using a wrench or pliers on chromed or brass surfaces, soften the jaws of the tool with a few turns of masking tape to reduce scratching.

PLUMBING MATERIALS

Troubleshooting

If faucet drips from spout
- Compression faucet: Replace washer and/or seat **24–25**

If faucet leaks from handle
- Compression faucet: For newer models, replace worn or damaged O-rings; for older models, tighten packing nut or replace worn packing **24–25**
- Reverse-compression faucet: Replace worn packing washer **26**
- Diaphragm or disk faucet: Replace worn O-ring **27–28**

If faucet leaks from collar (under handle)
- Ball or cartridge faucet: Replace worn O-rings **29, 33**

If faucet leaks around base or has reduced flow
- Disk faucet: Replace cracked or pitted disk assembly or worn inlet seals **28**

If there is water under sink
- Tighten faucet-set locknuts under the sink **35**
- Replace putty or gasket **34**
- Replace worn faucet **34**
- Replace leaky supply tubes **34**

If flow from spout is reduced
- Clean the aerator **36–37**

ou're faced with. And there, each repair is explained, step-by-step, using the same techniques pros use. We wrote the directions with the help of expert electricians, plumbers, carpenters, painters, and repairmen. We watched them work, photographed them doing actual repairs, and drew clear, easy-to-follow illustrations based on the photos. What you see is what they do. What you read describes it in detail.

A lot of homeowners are afraid of doing repairs themselves. They look at all the things that can go wrong. They imagine the pipes, plaster, framing, and wiring behind a wall, and they decide it's more than they can handle. But it isn't. Even the most complicated repair is a series of smaller ones. When a leaky pipe damages a wall, you fix the pipe first, then you patch the wall, and then you paint it. A pro knows this, and undertakes the job one piece at a time. A pro, no doubt, is more experienced than the homeowner. And pros have spent time in

school learning about some of the finer points—the building code, Ohm's Law, the live-load limits of deck framing.

If you were designing a house, you might need to know those things. But if you're making a repair, the things you need to know are far more basic. You need to know how to find a stud; how to fasten a wire; how to prep a wall for painting. This book shows you. You may make a lot of repairs before you can make them as quickly as a pro. You will make a lot of repairs before you can make them without having to look up a detail or two. But in the end, that doesn't matter. If you're willing to take your time and follow directions, the job you do will look as good and work as well as that done by a pro. And you'll have the added comfort of knowing what's behind those walls—the studs, the vents, the wires, and pipes—and knowing that whatever the repair, it was done right, and was done by the person to whom the repair mattered most. You.

*Step-by-step instructions
use the same techniques
the pros use*

*Clear, easy-to-follow
illustrations show you
what you will be seeing*

Clearing a Trap and Branch Drain

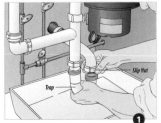

1. Removing the trap

- This is a messy job, so place a pan or pail under the trap. Support the trap with one hand and loosen the slip nuts on each end with adjustable pliers. Pull the trap free (left), and pour out any water. If the trap is blocked up, push out the debris, rinse, and reinstall the trap. Test the drain; if it is still blocked, remove the trap again and move on to the next step.

2. Removing other trap fittings

- Loosen slip nuts to remove any other drain pieces that may be blocked, and clear out any debris. Replace all the rubber compression washers. If any piece is corroded, replace it; better yet, replace all the pieces, because the others may soon rust out as well.

- To remove the trap arm, you may have to use a pipe wrench to loosen the nut that connects it to the pipe in the wall. Apply penetrating oil if the joint is rusted. If it's frozen with mineral deposits, wrap a vinegar-

PLUMBING

Stopping Leaks under a Bathroom Sink

Tighten the lift-rod retaining nut

- If water is leaking around the retaining nut, tighten the nut with pliers or an adjustable wrench (right).

- If leaks continue, remove the retaining nut, slide the pivot rod out, and replace the washer or gasket under the retaining nut.

Tools for Home Repairs

Contents

INTRODUCTION

These days, television home-repair shows and glitzy showrooms have turned many homeowners into tool junkies. Countless basements are filled with expensive tools that have been used only a few times, if at all.

Other homeowners resist buying tools at all, not wanting to waste money on something they will not use very often. As a result, they struggle for hours with a task that would have taken only minutes if they'd had the right tool.

This chapter will help you find the golden mean so that you buy the tools you need, the tools that will save you time and money.

Buying What You Need

Think of tool buying as a two-step process: First, decide which sort of work you will be doing often—plumbing, for example—and buy a basic set of tools so you will be prepared for most jobs. Second, buy or rent specialized tools as the need arises.

If a special tool costs $25 or less and you definitely need it for the job at hand, don't hesitate to buy it. If it costs more, ask yourself: Is it likely I will use the tool again? How much time will it save? Can I rent or borrow it instead of buying it? And, will it ensure a better quality job, as well as making the job go faster?

Choosing The Right Quality

For home repairs, you want tools that perform well, but you don't necessarily need tools designed to endure long years of heavy use. And unless a repair requires exact precision, the best choice may be a mid-priced tool made by a reputable company. Most importantly, the tool should feel comfortable in your hand, and all of its operating parts should move smoothly.

Carpentry Hand Tools

TOOLS FOR MEASURING

Hand tools are inexpensive, so assemble a tool kit that includes most if not all of these tools. All these tools will fit comfortably in a bucket equipped with a tool apron.

25-Foot Tape Measure

A 25-foot tape measure with a 1-inch-wide blade will handle all your measuring needs. The blade's hook slides back and forth slightly, so you get the same measurement whether you are hooking onto something or butting up against it.

To make sure your cuts are at a right angle, use a triangular speed square or a combination square with a sliding blade. Use a carpenter's square, also called a framing square, to mark longer lines.

Check to see whether installations are level (perfectly horizontal) or plumb (perfectly vertical) with a level. A torpedo level comes in handy in tight spots. Check a level for accuracy: Place it on a flat surface, and note the position of the bubble. Flip it over; if the bubble is not in the exact same place, the level is out of whack. Adjust the bubble if possible; or replace the level.

TOOLS FOR CUTTING AND SHAPING

Keep a utility knife in an easily reached tool belt pocket. A retractable model is safer than one with a fixed blade. To make accurate cuts on moldings and small boards, a modestly priced backsaw and miter box will do a serviceable job. For greater precision, buy a metal miter box with adjustable guides, or use a power miter saw (page 12). Choose a general-purpose handsaw to cut larger boards.

To shave the top or bottom of a door, or to shape a board along its length, a plane produces the smoothest results. A 6-inch-long "block plane" handles most jobs. Keep the blade sharp, and take care to set it at just the right depth, so it cuts but does not bind.

A Surform tool is cheaper and easier to use than a plane, but the results are not nearly as smooth. You may choose to use a Surform and then sand thoroughly. Surforms come in a variety of shapes and sizes.

Use a chisel to cut mortises for locksets and door latches or to cut where a saw cannot reach. A 1-inch-wide chisel is the most useful, but sometimes you need a wider or narrower blade, so you may want to purchase a set.

Don't attempt to sand boards smooth using a piece of sandpaper and your hand; the work will be hard and the result will be uneven. Buy a simple sanding block, designed so you can quickly change pieces of sandpaper. Keep sheets of sandpaper or emery cloth on hand, in a variety of grits—80, 100, 120, and 240.

Chisel

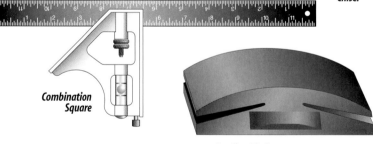

Combination Square

Sanding Block

Block Plane

Torpedo Level

Carpenter's Level

Framing Square

TOOLS FOR FASTENING AND UNFASTENING

Choose a hammer that feels comfortable in your hand. A 16-ounce model with curved claws and a smooth nailing face is the most useful. For heavy demolition work, a 32- or 48-ounce baby sledge (page 18) is essential.

Use a nail set to drive the heads of finishing nails just below the surface. Fill the resulting holes with wood putty, using a putty knife.

A four-way screwdriver is easier to keep track of than separate screwdrivers. Always use the screwdriver tip that fits most tightly into the screw head. Use an adjustable crescent wrench (page 15) to tighten and loosen nuts and bolts.

Clamps hold materials tight while you work on them or until glue dries. Have a few different types on hand.

When pulling things apart, nothing takes the place of a flat pry bar, which can be wedged into tight spots before prying.

A staple gun attaches sheets of tar paper or plastic in a hurry. Along with the gun, have several sizes of staples on hand.

An electronic stud finder will easily find studs or joists hidden behind drywall or plaster, so you won't have to make a lot of exploratory holes that have to be patched and painted.

C-Clamp

Staple Gun

Hammer

WARNING·WEAR SAFETY GOGGLES

Nail Set

Pry Bar

Stud Finder

Basic Tool Kits

CARPENTRY, EXTERIOR WORK, AND FLOORING

Tape measure; square; level; utility knife; backsaw with miter box; plane, chisel, sanding block; hammer; nail set; screwdrivers; putty knife; flat pry bar; staple gun; electronic stud finder; drill; saber saw

PAINTING AND WALL PREPARATION

Drywall-type hand sander; putty knife; several taping knives; hammer, paint scraper; dust mask; trim paintbrush; large paintbrush; paint roller frame with roller sleeve and tray

PLUMBING

Channel-joint pliers; adjustable wrench; screwdrivers; pipe wrench; plunger, auger

ELECTRICAL REPAIRS

Multitester, or voltage tester and continuity tester; receptacle analyzer; multipurpose electrical tool (combination strippers); lineman's pliers, long-nose pliers; rubber-gripped screwdrivers

MECHANICAL WORK

Multitester; multipurpose electrical tool (combination strippers); lineman's pliers; long-nose pliers; rubber-gripped screwdrivers; nut drivers; socket wrench with sockets; wrenches; locking pliers; hex wrenches; wire brush

11

Carpentry Power Tools

DRILL

For most household projects, get a variable-speed, reversible drill with a ⅜-inch chuck (the opening into which you put the drill bits). It should be rated at 3.5 amps or greater, and rev to at least 2,000 rpm.

A cordless drill is mighty handy, freeing you from hassling with cords. Get one that uses at least 12 volts; any less power, and you'll have trouble driving screws. It should come with two rechargeable batteries so you'll always have one ready to use.

Some people prefer a keyless chuck, which allows you to change bits quickly. However, it requires a good deal of hand strength to operate, and may not grab the bit as tightly as you would like. A keyed chuck is slower to use but grabs the bits with authority.

For holes smaller than ⅜ inch in diameter, buy a set of twist drill bits. "Titanium" bits cost more but last longer. A countersink bit reams out the top of a hole so a screw head nestles flush with the surrounding wood. To drill holes in brick or concrete, use a masonry bit.

To drive screws quickly and firmly, you can't beat a drill equipped with a screwdriver bit. If you buy a magnetic sleeve, which holds interchangeable bits, the screw will stick to the bit, allowing you to work with one hand.

SABER SAW

A saber saw cuts more slowly than a circular saw and is not ideal for making long, straight cuts. But it cuts curves with ease, and it makes much less mess than a circular saw.

Choose a saw that pulls at least 3 amps. A cheap saw will have a flimsy baseplate and adjusting mechanism, meaning that the saw will wobble or go out of adjustment as you cut. Look for a thick baseplate and sturdy adjusting knobs.

Saber saw blades break easily, so keep plenty on hand. Have some for fine cutting, some for rougher cutting, and a few for cutting metal.

Saber Saw

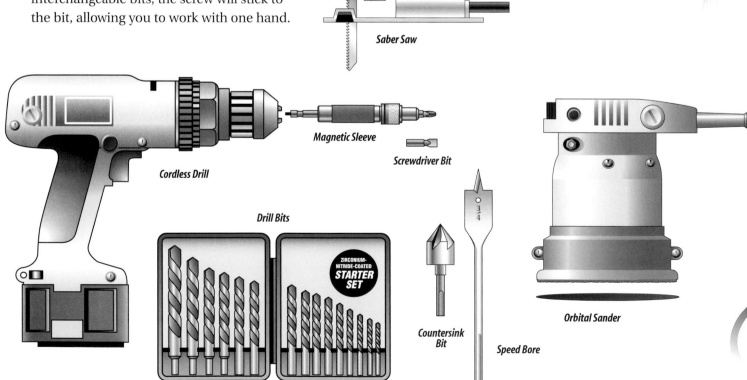

Cordless Drill

Magnetic Sleeve

Screwdriver Bit

Drill Bits

ZIRCONIUM-NITRIDE-COATED STARTER SET

Countersink Bit

Speed Bore

Orbital Sander

CIRCULAR SAW

Use a circular saw for serious cutting of straight lines. The standard size uses a 7¼-inch blade, plenty large for cutting through 2-by lumber. A high-quality saw will use 12 amps or more, and run on ball bearings.

Keep several blades on hand. A carbide-tipped blade with 24 or more teeth per inch will handle most jobs admirably. For very fine cutting, use a plywood blade.

SPECIALIZED POWER TOOLS

These tools may not come in for constant use, but they are indispensable for certain jobs. Some are very expensive, so research your purchases before buying, to get a tool that is powerful enough, easy to operate, and solid enough to produce professional results.

A belt sander smooths wood in a hurry but may gouge the wood if not used carefully. Buy sanding belts of various grits, sized to fit your sander.

For final sanding, use a hand sander or, for quicker results, an orbital sander. (Much the same results can be achieved with a vibrating sander or random-orbit sander.) Choose a model that allows you to change sanding disks easily.

To get into nooks and crannies when stripping or smoothing furniture or woodwork, a detail sander can't be beat. Before buying, check the price of the fitted pieces of sandpaper as well as the tool itself.

If you have demolition work to do, a reciprocating saw can cut your work by more than half. Its blade sneaks into tight spaces and cuts wood or metal with ease. Equipped with a metal-cutting blade, it quickly slices through even thick pipes. Buy blades of several sizes and types.

For quick and precise cutting of wood moldings, as well as standard lumber, you can't beat a power miter saw (also called a chopsaw). Make sure the blade guard slides smoothly so you will be protected when cutting.

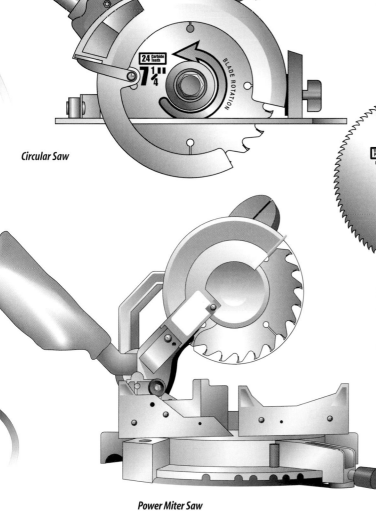

Circular Saw

Power Miter Saw

Detail Sander

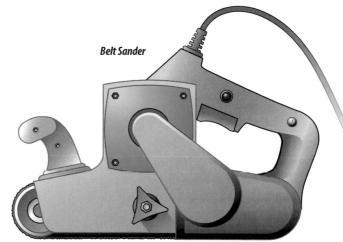

Belt Sander

Painting and Wall-Preparation Tools

TOOLS FOR PATCHING AND SMOOTHING WALLS AND WOODWORK

A narrow putty knife plus 4-, 8-, and 12-inch taping blades will equip you to solve nearly every wall patching and smoothing job. Fill small cracks in walls with a caulking gun.

When working on a ceiling or high up on a wall, stand on a sturdy 6-foot stepladder. Fiberglass ladders remain steady and do not conduct electricity (in case you touch a bare wire).

Don't try to sand walls or ceilings with a power sander or with a small carpenter-type sanding block; you will end up with a wavy surface. For most jobs, a hand-held drywall sander does the trick. For big jobs, get a pole-type drywall sander. Have plenty of 80-grit and 100-grit sandpaper or screen sheets designed to fit in the sander. Protect your lungs from fine joint-compound dust by wearing a dust mask while sanding.

To smooth woodwork in tight places, or to remove alligator-skin paint buildup, use a paint scraper with removable blades.

TOOLS FOR PAINTING

A good brush lays a thick coat of paint, possibly allowing you to finish the job with one coat instead of two; it minimizes brush-stroke marks; and its bristles are anchored securely, so bristles will not come loose. Signs of a good brush include: hardwood handle, bristles that are split at the ends to hold more paint, and a sturdy metal ferrule to hold the bristles.

For most jobs, all you need is a 2½-inch angled brush for tight spaces and a 4-inch straight brush for larger areas. Use natural-bristle brushes for oil paint or finish, and synthetic bristles for latex paint.

Paint most of a wall or ceiling with a paint roller attached to a pole. A professional-quality roller frame rolls smoothly, without binding. The thicker the nap of the roller sleeve, the more paint it will lay down and the more pronounced will be the stipple (little bumps on the painted surface). A roller-cleaning tool scrapes away a surprising amount of paint from a roller.

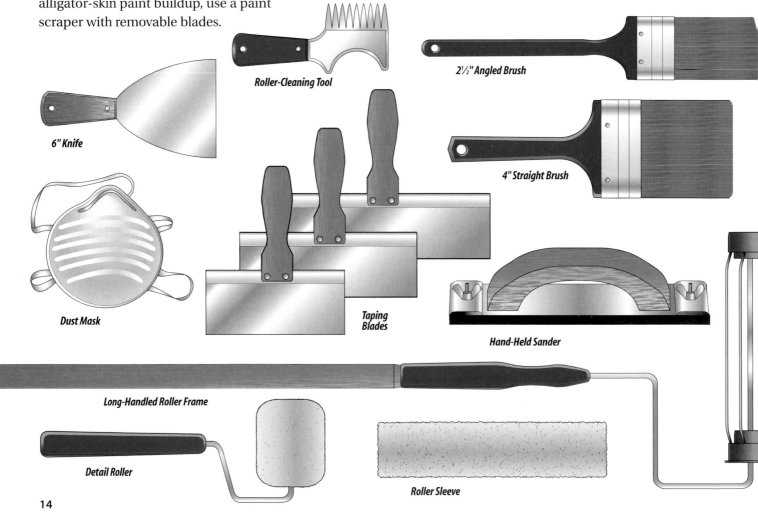

Roller-Cleaning Tool

2½" Angled Brush

6" Knife

4" Straight Brush

Dust Mask

Taping Blades

Hand-Held Sander

Long-Handled Roller Frame

Detail Roller

Roller Sleeve

Plumbing Tools

BASIC REPAIR TOOLS

Most of the unscrewing and fastening required for plumbing repairs can be done with a pair of 12-inch channel-joint pliers. Pay extra for high quality, because you will use this tool often. Occasionally, the going will get tough and you will need a pipe wrench. For removing nuts, use an adjustable crescent wrench or a socket and ratchet (page 17). You'll also need screwdrivers.

To clear out clogs, first use a plunger. The type shown has a flange at the bottom that makes a tight seal in a toilet and can be folded back for sinks. When a plunger fails to do the job, use a hand-crank auger, also called a snake. For clogged toilets, get a special toilet auger.

SPECIAL-DUTY TOOLS

Sometimes a faucet handle pulls out easily after you tap it, and other times you need a faucet puller. When fixing a dripping compression faucet—either in a sink or in a tub—you may need to remove and replace a worn seat; with a seat wrench, you can pull it out easily.

Often it is difficult to reach the nut that holds a faucet to a sink. The only way to get at it is with a basin wrench.

When working with copper or chrome-plated supply tubes, cut them with a tubing cutter and bend them with a tubing bender.

Sometimes the only way to dismantle faulty plumbing is to first cut with a hacksaw. To loosen joints in copper lines, or to thaw frozen pipes, use a propane torch.

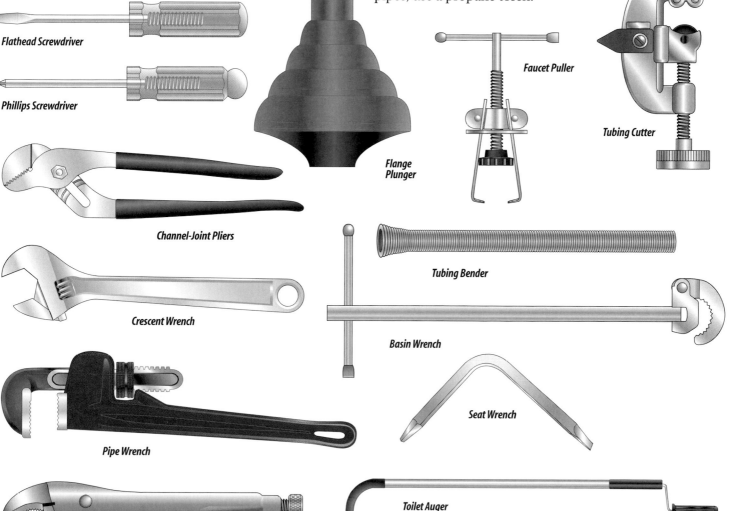

Flathead Screwdriver

Phillips Screwdriver

Channel-Joint Pliers

Crescent Wrench

Pipe Wrench

Locking Pliers

Flange Plunger

Faucet Puller

Tubing Cutter

Tubing Bender

Basin Wrench

Seat Wrench

Toilet Auger

Tools for Electrical Repairs

TESTERS

You can handle most electrical repairs with surprisingly few tools. The most expensive is a multitester. This will test for the presence of power or for continuity—whether or not the wiring or circuitry of a device is broken at any point. Use it for household wiring as well as for testing appliance switches and components. An analog multitester has a dial; a digital tester gives a numerical readout. See page 96 for general instructions on using a multitester, and study the manual that comes with the tester.

If you will be testing household wiring only, and not appliance parts, consider buying two simple tools instead of a multitester: A 4-level voltage tester tells you whether power is present. (Don't use a cheap little neon tester; its bulb easily burns out, so you may think there is no power when there really is—a dangerous situation). Use a continuity tester to see whether the wiring or circuitry of a fixture or device is damaged; if the light comes on, there is continuity.

Even people scared to work with power can use a receptacle analyzer. Just plug it in, and it will tell you whether a receptacle is safely wired.

If your service panel is a fuse box, leave a fuse puller nearby so you can safely remove cartridge-type fuses.

TOOLS FOR STRIPPING AND JOINING WIRES

To save hassle and produce safe electrical connections, buy the right tools for cutting, stripping, and twisting wires. A multipurpose electrical tool, also called combination strippers, will strip insulation without nicking the wire. It also cuts wire and bends it.

Use lineman's pliers to twist wires together. Long-nose (or needlenose) pliers reach into tight spots and bend wires into loops for connecting to terminals. A pair of diagonal-cutting pliers snips wire and cable with ease.

For an extra measure of safety, see that all your tools have rubber grips so you never touch metal while working on wires. Buy a set of rubber-gripped screwdrivers and keep them separate so they will always be on hand for electrical work.

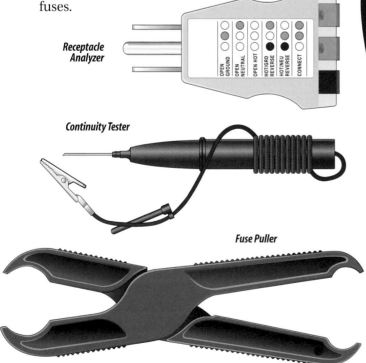

Receptacle Analyzer

OPEN GROUND · OPEN NEUTRAL · OPEN HOT · HOT/GRD REVERSE · HOT/NEU REVERSE · CONNECT

Continuity Tester

Fuse Puller

Lineman's Pliers

Long-Nose Pliers

Diagonal-Cutting Pliers

Cable Cutter · Spade · Spade · Crimper

20 · 18 · 16 · XP · SF · MC

Multipurpose Electrical Tool

Tools for Mechanical Work

WRENCHES AND SOCKETS

When working on appliances or a heating/cooling system, you'll need basic electrical tools (opposite page) as well as mechanical tools.

For a little more than the price of bargain-basement tools, you can buy mechanical tools that are guaranteed for life.

A nut driver fits onto a bolt head and works like a screwdriver. Buy a set with various sizes. A socket wrench has a reversible handle to tighten or loosen nuts and bolts. You may need a set of American and a set of metric sockets. An extension reaches the socket into otherwise inaccessible places.

Combination wrenches have an open-ended wrench at one end and a box-end wrench at the other. Again, you may need both American and metric sizes.

Use locking pliers (page 15) to hold one end of a piece in place while you work on the other end.

Hex wrenches fit the heads of some mechanical bolts, especially setscrews. The long end reaches into tight places; when you insert the short end, you have greater leverage.

TOOLS FOR CLEANING, LUBRICATING, AND DISCHARGING

Often the way to fix a mechanism is to clean it. Have cotton swabs on hand, as well as clean rags. A wire brush quickly removes built-up dirt and rust or flaking paint. Keep it dry or the bristles will rust.

Some motors and pumps need to be oiled, and the oil ports may not be easily reached. Use a flexible-spout oil can that's filled with the oil recommended by the manufacturer.

A multi-headed fin comb straightens bent coil fins.

Make a simple capacitor discharging tool to avoid injury and damage to capacitors. Assemble a screwdriver, two jumper cables, and a 20,000-ohm, 2-watt resistor as shown on page 192.

Wire Brush

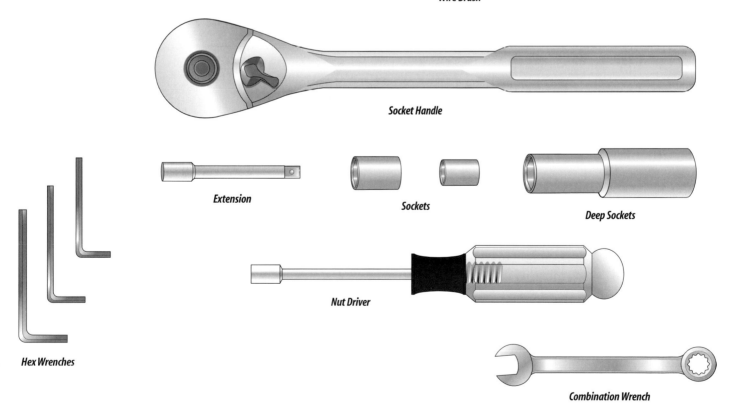

Socket Handle

Extension

Sockets

Deep Sockets

Nut Driver

Hex Wrenches

Combination Wrench

Tools for Exterior Work

MASONRY TOOLS

Use a hammer and cold chisel to chip away mortar for repointing or to remove damaged bricks or blocks. (Rent a power grinding tool if you have a lot of mortar to grind away.)

Mix mortar on a board and smooth the surface of mortar or concrete using a mason's trowel. Fill cavities with mortar, using a pointing trowel. Stuff mortar into joints with a joint filler, and shape the joint with a finishing jointer.

Break up damaged concrete and masonry with a baby sledge or a full-sized sledgehammer and some large prying tools.

TOOLS FOR SIDING AND ROOFING REPAIRS

Use carpentry and painting tools to work on siding, as well as these: Fill cracks and gaps with a caulking gun; have plenty of caulk tubes on hand. A paint scraper with removable blades can take paint off in a hurry as long as the blade is sharp; so keep extra blades around, or use a file to sharpen them. Use a linoleum knife to cut through aluminum siding when you want to remove a section.

Before working on a steep roof, nail down a pair of roof jacks and lay a board on top of them, to provide a stable surface.

Buy or rent an extension ladder that is at least 3 feet longer than the height to which it must reach. It should have a rope-and-pulley system that works smoothly, and it should not sway even when fully extended.

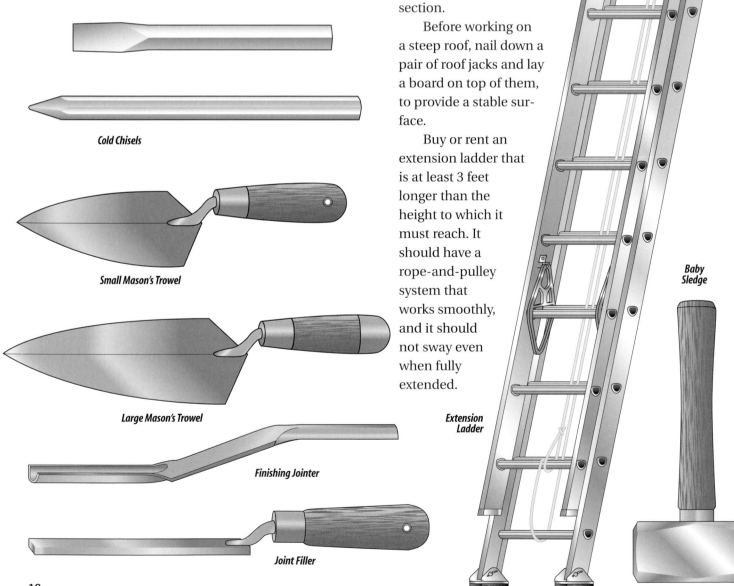

Cold Chisels

Small Mason's Trowel

Large Mason's Trowel

Finishing Jointer

Joint Filler

Extension Ladder

Baby Sledge

Flooring Tools

TILE AND CARPET TOOLS

If grout on a ceramic-tile surface is damaged or hopelessly discolored, remove it using a grout saw. Make a straight cut in ceramic tile with a snap cutter. If you need to cut a curve or a notch, nibble the area away with tile nippers.

Spread tile adhesive using a trowel of the size recommended by the tile manufacturer. For floor tiles, a square-notched trowel lays down plenty of adhesive. A wall-tile trowel has smaller notches. Fill grout joints with a grout float, and clean up using a large sponge.

To stretch carpeting tight, buy or rent a knee-kicker. Insert the teeth into the carpeting, and jam your knee against it to move the carpet forward.

TOOLS FOR WOOD FLOORING AND STAIRS

Use carpentry tools for flooring repairs. Test for the presence of termites by poking an awl into suspect areas; the damage is almost always below the surface.

Rent a floor polisher to buff a wax finish. You can also equip it with a sanding screen to remove varnish and minor imperfections before refinishing the floor.

To refinish a floor, take off the old finish with a drum sander for the main area and an edger for the perimeter and corners. You'll need to buy sanding pads of three different grits, and sand three times to achieve a smooth surface.

Awl

Tile Nippers

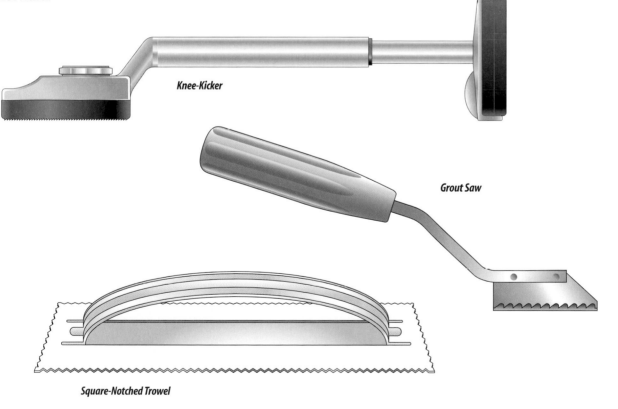

Knee-Kicker

Grout Saw

Square-Notched Trowel

Plumbing

Contents

INTRODUCTION

Plumbing repairs may be wet and nasty, but they are also easy. Plumbing is a simple, straightforward system for getting water in and out of your home. When a problem develops, often all it takes is a little common sense to diagnose the cause and find the solution. It's well worth your time and trouble to fix a faucet or toilet, unclog a sink, or replace a section of pipe instead of calling in a plumber.

An obvious but very important fact: Water in your pipes is pressurized. If you disassemble your plumbing while the pipes are still under pressure, you're in for a very wet and exciting surprise. The pressure is relieved only when a valve—such as a shutoff valve—is turned off. So for most plumbing repairs, it is essential that water be shut off prior to disassembling the pipe or fixture in need of repair.

Always turn the water off at the shutoff valve, then open the faucets at the other end of the plumbing run and let all the water in the pipes run out to relieve the pressure. If you will be fixing a faucet, open that faucet. If you are working on pipes, open a faucet below or on the same level as the pipes.

Every adult in your home should know how to shut off the water to your house in case of emergency.

The main shutoff is usually located inside where a large pipe enters your home through the basement floor or a wall, probably near the water meter. You will see either one large valve (after the meter) or two (one before and one after). On two-valve systems, you can close either valve. You may have to crank a valve handle clockwise for quite a few revolutions before the water shuts off. Some homes have the main shutoff ouside. Many homes have shutoffs both in the house and outside.

Faucets

HOW THEY WORK

Kitchen and bathroom faucets use simple valves to control the flow of water. There are several types of valves—compression, disk, ball, and cartridge are the most common. Faucets also use different configurations of levels and handle to open and close the valves—single-lever

and two-handle faucet are shown below. All faucets are fed from below by hot- and cold-water supply tubes. Shutoff valves make it possible to work on the faucet without interrupting the flow of water to other fixtures in the house.

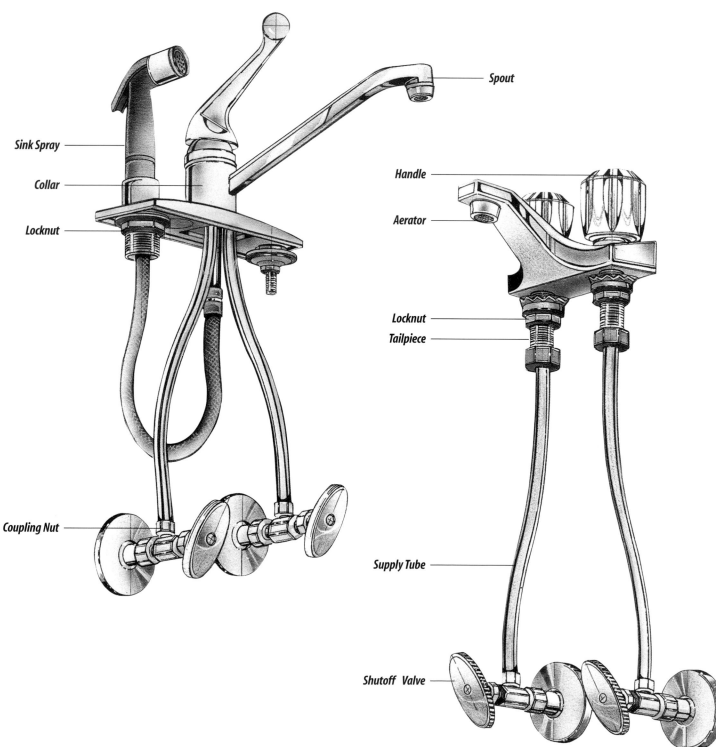

Sink Spray

Collar

Locknut

Coupling Nut

Spout

Handle

Aerator

Locknut

Tailpiece

Supply Tube

Shutoff Valve

BEFORE YOU START

To repair a faucet, you often have to know what kind of valve is inside. Begin by looking for a brand name. If you find one, a plumbing supply store or home center can usually find the parts needed to repair it.

If you can't find a brand name, do a little detective work. If the faucet has two handles and rises when you turn the water on, it is a compression or diaphragm faucet. If the handles rise when you turn the water off, it is a reverse-compression faucet. If a single-lever faucet has a lever that rises and falls as you open and close the faucet, it likely has a cartridge.

If none of this is conclusive, take off the handle and compare what you see to the exploded views that appear on the following pages.

TIPS

- Before disassembling a faucet, turn off the water supply, open the faucet slightly to let water escape, and close the sink drain to keep from losing small parts.

- When using a wrench or pliers on chromed or brass surfaces, soften the jaws of the tool with a few turns of masking tape to reduce scratching.

If faucet drips from spout
- Compression faucet: Replace washer and/or seat **24–25**

If faucet leaks from handle
- Compression faucet: For newer models, replace worn or damaged O-rings; for older models, tighten packing nut or replace worn packing **24–25**
- Reverse-compression faucet: Replace worn packing washer **26**
- Diaphragm or disk faucet: Replace worn O-ring **27–28**

If faucet leaks from collar (under handle)
- Ball or cartridge faucet: Replace worn O-rings **29, 33**

If faucet leaks around base or has reduced flow
- Disk faucet: Replace cracked or pitted disk assembly or worn inlet seals **28**

If there is water under sink
- Tighten faucet-set locknuts under the sink **35**
- Replace putty or gasket **34**
- Replace worn faucet **34**
- Replace leaky supply tubes **34**

If flow from spout is reduced
- Clean the aerator **36–37**

If aerator (at tip of spout) leaks around edge
- Replace washer in aerator **37**

If spray hose leaks or has reduced flow at spray head
- Replace worn O-ring on diverter valve **37**
- Replace worn washer at base of spray head **37**
- Clean diverter valve and spray head . . **37**

Compression Faucets

ANATOMY

In a compression faucet, the spindle moves within the stem and lifts the washer from its seat. This allows water to flow to the spout. As the stem turns in the opposite direction, the washer is pressed tightly against the seat to block the flow of water. Beneath each handle on a compression faucet, you may find a sleeve to separate the stem assembly from the handle.

If the spout leaks, it's most likely a worn or damaged washer, or perhaps a pitted seat. Leaks from the handle indicate problems with the O-ring on newer models (right) or with the packing on older models (opposite).

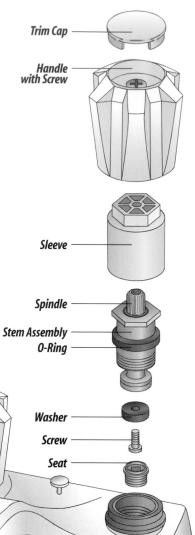

Trim Cap
Handle with Screw
Sleeve
Spindle
Stem Assembly
O-Ring
Washer
Screw
Seat

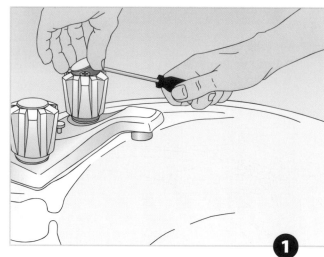

1. Getting at the stem

- Turn off the water supply, then turn the faucet on to reduce water pressure to the faucet. Carefully pry off the trim cap with a knife or small screwdriver (above), and remove the handle screw by turning it counterclockwise. If the faucet has a sleeve, remove it.

- If the handle or the sleeve is stuck, apply penetrating oil and tap gently in several directions. Wrap the handle with a cloth or with tape to protect it, then pull with adjustable pliers until it comes loose; this may take a while. You can also wrap the frozen parts with a cloth dipped in vinegar. Cover the cloth with a plastic bag to prevent the vinegar from evaporating, and let the faucet set overnight. The vinegar slowly dissolves the minerals that cause plumbing parts to freeze together.

2. Replacing the O-ring and washer

- Use an adjustable wrench to remove the locknut. Grasp the spindle with pliers and lift it out.

- To stop leaks around the handle, remove and replace the O-ring. Coat the stem lightly with heat-proof grease before sliding the new O-ring on.

- To stop leaks around the spout, remove the retaining screw and pry out the washer. (If the screw is tight, place the faucet handle on the stem for better leverage.) Install a new washer the exact same size and shape, with the flat side against the stem, and secure it with the screw.

- Screw the stem into the faucet body and tighten it snugly with a wrench. Reinstall the handle, turn on the water, and test the faucet.

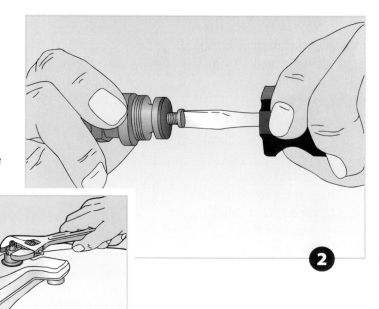

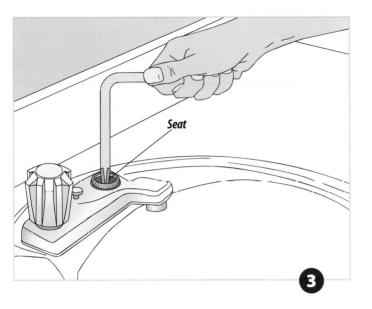

3. Replacing the seat

- If the faucet still leaks at the spout, the seat is probably damaged. Remove the stem as before, and inspect the seat. If the damage is light, you may be able to recondition the seat with a seat reamer. If the damage is heavy, unscrew the seat (left) with a special seat wrench or a hex wrench. If the seat is stuck, apply penetrating oil and wait an hour before trying again. Or put the stem in a plastic bag with a vinegar-soaked rag and let it rest overnight.

- Lift out the old seat. Fit an identical replacement seat into the faucet body by hand or with a pair of long-nose pliers, and tighten.

Older Compression Faucets

ANATOMY

In older-style compression faucets, the stem-and-seat design works much as it does in newer compression faucets, but the faucet relies on packing instead of an O-ring to keep water from leaking around the handle. Packing may be either a rubber or cork washer, graphite-impregnated string, or waxed cord. If the leak is at the handle, first try tightening the packing nut. If that doesn't solve the problem, disassemble and replace the packing.

　　To take apart the faucet, turn off the water supply, pry off the trim cap (if any), and remove the handle screw. Pull off the handle.

　　If the spout drips, replace the washer and perhaps the seat, as for a newer compression faucet (opposite page).

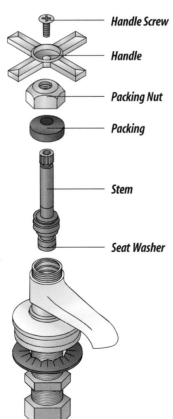

- Handle Screw
- Handle
- Packing Nut
- Packing
- Stem
- Seat Washer

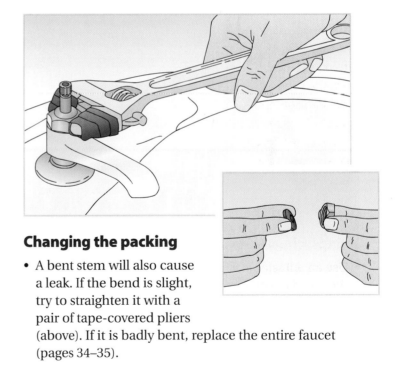

Changing the packing

- A bent stem will also cause a leak. If the bend is slight, try to straighten it with a pair of tape-covered pliers (above). If it is badly bent, replace the entire faucet (pages 34–35).

- Pry off the packing washer or unwind the packing string. Remove the remnants of the old packing, and clean away any mineral deposits with vinegar.

- Insert a new packing washer into the packing nut (inset), or wrap new packing string around the stem several times before replacing the stem and threading the packing nut back on. Do not overtighten. Reassemble the handle and test.

Reverse-Compression Faucets

ANATOMY

When this faucet is turned on, the spindle moves downward to open a space between the washer and the seat, allowing water to flow. (This is the opposite of the way a compression faucet works.) The seat is not designed to be removed in this type of faucet because it is subjected to little wear.

If the spout leaks, remove and replace the seat washer, or replace the entire stem assembly. To stop water from leaking around the handle, remove and replace the washer under the packing nut.

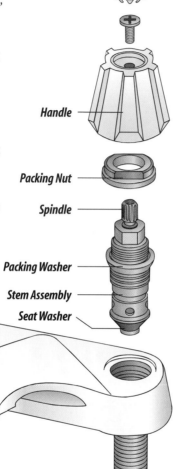

Trim Cap

Handle

Packing Nut

Spindle

Packing Washer

Stem Assembly

Seat Washer

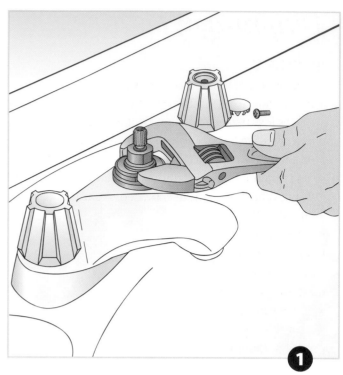

1. Taking apart the faucet

- Turn off the water supply. Open the faucet handle to relieve water pressure.

- Carefully pry off the trim cap with a knife or a small screwdriver, and remove the handle screw. Unscrew the packing nut (above) and lift out the stem assembly.

2. Replacing packing or the seat washer

- To stop water from leaking around the handle, pry out the washer under the packing nut and replace it (right).

- If water drips from the spout, remove the seat washer (inset) by turning the spindle with your hands (or with pliers) to release the cap. Remove and replace the washer with one that fits exactly. Rethread the spindle and washer back onto the stem, and then reassemble the faucet.

- If the spindle has grooves in it, replace the spindle.

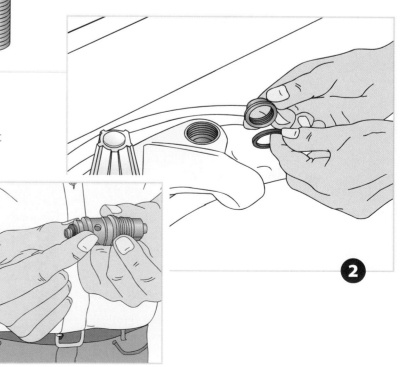

Diaphragm Faucets

ANATOMY

A diaphragm faucet is a type of compression faucet and operates much like its relatives, except that it requires less maintenance. A rubber diaphragm is located on the bottom of the stem. Its edges are in contact with the walls of the valve body, sealing the stem from the water — there's no need for a packing washer. When the handle is turned to shut off the water, the diaphragm presses against the seat inside the valve body and stops the water flow. Some models have a sleeve that supports the handle.

If the handle is loose because the O-ring is stiff or damaged, you don't need to shut off the water when making a repair. Remove the handle and O-ring, coat them lightly with heat-proof grease, and replace the O-ring.

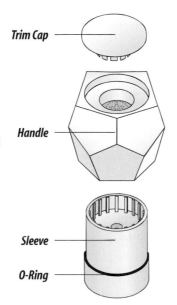

Trim Cap
Handle
Sleeve
O-Ring
Stem Locknut
Stem
Diaphragm

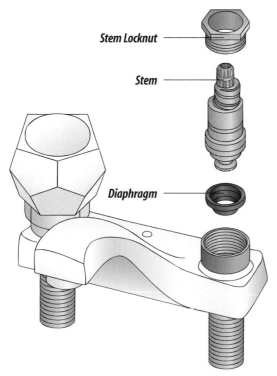

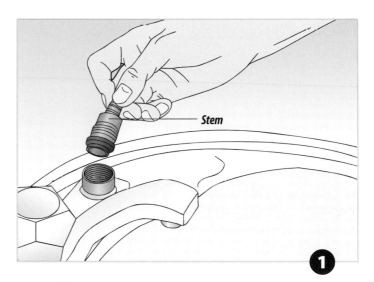

1

1. Getting at the diaphragm

- Turn off the water supply and open the faucet to relieve water pressure. Close or cover the drain so it won't swallow small parts. Remove the handle the same way you would from a compression faucet (pages 24–25).

- If your faucet has a sleeve, lift it off by hand or use pliers. Unscrew the stem locknut (see anatomy) with an adjustable wrench, and lift the stem from the body (above).

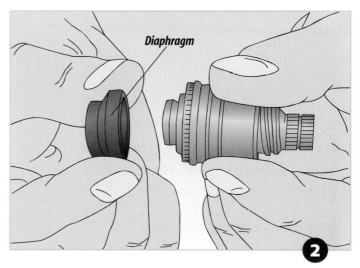

Diaphragm

2

2. Replacing the diaphragm

- Pry off the hat-shaped diaphragm with your fingers (above), then press an exact replacement in its place.
- Insert the stem in the faucet, then tighten the locknut firmly with a wrench. Reinstall the handle and test the faucet.

Disk Faucets

ANATOMY

In a disk-type faucet, a disk assembly takes the place of a stem. As the faucet is opened, the assembly rises and breaks contact with the spring-loaded seat, allowing the water to flow. An O-ring prevents water from leaking around the handle.

A defective disk assembly may cause a leak from the handle or spout. If the assembly is not damaged, a spout leak is the result of a faulty seal. A handle leak points to a worn O-ring. You can replace parts one at a time, but you may choose to replace both the seal and the O-ring to avoid having to dismantle the faucet again soon.

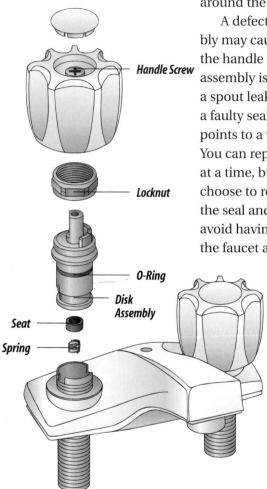

Handle Screw

Locknut

O-Ring

Disk Assembly

Seat

Spring

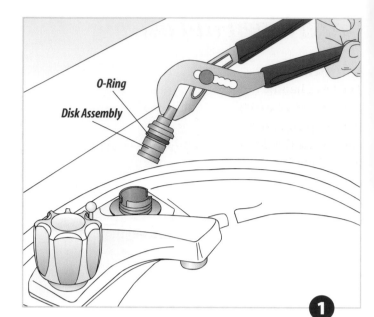

O-Ring

Disk Assembly

1

1. Lifting out the disk assembly

- Turn off the water and open the faucet to relieve water pressure. Close the drain to prevent loss of parts.

- Taking care not to mar the handle, pry off the trim cap with a knife or small screwdriver. Remove the handle screw and pull off the handle.

- Unscrew the locknut with an adjustable wrench, then lift the disk assembly from the faucet body (above). If the assembly is cracked or pitted, buy a new assembly and install it, lining up its slots with those on the faucet body. Tighten the locknut firmly.

2. Servicing the seat and spring

- If the faucet drips from the spout and the disk assembly is not damaged, buy a spring-and-seat repair kit for your make and model of faucet.

- Remove the rubber seat and the spring out of the faucet body with long-nose pliers (right). Note the orientation of the springs; some springs are tapered.

- Replace these parts with new ones from the repair kit. Insert the disk assembly, lining up its slots with the faucet body. Tighten the locknut, reinstall the handle, and test the faucet.

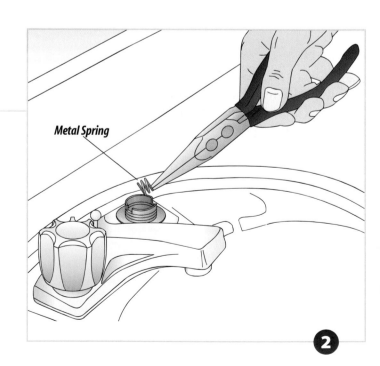

Metal Spring

2

Cartridge Faucets

ANATOMY

The lever handle moves the stem of a cartridge faucet up and down, controlling the flow of water. Rotating the cartridges adjusts the mix of hot and cold water, changing the temperature. O-rings create a watertight seal between the cartridge and the faucet body.

To repair a leaking handle or a dripping spout, replace the O-rings or the entire cartridge (Step 2). To stop leaks coming from the spout collar, replace the spout O-rings (Step 3).

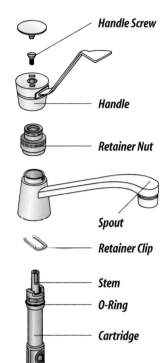

Handle Screw
Handle
Retainer Nut
Spout
Retainer Clip
Stem
O-Ring
Cartridge
O-Ring
Faucet Body
Spout O-Ring

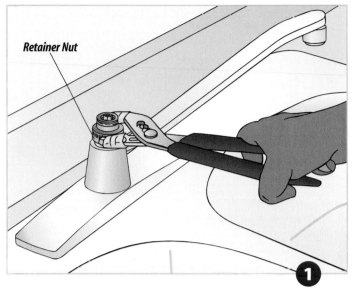

Retainer Nut

1. Removing the handle and retainer nut

- Turn off the water supply, then raise and lower the handle several times to empty the faucet. Close the drain to prevent the loss of small parts.

- Pry off the trim cap with a small screwdriver or knife. Remove the handle screw.

- The faucet handle is held in place by a lip that secures it to the retainer nut. Tilt the handle lever up sharply to unhook it from the nut, and lift the handle free.

- Unscrew the retainer nut with adjustable pliers, and lift off the faucet (above). If the nut will be visible after the handle is put back in place, tape the jaws of the pliers to prevent scratching the nut.

2. Servicing the cartridge

- Locate the U-shaped retainer clip that holds the cartridge in the faucet body. Only the base will be visible. Pull the clip from its slot using long-nose pliers or tweezers (inset). The clip is small and easily lost; put it in a safe place until you need it for reassembly.

- Using taped pliers to avoid scratching the stem, grasp the cartridge stem and lift it out of the faucet body (right).

- If the cartridge is worn or damaged, replace it, being sure to align its ears with the slots in the faucet body. If only the O-rings are worn or cracked, keep the cartridge but replace the rings. Make sure that the new O-rings rest in the correct grooves.

(CONTINUED)

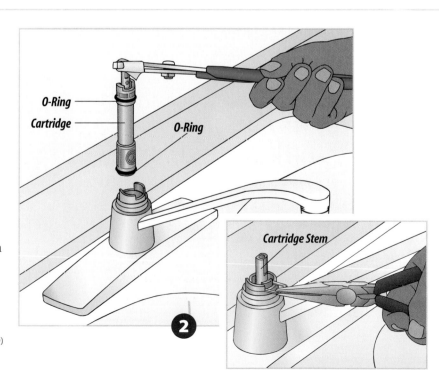

O-Ring
Cartridge
O-Ring
Cartridge Stem

Cartridge Faucets—continued

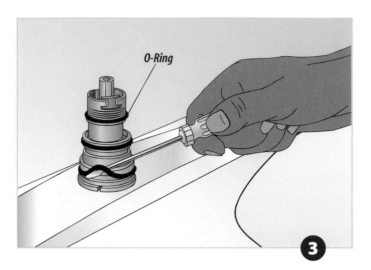

3. Replacing the spout O-rings

- Lift the spout from the faucet body and pry off the cracked or worn O-rings (left). Lubricate new O-rings with heat-proof grease, and roll them into the appropriate grooves.

- Slip the spout back onto the faucet body, then reassemble the faucet. Test the faucet. If the hot and cold water are reversed, disassemble the faucet again and rotate the cartridge stem one half-turn.

Ceramic-Disk Faucets

ANATOMY

A ceramic-disk faucet has two disks. When you lower the lever of a ceramic-disk faucet, the upper disk is positioned at the rear of the lower disk, covering all the inlet ports and preventing water flow. As the lever is raised, the upper disk slides forward, uncovering the hot- and cold-water inlet ports. Pushing the lever side to side adjusts the mix of hot and cold water.

If dirt or debris gets between the two disks, it can reduce their ability to seal the inlet ports. You can fix other leakage problems by replacing the seal on each port, or by replacing the entire cartridge.

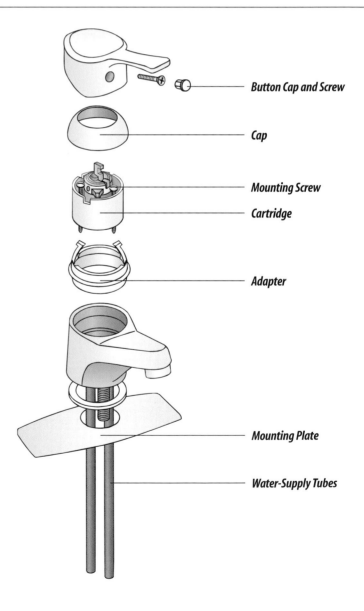

Button Cap and Screw

Cap

Mounting Screw

Cartridge

Adapter

Mounting Plate

Water-Supply Tubes

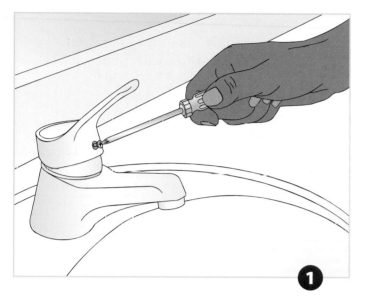

1. Loosening the setscrew

- Turn off the water supply, then drain the faucet by lifting the lever to its highest position. Close the sink drain to prevent the loss of small parts.

- Pry off the button cap, if you find one, with a knife or small screwdriver. Loosen the handle screw (left).

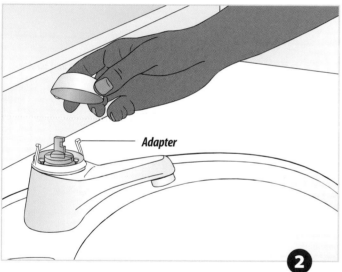

Adapter

2. Freeing the cartridge

- Lift off the handle, exposing the cap and cartridge inside the faucet body.

- Remove the cartridge cap. On some models, gently pry it loose from the adapter (left). On others, unscrew it from the faucet body.

- Loosen the screws or the retainer that holds the cartridge to the faucet body. Lift out the cartridge.

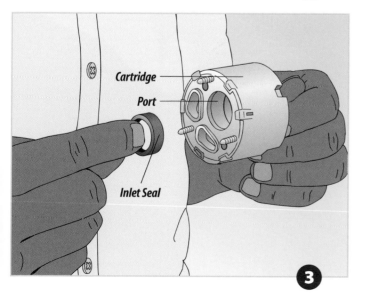

Cartridge

Port

Inlet Seal

3. Repairing the cartridge

- Check to see whether the leak is caused by particles of dirt between the ceramic disks. Clean the inlet ports and the surface of the lower disk inside the faucet.

- If the upper disk is cracked or pitted, buy a replacement cartridge for the same make and model of faucet. Replace any faulty seals (left).

- Position the new cartridge in the faucet body. Check that the ports on the bottom of the cartridge align with those of the faucet body. Screw the cartridge into place. Reinstall the cap and handle, and test the faucet.

Rotating-Ball Faucets

ANATOMY

A rotating-ball faucet relies on the position of the ball to control water flow and temperature. When the faucet is off, the ball depresses spring-loaded seats, closing them. When the faucet is turned on, the ball lifts and allows water to flow through the seats and out of the faucet. Pushing the handle to the left or right allows more hot or cold water to flow through the ports in the ball.

This faucet has no washers, but it does have other parts that will eventually need to be replaced. When it leaks from the handle, you may be able to fix it with Step 1. If the leak persists, the best remedy is to rebuild the faucet, using a repair kit.

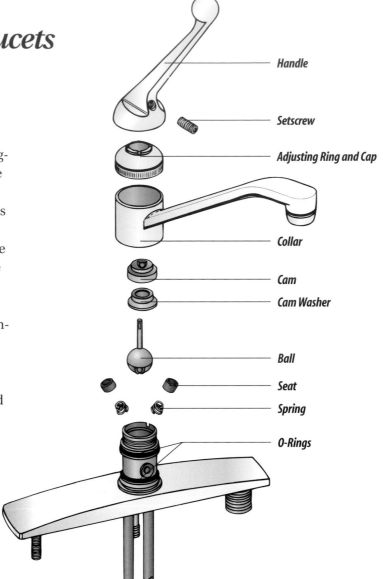

Handle

Setscrew

Adjusting Ring and Cap

Collar

Cam

Cam Washer

Ball

Seat

Spring

O-Rings

1. Tightening the adjusting ring

- Loosen the setscrew under the handle (see anatomy) using a small hex wrench. Lift the handle from the ball lever to expose the adjusting ring.

- Turn the adjusting ring clockwise. Use the edge of an old dinner knife, or a special wrench (right) included in a repair kit. Do not overtighten; the ball should move easily without the handle attached.

- Reinstall the handle, aligning the setscrew with the flat spot on the ball lever (inset), and test the faucet. If the leak persists, go to Step 2.

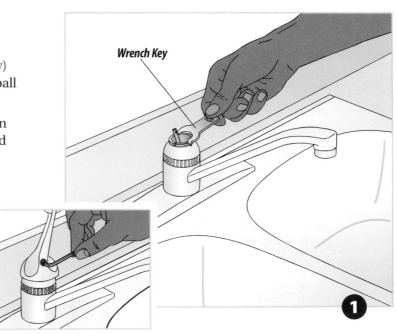

Wrench Key

①

2. Removing the cap

- Turn off the water supply and open the faucet. Close the drain to prevent loss of small parts.
- Unscrew the adjusting ring and cap (right) by hand or with a pair of adjustable pliers that have been taped to protect chrome parts.
- Once the adjusting ring and cap are off, lift off the plastic cam, exposing the cam washer and rotating ball (see anatomy).

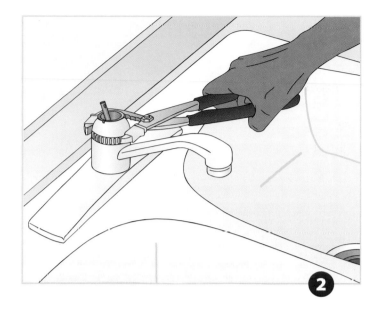

3. Replacing the seats, springs, and ball

- Lift the rotating ball from the faucet body (left). With a small marking pen, mark the right and left side of the ball so you can align it correctly for reassembly.
- With long-nose pliers or the tip of a screwdriver or pencil, remove the rubber seats and metal springs, or the ceramic seats and O-rings, if your faucet has them.
- Replace the old parts with new ones, making sure they are properly seated in the faucet body before you reassemble the faucet.

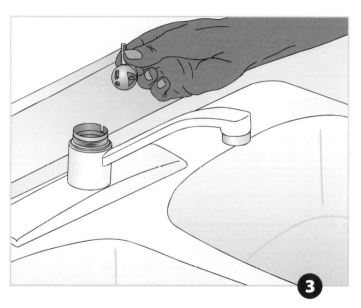

4. Replacing the spout O-rings

- Twist the spout off the faucet body. Pry off the O-rings with a small screwdriver, taking care not to scratch the faucet body.
- Lubricate the new O-rings with heat-proof grease, then roll them into place. Lower the spout straight down over the body (right) and rotate until it rests on the bottom O-ring. Reassemble and test the faucet.

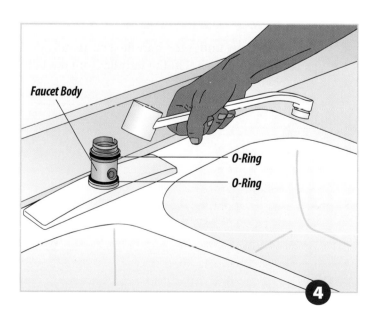

Faucet Body

O-Ring

O-Ring

Replacing a Faucet

1. Removing the supply tubes

Sometimes it's less trouble and not much more expensive to replace a faucet rather than fix it.

- Shut off water to the old faucet and open the faucet to relieve pressure inside it. Use towels to make the work space under the sink as comfortable as possible.

- You will probably have six nuts to loosen. Use a taped adjustable wrench to loosen the coupling nuts at the shutoff valves, and a basin wrench to loosen the coupling nuts and the locknuts attached to the faucet (right).

- If you have rigid supply tubes like those shown at right, remove them very carefully; one wrong twist and they will be kinked beyond repair.

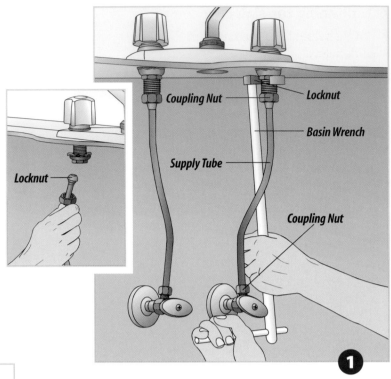

Coupling Nut · Locknut · Basin Wrench · Supply Tube · Locknut · Coupling Nut

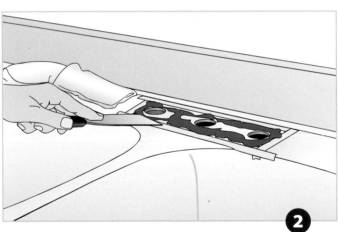

2. Preparing the sink

- Once the supply tubes are removed, remove the locknuts and carefully lift the faucet out.

- Protect the sink with masking tape, then scrape away any old putty with a putty knife (left). Scour off any remaining putty residue, using fine steel wool or a fine abrasive pad.

3. Dropping in the new faucet

- Single-lever and two-handle faucets are available for three-hole bathroom sinks with the outer holes spaced 4 inches apart, and kitchen sinks with 6- or 8-inch spacing.

- Feed the spray hose and supply tubes, if any, through their holes. If you have copper supply tubes like those shown (left), take care not to kink them.

- Some faucets require you to embed the faucet's mounting plate in a continuous rope of plumber's putty; others come with a gasket. Push the faucet into position on the putty, or position the gasket carefully. Many plumbers prefer to use silicone caulk, not putty, and some put a little bead of silicone around the perimeter of the gasket to improve the seal.

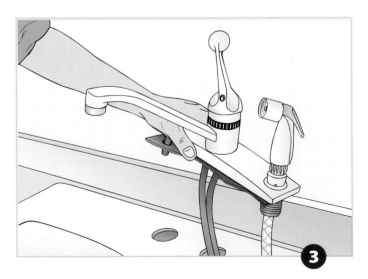

4. Tightening the sink connections

- Have a helper hold the faucet in the correct position above while you work below.

- If your new faucet has locknuts for each tailpiece like that shown (opposite page), just slip the nuts on and tighten with a basin wrench. (Tighten a plastic locknut by hand.)

- For the type shown (right), slip the flange onto the threaded mounting stud or the tailpiece. Thread a locknut onto the stud and tighten it with a basin wrench. Thread a second locknut onto the sprayer hose tailpiece and tighten it in the same way.

- Scrape away excess putty from around the mounting plate. If you used silicone, wipe it up with a vinegar-soaked paper towel before it dries.

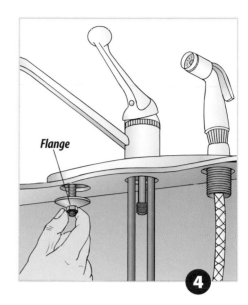

Flange

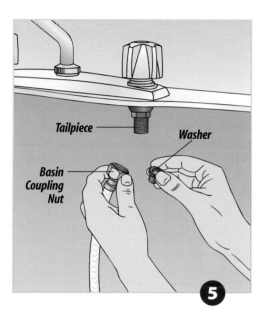

Tailpiece
Washer
Basin Coupling Nut

5. Attaching the supply tubes

- Use a tubing bender to reshape the tubes without kinking them. Use a tubing cutter to make any cuts. Make sure the tubing goes straight into the shutoff valve with no abrupt bends. Slide a top coupling nut, bottom coupling nut, and compression ring onto the tube (below right), slip the tube into the valve, and tighten the bottom nut over the ring. Fit the top of the tube against the faucet tailpiece and tighten the top nut.

- Flexible supply lines are easier to install; just twist on the coupling nuts. Purchase one that will fit your shutoff valve (either ½ or ⅜ inch). At the faucet tailpiece you may need to place a washer in the large coupling nut; some flexible tubes come with washers already installed.

- Turn on the shutoff valves. If there are any leaks, tighten the leaky coupling nut another quarter-turn. Remove the aerator and run water for a minute to flush the lines.

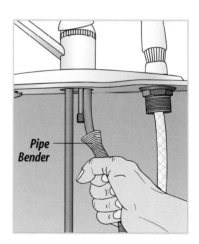

Pipe Bender

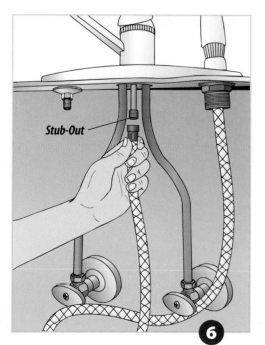

Stub-Out

6. Connecting the hose

- To attach a spray hose, screw its coupling nut onto the stub-out behind the supply tubes (left). Tighten the nut with a basin wrench.

- To check the installation, unscrew the aerator on the faucet and on the sprayer (page 32). Turn on the water, slowly at first, and run it alternately through the faucet and the sprayer. If it leaks, tighten the coupling nuts another quarter-turn.

- Run water full force for a minute to flush the lines, and replace the aerators.

Sink Sprays and Aerators

ANATOMY

Sink spray systems connect to the faucet at a diverter valve, which is often housed within the faucet body. When the faucet is turned on, water in the spray hose keeps the diverter closed so that all the water flows through the spout. When the spray lever is depressed, back pressure is released and the diverter valve pops open, allowing water to flow through the spray head. This pressure balance is easily upset by sand, rust, or grit in the aerators, in the diverter valve, or in the spray shutoff valve.

Both faucet spouts and sprayers have aerators. An aerator mixes air with water to provide a softer flow that is less likely to splash than a non-aerated flow. Like spray nozzles, aerators are prone to disruption by debris. When reassembling an aerator, take care to keep the various seals, screens, and disks in exactly the same order as you removed them.

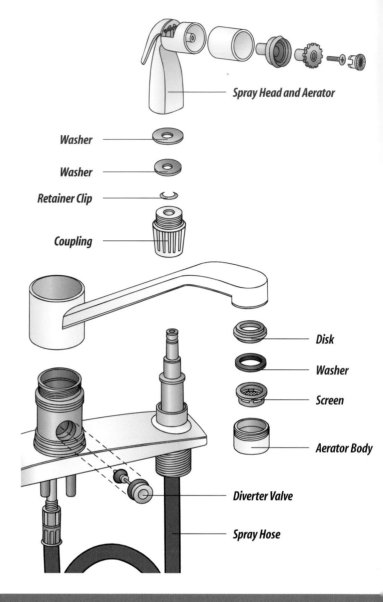

Spray Head and Aerator

Washer

Washer

Retainer Clip

Coupling

Disk

Washer

Screen

Aerator Body

Diverter Valve

Spray Hose

Faucets with Integral Sprayers

One of the newest innovations in kitchen plumbing is a faucet in which sprayer and spout are combined. The spray head sits in the faucet body for normal use, but pulls out to function as a conventional sprayer. With this arrangement, the sink does not require a separate hole for the sprayer.

Installing a new integral-spray faucet involves most of the steps for standard faucets (pages 34–35), with an additional wrinkle: The chrome hose, with a weight slipped over it, must hang down below the faucet with no impediments, so it can freely slide up and down.

Repairing these units calls for the same techniques used on standard faucets and sprayers. As with any kind of faucet, quality varies from one model to another. The best have brass bodies and cartridges. Lesser faucets use more plastic, and tend to be lighter and less durable.

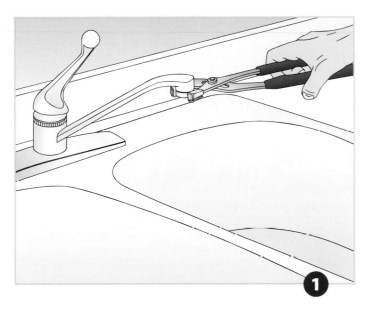

1. Cleaning an aerator

- Using tape-wrapped pliers, unscrew the aerator from the spout (left).

- Disassemble the aerator, taking care to note the exact order of parts. Replace the washer if it is worn or cracked.

- Soak the screen and aerator disks in vinegar for an hour or more, and scrub them with a small brush. Turn on the faucet to flush sediment from the spout.

- Reassemble the aerator and thread the assembly back onto the spout. Tighten it one-quarter turn with pliers.

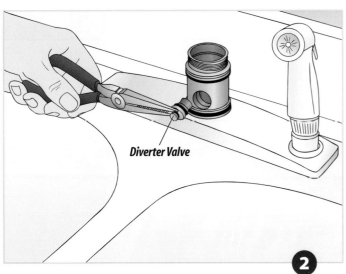

Diverter Valve

2. Servicing the diverter valve

- Turn off the water supply to the faucet and remove the spout (pages 29, 33). Pull out or unscrew the diverter valve, located on the faucet body for a single-lever faucet (left) and under the spout nut on a double-handle faucet.

- If the valve is bent or if the conical washer is loose, buy a new valve. Otherwise, rinse off the valve, pry off the O-ring, and roll a replacement onto the valve.

- Flush the diverter socket with water. Insert the diverter valve, reassemble the faucet, and turn on the water. If leaks persist, clean the spray head (below).

3. Cleaning the spray head

- Pry the screw cover from the nozzle with a knife or small screwdriver. Remove the screw to free the perforated disk, seat, and sleeve. Set these parts aside in the exact order in which you removed them. Buy replacements for all washers.

- To remove mineral deposits, soak the disk and seat in vinegar for at least an hour, then scrub with a small brush (left). Reassemble the sprayer.

Kitchen and Bathroom Sinks

HOW THEY WORK

Sinks come in a variety of shapes and sizes, but the plumbing hookups are all the same. Many modern kitchen sinks are equipped with a garbage disposal, through which water drains from the sink and from the dishwasher, if there is one.

In double-sink installations like the one shown (below), a drainpipe from the second sink joins the garbage disposal drainpipe at an intersection called a continuous waste "T." From there, waste water passes through a trap (which blocks sewer gas from entering the house) and into a trap arm leading to the drainpipe in the wall. Some plumbing codes require that a dishwasher be fitted with an air gap—a simple device mounted next to the faucet that prevents back-siphoning of wastewater into the water supply.

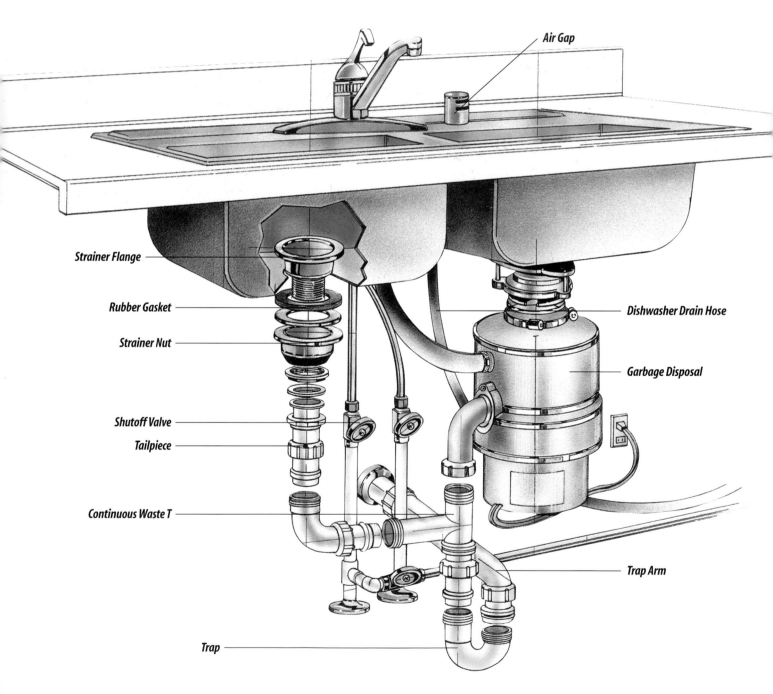

Air Gap

Strainer Flange

Rubber Gasket

Strainer Nut

Shutoff Valve

Tailpiece

Continuous Waste T

Trap

Dishwasher Drain Hose

Garbage Disposal

Trap Arm

BEFORE YOU START

Clogs and leaks are sometimes easily fixed with a plunger or a pair of pliers. At other times, you may have an all-day job on your hands.

DEALING WITH CLOGS

You can avoid most clogs by placing strainer baskets in the drain openings. Also, pour grease and coffee grounds into the trash instead of down the drain. If your drain does become stopped, be aware that chemical drain openers may free up a sluggish drain, but they should not be poured down a drain that is completely stopped up. You must clear the clog mechanically.

Plunging (below right) clears up many clogs. For more stubborn problems, disassemble the drain plumbing and clean out the trap. If that does not work, you may have to employ an auger or "snake" (page 40).

STOPPING LEAKS

Page 41 shows how to perform repairs for leaks under the sink. Many leaks dry up if you simply tighten the slip nuts on the drain assembly. If that doesn't work, remove the section of the trap nearest the leak and install a new washer. If a part is corroded, replace it.

Clearing Clogs with a Plunger

Before you plunge, seal off the rubber dishwasher drain hose that leads to the garbage disposal, if you have one, by pinching it with a C-clamp and two pieces of wood. Lift out the sink basket and clear any debris caught in the drain opening. Fill the sink with water to cover the plunger cup. On a double sink, pack rags wrapped in plastic into the other drain opening, or have a helper hold the strainer in place.

Set the plunger squarely over the drain and pump vigorously up and down at least a dozen times, then pull away sharply. Repeat if necessary.

Air Gap

Clearing a Trap and Branch Drain

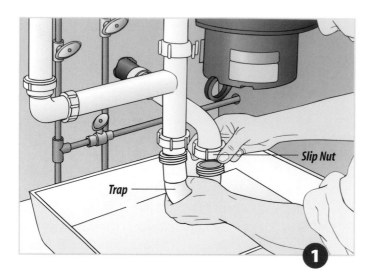

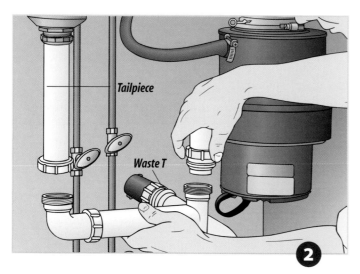

1. Removing the trap

- This is a messy job, so place a pan or pail under the trap. Support the trap with one hand and loosen the slip nuts on each end with adjustable pliers. Pull the trap free (left), and pour out any water. If the trap is blocked up, push out the debris, rinse, and reinstall the trap. Test the drain; if it is still blocked, remove the trap again and move on to the next step.

2. Removing other trap fittings

- Loosen slip nuts to remove any other drain pieces that may be blocked, and clear out any debris. Replace all the rubber compression washers. If any piece is corroded, replace it; better yet, replace all the pieces, because the others may soon rust out as well.

- To remove the trap arm, you may have to use a pipe wrench to loosen the nut that connects it to the pipe in the wall. Apply penetrating oil if the joint is rusted. If it's frozen with mineral deposits, wrap a vinegar-soaked rag around the joint and wrap a piece of plastic wrap around that. Let this sit overnight to dissolve the minerals.

3. Augering the branch drain

- If none of the drain pipes were clogged, the blockage is inside the wall. Purchase an inexpensive hand-crank auger or plumber's "snake."

- Probe into the branch drain carefully; ramming the auger too vigorously can loosen fittings and damage pipes inside the wall.

- Loosen the setscrew on the auger, and push the auger cable in as far as it will go. Tighten the setscrew, and push as you crank the handle clockwise. Cranking or turning the snake usually helps the cable snake its way around a bend so you can push it forward again.

- Keep working until you meet a clog. The auger may push a clog into a larger pipe, or it may grab a clog, so you can pull it out. If hand-augering does not clear the clog, call in a pro.

Fixing a Leaky Drain or Strainer

1. Removing the drain assembly

Leaks develop when the drain assembly wears through or when the putty that seals the drainpipe in the sink dries out.

- Remove the tailpiece. You may have to loosen or remove other trap fittings as well (page 40).

- Have a helper wedge the handles of a screwdriver into the drainpipe from above and hold it while you loosen the locknut below, using large adjustable pliers or a pipe wrench (right). If the drainpipe is held by a plastic retainer, remove its screws and twist the retainer a quarter-turn to unlock the pipe.

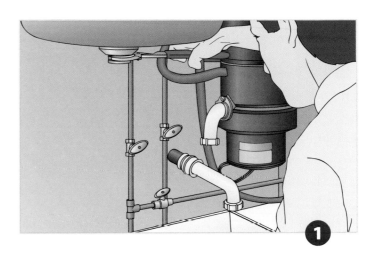

2. Reinstalling the drain assembly

- Scrape the putty from the drain hole, and from the drainpipe if you plan to reuse it. Apply a ½-inch-thick rope of plumber's putty or silicone caulk under the lip of the drainpipe. (Some drain assemblies come with adhesive-coated rubber gaskets and need no putty or caulk.)

- Lower the drainpipe into the drain opening from above. From underneath the sink, slip the rubber and metal washers over the neck of the pipe (left), then secure the locknut or retainer and screws. From above, scrape away excess putty. Reinstall the other drain fittings.

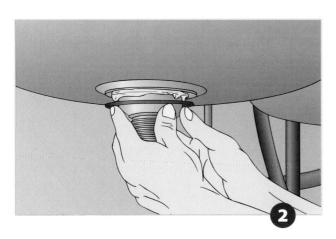

Stopping Leaks from a Garbage Disposal

- Unplug the garbage disposal and place a bucket under it. Loosen the slip nut at the end of the disposal's drainpipe. You may need to loosen and remove other trap fittings as well (page 40).

- Support the disposal with one hand or, if it's large and heavy, place a number of wood scraps beneath it to support it. Turn the lower support ring to unlock it from the mounting assembly, and then lower the disposal. You may have to use a screwdriver to turn the support ring.

- Remove the screws on the mounting assembly and push up on the mounting flange. Pop the snap ring out of the flange with a screwdriver. The mounting flange and gasket will now come out.

- Replace any cracked putty or worn gaskets. Reinstall the mounting flange and snap ring and tighten the retaining screws, then lift the garbage disposal and support ring back into place.

Support Ring

Disposal Drainpipe

Adjusting a Bathroom Sink Stopper

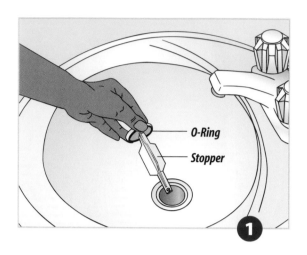

O-Ring

Stopper

1. Removing the pop-up stopper

- Pull the stopper from the drain (left). If necessary, twist the stopper to free it from the pivot rod, or unscrew the retaining nut on the back of the drainpipe (below) and pull out the pivot rod.
- Clean the stopper and replace the O-ring.
- Reinsert the stopper, reconnect the pivot rod if necessary, and tighten the retaining nut. Fill the basin. If the stopper does not hold water in the basin, adjust the lift mechanism (Steps 2 and 3).

2. Adjusting the pivot rod

- First, try moving the metal spring clip along the pivot rod. Pinch the spring and move it in along the rod, toward the drainpipe, to seat the stopper more firmly. If that doesn't work, slip one side off the end of the pivot rod (right). Slide the end of the pivot rod out of its hole in the clevis strap. Move the rod up one hole and reinsert the rod through the strap.
- Reinstall the metal spring clip and test the lift assembly. Adjust the position of the pivot rod in the strap and the spring clip on the pivot rod as needed until the stopper seats properly.

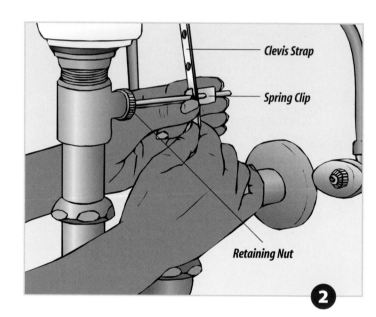

Clevis Strap

Spring Clip

Retaining Nut

3. Adjusting the lift rod

- If the stopper still doesn't seal the drain, the stopper may not be going down all the way. If that is the case, loosen the clevis screw with pliers, then unscrew it by hand (right). Push the clevis strap up the lift rod to shorten the assembly.
- Tighten the clevis screw and test, readjusting if necessary. If water continues to leak out of the sink, buy a new drain assembly and install it (page 41).

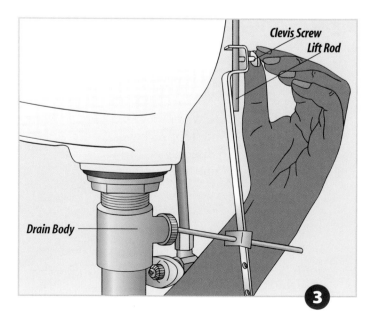

Clevis Screw

Lift Rod

Drain Body

Stopping Leaks under a Bathroom Sink

Tighten the lift-rod retaining nut

- If water is leaking around the retaining nut, tighten the nut with pliers or an adjustable wrench (right).

- If leaks continue, remove the retaining nut, slide the pivot rod out, and replace the washer or gasket under the retaining nut.

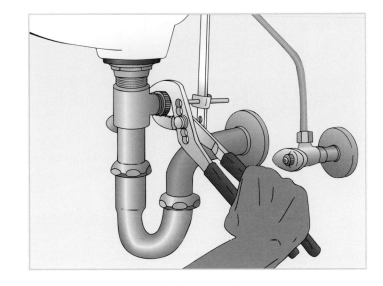

Tighten the tailpiece

- If water is leaking around the tailpiece, loosen the slip nut at the bottom of the tailpiece.

- Tighten the tailpiece by hand (right).

- Using a wrench, tighten the slip nut at the bottom of the tailpiece.

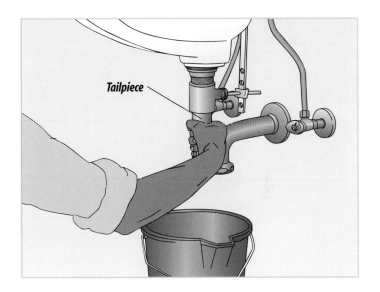

Tailpiece

Repack the drain flange

- A worn washer or cracked putty under the drain flange may allow water to seep down below the sink. Remove the stopper (pages 40–41) and drainpipe, and disconnect the lift rod (page 42). Free the drainpipe from the sink.

- Press a thin rope of plumber's putty or apply a bead of silicone caulk under the lip of the flange (right).

- Reinstall the parts and wipe away any excess putty or caulk around the flange. If leaks persist, tighten the guilty connections a quarter-turn.

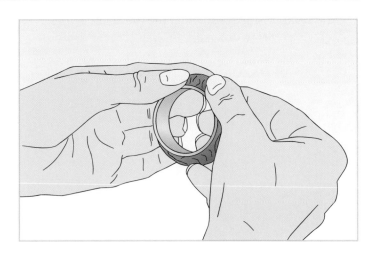

Toilets

HOW THEY WORK

Two mechanisms operate simultaneously when a toilet is flushed: a flush valve and a fill valve (often called a ball cock). The illustration (below) shows a flapper-style flush valve and a ball cock with a float ball. Page 51 shows two other common styles.

Tripping the flush handle raises the flush valve, releasing water from the tank to the bowl. The rushing water creates a siphoning action in the bowl that forces wastewater down the drain. As the tank empties, the falling water level lowers a float. The float is connected to the ball cock by a rod. As the float falls, it opens the fill valve inside the ball cock. Meanwhile, the flush valve closes itself after the water drains from the tank. With the fill valve open and the flush valve closed, the tank fills and the rising water lifts the float. When it reaches a preset level, the float closes the fill valve in the ball cock. At that point, the tank should be full and ready to flush again.

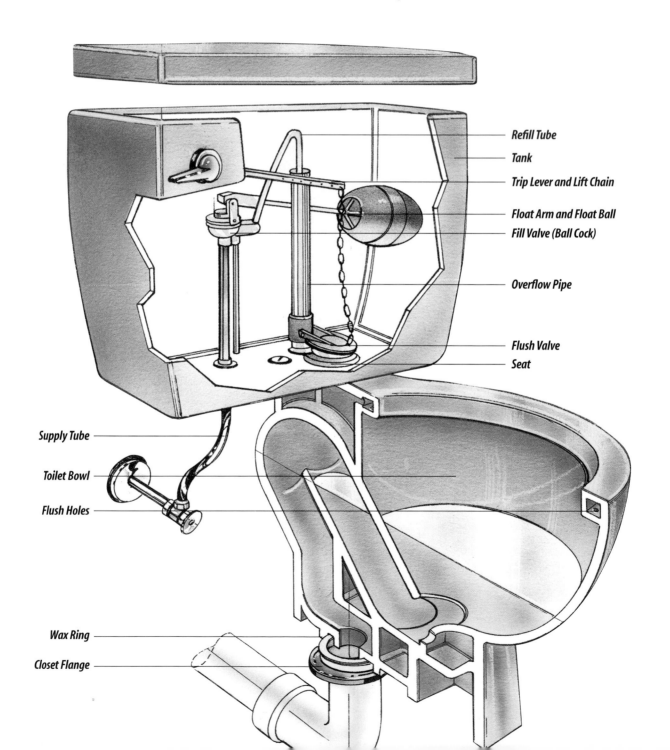

- Refill Tube
- Tank
- Trip Lever and Lift Chain
- Float Arm and Float Ball
- Fill Valve (Ball Cock)
- Overflow Pipe
- Flush Valve
- Seat
- Supply Tube
- Toilet Bowl
- Flush Holes
- Wax Ring
- Closet Flange

BEFORE YOU START

The toilet is the most heavily used plumbing fixture in the house. While the porcelain bowl and tank will last indefinitely, the working parts inside will not.

CHECK THE WATER LEVEL

A toilet tank's water level should be ½ to 1 inch below the top of the overflow pipe. A low water level results in an incomplete flush. If the level is too high, the water will drain into the overflow pipe and the toilet will run continuously.

CHOOSING PARTS

In some cases, the only lasting solution to flushing problems is to replace the ball cock or flush valve. Usually, you can substitute parts made of plastic for the brass variety. Plastic is less expensive and does not corrode as brass does.

TIPS

- When working on a toilet, take care to place the tank cover in a safe place; porcelain cracks easily.

- Have plenty of rags, a sponge, and a pail nearby to catch water or clean up spills.

Replacing a Toilet Seat

- Toilet seat bolts may be hidden under plastic caps (right). Pry open each cap. Hold each bolt with a screwdriver, and unscrew the nut with adjustable pliers. Some nuts have plastic "wings" that make pliers unnecessary.

- If the bolts are corroded, apply penetrating oil, wait overnight, and then try again. If the bolts still will not budge, apply tape to the toilet rim to protect it and then cut through them with a hacksaw.

- Replace the seat and bolts, then hand-tighten the nuts. Align the seat with the bowl and tighten the nuts one-quarter turn.

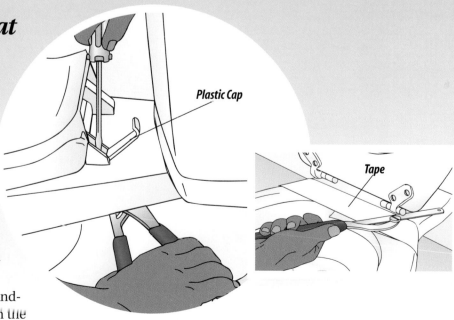

Plastic Cap

Tape

Unclogging the Toilet

1. Using a plunger

A flange-type plunger fits into the toilet drain and exerts more pressure than an old-style cup plunger.

- If the bowl is full or overflowing, put on rubber gloves and use a plastic container to bail out half the water. If the bowl is empty, add water to half-full.

- Place the plunger over the drain opening (the larger one, if there are two). Keeping the plunger below water level and firmly in place (right), pump up and down rapidly about eight times. If the water rushes away, you may have removed the blockage.

- Use the plunger again to be sure the water is draining freely. Then pour in a pail of water and plunge one more time before flushing the toilet to refill the bowl.

- If the blockage remains after plunging, use a closet auger. You can also use a drain auger or "snake," but the closet auger is much easier (Step 2).

Plunger

1

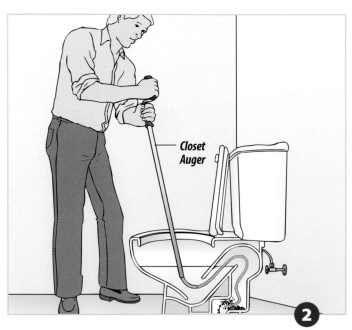

Closet Auger

2

2. Using a closet auger

- Determine the direction in which to guide the auger. Some toilets are rear-draining (left), while others are front-draining.

- Feed the curved tip of the auger into the drain opening. Crank clockwise and push with moderate pressure until the auger tightens up, then crank in the other direction. When the auger tightens again, reverse the direction until the auger is as far in the drain as it will go.

- Pull the handle up and out to remove the auger. If it jams, push gently, then pull again. You may have to turn the handle as you pull up.

- Augering may either push the blockage through or pull gunk up into the bowl. After augering, remove any large pieces, wearing rubber gloves. Finish with a plunger (Step 1) to ensure that the drain runs freely.

Adjusting the Water Level

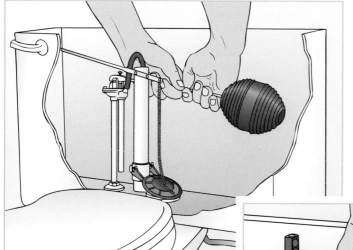

Bending a float arm

- To lower the water level, gently lift the float arm (left) and bend it down slightly to keep the water level ½ to 1 inch below the top of the overflow pipe.

- To raise the water level, bend the float arm to raise the float ball, making sure that the ball does not rub the tank.

- To raise or lower a plastic float arm, turn the knob at the ball cock.

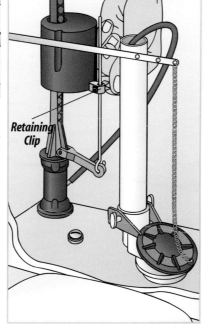

Retaining Clip

Raising or lowering a float cup

Pinch the retaining clip (right) and slide the float cup up or down along the ball-cock assembly. Lower the water level by lowering the float cup; raise the water level by raising the cup. Make the adjustment in increments, moving the cup no more than ½ inch until the water level is where you want it.

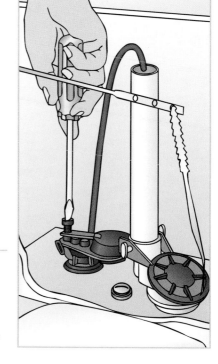

Regulating a metered fill valve

On this variety of flush valve, the water level is raised or lowered by turning the adjustment screw (above). Lower the water level by turning the screw counterclockwise; raise the level by turning it clockwise. Make the adjustment in small increments, turning the screw one-half turn each time. Test the toilet by flushing, and readjust the water level if necessary.

Servicing the Flush Assembly

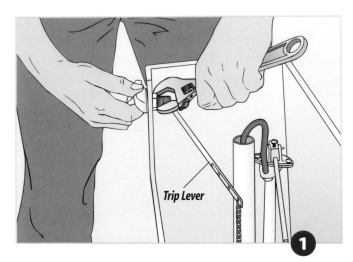

Trip Lever

1

1. Adjusting the handle

- Remove the tank cover. If the handle is loose, tighten the locknut with a wrench (left). If the nut won't budge, even after treatment with penetrating oil, cut through the handle shaft with a hacksaw and replace the handle and trip lever.

- Unhook the chain from the trip lever and slide the trip lever, with the handle attached, through the hole in the tank.

- Soak the handle threads in vinegar for an hour or so to remove mineral deposits, and scrub with a toothbrush.

- Reinstall the assembly, then tighten the locknut and adjust the lift chain (Step 2).

2. Adjusting the lift chain

- If the handle must be held down while the toilet is flushing, the chain may be too long. Shorten it by hooking the upper end through a different hole in the trip lever (right), or use long-nose pliers to open and remove some chain links.

- Some older flush assemblies have a lift wire instead of a chain. If the wire binds against its guide, flushing is impaired. Loosen the guide with a screwdriver, then adjust it so that the flush valve falls freely onto the seat.

2

3. Cleaning the valve seat

- Turn off the water supply and flush the toilet to drain the tank. Wearing rubber gloves, use a large sponge to mop out most of the remaining water. Disconnect the refill tube and slide the flapper valve off the overflow pipe.

- With emery cloth, gently scour inside the seat and along its rim, removing any debris. If the seat is badly pitted, replace it or install a rebuild kit (opposite page).

- Reassemble the mechanism, turn on the water supply, and flush to check for leaks.

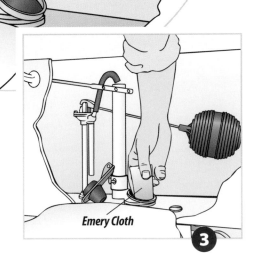
Emery Cloth

3

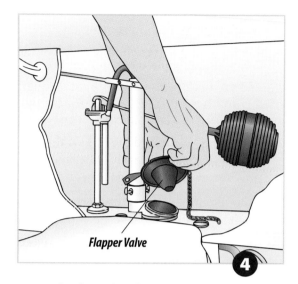

Flapper Valve

4

4. Replacing the flapper valve

- Unhook the refill tube and lift chain, then remove the flapper valve (above).

- Buy a replacement that fits the valve seat in your tank. Install it in the tank and attach the lift chain. If you cannot find a valve that fits your seat, or if leaks persist after replacing the flapper valve, install a rebuild kit (see below).

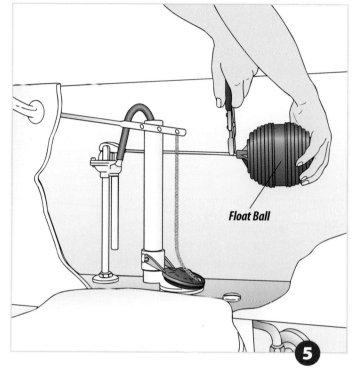

Float Ball

5

Rebuild Kits

If a toilet flush valve doesn't work properly, even after you've scoured the seat and replaced the flapper, buy an inexpensive rebuild kit that consists of a new flapper valve and valve seat. Under the new seat is a putty-like collar. When pressed against the old seat, it makes a watertight seal. The new seat and valve ordinarily stop a constantly running toilet.

5. Replacing the float ball

- Grasp the float arm with locking pliers, and unscrew the float ball (above). If it will not come off, use pliers or a wrench to remove the float arm from the ball cock.

- Coat the threads with petroleum jelly, and screw a new ball onto the float arm. Screw the arm back onto the ball cock.

- Flush the toilet and adjust the water level as necessary (page 47).

Replacing the Flush Mechanism

1. Preparing the tank

- Shut off the water supply and flush the toilet. Remove the tank cover and place a container on the floor beneath the tank to catch water runoff. Wearing rubber gloves, sponge up any water remaining in the tank.

- With an adjustable wrench (right) or adjustable pliers, unscrew the nut and disconnect the supply line where it enters the tank.

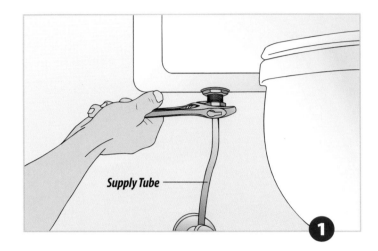

2. Removing the flush mechanism

- Attach locking pliers to the nut at the base of the ball cock (right), and loosen the locknut under the ball cock with an adjustable wrench or adjustable pliers. Unscrew the nut, and lift the ball cock up from the tank.

- Use a bristle brush or a nylon scrubbing pad to clean the opening in the tank where the ball cock was.

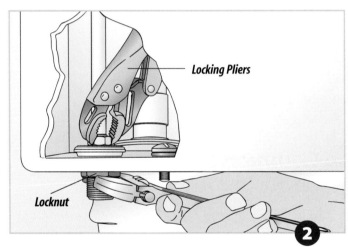

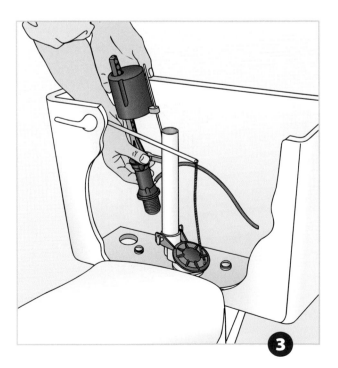

3. Installing new parts

- Position the assembly in the tank (left), with the cone-shaped washer of the new ball cock centered over the hole, and tighten the locknut snugly; do not overtighten, or it may crack.

- Place the refill tube into the overflow pipe, reconnect the supply tube, and slowly turn on the water. Tighten the locknut slightly if the new hardware leaks.

- Adjust the water level in the tank as necessary (page 47).

Stopping Leaks at the Tank

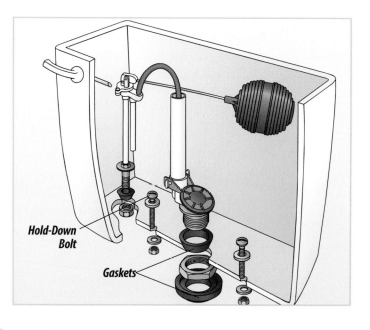

Hold-Down Bolt

Gaskets

Tighten bolts or replace washers

- If water is leaking from the bottom of the tank, first try tightening the tank hold-down bolts. Shut off the water and drain the tank. Use locking pliers or a wrench to keep the nut under the tank from spinning, and turn the screw inside the tank with a screwdriver. Turn the water back on and test.

- If that doesn't work, shut off the water again, flush the tank, and mop any remaining water from the tank. Disconnect the supply line (page 50), unscrew the hold-down bolts, and remove the tank. Replace the gaskets and rubber washers, and reassemble.

Two Common Flush-and-Fill Mechanisms

When you remove the cover of your toilet tank, you may find, instead of the float-ball fill mechanism shown on page 44, one of the two types shown here. In the float-cup type, the flush handle lifts a flapper valve to begin the flush. As the flapper valve returns to its seat after the flush, the rising water floats a plastic cup that is connected by a shaft to a lever that turns off the water. In the model shown, the lever is near the bottom of the flush mechanism; other models have the lever near the top. Note: Float-cup assemblies may not conform to the anti-siphon regulations that some local plumbing codes contain.

A tilt-cup flush valve is essentially a time-delay mechanism. When the flush handle is pulled, it lifts the float cup and flapper valve to begin the flush. As the tank empties, water remains in the upturned cup but gradually drains through a small hole in its bottom. When the cup is empty, it falls forward, closing the flapper valve. The delay ensures that the tank will empty completely before the flapper closes.

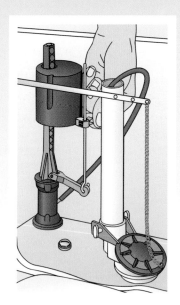

FLOAT-CUP MECHANISM

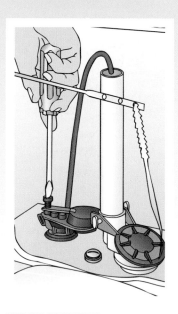

TILT-CUP MECHANISM

Tubs and Showers

HOW THEY WORK

The heart of a shower and/or tub supply system is the faucet/diverter, fed by hot- and cold-water pipes. The faucet determines the temperature and volume of water, and the diverter acts like a switch to direct the flow down through the spout or up to the showerhead. Faucets eventually succumb to wear; the diverter and showerhead may become clogged with mineral deposits.

Drains clog easily but are mechanically simple and easy to clean. A pop-up drain (below) has a stopper that blocks the drain opening when lowered and permits water to flow down the drain when raised. It accumulates debris quickly and requires frequent cleaning. A trip-lever drain (below) is capped by a strainer plate instead of a stopper. Inside the overflow tube, a hollow metal plunger moves up or down to block or unblock the end of the drain.

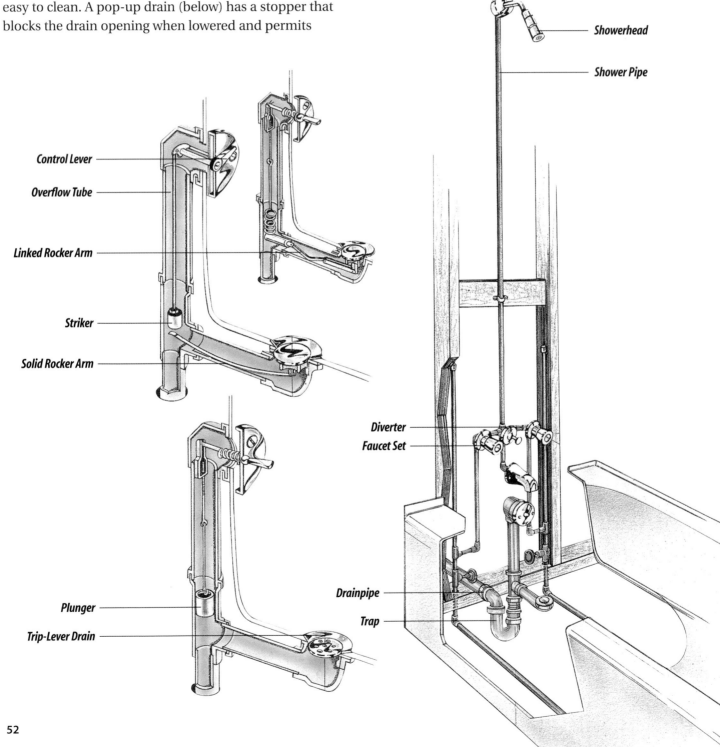

Control Lever

Overflow Tube

Linked Rocker Arm

Striker

Solid Rocker Arm

Plunger

Trip-Lever Drain

Showerhead

Shower Pipe

Diverter

Faucet Set

Drainpipe

Trap

BEFORE YOU START

About one-third of the water used by a typical household pours down the bathtub drain. Little wonder, then, that these drains sometimes clog and fixtures sometimes drip.

GETTING AT THE PLUMBING

Fixing leaky faucets in the tub and shower is similar to repairs in the kitchen and bathroom, except that the plumbing is usually harder to get at. If the wall has no access panel behind the faucets (in the adjoining room), have a plumber cut a hole and install a panel. If a clogged trap cannot be cleared with a plunger or auger, a pro may have to cut a hole in the ceiling of the room below to get at the plumbing.

SHUTTING OFF THE WATER

Before repairing supply pipes and fixtures, turn off the water supply. You may find shutoff valves behind an access panel, or in the basement directly below. If you find none, close the main shutoff valve for the house.

Preventing Clogs in the Tub

The most common cause of clogged drains in bathtubs and showers is hair and soap sludge. Prevention is the best medicine. One strategy is to replace the pop-up with a rubber stopper and basket strainer (right). Regularly remove and clean the strainer.

If a drain begins to empty slowly, act immediately to clear the developing clog. Examine the lift assembly and the underside of the stopper; if gunk is starting to build up, use a plunger or a hose to clear the line (page 56).

Fixing the Drain Assembly

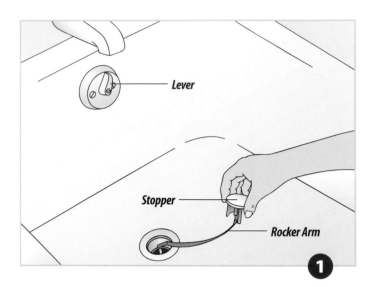

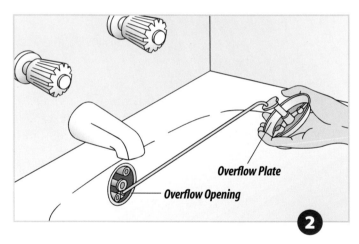

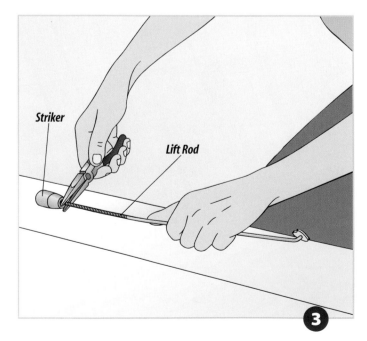

1. Cleaning the pop-up stopper

See the drawings on page 52 for three types of drain assemblies. Repair a plunger assembly using the methods shown in Steps 2 and 3.

- To remove the stopper, turn the control lever to open the drain, pull up on the stopper (left), and work the rocker arm clear of the drain opening. Remove accumulated hair and soap, then clean the assembly with fine steel wool.

- If the rocker arm is curved, feed it back into the drain with the arm curving downward in the drainpipe. If the rocker arm is linked, wiggle it until it seats itself.

2. Removing the lift assembly

- Cover the drain with a bath mat to protect the tub and to keep from losing small parts.

- Remove the screws securing the overflow plate to the tub, then pull the lift assembly up through the overflow opening (left).

- Wash debris from the assembly. Scrub away corrosion, using vinegar and an old toothbrush.

3. Repositioning the striker

- Remove the lift rod from the overflow plate, if possible. Loosen the locknut that holds the striker in place (left).

- Rotate the striker so it moves along the threaded rod. Depending on which way you turn it, this will lengthen the lift assembly (and raise the stopper higher) or shorten it (seating the stopper deep in the drain). Retighten the locknut, reassemble, and test.

- If problems persist, replace the drain assembly. When a drain assembly of the same make and model as the old one is not available, substitute a rubber plug, or a new flange and stopper (opposite page, top).

Replacing a Drain Flange

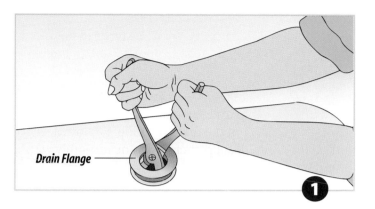

Drain Flange

1. ❶

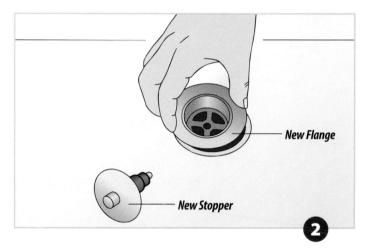

New Flange

New Stopper

❷

1. Removing the old flange

- Pull out the pop-up stopper (or unscrew the trip-lever strainer; see page 52), and then remove the overflow plate and lift assembly. Disconnect or cut off the lift rod. Screw the overflow plate back in place.

- With the stopper or strainer removed, use pliers to unscrew the drain flange (left).

2. Installing the new flange

- Take the flange to a home center or plumbing supply store and find a replacement whose threads match those of the original. It will come with a matching stopper.

- Apply a strip of plumber's putty or a bead of silicone caulk under the lip of the new flange.

- Screw the flange into the drain opening and thread the metal stopper into the cross piece. On some models, you depress the stopper once to close the drain, and again to open it. With others, you lift the stopper and twist to open or close.

Unclogging a Showerhead

Wrap the showerhead collar with tape, and unscrew it with adjustable pliers or a pipe wrench. If the shower arm turns when you do this, wrap it with tape as well and use two wrenches as shown (right).

Disassemble the showerhead. On many models, there is a screw in the faceplate that must be removed. Keep track of where all the parts go and which way they face so you can reassemble correctly. If the parts are worn, either replace them or replace the entire showerhead.

Soak the parts overnight in vinegar to remove mineral deposits. Scrub with steel wool and an old toothbrush, and clear the spray holes with a needle or toothpick (inset).

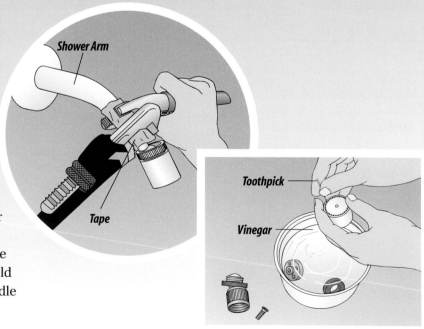

Shower Arm

Tape

Toothpick

Vinegar

Clearing a Clogged Tub

A plunger

- If there is a tub stopper, remove it and the overflow plate (page 54). Plug the overflow opening with a large, wet rag. Run enough water into the tub to cover the plunger cup.

- Place the plunger so it completely seals up the opening. Work the plunger vigorously up and down over the drain opening (right). Continue plunging for one or two minutes.

- If the clog remains, try one of the following methods.

Wet Rag

An auger

- Have a pail ready to catch any debris snagged by the end of the auger.

- In a shower stall, pry up or unscrew the strainer so you can work through the opening. In a bathtub (right), remove the stopper and the lift assembly (page 54), and feed the auger down the overflow tube.

- Maneuver the drain auger through the bends in the drain, rotating it clockwise as you push. (See page 40 for more augering instructions.) Slowly remove the auger, then run water to test the drain.

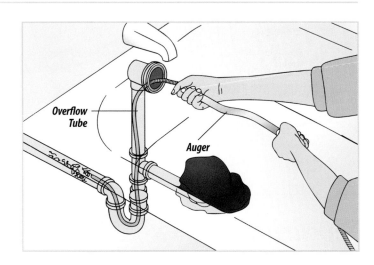

Overflow Tube

Auger

An expansion nozzle

- Buy an expansion nozzle that is the right size for your drainpipes, and attach it to a garden hose. Attach the hose to a faucet.

- Seal off all nearby drains. Insert the nozzle (right), and turn the water slowly to full force. This will inflate the nozzle so it seals the drain. At the same time, the nozzle begins to shoot water down the drain in spurts, actually "hammering" a column of water down the drain and freeing the clog.

- After 10 seconds or so, turn the water off. Detach the hose from the faucet to let the nozzle deflate before removing it.

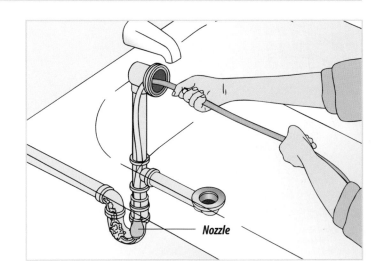

Nozzle

Repairing Ball Faucets

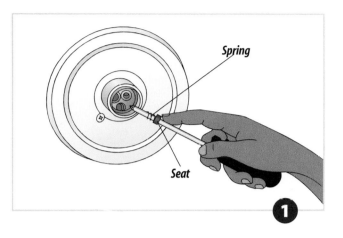

1. Replacing seats and springs

Pages 32–33 show repairs for ball faucets mounted on sinks; shower ball faucets work much the same way but are horizontal rather than vertical.

- Shut off water to the faucet, and open the faucet to relieve water pressure. Remove the handle, cap, and ball. Use a small screwdriver or a nail to extract the rubber seats and springs from the two small sockets in the faucet body (left).

- Install new springs. If the springs are cone-shaped, insert the large end first. Place new rubber seats over the springs.

- To reassemble, set the ball in the faucet body, adjust the cam assembly over the ball, and screw on the cap.

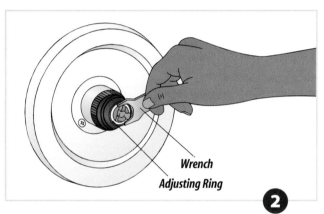

2. Tightening the adjusting ring

- Using pliers (or a special wrench often included in the repair kit), turn the adjusting ring inside the cap clockwise (left).

- Turn on the water supply, then use the ball stem to turn on the faucet. If water leaks from around the stem, tighten the adjusting ring.

- Reinstall the handle once the leaks have been corrected.

Repairing Cartridge Faucets

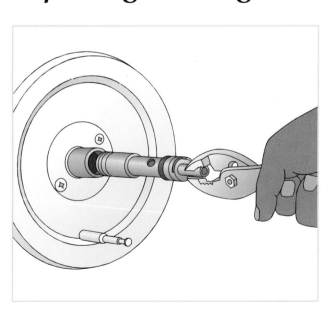

Replacing a cartridge

- See pages 29–30 for information on cartridge faucets. Shower cartridge faucets operate in much the same way as cartridge faucets on sinks. After removing the handle, slide out a metal sleeve called a stop tube in order to get at the retaining clip. Remove the retaining clip.

- Grip the cartridge stem with pliers (left), then pull it from the faucet body by rotating it from side to side.

- Insert a replacement cartridge with the flat part of the stem facing up (otherwise, the hot and cold water will be reversed). Reinstall the retaining clip, the metal sleeve, and the handle.

Rebuilding Two-Handle Faucets

1. Removing the handles and escutcheons

- Turn off the water supply and open the faucets. Close the drain and cover the tub with a cloth or bath mat to protect the tub and to keep from losing small parts.

- Pry off the handle cover, if any, using a small screwdriver or knife. Remove the retaining screw, and pull the handle off. If the handle is stubborn, pour hot water over it and pry the base with a screwdriver.

- If there is a setscrew in the escutcheon, loosen it with a hex wrench. Pry the escutcheon off carefully so as not to damage the wall tiles.

- There are often thin metal pipes or collars around the stems that are threaded onto the faucet, back in the wall. If you can perform the repairs without disturbing these collars, leave them alone. If not, scrape away the caulk on the outside and turn them counterclockwise until they come loose.

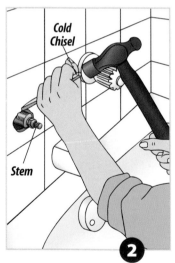

2. Trimming back the wall surface

- If the bonnet nut (the larger of the two nuts on the stem) is behind the surface of the wall, you may have to trim back the wall surface so you can get a socket wrench on it. If the tub or shower enclosure is made from fiberglass, you can enlarge the opening with a rasp. If it's tile, chip it away with a hammer and cold chisel.

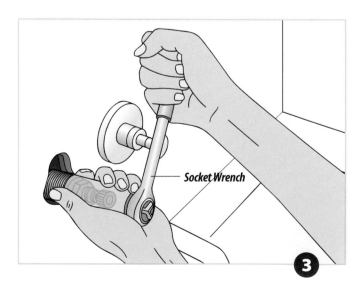

3. Removing the stem

- Fit the socket over the stem and onto the nut, then turn the wrench counterclockwise (left). If the stem stays in the faucet, which it may in old sets, unscrew and remove it as well. If it's frozen in place, spray on penetrating oil and wait 15 minutes before trying again.

- If you are using an adjustable wrench, be careful not to damage the soft brass bonnet nut.

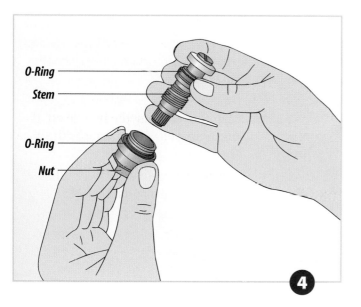

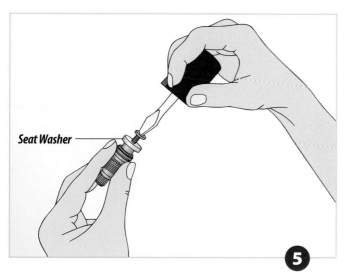

4. Curing leaks around the handle

- Repair shower compression stems much as you would stems for a compression faucet on a sink; see pages 24–25.

- Separate the stem from the nut (left). For better leverage, reattach the faucet handle.

- Pry off and replace any O-rings. On an older faucet, replace the packing string or washer (see page 25). While you have the stem out, you may as well replace other serviceable parts (Steps 5 and 6), to prevent future leaks from the spout. If the stem appears worn, pitted, or corroded, replace the entire assembly.

- When you reassemble the faucet, apply silicone caulk around the outside of the collars (if you removed them). This prevents water from running down inside the wall.

5. Curing leaks from the tub spout or showerhead

- Remove the screw that holds the seat washer to the stem (left). Replace the old washer with a new one of the same size.

- While the stem is out of the faucet body, inspect the valve seat in the wall. If it appears damaged, replace it or recondition it (Step 6). Lubricate the stem with heat-proof grease before installing it.

6. Replacing the seat

- Some seats are built into the faucet and cannot be removed for replacement. In that case, use a valve-seat dresser (also called a "reamer") to smooth the seat surface.

- To replace a removable seat, unscrew the worn seat with a valve-seat wrench or a large hex wrench (right); use a tool that fits tightly into the hole in the center of the seat. Buy an exact replacement, lubricate the threads with pipe-joint compound, and then screw it into the faucet body. Reinstall the stem and handle, and test.

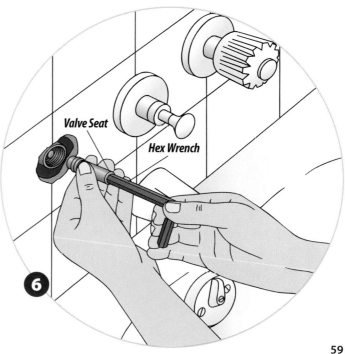

Replacing a Screw-On Tub Spout

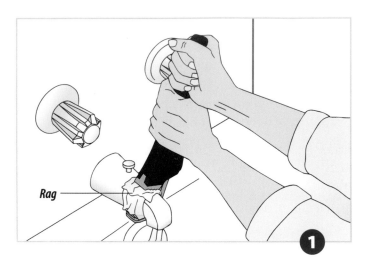

Rag

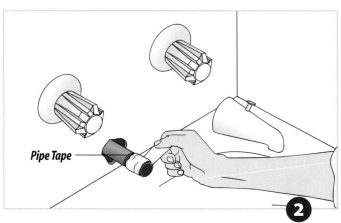

Pipe Tape

1. Removing the old spout

- Check under the spout for the head of a clamp screw; if there is one, the spout is a slip-fit type (opposite page, bottom). Otherwise, protect the spout with a rag, grip it with a pipe wrench, and turn counterclockwise (left). If the spout will not move and there is access from behind, apply penetrating oil, wait 15 minutes, and try again.

- Twist the loosened spout off the nipple (a short length of pipe) or off an adapter attached to a nipple.

2. Mounting the new tub spout

- Clean the threads of the nipple with a wire brush. Apply pipe tape to the threads (left), unless the instructions on the new spout advise otherwise. Spread a bead of silicone caulk on the base of the spout.

- Thread the new tub spout onto the nipple and tighten it by hand. Wrap the new spout with a rag and tighten with a pipe wrench. Avoid overtightening, or you may damage the spout. Make sure the caulk seals the back of the spout so no water runs down into the wall.

Replacing a Slip-Fit Tub Spout

If there is a clamp screw under the spout near the wall, use a hex wrench to loosen it. Grasp the spout firmly and twist it back and forth while you pull it off the pipe.

- Clean the copper pipe with steel wool and spread silicone caulk on the surface, all around the circumference. Also apply caulk to the back of the spout. Loosen the clamp screw on the new spout with a hex wrench (right), then twist the spout onto the copper pipe.

- Turn the spout so that the clamp screw faces up, and partially tighten the screw. Twist the spout into position, and finish tightening the screw with the hex wrench.

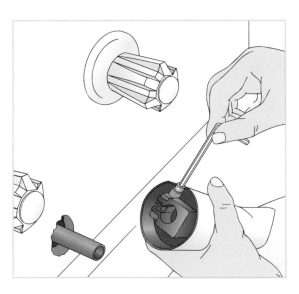

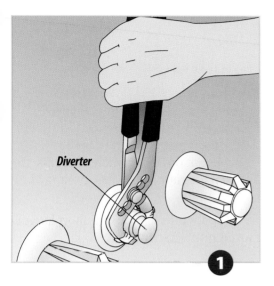

Diverter

①

Push-Pull Diverters (Two-Handle Faucets)

1. Loosening the diverter

If you have a three-handle faucet, with a diverter that looks and turns like a faucet handle, you can remove it and replace the worn parts much as you would the handles of a cartridge faucet (page 57).

- Turn off the water supply and open the faucets. Close the drain and set a bath mat down to prevent loss of small parts and to protect the tub.
- Wrap the jaws of a pair of adjustable pliers with plenty of tape, and unscrew the diverter.

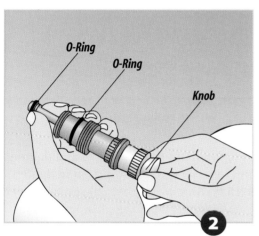

O-Ring

O-Ring

Knob

②

2. Cleaning the mechanism

- Unscrew the diverter knob by hand (left). You will see two or more O-rings and a spring inside the housing.
- Clean the spring and lubricate it lightly with heat-proof grease. Replace all of the O-rings if any appear cracked or worn.
- Reinstall the diverter knob, then screw the entire assembly back into place. Turn on the water supply. If problems persist, replace the entire diverter with an identical part.

Push-Pull Diverter for a Single-Handle Faucet

These operate much the same way as the diverter shown above but are more likely to get clogged up with sediment.

- Remove the faucet handle and escutcheon (inset). Unscrew the diverter, using an adjustable wrench or adjustable pliers.
- If water is not being properly diverted from the tub spout to the showerhead, clean any sediment off the diverter with vinegar and an old toothbrush (right).
- If water leaks around the diverter, or if its parts are worn, replace the entire mechanism with one of the same make.

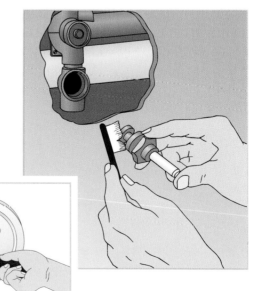

Pipes and Fittings

HOW THEY WORK

Although it may seem a puzzling maze of pipes and fittings, a home's plumbing system works in a simple, straightforward way: Supply pipes bring water to fixtures, and drainpipes carry water away.

The supply system consists of copper, galvanized steel, or plastic pipes, fittings, and valves that carry potable water through the house. A single cold-water main line enters the house and branches off. One line goes to the water heater (or, as shown here, to a water softener and then to the water heater) and then delivers hot water throughout the house; the other branch delivers cold water.

The plumbing fixtures include sinks, toilets, and anything else that dispenses water and drains it away.

Drainpipes comprise the drain-waste-vent (DWV) system. Strict plumbing codes demand that each fixture have a trap that prevents harmful sewer gas from entering a home. Nearby every fixture must be a vent pipe, which carries gases out the roof and ensures a smooth flow through the drainpipes.

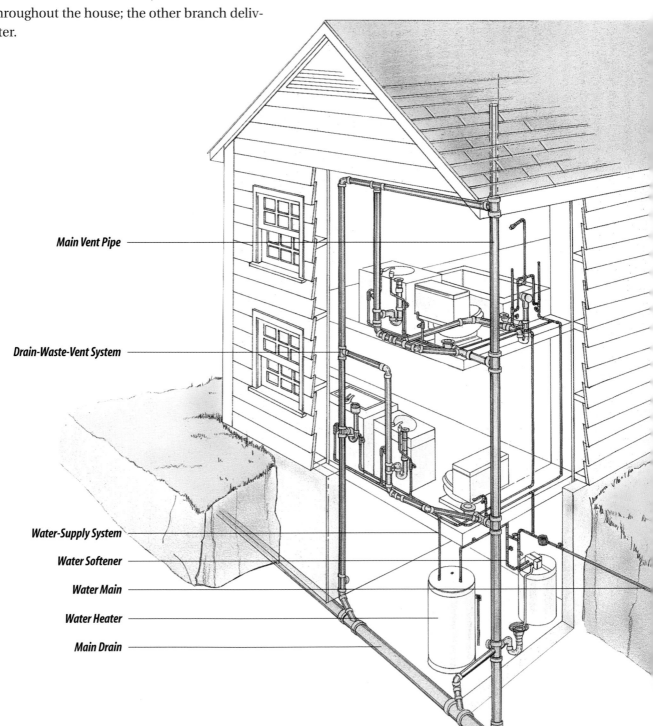

Main Vent Pipe

Drain-Waste-Vent System

Water-Supply System

Water Softener

Water Main

Water Heater

Main Drain

BEFORE YOU START
Copper, Steel, and Plastic

- For piping repairs, you can match the existing material or switch to another. Special fittings make the transition from one material to another easy.

- Copper is easy to work with and comes in rigid, 10-foot lengths. Use medium-thick Type L or thinner Type M.

- Galvanized steel pipe corrodes and gets stopped up with sediment over time, so switching to copper makes sense. "Black" steel pipe isn't plumbing pipe; it's normally used for natural gas lines.

- Plastic supply pipe was once popular but is not now, because it develops leaks over time. Use it only where it can be easily reached for repairs.

- Plastic is actually the best material for drainpipe. However, black ABS pipe is no longer accepted by most building codes; use white PVC pipe instead.

If a pipe has a small hole

If a joint leaks

If a supply pipe is cracked or corroded

If a drainpipe is cracked

If a pipe or faucet is noisy

Calculating Pipe Dimensions

	Outside Diameter	Inside Diameter	Depth of Fitting
COPPER 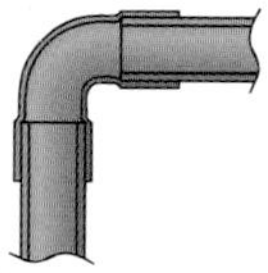	½ in.	⅜ in.	⅜ in.
	⅝ in.	½ in.	½ in.
	⅞ in.	¾ in.	¾ in.
	1⅝ in.	1½ in.	1⅛ in.
GALVANIZED STEEL 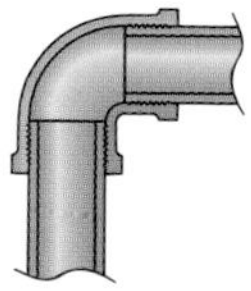	⅝ in.	⅜ in.	⅜ in.
	¾ in.	½ in.	½ in.
	1 in.	¾ in.	9/16 in.
	1¼ in.	1 in.	11/16 in.
	1¾ in.	1½ in.	11/16 in.
PLASTIC 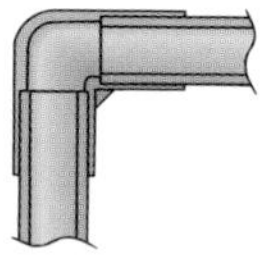	⅞ in.	½ in.	½ in.
	1⅛ in.	¾ in.	⅝ in.
	1⅜ in.	1 in.	¾ in.
	1⅝ in.	1¼ in.	11/16 in.
	1⅞ in.	1½ in.	11/16 in.
	2⅜ in.	2 in.	¾ in.
	3⅜ in.	3 in.	1½ in.
	4⅜ in.	4 in.	1¾ in.

Pipe is usually measured according to its inside diameter ("I.D."), so you may have difficulty selecting the right size if you can see only the outside. It is also often helpful to know the depth of the fitting—how far a pipe will slide into a fitting like an elbow or a coupling.

Repairs for Small Leaks

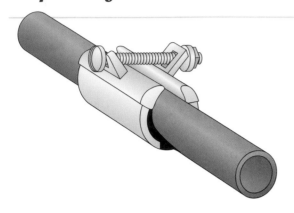

Pipe clamp

A pipe clamp allows you to fix a leak in the middle of a pipe quickly and without shutting off the water. The repair will probably last for years, but—except in emergencies—use this only in places where you can get at it easily, in case it fails.

- Sand away any burrs from the area around the leak so the gasket can rest on a smooth surface. Center the gasket over the hole. Place the clamp pieces around the gasket, and tighten the screws or nuts.

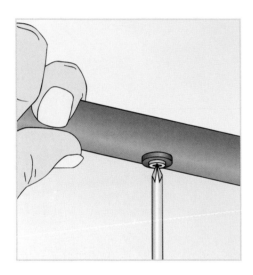

Screw-and-washer plug

This works only for pinhole leaks. Use it as a temporary fix, and plan to replace the affected pipe section soon. The repair can be made while water continues to leak out, but it will be easier if you shut off the water to the pipe.

- Insert a short sheet-metal screw through the hole of a faucet washer. The screw should fit tightly into the washer's hole.

- Push the tip of the screw into the leak, and tighten the screw gradually (left). You may have to drill out the hole slightly, depending on the diameter of the screw. Take care not to over-tighten the screw. *Note:* If the screw is a different metal than the pipe, both the screw and the surrounding pipe will corrode quickly. Plan to make a permanent repair as soon as you can.

Replacing Copper Pipe

1. Cutting copper pipe

- Close the main shutoff valve, and drain the supply lines by opening a faucet located below the pipe you are working on.

- Fit a tube cutter around the pipe next to the break. Turn the knob clockwise until the cutting disk begins to bite into the pipe (right). Rotate the cutter once around the pipe, then tighten the knob and rotate again. Continue tightening and turning the tube cutter until the pipe is severed.

- Loosen the knob, slide the cutter down the pipe, and cut the pipe on the other side of the break. Use the triangular blade attached to the cutter to ream out the burrs inside the pipe (inset).

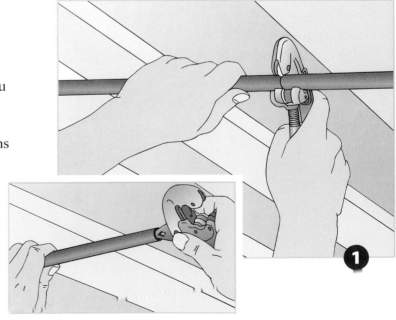

2. Measuring pipe

- Fit standard couplings (right) on the ends of the old pipe, hold the new pipe against the gap, and mark it at the coupling ridges (see the chart on page 63 for depth of couplings).

- Alternatively, use slip couplings, which slide all the way onto the pipe. In that case, cut the pipe to completely fill the gap between the two cut ends of the old pipe.

- Cut the replacement pipe at the mark with a tube cutter.

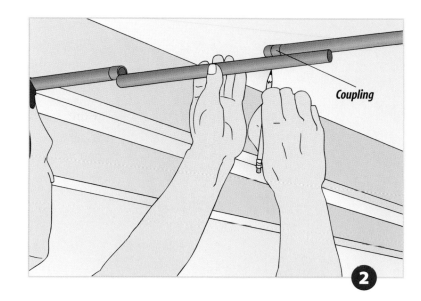

Coupling

3. Preparing the joints

- Rub the inside of the couplings and the ends of the old and new pipes with emery cloth until they are bright and shiny (right). This is an important step; solder will not adhere to copper if it is not sanded.

- Remove any grit left on the surface with a clean, dry cloth.

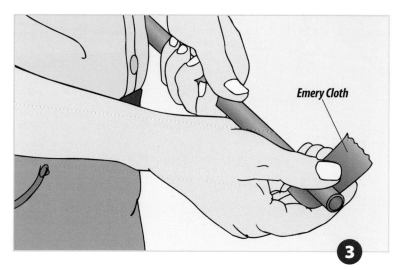

Emery Cloth

4. Brushing joints with flux

Soldering flux for copper pipe typically comes with a small brush. Take care to keep the bristles free of dirt and grit.

- With the brush, spread a thick and even coat of soldering flux on all the cleaned pipe surfaces (right)—both the outsides of the pipes and the insides of the fittings. Also dry the insides of the standing pipes at their ends.

(CONTINUED)

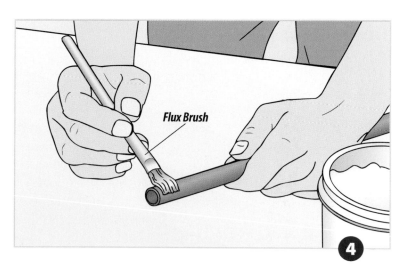

Flux Brush

Replacing Copper Pipe—continued

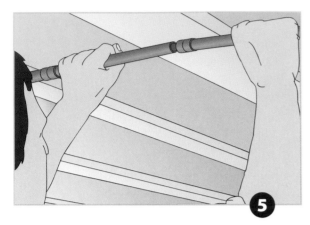

5. Fitting the replacement pipe

- If you are using standard couplings, slide them onto the standing pipes until they bottom out. Insert the replacement pipe into one coupling. Gently pull the pipes apart (left) so you can slip the other end into the second coupling. Give the new pipe and the fittings a quarter-turn to evenly distribute the flux.

- If you are using slip couplings, slide them all the way onto the standing pipes. Hold the replacement pipe in place, and slide each coupling over its joint. Give the new pipe and fittings a quarter-turn to evenly distribute the flux.

6. Soldering the joint

- Wear safety goggles and work gloves, and protect flammable materials in the area with a fireproof shield.

- Light a propane torch and dance the flame over the fitting—not the pipe. Heat the fitting all around, if possible. It typically takes half a minute to heat the fitting enough to melt solder.

- Touch the tip of the wire solder to the joint until it melts and is sucked (via capillary action) into the fitting (left). Do not let the flame touch the solder.

- Keep feeding solder into the joint until a bead of metal appears around the edge. Repeat for both sides of the fitting. Before the solder has a chance to cool, wipe the joint with a damp towel.

Achieving Strong, Long-Lasting Solder Joints

A strong solder joint (far right) is smooth and shiny; a poor one (near right) looks burned and lumpy and has tiny pinholes in the solder that probably will leak sooner or later.

When soldering, remember that the tip of the inner (darker) cone of flame is the hottest. Keep the torch moving evenly over the joint; if you apply too much heat, flux will burn away and the copper will darken. If this happens, clean the joint and then flux it again. The perfect joint results when the heat is maintained at just the point were the solder flows evenly.

Practice your soldering technique on some spare pipe and fittings. To check a practice joint, use a hacksaw to cut it apart after it cools. Solder should completely fill the gap between the pipe and the fitting.

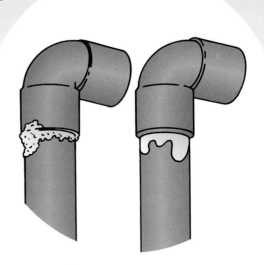

Fixing Steel Pipe

1. Cutting out a defective pipe

- Close the main shutoff valve, and drain the supply lines by turning on a faucet located below the pipe being repaired.

- You cannot simply unscrew the damaged pipe, since loosening it at one fitting will tighten another fitting. Look for a nearby union (see the inset for Step 3). If you find one, unscrew the pipe from it. Unscrew the other end from its coupling.

- If there is no union, cut through the pipe with a hacksaw or small hacksaw (right) and unscrew each piece from its coupling.

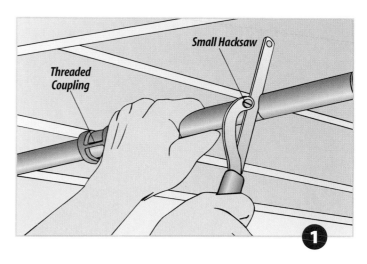

2. Removing the defective pipe

- To unthread pipe from a union or coupling, grip the coupling with one wrench and turn the pipe with another (left) so that the rest of the plumbing run will not be twisted or strained. Turn the jaws of the wrenches to face the direction in which force is applied.

- Purchase a replacement pipe—threaded on both ends—to fill the gap. Measure, taking into account the depth of fitting (see the chart on page 63). Or, buy a pipe the same length as the old one. *Note:* If you cut a pipe in two to remove it from the middle of a plumbing run, you may buy two pieces of pipe and a coupling to replace it. The new pieces, when coupled together, should be the same length as the pipe you cut.

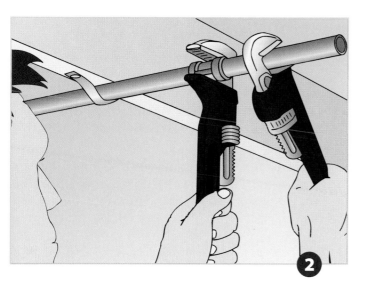

3. Connecting with a union

- Wind two to three turns of pipe tape clockwise over every exposed pipe thread, tightly enough so that the threads show through.

- On one end of the new pipe, slip on the union ring nut and screw on one union nut (right). Screw the other union nut onto the standing pipe.

- Screw the pipe into the fitting at the non-union end (inset). At the other end, hold the two union nuts together, aligned so the two pipes form a straight line, and screw on the ring nut. Tighten all the joints with a pipe wrench, saving the union's ring nut for last.

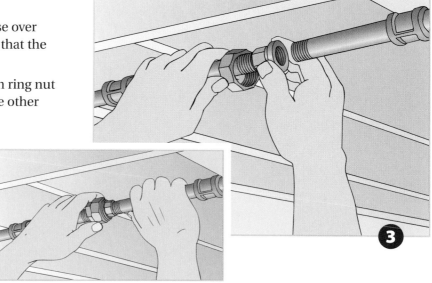

A Fix for Plastic Drainpipe

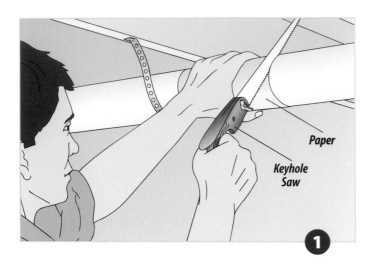

1. Removing the damaged section

- Do not run water or flush toilets in the house during this repair.

- Wrap a sheet of paper around the pipe as a saw guide, and cut squarely through the pipe with a keyhole saw or handsaw (left). Repeat at the other end of the damaged section.

- As you proceed, stuff newspapers or paper towels into the standing pipes to block sewer gas.

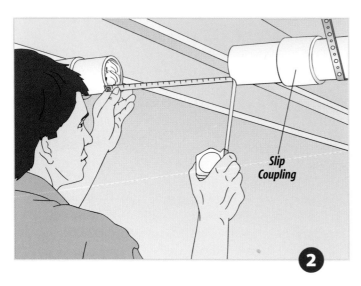

2. Cutting the replacement pipe

- With a knife or sandpaper, remove burrs from the cut ends. Slide a slip coupling over each of the pipe ends. Carefully measure the gap (left) and cut the replacement section to length. Use a handsaw and miter box to make a square cut, then remove the burrs.

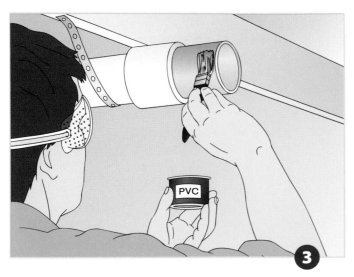

3. Applying primer and cement

- Remove the slip couplings from the standing pipes. Clean all four ends of the pipes and apply primer (usually purple-colored) to all four pipe ends. Slide the slip couplings onto the two standing pipe ends as well as the insides of the fittings. (Do not apply primer to black ABS pipe.)

- Position the new pipe between the cut pieces, and slide one slip joint over to temporarily hold the new piece in place. Apply a thick coat of cement half the width of the slip coupling to the other end of the new pipe, and to the adjoining standing pipe (left).

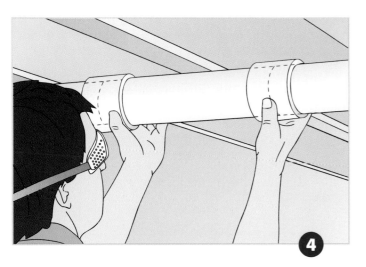

4. Fitting the replacement pipe

- Working quickly, hold the new pipe in place and slide the coupling so it is half on the old pipe and half on the new.

- Give the coupling a quarter-turn to spread the cement (left), then wipe away excess cement with a cloth. Wait a couple of minutes for the cement to set, then glue the other joint in the same way.

- Allow the cement to cure at least two hours, then run water through the drainpipe. If it leaks, the couplings were not properly cemented. Cut out the replacement pipe and start again with new parts.

Silencing Water Hammer

Water hammer is a banging noise caused by vibrating pipes, which is amplified when the pipes are in contact with framing or walls. Wrapping supply pipes with pipe insulation may be enough to dampen the noise.

If not, install an air chamber, also called a shock absorber (below). This simple and inexpensive device contains a flexible diaphragm to dampen the shock wave.

To install one, you don't need to solder copper joints, since the device comes equipped with compression fittings. Cut out a section of pipe where you want to install the air chamber. Slide a nut and ferrule onto the ends of the cut pipes, insert the pipe ends into the air chamber, slide the ferrules over to the chamber, and tighten the nuts. (See pages 64–66 for working with copper pipe, and page 67 for steel pipe.)

T Fitting

Cast-Iron Drainpipe

- Black-colored cast-iron drainpipe is found in many old homes. It is durable and it muffles the sound of water rushing through the pipes. Repairing it, however, is very difficult and probably should be left to a professional.

- To make a repair, the heavy pipe must first be supported so it will not fall down after being cut. Make the cut with a circular saw equipped with a metal-cutting blade, or rent a soil-pipe cutter, a sort of heavy-duty tubing cutter.

- Insert a length of either cast-iron or plastic drainpipe between the standing pipes, and connect the ends with "no-hub fittings." These are neoprene sleeves encased in large hose clamps. Tighten the clamps with a screwdriver.

Water Heaters

HOW THEY WORK

Water heaters typically warm water to a temperature between 120° and 140°F. When a hot-water faucet is opened, hot water flows from the top of the tank toward the faucet, and cold water enters via the dip tube to replace it. Sensing a drop in temperature, a thermostat opens a valve that sends gas to the burner, where it is ignited by a pilot flame or electric spark. *Note:* A gas water heater is shown below; for details on electric water heaters, see page 79.

Combustion gases are vented from the burner chamber through the flue and its heat-retaining baffle, then out the draft hood and vent. In the unlikely event that the temperature or water pressure rises too high inside the water heater, a relief valve opens to prevent the tank from exploding. The anode rod is a magnesium bar that attracts impurities in the water that would otherwise attack the metal tank. A water heater may be joined to the gas line by a flexible connector or by a rigid pipe, as this one is.

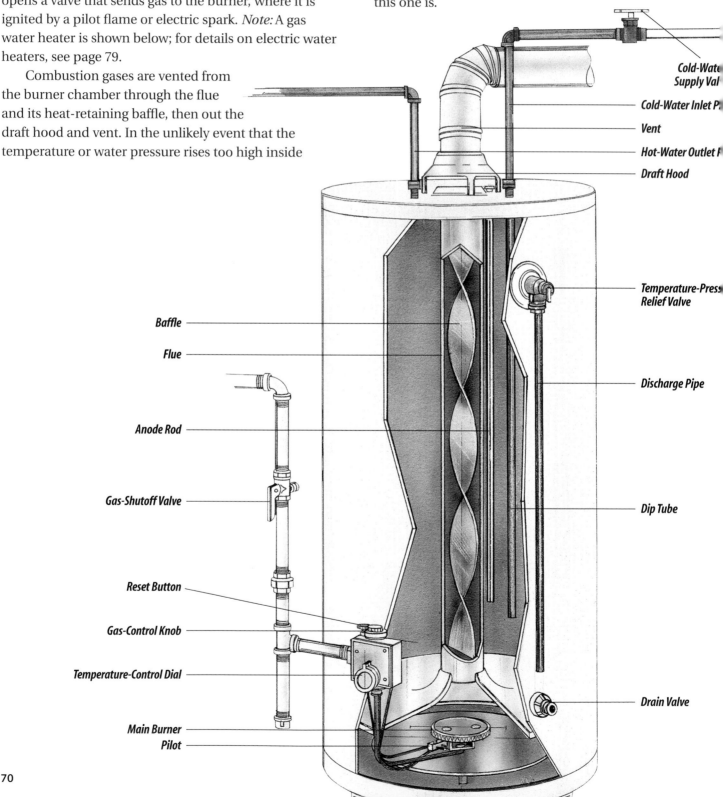

Cold-Water Supply Val

Cold-Water Inlet P

Vent

Hot-Water Outlet P

Draft Hood

Temperature-Press Relief Valve

Discharge Pipe

Dip Tube

Drain Valve

Baffle

Flue

Anode Rod

Gas-Shutoff Valve

Reset Button

Gas-Control Knob

Temperature-Control Dial

Main Burner

Pilot

BEFORE YOU START

A problem with your water heater may be due to overwork, not mechanics. If your water heater holds less than 15 gallons per family member (tank volume is stamped on a metal plate affixed to most water heaters), consider a larger unit or staggering your use of hot water.

GAS WATER HEATERS

All gas water heaters have a flue-and-vent system that carries dangerous carbon monoxide outside. Clean the vent, baffle, and combustion chamber once a year to ensure good ventilation (pages 74–75).

Some gas water heaters have a constantly burning pilot light to light the burner; others use electronic ignition. If your water heater has electronic ignition, or if it has parts that differ from the model shown on page 70, seek the advice of a professional.

ELECTRIC WATER HEATERS

These have many of the same parts and require many of the same maintenance procedures as a gas water heater. The difference is that they use an electric element to heat the water. See page 79 for specific information and maintenance tips.

TIPS

- Your household will be without hot water while you work on the water heater. Inform your family in advance of any repairs.
- Removal of parts such as drain valves and anode rods may require a helper to steady the water heater while you apply a wrench.
- Take old water-heater parts—as well as the brand and model number—with you when you buy replacements.

If there is no hot water
- Gas: Relight pilot light **72**
- Replace a faulty thermocouple **73**
- Test and replace upper thermostat or element **80, 83**
- Reset or replace high-limit cutoff **82**

If there is not enough hot water
- Raise temperature, or use a larger water heater
- Drain tank to remove sediment **76**
- Gas: Clean the combustion chamber **75**
- Electric: Test and replace lower thermostat or element **80, 83**
- Test and replace high-limit cutoff **82**

If water is too hot
- Gas: Lower temperature, or have a professional inspect the control unit . . **80**
- Electric: Lower temperature settings on thermostats **80**
- Test and replace thermostats or elements **80, 83**
- Test and replace high-limit cutoff **82**

If relief valve or drain valve leaks
- Test and replace the relief valve **77**
- Replace the drain valve **78**

If water heater makes noise
- Drain sediment from the tank **76**
- Electric: Remove accumulated scale from heating elements **83**

If hot water is dirty
- Drain sediment from the tank **76**

If water heater tank leaks
- Replace the water heater; no repairs are possible

Lighting a Pilot

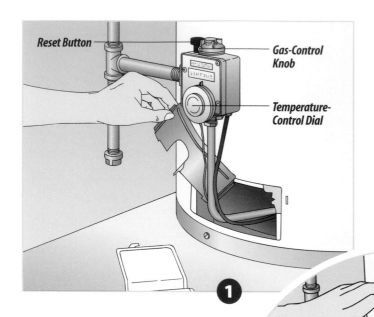

Reset Button

Gas-Control Knob

Temperature-Control Dial

1

1. Gaining access to the pilot

- Remove the burner access panel by lifting it off the heater (left) or sliding it sideways. Specific lighting directions may be printed on or near this cover.

- To light a pilot that has blown out, turn the temperature-control dial to its lowest setting and the gas-control knob to OFF. Wait at least 5 minutes for the gas to clear. If gas odor lingers, close the gas-shutoff valve supplying the water heater, ventilate the room, and call the gas company.

2. Lighting the pilot

- Tightly twist a piece of paper and light it. Turn the gas-control knob to PILOT. Depress the reset button (or the gas-control knob if there is no reset button) while holding the burning paper near the pilot burner (right). The pilot may be hard to reach.

- If the pilot fails to light after a few seconds, close the gas-shutoff valve and call the gas company. If it lights, continue to depress the reset button or knob for one minute, then release it.

- If the pilot stays lit, turn the gas-control knob to ON; the main burner should light when the temperature-control dial is set above 120°F.

- If the pilot does not stay lit, turn the gas-control knob to OFF. Check that the thermocouple's tip (inset) is positioned so the pilot's flame touches it (page 73), and tighten the nut holding it in place. Try lighting it once more. If the flame goes out again, replace the thermocouple (page 73).

2

Thermocouple Lead

Thermocouple Tip

Installing a Thermocouple

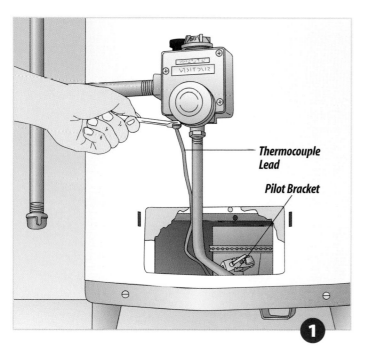

1. Disconnecting the lead

- Turn the gas-control knob to OFF and close the gas-shutoff valve. With an open-ended wrench, loosen the nut that secures the thermocouple lead to the control unit (left), then unscrew it by hand.

- Pull down on the copper tubing to detach the end of the thermocouple from the control unit. There may be a second nut attaching the thermocouple tip to the pilot bracket; unscrew the nut and slide it back along the copper lead.

- Grip the base of the thermocouple and slide it out of the pilot bracket.

Thermocouple Lead

Pilot Bracket

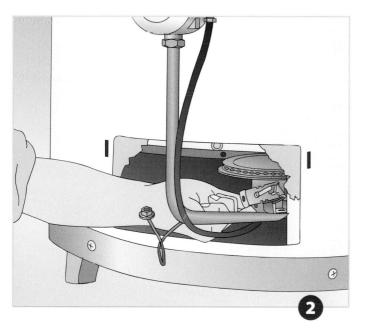

2. Installing the new thermocouple

- Buy an exact replacement for the old thermocouple. Make sure it is long enough.

- Push the tip of the new thermocouple into the pilot bracket clip as far as it will go (left). If there is a nut at its tip, screw it to the bracket.

- Uncoil the lead and gently form it into a curve. Screw the nut at the end of the lead to the control unit by hand, then give it a quarter-turn with an open-ended wrench.

- Open the gas-shutoff valve, and relight the pilot (page 72). If it goes out, close the gas-shutoff valve and call a professional.

Maintaining the Flue and Vent

1. Testing the vent

- Temporarily set the water heater at a high temperature to light the burner.

- Wait 10 minutes, then hold a lighted match at the edge of the draft hood (right). A properly working vent will draw the flame under the edge of the hood; when you blow out the match, the hood should suck up the smoke. If the flame or smoke is blown away from the hood, the vent may be blocked.

2. Disassembling the vent

- Turn the gas-control knob to OFF and close the gas-shutoff valve; then let the burner, draft hood, and vent cool.

- Remove the burner access panels (page 72), and cover the burner and floor with newspapers to catch soot and debris.

- Mark the vent sections for reassembly. For support, wire any overhead ductwork to joists.

- Unscrew and remove the draft hood from the top of the tank (right). Shake the hood and vent sections over the newspapers to release soot, then scrub the insides gently with a wire brush.

- Replace any rusted or damaged ductwork.

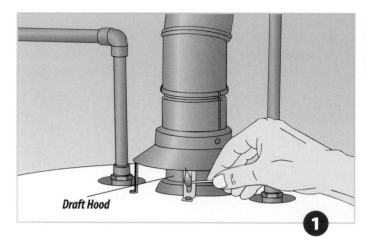

Draft Hood

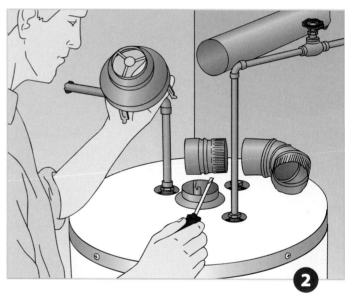

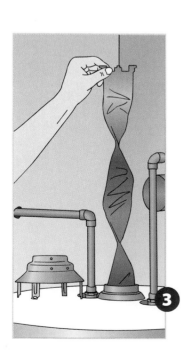

3. Cleaning the baffle

- With the vent removed, lift the baffle from the flue (far left) and scrub it with a wire brush to remove dust and soot (near left). If there is not enough room to pull the baffle all the way out, lift it as high as possible. Cover the flue opening with a rag or newspaper, then brush the baffle and rattle it to dislodge debris.

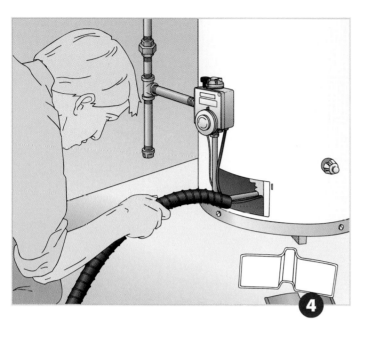

4. Cleaning the combustion chamber

- Reinstall the baffle, draft hood, and vent, then vacuum the inside of the combustion chamber (left).

- Clean the burner and its ports with a soft brush. Use an old toothbrush to clean around the pilot. Vacuum the combustion chamber again.

- Relight the pilot (page 72). Test the vent with a match as in Step 1. If the flame or smoke is not drawn up, there may be a blockage in the main chimney; call for service.

Replacing an Anode Rod

An anode rod attracts harmful sediment that would otherwise attack the lining of the tank. If you have hard water, check yours once a year or so and replace it if it is encrusted.

To do this, close the cold-water supply valve (page 76) and turn the gas-control knob to OFF. Drain several gallons of water from the tank (page 76). While a helper braces the tank to keep it from moving, loosen the anode rod with a pipe wrench or large socket wrench (inset). If it is stuck, squirt the joint with penetrating oil and wait a few minutes.

Lift the rod out (right). Apply pipe tape to the threaded upper end of the new rod, insert it into the tank, and screw it in. Tighten with a wrench. Open the cold-water supply valve and relight the pilot (page 72).

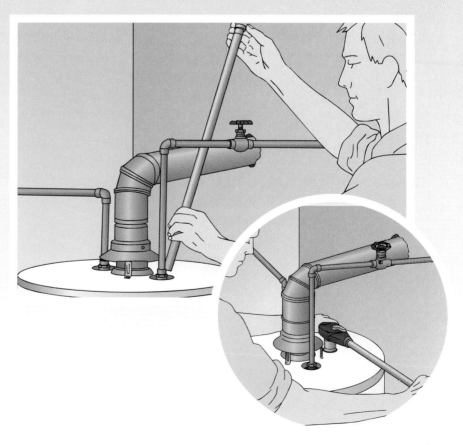

Draining a Tank

1. Shutting off the water supply

- For a gas water heater, turn the gas-control knob to OFF and close the gas-shutoff valve. For an electric water heater, shut off power at the main service panel (page 79).

- Close the cold-water supply valve (right) and open a hot-water faucet somewhere in the house. This will speed draining.

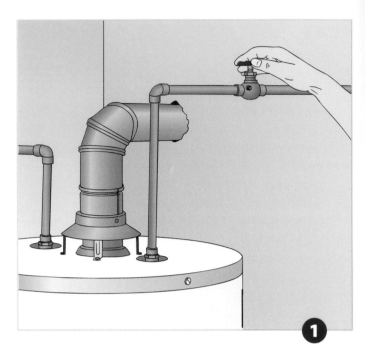

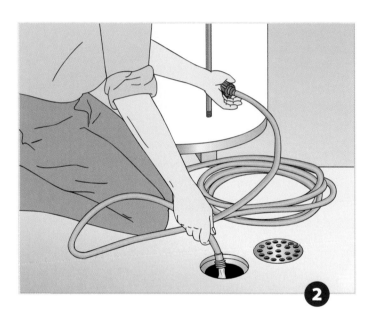

2. Draining and filling the tank

- Attach a garden hose to the drain valve (above) and run it to a nearby floor drain, outdoors, or into a bucket. (Using a bucket will be time-consuming.)

- Open the drain valve. As the tank empties, the valve may clog with sediment; if so, open the cold-water supply valve for a few minutes to allow water pressure to clear the blockage.

- To refill the tank, close the drain valve tightly, open the cold-water supply valve, and open any nearby hot-water faucet. When a steady stream of water flows from that faucet, the tank is full; close the faucet.

- Only after the tank is full, turn on the gas and relight the pilot (page 72) or turn the electrical power back on.

Controlling Sediment

If you live in an area with hard water, then sand, mineral scale, and other contaminants in the water supply will build up, creating a layer of sediment on the bottom of a water tank. This will hinder the performance and shorten the life of the water heater. You can slow—but not stop—this process by softening hard water and by lowering the temperature to 130°F or less. To keep sediment from accumulating, purge your tank every few months. Drain off 2 or 3 gallons of water from the tank, then refill as described at left.

Installing a Relief Valve

1. Testing the relief valve

- Lift the spring lever on the valve (right) long enough for a cup or so of water to spurt out. Lift the lever several times to clear the valve of mineral scale. Keep clear of the discharge pipe as hot water escapes.

- If no water spurts out, or if water continues to drip after the valve is released, replace the valve.

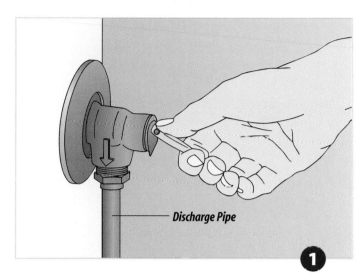

Discharge Pipe

2. Removing the relief valve

- For a gas unit, turn the gas-control knob to OFF and close the gas-shutoff valve. For an electric water heater, cut power at the main service panel (page 79). Close the cold-water supply valve (page 76).

- Drain a gallon of water from the tank if the relief valve is on top of the water heater, or 5 gallons if it is on the side (page 76).

- Unscrew and remove the discharge pipe (left), if there is one.

- Fit a pipe wrench over the relief valve and unscrew it. The valve may be difficult to remove; use steady pressure and have a helper brace the tank. Once it's loose, finish removing it by hand.

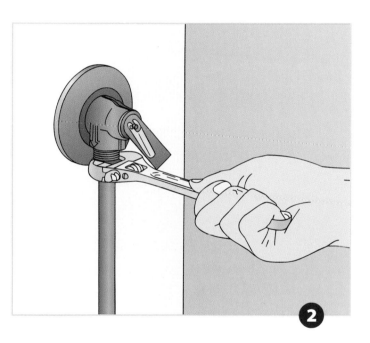

3. Installing a new relief valve

- Take the old valve with you to buy a replacement. Apply pipe tape to the threads of the new valve and screw it into the tank by hand, then tighten with a pipe wrench.

- Screw the discharge pipe (if any) into the valve outlet.

- Refill the water heater (page 76) and relight the pilot (page 72) or restore electrical power (page 79). If the valve leaks, have a plumber check for high water pressure in the house.

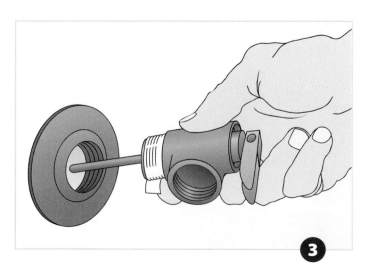

Replacing a Drain Valve

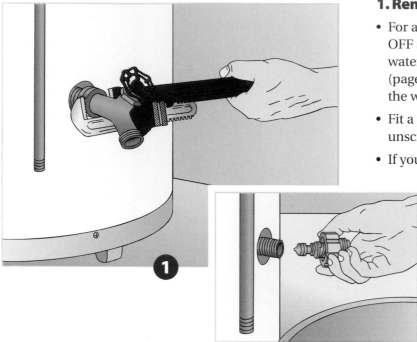

1. Removing the defective valve

- For a gas water heater, turn the gas-control knob to OFF and close the gas-shutoff valve. For an electric water heater, shut off power at the main service panel (page 79). Close the cold-water supply valve and drain the water heater completely (page 76).

- Fit a pipe wrench over the base of the drain valve and unscrew the valve (left).

- If you have a plastic valve (inset), turn the handle counterclockwise by hand, four complete revolutions. Then pull and turn clockwise six revolutions to free it from the tank.

2. Assembling a new valve and coupling

- Replace a metal or plastic valve with a durable sillcock valve. Select a ¾- or ½-inch valve with male threads; also buy a ¾- to ½-inch reducing coupling to mate the ½-inch valve to the tank.

- Wrap pipe tape around the threaded end of the sill-cock valve and screw it into the ½-inch end of the coupling (right).

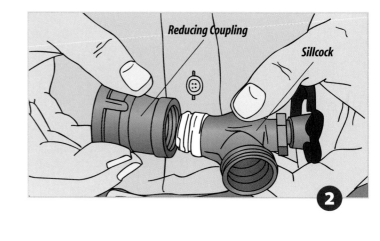

Reducing Coupling

Sillcock

3. Installing the valve

- Apply pipe tape to the pipe threads that emerge from the water heater. Screw the coupling and valve onto the nipple and tighten as far as possible by hand. Finish tightening the coupling with a pipe wrench.

- Fit an adjustable wrench over the body of the sillcock valve (but not over its outlet), and turn it clockwise to tighten the valve so that it faces down toward the floor.

- Refill the tank (page 76) and relight the pilot (page 72) or turn the electricity back on (page 79).

Understanding an Electric Water Heater

An electric water heater shares many features with gas-heated units. Instead of a flame, however, it uses curved rods called heating elements to heat the water.

Electric water heaters usually have both an upper and a lower heating element; each is controlled by a separate thermostat. When the thermostats sense a drop in the water's temperature, they close to complete an electrical circuit and the elements heat up. The circuit is designed to prevent operation of both elements at the same time. When water in the tank reaches a suitable temperature, the thermostats open to break the circuit.

The upper element has a high-limit temperature cutoff to keep hot water at the top of the tank from reaching the boiling point.

Safety First

Electric water heaters are 240-volt appliances whose exposed wires can deliver a fatal shock. Always turn off power to the water at the main service panel before beginning work, verify that power has been shut off, and post a sign to warn others not to restore electricity prematurely. (See pages 88–89 for shutting off power, and page 96 for using a multi-tester to test for power.) If you have any doubt as to whether electricity has been turned off, seek professional assistance.

Before restoring power, even to test a repair, replace any insulation that was moved and reattach access panels to prevent shock.

Cold-Water Supply Valve

Hot-Water Outlet Pipe

Cold-Water Inlet Pipe

Temperature-Pressure Relief Valve

Power Cable

Outer Jacket

Upper Heating Element

Upper Thermostat

Anode Rod

Overflow Pipe

Dip Tube

Lower Thermostat

Access Panel

Drain Valve

Troubleshooting Thermostats

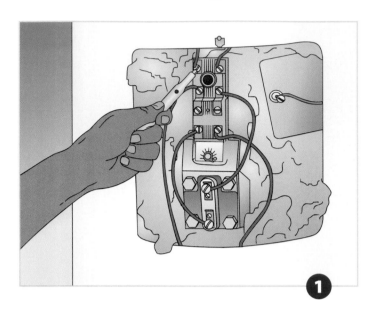

1. Verifying power shutoff

- Shut off power to the heater, and post a sign warning others not to turn it on. Unscrew and remove the access panels (below right). Wearing gloves, carefully push insulation aside or lift it out without touching any wires or components.

- Touch the tip of a power pen to the upper terminals of the high-limit cut-off and to each incoming power supply wire (left). If voltage is still present, check the circuit box again.

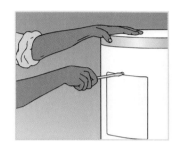

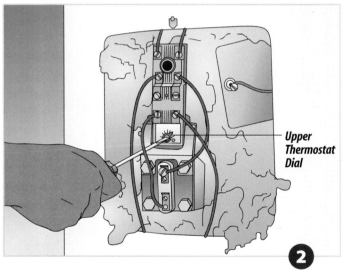

Upper Thermostat Dial

2. Adjusting the temperature

A water heater set too high wastes electrical energy, while one that's set too low won't provide enough hot water.

- Using a small screwdriver (left), turn the thermostat dial counterclockwise to lower the temperature, or clockwise to raise it. If the water heater doesn't maintain the proper temperature, test the thermostat (Step 3).

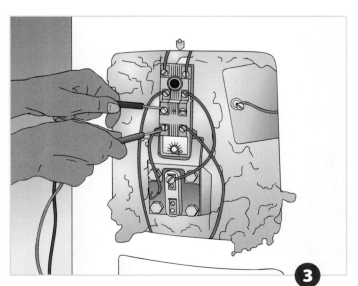

3. Testing the upper thermostat

If either thermostat fails any of the following tests, replace it (Steps 5 and 6).

- Disconnect one wire to the upper element. Set a multitester to RX1 and touch a probe to each of the left thermostat terminals (left). The tester should show infinity when the tank is warm.

- Touch a probe to each of the two right terminals (or to the upper left and upper right terminals on a three-screw model). The tester should display 0.

- Adjust the thermostat to its highest setting. Repeat the two tests; the results should be reversed.

4. Testing the lower thermostat

- Turn the lower thermostat dial to its lowest setting and test it (right); the multitester (still at RX1) should read infinity when the tank is warm. (See page 96 for more instructions on using a multitester.)

- Turn the dial to the highest setting; the needle should swing to 0.

- If any results differ, replace the faulty thermostat (Step 5). If the thermostats test OK, test the elements (page 83).

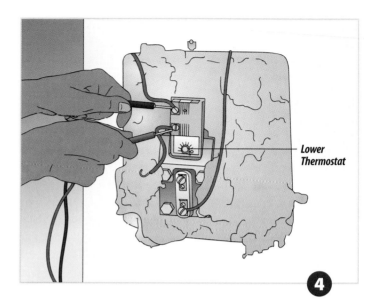

Lower Thermostat

4

5. Removing the thermostat

- Remove the high-limit cutoff (page 82). Label and disconnect the wires to the thermostat.

- Using a socket wrench (right), loosen the two bolts on the thermostat mounting bracket. Slip the thermostat up and out of the bracket.

- Buy a new thermostat of the same make and model at a heating or plumbing supply store. Before accepting the part, have the supplier check it for continuity.

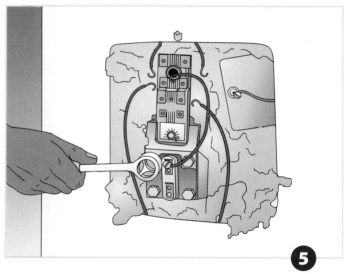

5

6. Installing the new thermostat

- Insert the new thermostat behind the bracket (right) and tighten the bolts.

- Adjust the thermostat or thermostats to the medium setting.

- Reinstall the cutoff (page 82), reconnect all the wires, repack the insulation (making sure none gets behind the thermostat and cutoff), replace the access panels, and turn on the power. If the tank does not feel warm after three hours, test the heating elements (page 83).

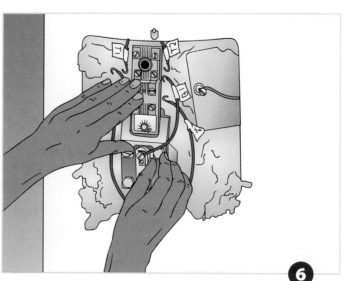

6

Testing and Replacing the High-Limit Cutoff

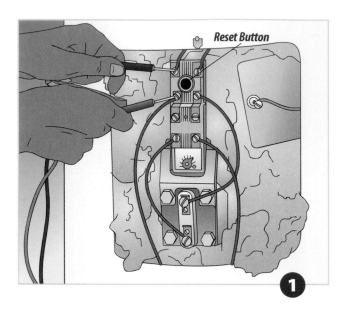

Reset Button

1. Checking the reset button and testing the cutoff for continuity

- Disconnect power to the heater (page 79), then remove the upper access panel and verify that power is off (page 80). Depress the reset button and listen for a click.

- If you hear no click, skip to Step 2. Otherwise, replace the insulation and access panel, then turn on the power. If you have warm water after three hours, you have solved the problem. If the water is cold, turn off the power and reopen the access panel.

- With a multitester set to RX1, touch the probes to the cutoff's left terminals (left), then to the right terminals. If the tester displays 0 each time, indicating continuity, test the thermostat (page 80). If not, go to Step 2. (See page 96 for more information on using a multitester.)

2. Removing the cutoff

- Tag the wires to each of the cutoff terminals to help when you reassemble the cutoff. Loosen the terminal screws and unhook the wires (right).

- Remove the screws that hold the metal straps connecting the cutoff to the thermostat; the straps may be at the front or on the side. Take off the straps.

- Pull the cutoff upward to release it from spring clips, or gently pry it free with a screwdriver.

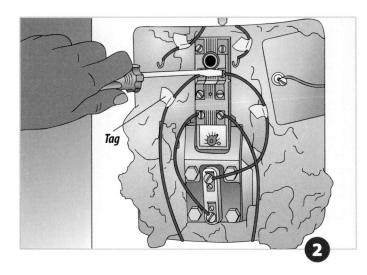

Tag

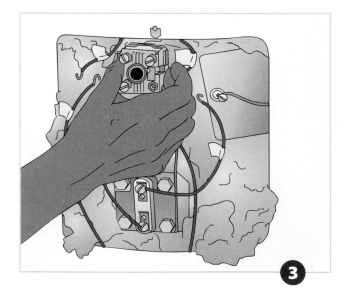

3. Replacing the cutoff

- Buy a new cutoff and have the supplier test it for continuity. Depress its reset button.

- Snap the new cutoff into place and return wires, straps, insulation, and access panels to their original positions. Turn the power on. If the water is not warm after three hours, check the thermostats (page 80) and elements (page 83).

Replacing Heating Elements

1. Checking resistance

- Turn off power and remove the appropriate access panel (page 80). The upper and lower elements are tested in the same way. Disconnect one of the element wires.

- Set a multitester (page 96) to RX1000. Touch one probe to an element mounting bolt and the other to each element terminal screw, in turn. If the tester displays anything but infinity, replace the element (Step 2).

- If the element passes the preceding test, set the multi-tester to RX1. Touch the probes to the terminal screws (right). If there is any resistance reading at all, then the element is good; otherwise, replace it.

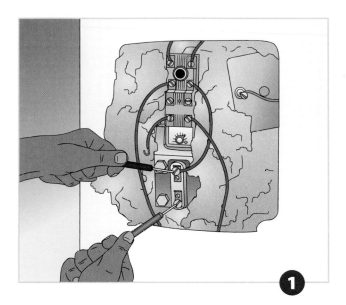

2. Removing the element

- Drain the heater (page 76). Disconnect the remaining element wire.

- Remove the mounting bolts with a socket wrench (or use a socket wrench or pipe wrench to unscrew the element itself, depending on the type). Gently work the element loose, and pull it straight out.

- If the element is faulty, purchase a replacement and a gasket to fit. If the element works but you're removing it because the water heater is noisy, you must clean it. Soak the element in vinegar for several hours, then chip off the mineral scale with an old knife.

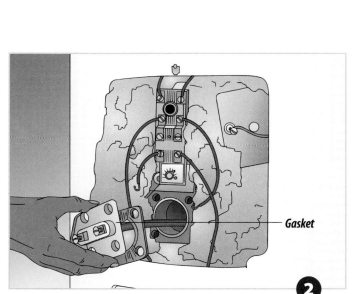

Gasket

3. Installing an element

- Using an old screwdriver, remove all remnants of the old gasket. Scrape mineral scale and rust from the inside surface of the element fitting. Place a new gasket on the element.

- Ease the element into the heater, then tighten the element mounting bolts (or tighten the element itself, depending on the type).

- Repack the insulation uniformly, reconnect the wires, replace the access panels, then turn the power back on.

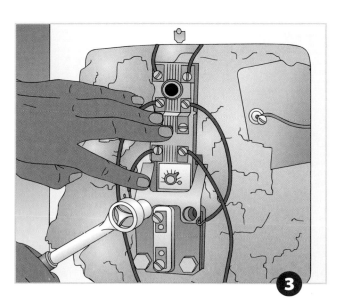

Lighting & Electricity

Contents

INTRODUCTION

Your home's electrical system may seem mysterious and dangerous, a confusing tangle of hidden wires and cables that are full of shocking power. You are right to be cautious, but there is no need for fear as long as you proceed methodically.

Work Safely

Most household wiring carries 120 volts of electricity. If conditions are dry and you are wearing rubber-soled shoes, a 120-volt shock will be painful but probably not harmful. If your feet are wet or you are simultaneously touching something metal, such a shock could do you serious harm or even kill you. Children, having smaller bodies, are at greater risk; even under otherwise ideal conditions, a 120-volt shock could kill them. Your house probably also has some 240-volt lines that can kill an adult.

So much for grim warnings. The fact is, a do-it-yourselfer who follows these safe procedures will keep out of harm's way.

- Shut the power off. Always turn power off at your home's service panel (pages 86–89). Then lock it or put a sign on it to ensure that a family member will not restore power while you are working.

- Check for the presence of power. You may have flipped the wrong breaker, or you may have turned off only some of the power.

- Work as if the wires were live. Wear rubber-soled shoes. Never wear anything wet or stand on a wet floor. Use a fiberglass or wood ladder and use tools with rubber grips.

- Always be sure. If you are at all in doubt about what you are doing, stop and get professional guidance.

Electricity in Your Home

HOW IT WORKS

Electricity comes into a home through a service entrance. From there it passes through the electric meter to a service panel, which distributes power to individual circuits. Most homes have two kinds of circuits: 120-volt circuits carry enough current for small devices—lamps, TVs, blenders, and the like—while 240-volt circuits supply the additional power needed for large appliances like central air conditioners, electric ranges, and dryers. Most circuits include a ground wire that links them to a water main or to a grounding rod. All wiring connections must be made within a metal or plastic box.

There's a limit to the amount of electricity any given circuit can carry. For safety, circuit breakers trip or fuses blow when the demand exceeds capacity—or when there's a short circuit caused by a loose connection, a broken wire, or a malfunction within an appliance.

When problems occur, you can diagnose them fairly easily by studying the service panel (page 88), evaluating the loads on the circuits (page 91), inspecting the wiring connections, and testing individual components.

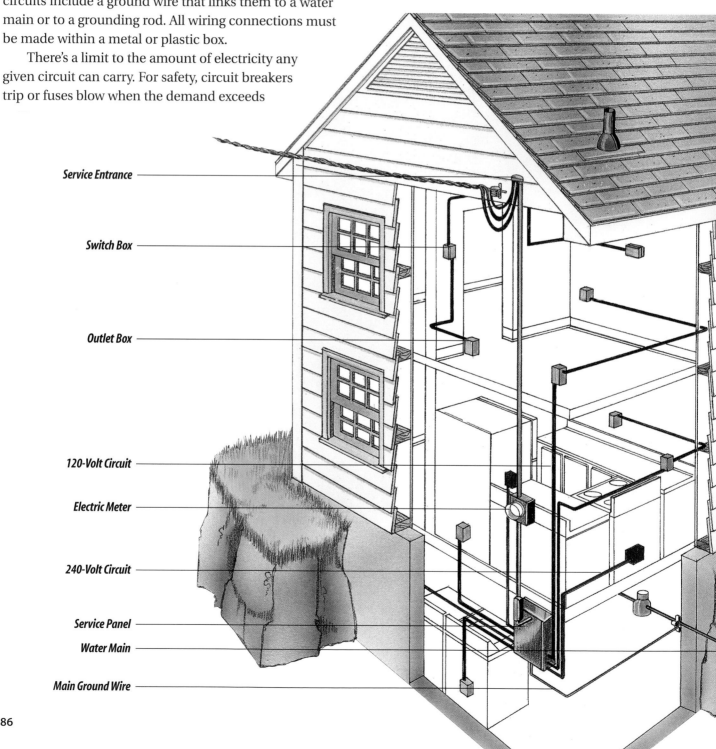

Service Entrance

Switch Box

Outlet Box

120-Volt Circuit

Electric Meter

240-Volt Circuit

Service Panel

Water Main

Main Ground Wire

BEFORE YOU START

Understanding how power is distributed to your home will help you diagnose and repair most electrical problems.

THE HEART OF THE SYSTEM

To begin understanding your home's electrical system, start at the service panel. If you don't know which breaker or fuse controls a given circuit in your home, map each circuit (page 90). This can help you isolate and repair problems when they occur.

TIPS

- Fuses and circuit breakers prevent fires by keeping wiring from overheating. Never replace a breaker or fuse with another of higher amperage.

- Use only lights, appliances, receptacles, and other electrical devices that have been approved by Underwriters Laboratory. The UL label indicates that a device has passed all standard safety tests.

- Have a pro inspect your system. If anything looks a bit odd to you, ask an electrician to look at it.

- Test your receptacles. You can perform one of the most important inspections yourself; all you need is a receptacle analyzer (page 139). Plug it into each of your home's electrical outlets and it will tell you whether your outlets are polarized and grounded—two essential safety features. See page 138 for correct grounding, or hire a pro to fix any problem receptacles.

- Install GFCI receptacles (page 141) wherever conditions are damp, as well as in outdoor locations.

- All wire splices must be enclosed in a box. If you see wires spliced together outside of an electrical box, you have a dangerous situation. Call in a pro to put the wires in a box. All cable entering a box should be attached firmly to the box with approved cable clamps.

If there is no power to a particular circuit

- Check the fuse or circuit breaker **88**
- Identify all loads on circuit **91**
- Compare capacity to total load **91**
- Move one or more loads to another circuit
- Check loads for a short circuit
- Check wiring connections

If a breaker trips or a fuse blows frequently

- Don't touch the panel
- Call the utility company to turn off power to the home
- Have an electrician check the panel before restoring power

If you see arcs or sparks at the service panel

- Pull the power cord or kill power to that circuit **90**

If an appliance, switch, or outlet sparks or is hot to the touch

- Cut power to the circuit **88**

If an appliance is submerged or outlet is wet

- Call the utility company to turn off power to the home

If your basement or room is flooded

- Call the utility company, police, or fire department

If a power line has fallen in your yard

- Call the utility company, police, or fire department

If someone is stuck to a live power source

- Cut power to the circuit **88**
- Use a wooden broom handle or chair to knock the person free **90**

If there is an injury due to electric shock

- Check whether the victim is breathing or has a pulse
- If not, begin CPR if you are qualified
- Call for help

Controlling Power at the Service Panel

Setting circuit breakers

A main service panel may have circuit breakers (right) or fuses (below). The main breaker controls power to all circuits; individual breakers control separate circuits.

• Before attempting any electrical repair, find the breaker that controls the circuit that you'll be working on (page 90). Switch off power to the circuit by pushing the breaker toggle to the OFF position.

• If power to a circuit fails, check the service panel for a tripped breaker (a flashlight might be helpful). Some breakers have three positions—ON, TRIPPED, and OFF. Reset the breaker by first turning it off, then on. If it trips again, turn off one or two appliances and reset it.

• If the breaker continues to trip, call in an electrician.

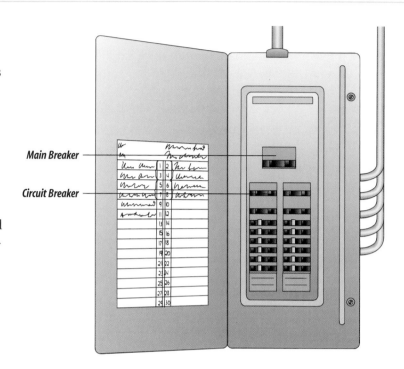

Main Breaker

Circuit Breaker

Removing and replacing a fuse

• Before attempting any electrical repair, find the fuse that controls the circuit you'll be working on (page 90). Cut power by removing the fuse. Unscrew plug fuses (right). Deal with fuse blocks and the cartridge fuses that they hold as shown on the next page.

• If power to a circuit fails, check for a blown fuse (a flashlight might be helpful). A complete break in the metal strip inside a plug fuse indicates a circuit overload; discoloration indicates a short circuit. Cartridge fuses often show no sign of failure.

• To correct an overload, disconnect one or two appliances from the circuit and replace the fuse (page 89). When you suspect a short circuit, find the problem and repair it before replacing the fuse.

• If problems recur, call an electrician.

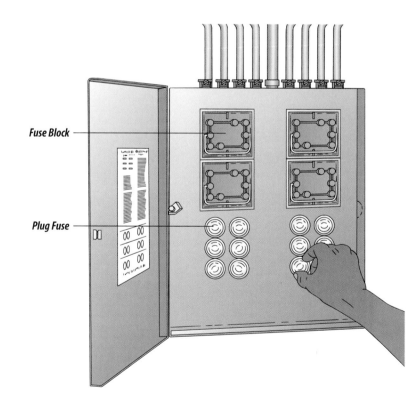

Fuse Block

Plug Fuse

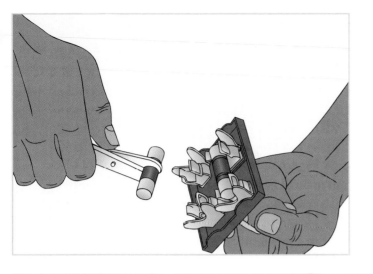

Removing cartridge fuses

A 240-volt circuit may be controlled by cartridge fuses housed either in fuse blocks or in a separate panel. Before removing a fuse block or cartridge fuse, turn off the appliance that it serves.

- To remove a cartridge fuse housed in a fuse block, pull the fuse block out of the service panel by its handle.

- Remove the fuse from the spring clips with a fuse puller (left). Don't touch metal ends—they may have overheated.

- For cartridges in a separate panel, simply remove them with the fuse puller.

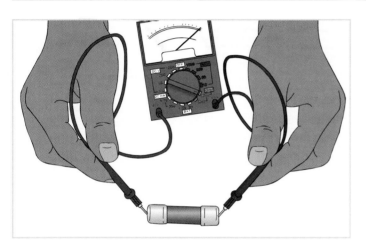

Testing a cartridge fuse

- Set a multitester (page 96) to RX1, and touch the probes to the fuse's metal ends (left). A reading of 0 ohms indicates that the fuse is good; an infinity reading indicates that the fuse is blown.

- If the fuse is good, reinstall it in the service panel, inserting it into the spring clips with the fuse puller.

- If the fuse is blown, replace it with a new fuse of identical design and amperage.

Fuse Types and Capacities

Replace blown fuses with fuses of the same type and amperage—never higher, or wires may start to burn before the fuse blows. Common types are shown (right).

    Standard plug fuses come in 15-, 20-, and 30-amp versions. The metal strip inside a time-delay fuse withstands the momentary power surge created when an appliance motor starts, but it blows if there is a sustained overload or a short circuit. A type-S fuse fits into an adapter, which guards against installation of a higher-amperage fuse. Ferruled-cartridge fuses, rated up to 60 amps, are used to protect circuits for large appliances. Knife-blade cartridge fuses, rated more than 60 amps, are used to protect the home's electrical system.

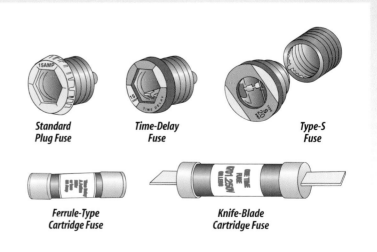

Standard Plug Fuse **Time-Delay Fuse** **Type-S Fuse**

Ferrule-Type Cartridge Fuse **Knife-Blade Cartridge Fuse**

Mapping Your Home's Electrical System

Tracing each circuit

Having a map of the circuits in your house can speed electrical repairs.

* Sketch a plan of each floor of the house; then mark the location of all outlets, switches, and light fixtures, using standard architectural symbols (right).

* Turn off all switches and appliances.

* At the service panel, stick a numbered label next to each circuit breaker or fuse.

* Turn off power to circuit No. 1 by shutting off the breaker or removing the fuse (page 88). Go through the house and find the switches, outlets, and fixtures that are not getting power. (Plug in a lamp to test the receptacles.) On the plan, write the circuit number beside each one.

* Repeat the process for each circuit breaker or fuse in the service panel.

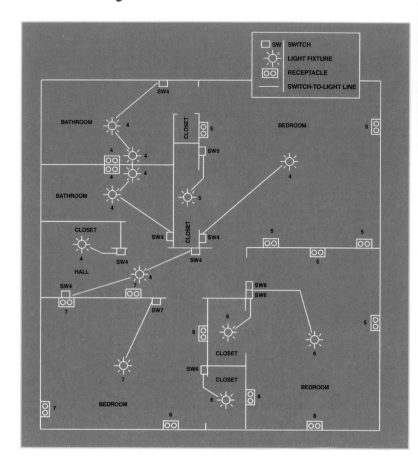

The Right Wire for the Circuit

Wire diameter is measured using the American Wire Gauge system: the smaller the number, the greater the diameter of the wire. The wire's size and type are marked on its insulation.

Wire sizes #12 and #14 are the most common types in homes, carrying 20 and 15 amps, respectively. Since the cost difference is minor, common proctice is to provide a safety margin by using #12 in both 15- and 20-amp circuits. These wire sizes are used in both 120- and 240-volt circuits, although some 240-volt circuits, particularly those for electric ranges or central air conditioners, use #8 and #6 wire. Smaller wires such as #16 and #18 are used for low-voltage systems such as door chimes or outdoor lighting.

Safe Responses to Electrical Emergencies

A person in contact with live current may appear stuck to the source. Do not touch the individual. Instead, shut off power to the house (pages 88–89), or unplug the appliance or lamp. If you can't cut power immediately, use a broomstick or other wooden object to knock the person free.

If a lamp or appliance sparks, shocks you, feels hot, or is smoking or aflame, pull its plug. Use a thick, dry towel or heavy-duty work glove to protect your hand.

If a switch, outlet, or fixture should spark or smoke, immediately kill power to the entire house.

Never touch a burning or sparking switch to turn it off. Flip off the toggle with a wooden spoon.

Calculating the Load on a Circuit

1. Determining circuit capacity

If breakers trip or fuses fail persistently—or if you plan to add another load to a circuit—compare the total load on the circuit with its designed capacity, expressed in amperes or amps. To do so:

- Find the amperage rating on the breaker or fuse that controls the circuit in question. On circuit breakers, the amperage rating is embossed on the tip of the toggle switches (right). Plug fuses are labeled and color-coded according to amperage rating (page 89).

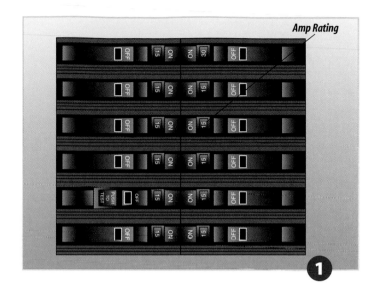

Amp Rating

2. Calculating the load

- Look for an Underwriters Laboratory label on each appliance (right). The label specifies how much voltage the appliance requires and the power it consumes in watts.

- Add the wattages of all the appliances and lightbulbs on the circuit.

- Use the wattage table below to compare the total load to the amperage of the breaker or fuse. For example, a 15-amp circuit breaker or fuse on a 120-volt circuit has a capacity of 1,800 watts.

- If the total load exceeds the capacity, disconnect some loads from the circuit, or consult an electrician.

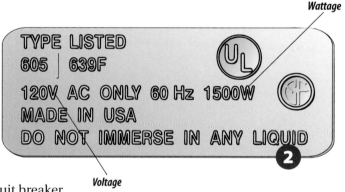

Wattage

Voltage

How many watts can a circuit handle?

Breaker/Fuse Rating	120-Volt Circuit	240-Volt Circuit
15 amps	1,800 watts	3,600 watts
20 amps	2,400 watts	4,800 watts
30 amps	3,600 watts	7,200 watts

Lamp Repairs

HOW THEY WORK

In its major components, the table lamp shown (below) is virtually identical to most other such lamps, regardless of size, shape, or type of bulb.

Every lamp has a cord that runs from a plug at one end, through the lamp, to a socket at the other. In this lamp, the socket accepts an ordinary incandescent lightbulb; other sockets accept fluorescent tubes or halogen bulbs.

A switch in the socket of this lamp turns it on and off; but switches can also be built into the base of a lamp, into the cord, or in many desk lamps, into the lampshade.

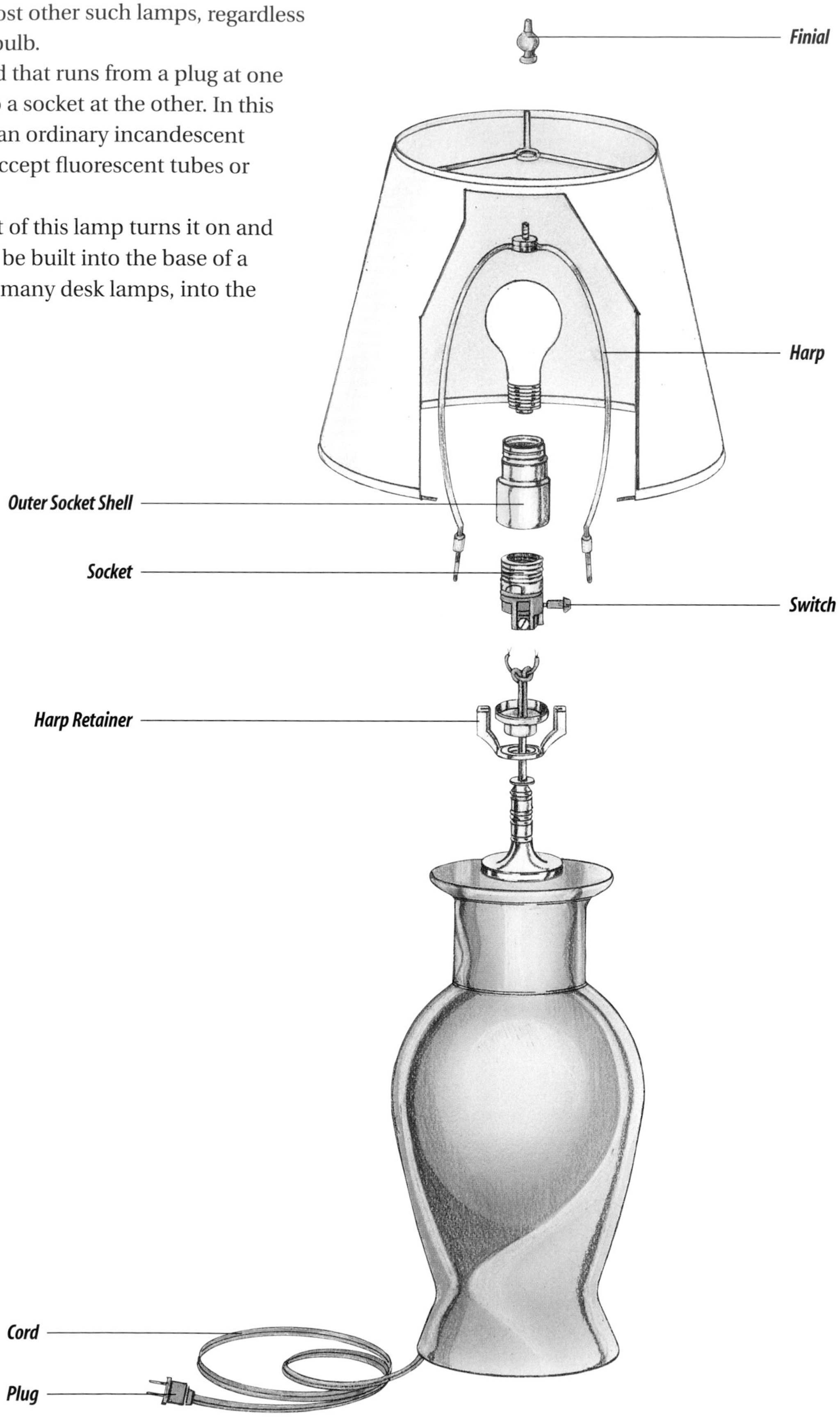

Finial

Harp

Outer Socket Shell

Socket

Switch

Harp Retainer

Cord

Plug

BEFORE YOU START

Look for simple problems first, then follow a thorough diagnostic procedure. If a lamp doesn't work, first make sure the bulb hasn't burnt out, that the lamp is plugged in, and that the fuse or breaker controlling the circuit hasn't blown or tripped (page 88). If you find nothing amiss, test the socket next, then look at the plug, and test for continuity in the cord. Never try to repair a worn lamp cord; install a new one that has wires of the same gauge as the original. And while you're at it, replace the plug, too.

TIPS

- Lamp cord is made of fine wire strands. Twist them together before making connections so there are no stray ends.

- Buy polarized replacement plugs, which have one narrow and one wide prong. Wired correctly, this kind of plug assures that metal parts of the lamp will be disconnected from the power when the lamp is off.

- Twisting on a wire cap is the best way to join wires. Check the package label to be sure you have the right size for the number and diameter of the wires at the connection.

Testing and Replacing a Socket

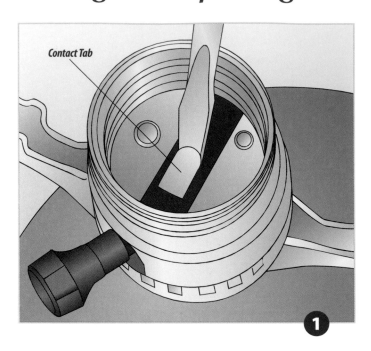

Contact Tab

1. Cleaning and adjusting the contact tab

To make a good electrical connection, the socket's contact tab must be clean, and it must fit tightly against the base of the bulb.

- With a flat-tip screwdriver, scratch any dirt off the surface of the tab. If it is corroded or broken, replace it.

- Check that the tab angles slightly upward from the base of the socket. If not, pry it gently upward (left).

- If the contact tab snaps off as you pry it—or if the bulb still doesn't light afterward—replace the socket.

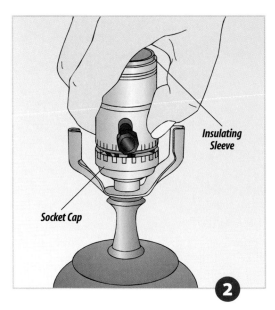

Insulating Sleeve

Socket Cap

2. Removing the outer shell and socket

- On the outer shell, look for the word PRESS. Push hard there with your thumb (above). Squeeze and lift the shell from the socket cap. You may have to wiggle the shell slightly, but don't twist it.

- Slip off the cardboard insulating sleeve if it doesn't come off with the shell. If it is damaged, replace the socket. Disconnect the socket by loosening the two terminal screws and removing the wires.

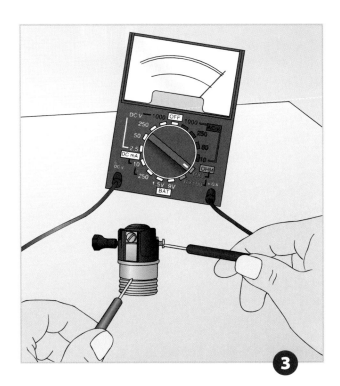

3. Testing the socket

- Set a multitester to RX1 for a continuity test (page 96).

- Touch one probe to the silver (neutral) terminal screw and the other to the socket's threaded metal base (above). The meter should read 0 ohms, indicating full continuity.

- If you don't get a 0 reading, the socket is faulty; replace it. Otherwise, continue by testing the switch (Step 4).

4. Testing the switch

A properly working switch will show continuity only when it is in the ON position.

Contact Tab

- To test a two-position ON/OFF switch (right), place the leads of a multitester on the brass terminal and the socket contact tab. The meter should read 0 ohms with the switch in ON position, infinity in OFF.

- To test a three-way switch, place the probes against the brass screw terminal and either the small tab in the socket base or the contact tab. Where you detect continuity depends on the switch position. In one of its ON positions, a properly working switch shows continuity with the probe touching the vertical tab; in another ON position, when it touches the contact tab; in the third ON position, when it touches either tab. When turned off, the switch shows no continuity.

- If the switch is faulty, replace the socket and the socket cap (below). If tests indicate that the switch and socket are good, test the cord and plug (page 100, Step 1).

5. Installing a new socket cap

- If the lamp cord is knotted inside the socket cap, untie it. Loosen the setscrew, if any, at the base of the cap, and unscrew the socket cap (inset). If the socket cap holds the lamp body to the center pipe, support the lamp so that it doesn't come apart.

- Thread the lamp cord through the cap, then screw the cap onto the center pipe. Tighten the setscrew, if present.

- If the cord is new, part the wires and strip the ends (page 97). Tie the ends of the parted cord in an Underwriters knot (right).

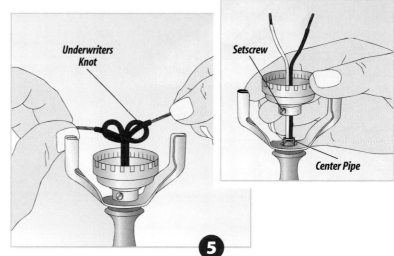

Underwriters Knot

Setscrew

Center Pipe

6. Wiring the new socket

One of the wires of a lamp cord has a ridge molded into the insulation to mark it as the neutral conductor; the hot-conductor insulation is smooth. These features help ensure correct connections to sockets, switches, and plugs.

- Connect the ridged wire to the silver socket terminal and the smooth one to the brass terminal. To do this, twist the wire strands clockwise so there are no frayed ends, and form a hook at the end of each wire. Use a screwdriver to help wrap each hook around its terminal screw (right). Tighten the screws, making sure there are no stray wire strands.

- Slip the insulating sleeve and outer shell onto the socket. Fit the notched opening over the switch, then push the shell into the rim of the cap, snapping it into place.

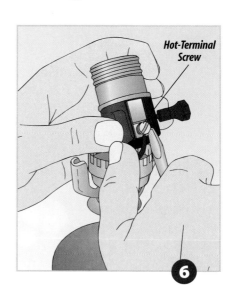

Hot-Terminal Screw

Using a Multitester

A multitester is an inexpensive but invaluable tool for diagnosing electrical problems. The analog type, shown here, has a needle indicator and printed scales. Digital multitesters give numerical readouts according to the test mode selected. All multitesters have probes connected to positive and negative leads.

Zeroing the needle

Set the selector dial to RX1 or any other ohms-range setting. Touch the probes together (below). On analog multitesters, the needle should sweep from left to right. Turn the ZERO OHMS adjustment dial until the needle rests directly over 0. Digital meters do not require zeroing.

Checking continuity

A continuity test determines whether a device has a broken connection at any point. Turn off power to the circuit and disconnect the wires or component to be tested. Set the selector to RX1 or any ohms setting, and touch the probes to two different terminals or to the ends of a wire.

The illustration below shows a continuity test on a switch. With the switch ON and probes touching the two terminals, the needle should indicate 0 resistance—a closed circuit. An infinity reading indicates an open one.

Testing for voltage

Voltage checks (below right) reveal whether a circuit is energized and how much voltage is present. A reading other than 0 indicates that voltage is present and that it would be unsafe to touch or disconnect the component without cutting power. When testing whether voltage flows within the correct range, for a 120-volt circuit, look for a voltage reading between 108 volts and 132 volts; for a 240-volt circuit, a reading between 216 volts and 264 volts.

CAUTION: *When testing for voltage, hold multitester probes by their plastic grips to avoid possible electrocution.*

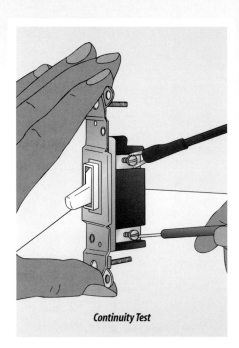

Scales

AC-Voltage Settings

Selector

Ohms-Range Setting

Negative Probe

Positive Probe

Continuity Test

Voltage Test

Dealing with a Switch in a Lamp Base

1. Testing the switch

Some lamps have a switch mounted in the base instead of in the socket or cord. If the bulb flickers or if the switch feels loose, take out the switch and test it.

- Unplug the lamp, set it on its side, and peel off the protective cover from the base. If the lamp has a bottom plate, remove the locknut holding it in place (inset), then pull off the plate. Disconnect the switch leads.

- Set a multitester to RX1 (page 96), and touch the probes to the ends of the switch leads (right). Note

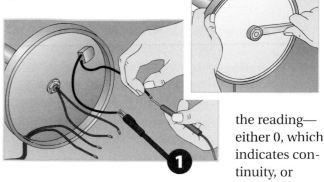

the reading—either 0, which indicates continuity, or infinity, which indicates an open circuit. Push or turn the switch once and note the multitester reading again. It should be the opposite of the result from the first test. If not, replace the switch (Steps 2–3).

2. Removing the switch

- Unscrew the switch-retaining ring, then pull the switch out of the base (left).

- Take the switch to a hardware store or electrical supplier, and get a compatible replacement.

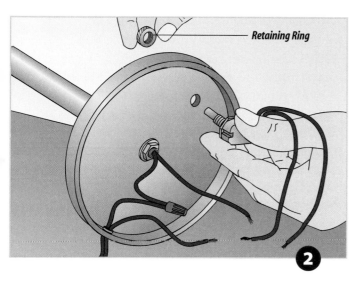

Retaining Ring

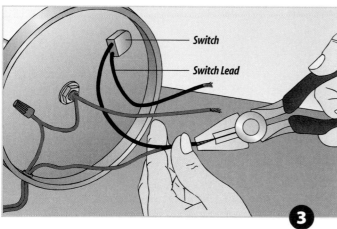

Switch

Switch Lead

3. Installing the new switch

- Place the new switch in the lamp base, and tighten the retaining ring.

- Twist each switch lead together with one of the wires to which the old switch was connected (above), and secure each connection with a wire cap.

- If you removed a bottom plate, reattach it with the locknut.

Working with Lamp Cord

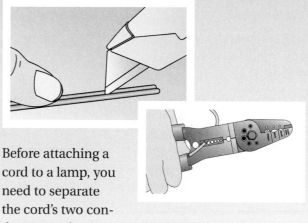

Before attaching a cord to a lamp, you need to separate the cord's two conductors and strip some insulation from each. To split the cord, insert the point of a utility-knife blade between the conductors about 1½ inches from the end of the cord (above), then pull the cord past the blade. Use a multipurpose tool (inset) to strip about an inch of insulation from the end of each wire.

How to Test and Replace Cord Switches

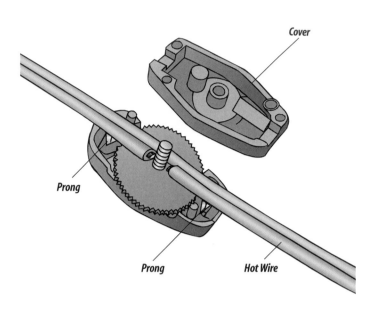

Cover

Prong

Prong

Hot Wire

Lamp-cord switches

- Unplug the lamp, remove the switch cover (left), and lift the cord out of the switch.

- Set a multitester to RX1, and touch the probes to the switch terminals to test for continuity. The meter should indicate continuity with the switch in the ON position, and no continuity after being clicked OFF. If your results are different, replace the switch.

- Check the lamp cord. If it is sound, install the new switch in the existing cord. If not, replace the cord (pages 100–105).

- Notch the hot wire (smooth insulation) of a new cord to fit around the switch's central screw. Make sure the switch's prongs pierce the hot-wire insulation.

- Add the switch cover.

Round-cord switches

- Unplug the lamp, remove the screws that hold the switch cover in place, and put it aside.

- Set a multitester to RX1, and touch the probes to the switch terminals to test for continuity (right). The meter should indicate continuity with the switch in the ON position, and no continuity after being clicked OFF. If your results are different, replace the switch.

- When installing a switch on a new cord, carefully cut the outer insulation to expose the conductors inside without damaging their insulation.

- Cut the black wire, strip the insulation off the ends (page 97), and connect them to the terminal screws. Trim excess wire, then attach the switch cover.

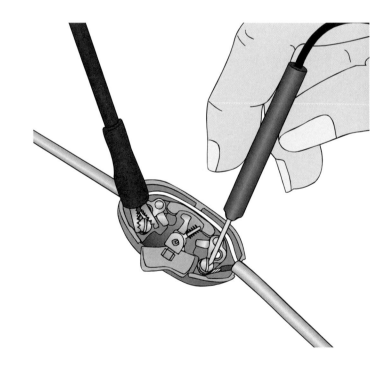

Replacing a Flat-Cord Plug

1. Threading the shell

- Unplug the lamp and cut off the old plug with wire cutters. Separate the core of the new plug from the shell, and slip the cord through the shell (right).

- Part the wire and strip about ½ inch of insulation from the ends (page 97).

- To protect the connections from strain, tie an Underwriters knot with the two wire ends (page 95).

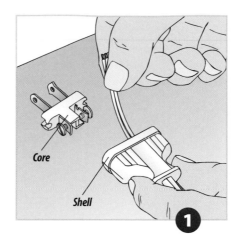

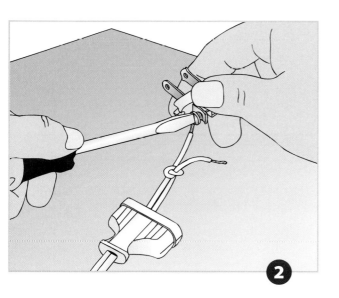

2. Connecting the terminals

- Twist the wire strands together and use a screwdriver to hook the end of each wire clockwise around a terminal screw (left). The hot wire (smooth insulation) should go to the plug's narrow prong; the neutral wire should go to the wide prong.

- Tighten the terminal screws, making sure there are no stray wire ends.

- Snap the core into the shell and tighten any retaining screws.

Quick-Connect Plugs

Inserting the wire and making the connection

- Unplug the lamp, and cut the old plug from the cord.

- Pull the two pieces apart and thread the cord through the shell of a new plug. Spread the prongs by hand (right) and insert the lamp cord, aligning the neutral wire with the wide prong.

- Squeeze the prongs together by hand. Slide the shell over the plug.

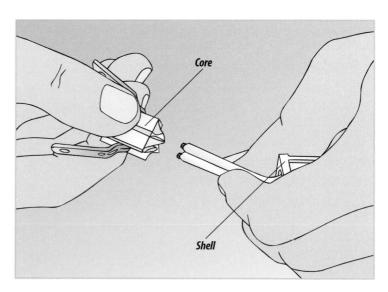

Rewiring a One-Socket Lamp

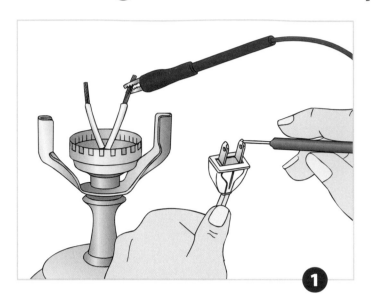

1. Testing the cord and plug

- Unplug the lamp and remove the socket (page 94).

- Set a multitester to RX1, and clip one probe on one wire end (left). Place the other probe against one plug prong and then the other. The meter should indicate continuity on one prong only (page 96).

- Repeat for the other wire end. If the cord and plug fail either test, rewire the lamp (Steps 2–3).

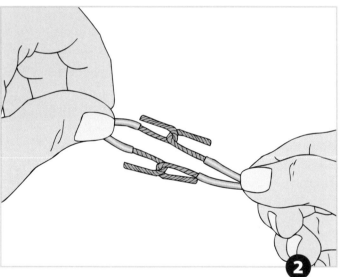

2. Tying the old cord to the new

- Strip the ends of the new cord (page 97), and twist the strands clockwise.

- At the top of the lamp, hook the ends of the old and new cords together (left).

- Wrap electrical tape around the connection. If it won't fit through the lamp, unhook one pair of wires and retape them alongside the remaining hooked pair.

3. Fishing the new cord

- With a paring knife, carefully peel back the base's felt cover far enough to uncover the cord in the lamp base.

- Feed the connection into the center pipe at the top of the lamp. From the base, pull on the old cord until the connection appears (right). Then pull on the old cord at the edge of the lamp base to bring the new cord through the channel.

- Untape the connection, and discard the old cord.

- Install a new socket (page 95) and plug (page 99).

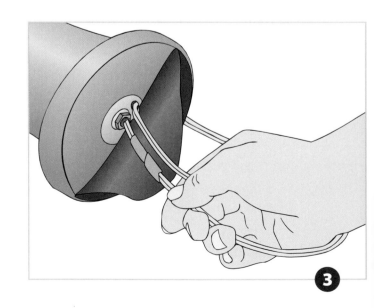

Rewiring a Multi-Socket Lamp

1. Disconnecting the wires

- Unplug the lamp and remove the shade. Remove the sockets (page 94). Test the wires for each socket (page 100, Step 1).

- Pull the socket wires out of the socket caps with long-nose pliers (right).

- One wire to each socket is connected to each of the lamp cord wires. Remove any electrical tape, twist off the wire caps, and disconnect the wires. Cut and fish new cord (page 100, Step 3).

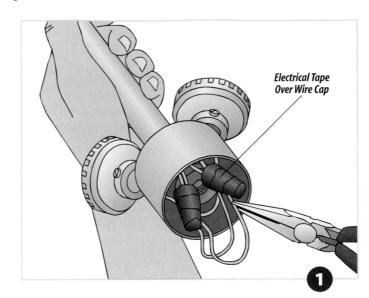

Electrical Tape Over Wire Cap

2. Rewiring the socket

- For each socket, cut a piece of lamp cord the same length as the old socket wires, then part and strip both ends of both socket wires, as well as the upper end of a new lamp cord (page 97).

- Connect the neutral wire—the one with the ridge in its insulation—to the silver socket terminal and the other wire to the brass socket terminal. Place the socket in the lamp, feeding the wires through the socket cap (left).

- Reinstall the socket's insulating sleeve and shell, pushing on the shell until it snaps into place.

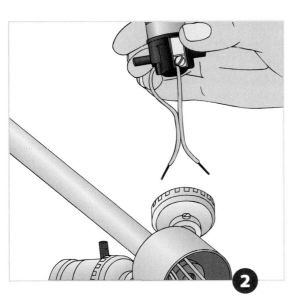

3. Connecting the socket wires to the lamp cord

- Twist the cord's neutral wire together with the neutral wires from each socket, and the cord's unridged wire with the unridged wires from each socket.

- Secure each connection with a wire cap and electrical tape (left).

- Fold the wires back into the top of the lamp and replace the cover.

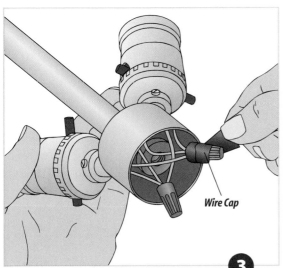

Wire Cap

Rewiring an Incandescent Desk Lamp

1. Disconnecting the socket-retaining ring

- If your lamp has a switch at the top of the shade, use pliers to unscrew the socket-retaining ring (right). The method for getting at the socket may vary for lamps with a switch in the base.

- Push the cord into the lamp at the base to gain some slack. Pull the socket out of its ceramic or plastic insulating sleeve.

- Use a screwdriver to loosen the terminals, and disconnect the wires.

- With a multitester, test the cord for continuity (page 96). If it fails, rewire the lamp (Steps 2–3).

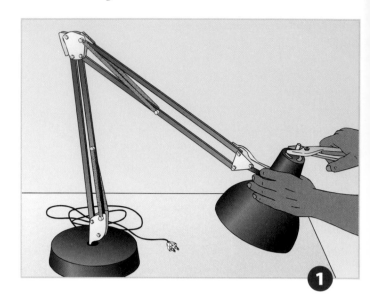

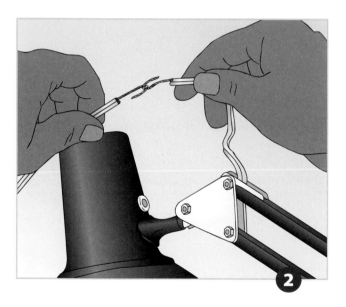

2. Tying the old cord to the new

- Pull the cord through the hole in the lampshade so that its wire ends are exposed at the top of the upper arm.

- To make a joint that's thin enough to fit through the channel of the lamp arm, hook together only one wire of the old and new cords (left). Secure the joint with electrical tape.

3. Fishing the new cord

- Feed the spliced cords into the upper lamp arm (left). Use the old cord to pull the new cord through the upper and lower arms.

4. Reassembling the lamp

- Feed the end of the new cord into the lampshade.

- Strip the wire ends, and attach them to the socket terminals (page 95).

- Pull the cord at the lamp elbow to create 3 or 4 inches of slack.

- Set the socket assembly inside the shade (right). Screw on the socket-retaining ring and tighten with pliers.

- Remove all but 2 inches of slack at the elbows by pulling the cord through from the base.

- Install a new plug (page 99).

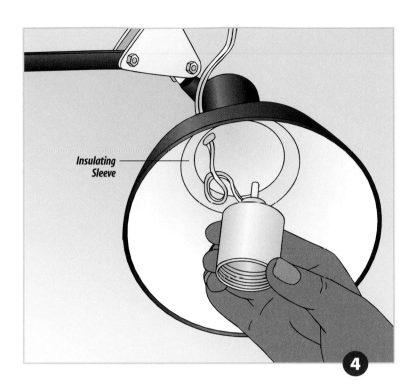

Insulating Sleeve

Troubleshooting a Halogen Lamp

Start with the same tests you would perform on an incandescent lamp (pages 94, 97, and 98). Then unplug the lamp and remove the bulb with a clean cloth (below). (Touching a halogen bulb with your fingers deposits oils that shorten its life; if you accidentally touch it, clean the spot with rubbing alcohol.)

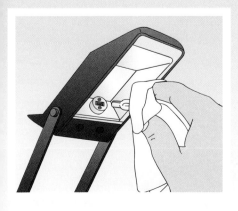

Set a multitester to the AC scale just above the lamp's rated voltage (test a low-voltage lamp on the 50-volt scale); then touch the probes to the socket terminals (right). If the meter shows the rated voltage, try a new bulb. If the meter shows a lower-than-rated voltage level, the problem may be a faulty transformer (on low-voltage lamps), a blown lamp fuse, a broken cord, or a damaged socket.

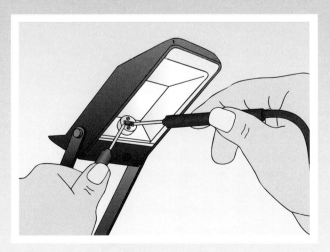

Models vary greatly, and replacement parts can be hard to find; so it's usually best to take halogen lamps to a dealer for repairs.

103

Troubleshooting a Fluorescent Desk Lamp

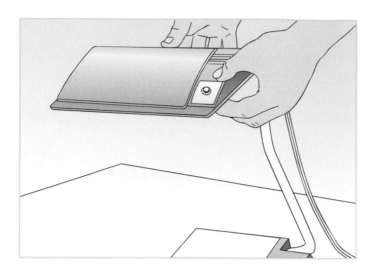

Checking the tube and removing the lamp head

- With the lamp switch in the OFF position, grasp the tube as close to the base as possible. Gently wiggle it back and forth until it pulls free.
- Take the old tube with you to purchase a replacement.
- Holding the new tube at the base, push it firmly into the socket.
- If the lamp still doesn't work, unplug it. Loosen any screws or clamps holding the lamp head on the stem, then slide it up and off (left).

Gaining access to key parts

- Remove any screws from the component case in the lamp head (right), and pry off the cover with a screwdriver.
- Make a sketch of how the parts are wired together so that you can reassemble the lamp correctly.

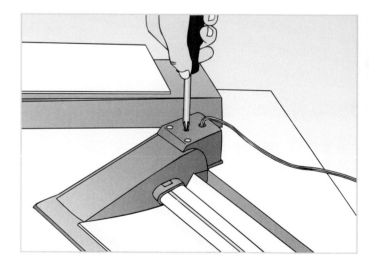

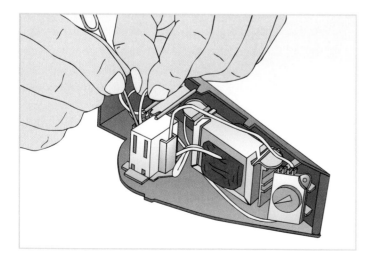

Testing and replacing the socket

- The single socket on this lamp has two push-in terminals. To disconnect the socket, push a pin or paper clip into the slot beside the wire and pull the wire free (left).
- Two plastic prongs secure the socket. Squeeze them together and pull the socket out of the lamp.
- Buy a replacement socket of the same wattage, and snap it into place.
- Reattach the cover plate, and return the assembled head to the lamp arm.

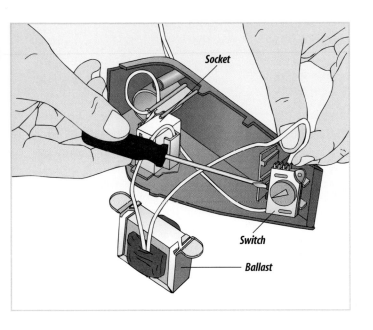

Socket

Switch

Ballast

Replacing the switch or ballast

- Disconnect the switch by detaching the wires from the two screw terminals (left). Detach the ballast wires from the switch and socket.

- Take the old ballast or switch to a lamp store for a matching replacement.

- Connect the new components to the same wires as the old.

- Set all of the parts back into the lamp head, tuck in the wires, and reattach the cover plate.

- If the lamp still doesn't work, test the cord and plug (page 100), and if either part fails a continuity test (page 96), replace it.

Repairing a Trigger-Switch Fluorescent Lamp

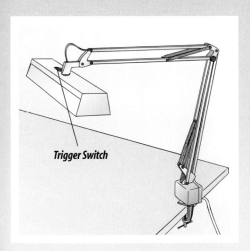

Trigger Switch

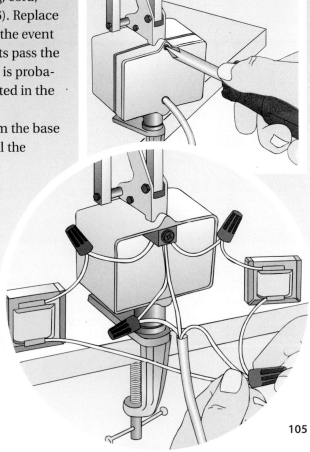

Trigger-switch fluorescent lamps, like the one shown (above), are similar to starter-type fixtures (page 116): Pressing the switch button for several seconds provides the necessary voltage surge to energize the gas in the bulb. If a trigger-switch lamp won't light, first replace the tube. If that fails, unplug the lamp and perform continuity tests on the plug, cord, socket, and switch (page 96). Replace components as needed. In the event that all of these components pass the continuity tests, the culprit is probably the ballast, usually located in the lamp base.

Remove the screws from the base plate (above right), and pull the wires from the base (below right). Remove the ballast; some lamps have two of them. Detach the two wires from one ballast at a time. If the wires aren't color-coded, twist them together to identify them as a pair. Take the ballasts to a lamp store for a correct match. Reverse this process to reassemble the lamp.

Lighting Fixtures

HOW THEY WORK

Incandescent ceiling lights come in two varieties—surface-mount fixtures (below right) and pendant fixtures, or chandeliers (below left). Both have leads that connect to house-circuit wires in a ceiling box. The leads (stranded wires) of a surface-mount ceiling fixture attach directly to the socket. In the pendant fixtures, leads from the sockets connect to fixture leads that run up the stem.

A surface-mount fixture fastens directly to the ceiling box with screws through the housing. Pendant fixtures and ceiling fans hang from a mounting strap fastened to the box. A threaded nipple screws into the strap and is attached to the stem with a fitting called a hickey. Other fixture-mounting variations include pull-chain sockets (page 110), track lights (page 112), and recessed fixtures (page 114). Fluorescent fixtures are explained on page 116.

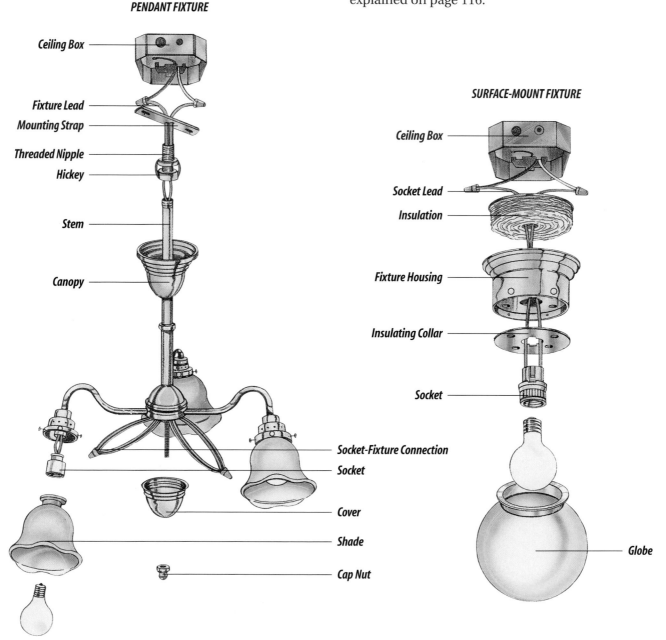

PENDANT FIXTURE

Ceiling Box
Fixture Lead
Mounting Strap
Threaded Nipple
Hickey
Stem
Canopy
Socket-Fixture Connection
Socket
Cover
Shade
Cap Nut

SURFACE-MOUNT FIXTURE

Ceiling Box
Socket Lead
Insulation
Fixture Housing
Insulating Collar
Socket
Globe

BEFORE YOU START

Always look for the simpler problems before dismantling a fixture to look for more challenging ones.

First check the bulb. If you're not sure whether the bulb is good, screw it into another fixture. If the bulb lights, the problem may be in the switch. Test the switch (page 122) before disassembling the light fixture to get at the sockets and wiring.

Most of the light fixtures shown in this chapter fasten to the ceiling, but the techniques for repairing them apply to wall fixtures as well.

TIPS

- Many light fixtures are wired with lamp cord. A ridge in the insulation of one of the two wires designates it as the neutral wire, which always goes to the silver socket terminal or to a white circuit wire.

- When rewiring a light fixture, select new wires that are the same gauge as the old ones, with insulation that's resistant to high temperatures.

SAFETY FIRST

Always cut power to a lighting circuit at the service panel as the first step in a light-fixture repair. But before doing so, turn on the switch that controls the fixture, to avoid misleading readings when testing for voltage.

Repairing Surface-Mount Fixtures

1. Dismounting the fixture

- Flip off the wall switch and loosen any retaining screws holding the globe in place, then remove the globe. Tighten a loose bulb or replace one that's burned out with a new one, and flip on the switch.

- If that doesn't solve the problem, flip on the switch, then turn off power to the fixture at the service panel by setting the circuit breaker to the OFF position or removing the fuse (page 88).

- Remove the mounting screws from the base, and gently lower the fixture (right).

- For a wall fixture, remove the globe for access to the locknut. Unscrew the locknut, then gently pull the fixture housing off the threaded nipple.

2. Checking for voltage

- With a helper, unscrew the wire caps from the black and white wire connections, being careful not to touch the bare wire ends.

- Set a multitester to 250 in the AC-voltage range (page 96). Touch one probe to the ground screw in the mounting strap and the other one first to the black wire connection (left), then to the white wire connection. Next touch probes to the white wire and black wire connections. If the needle moves during any test, return to the service panel and turn off the correct circuit.

  CAUTION: *Since there is a possibility that current may be flowing to the circuit, hold the multitester probes by their insulated grips.*

- After confirming that power is off, untwist the connections and take down the fixture.

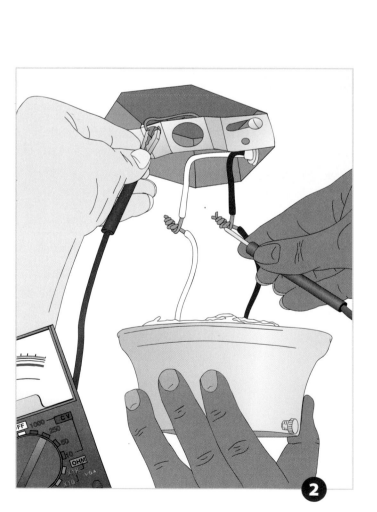

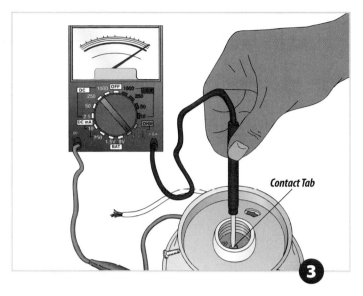

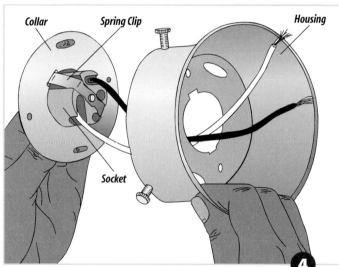

3. Testing the socket

- Expose the base of the socket by pulling away any insulation. Scrape any corrosion from the socket contact tab and pry it up slightly to make better contact with the bulb (page 94).

- Set a multitester to RX1 and test for continuity (page 96). To do so, clip one probe to the bare end of the black wire and touch the second probe to the contact tab (left). A reading of 0 ohms indicates continuity between the wire and the contact tab.

- Clip a probe to the bare end of the white wire, and touch the probe to the socket's threaded metal tube. The meter should indicate continuity.

- Replace the socket and its leads if you obtain different results.

4. Replacing the socket

- Press the spring clip or unscrew the retaining ring to remove the socket. Buy a compatible replacement socket, and thread the socket wires through the insulating collar (if any), then through the fixture housing (left).

- Snap or screw the new socket into place.

5. Connecting the wires

- Suspend the fixture from the electrical box by a hook fashioned from a wire coat hanger, and restore any insulation that you removed (right).

- Twist together the black socket lead with the black wire from the ceiling box, and the white socket lead with the white wire from the box; screw a wire cap onto each connection. Make sure the cable's ground wire is secured to the ground terminal on the mounting strap.

- Remove the coat hanger, and fold the wires into the ceiling box. Align the mounting slots with the mounting holes on the ceiling box, then insert and tighten the mounting screws. Screw in the bulb, set the globe in place, and retighten the retaining screws.

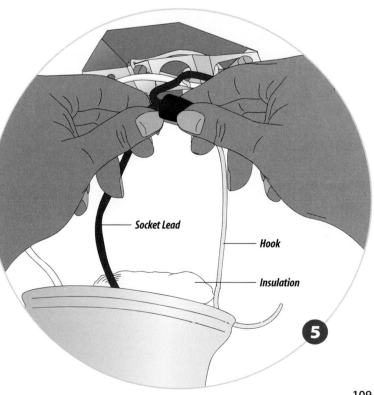

Replacing a Pull-Chain Socket

1. Testing for voltage

- Turn off power to the fixture by unscrewing the fuse or tripping the circuit breaker (page 88). Remove the bulb from the socket.

- Take out the screws that hold the fixture to the ceiling, and unscrew the cap from the socket (inset). Lower the fixture, taking care not to touch the socket or any metal parts.

- Set a multitester to 250 in the AC-voltage range (page 96). Clip one probe to the brass socket terminal, and touch the other to the ground wire. Repeat the test between the silver terminal and the ground wire (right). If the needle moves during either test, return to the service panel and cut power to the correct circuit.

- After confirming that the power is off, disconnect the wires from the socket terminal screws.

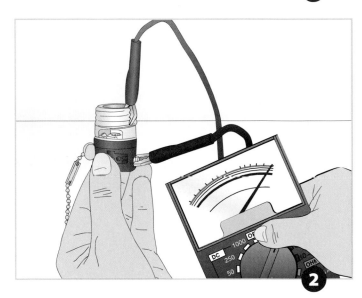

2. Testing the socket and switch

- Set a multitester to RX1 for a continuity test (page 96). Clip one probe to the threaded metal tube, and the second probe to the silver terminal (right). The meter should indicate continuity.

- Next clip one probe to the brass terminal screw, and the second probe to the socket contact tab.

- Pull the switch. The meter should indicate continuity when the switch is in one position and no continuity in the other. Get a new socket if your results differ.

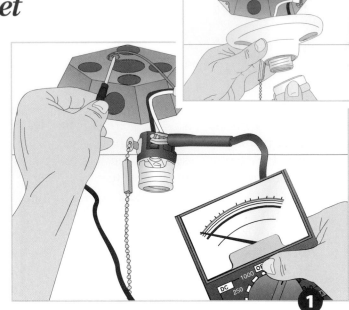

3. Replacing the socket

- Trim and restrip burned wire ends, then bend them into hooks to make a solid contact with the terminals.

- Connect the black wire to the brass socket terminal, and the white wire to the silver one. Carefully fold the wires into the ceiling box, and thread the pull chain through its hole in the fixture (right).

- Align the mounting slots with the mounting holes on the ceiling box, then insert and tighten the mounting screws.

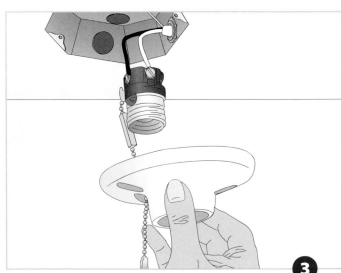

Testing and Repairing a Pendant Fixture

1. Opening up the fixture

If a single socket fails to work, see pages 108–110 for tests and repairs. If replacing a socket does not solve the problem, move on to the steps below.

- Flip on the switch, and turn off power to the circuit at the service panel (page 88). Loosen the canopy screws and lower the canopy. Unscrew the wire caps from the connection, taking care not to touch the wires. Check for power in the box (page 108, Step 2).

- Unscrew the socket from the fixture. Locate the word PRESS on the socket, and apply pressure to remove the outer shell. Slip off the socket insulating sleeve (page 94). Pull the socket away from the cap to expose at least 1 inch of wire.

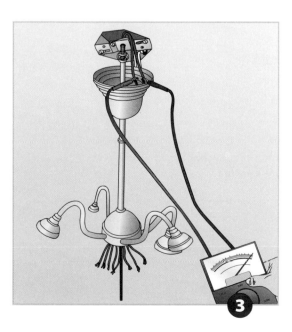

Canopy

2. Testing socket wires

- Remove the cover at the base of the fixture. Pull out and disconnect the wires. If none of the sockets work, go to Step 3.

- To test the wires to a single socket, first confirm that the ridged wire goes to the silver terminal. If not, reverse the connections.

- Set a multitester to RX1, and clip one probe on the ridged socket wire at the fixture base (left). Touch the other probe to the silver terminal. Next, place the alligator clip on the unridged wire and touch the probe to the brass terminal. Both tests should indicate continuity (page 96).

- Replace the socket wires if they fail the test. Disconnect the socket, and fish new wires to the socket (page 100).

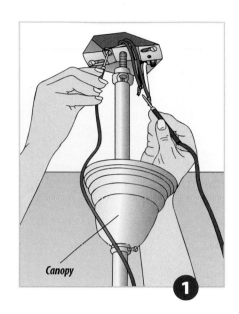

3. Testing the stem wires

- Twist the two stem wires together at the fixture base. Clip one multitester probe to each of the wires at the top of the stem (right). The meter should indicate continuity.

- If the wires fail the test, fish new wires through the stem (page 100).

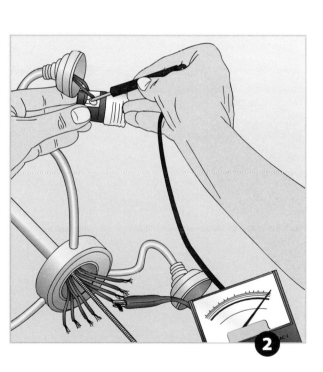

Troubleshooting Track Lights

TRACK-LIGHT ANATOMY

A track is wired to a house circuit at a ceiling box (right), which serves as the power source for two metal conductors that run the length of the track. Each fixture has a contact arm with two track contacts at the top. When a fixture is mounted to the track, the two contacts bridge the conductors to complete a circuit through a pair of wires to the socket and lightbulb.

Shut off power at the service panel before working.

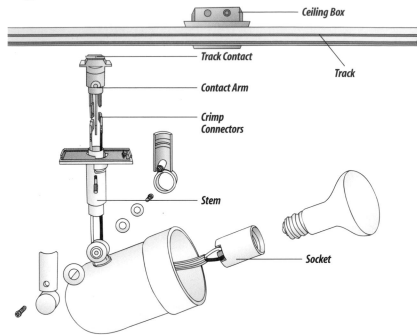

Ceiling Box
Track Contact
Track
Contact Arm
Crimp Connectors
Stem
Socket

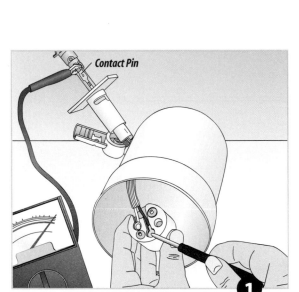

Contact Pin

1. Testing the socket

- To remove a light fixture, you may need to turn a lever, or rotate the entire fixture.
- Remove the screws holding the socket to the shade, and pull the socket free of its mounting.
- Crimp-on connectors join the socket leads to contact pins protruding from the contact arm. Set a multi-tester to RX1, and clip one probe to the brass contact pin. Touch the other probe to the black wire connection at the socket (above). The meter should indicate continuity (page 96).
- Place the alligator clip on the silver contact pin, and touch the tester probe to the white wire connection. The meter should indicate continuity. If the socket fails either test, replace it (Step 3).

Splicing Lamp Cord to Solid Wire

To get a good, permanent connection between stranded lamp cord and solid copper house wires, first strip about an inch of insulation from each wire. Then wrap the stranded wire around the solid one and hold the two wires together near the ends with lineman's pliers (below left). Use the pliers to fold the splice in two and squeeze it flat (below right). Finally, twist on a wire cap of the appropriate size, leaving no copper visible. This technique provides a solid connection and won't let the stranded wire slip.

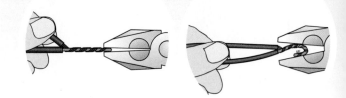

2. Removing the old socket

- Gently pull the socket wires from the contact pins (right).

- Extract the socket, wires, and insulating sleeve from the shade. Slip the wires out of the insulating sleeve, and set it aside.

- Purchase a comparable replacement socket with preattached wires. Also buy crimp-on connectors the same size and shape as the old ones.

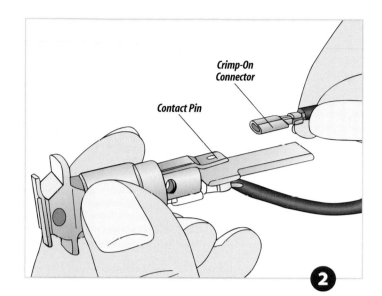

3. Installing the new socket

- Slip the insulating sleeve over the new wires, and thread the wires first through the hole in the shade, then through both parts of the stem.

- Twist the strands of the socket wires tightly together, and push a crimp-on connector onto the end of each. Use a multipurpose tool to crimp the connectors tightly onto the socket wires.

- Slide the black wire connector onto the brass contact pin and the white wire connector onto the silver contact pin (right).

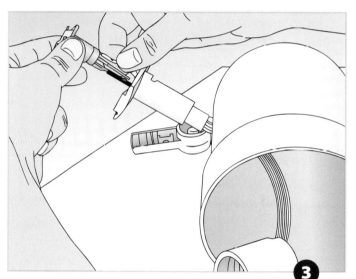

4. Reassembling the fixture

- Set the socket in the shade, and tighten the screws that secure it.

- Screw the lever (if any) into the stem by hand, then reassemble the stem and screw it together (right).

- Fit the fixture into the track, turn it a quarter-turn, and lock it in place with the lever. Or, twist the entire fixture a half-turn to lock it firmly in place.

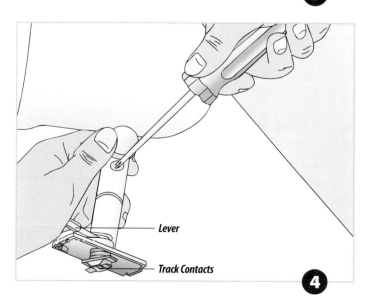

Ceiling Fan Repairs

CEILING FAN ANATOMY

A ceiling fan is an electric motor with blades attached. A shaft connected to the motor housing extends up and locks into place on a mounting ball; the mounting ball rests in a bracket that supports the fan's weight. A canopy covers the mounting assembly. Many ceiling fans have an integral light fixture with wiring and mounting features similar to those of pendant lights (page 111).

1. Taking down the fan

- Flip on the switch and cut power to the circuit at the service panel (page 88).

- Loosen the screws holding the canopy, and slide it down the shaft to expose the wire connections and the mounting bracket.

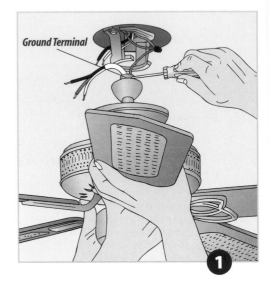

- Pull the black and white wire connections and the blue lighting wire, if any, out of the ceiling box. Unscrew the wire caps from the connections with the black and white cable wires, taking care not to touch any exposed wire ends. Leave the ground-wire connections in the box.

- Set a multitester to 250 in the AC-voltage range (page 96). Holding the probes by their plastic handles, touch one probe to the mounting plate and the other to the black and white wire connections in turn. The meter should not register voltage. After confirming the power is off, disconnect the wires.

- Have a helper raise the fan, then slip the mounting ball out of the bracket. Push the ball downward to expose the ground wire connected to a terminal at the top of the shaft. Loosen the screw (above), detach the wire, and lower the fan.

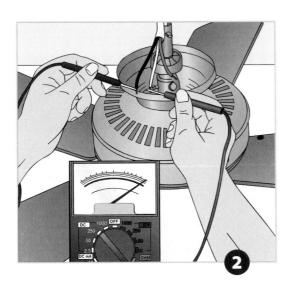

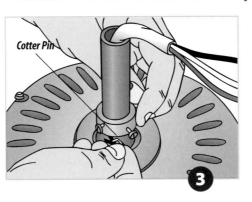

2. Testing the motor

- Set a multitester to RX1 and test the motor for continuity (page 96). To do so, set the pull-chain to the ON position and touch one probe to the black lead and the other to the white lead (above). The meter should register between 20 and 30 ohms.

3. Inspecting the pins and blades

- Pull out the cotter pin that secures the motor housing to the fan shaft (above) and the pin that holds the mounting ball in place; inspect each pin. Replace either pin if it appears worn.

- Check the blades and blade holders. If any blades are warped or broken, replace the entire set. Tighten any loose blade screws.

- Reinstall the fan and restore power to the circuit.

Repairing Recessed Fixtures

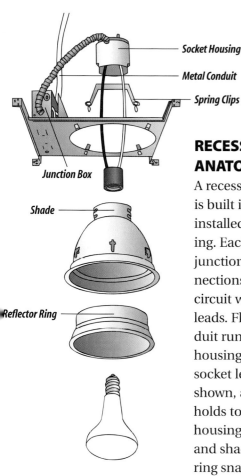

Socket Housing

Metal Conduit

Spring Clips

Junction Box

Shade

Reflector Ring

RECESSED-FIXTURE ANATOMY

A recessed ceiling fixture is built into a housing installed above the ceiling. Each housing has a junction box for the connections between house-circuit wires and socket leads. Flexible metal conduit runs to the socket housing and protects the socket leads. In the type shown, a spring clip holds together the socket housing, fixture housing, and shade. A reflector ring snaps into the shade.

1. Removing the shade

- Flip on the switch and cut power to the circuit (page 88). Unscrew the bulb, then snap out the reflector ring.

- Gently pry around the shade with a stiff putty knife to work it loose.

- Push hard on the spring clips that hold the shade to the socket housing. Lower the shade to expose the socket housing and ceiling box (right).

CAUTION: *Do not touch the socket until you have confirmed with a voltage test that the power is off.*

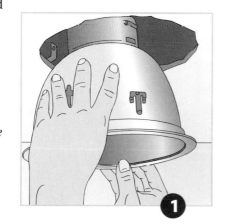

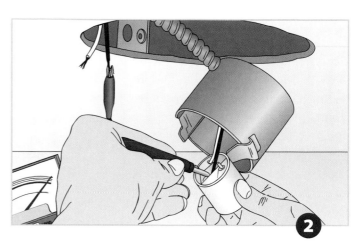

2. Testing for voltage

- Unclip the cover from the junction box; twist off the wire caps, taking care not to touch any bare wire ends.

- Set a multitester to 250 in the AC-voltage range (page 96). Touch one probe to the black wire connection, and the other first to the ground wire and then to the white wire connection. Then test between the white wire connection and the ground. If the meter registers voltage, return to the service panel and cut power to the correct circuit.

- Untwist the wire connection in the junction box. Set a multitester to RX1, and clip one probe to the black socket lead. Touch the other to the socket contact tab. Repeat this test between the white socket wire and the threaded metal socket tube. There should be continuity in both tests (page 96).

3. Replacing the socket (not shown)

- With diagonal-cutting pliers, cut the socket leads.

- Temporarily splice the new wires to the old wires at the socket housing, and secure the connection with tape. Pull the old wires from the box end of the flexible metal conduit to bring the new wires with them. Leave 8 inches of new wire in the electrical box.

- Untape the old wires and discard them. Twist together the new black wire with the black wire in the box and the new white wire with the white wire in the box. Screw a wire cap onto each connection.

- Gently fold the wires into the electrical box, and snap the cover onto the box. Reassemble all the parts and secure the fixture to the ceiling.

Fluorescent Fixtures

THREE TYPES OF FIXTURES

The illustrations on this page show typical ceiling-mounted fluorescent fixtures. All work on the same principles and have most parts in common, but there are subtle differences.

In every one, power from a 120-volt household circuit enters the fixture through the top. A ground jumper connects the circuit's ground wire to a ground terminal on the fixture housing. The black and white wires go to the ballast, a transformer-like device that feeds current to the sockets.

In a rapid-start fixture (top right), the ballast boosts voltage to start the tube, then limits current once the tubes are lit. Older fixtures, like the one below, employ a component called a starter and two ballast circuits, one to provide the initial surge of voltage and the other for continuous operation. A socket at each end holds a straight tube. Circular tubes plug into a single socket (right).

Many of the newest fluorescent fixtures have electronic ballasts, which are very durable. If replacing a tube does not solve the problem for one of these models, replace the entire fixture.

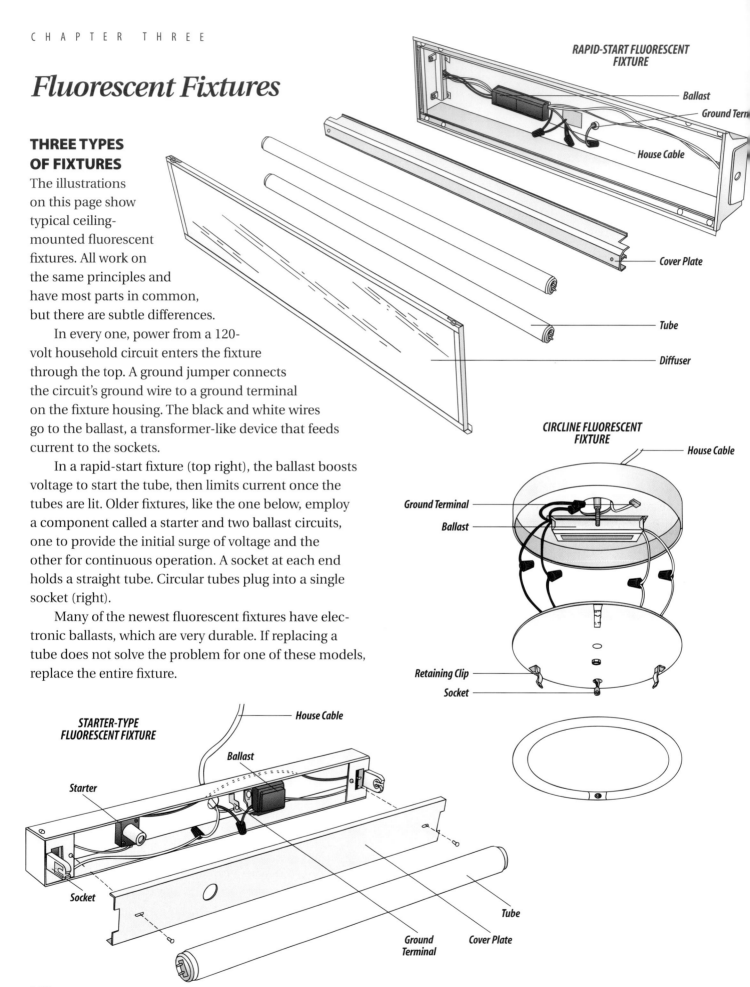

RAPID-START FLUORESCENT FIXTURE
Ballast
Ground Term
House Cable
Cover Plate
Tube
Diffuser

CIRCLINE FLUORESCENT FIXTURE
House Cable
Ground Terminal
Ballast
Retaining Clip
Socket

STARTER-TYPE FLUORESCENT FIXTURE
House Cable
Ballast
Starter
Socket
Ground Terminal
Cover Plate
Tube

Changing Tubes and Starters

1. Tightening or removing the tube

- Remove the diffuser—the plastic shield covering the tube(s). If the fixture does not light, first try gently twisting the tube to tighten it. If it still does not light, or if the tube has dark spots at either end, replace it.

- Hold a straight fluorescent tube at both ends; then rotate the tube a quarter-turn in either direction, and lower the pins from the sockets (right).

- Detach a circline tube by pulling the socket off the tube pins and releasing the tube from the retaining clips on the fixture.

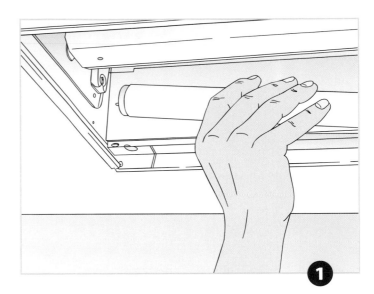

2. Replacing a starter

If the fixture is the rapid-start type, skip this step and go to Step 3.

- Push in the starter and twist it counterclockwise a quarter-turn; then pull it out (right). Take the old starter to a lighting store; the wattage of the new starter must match that of the tube and ballast.

- Insert the new starter so that the pins on one end enter slots in the fixture; then turn the starter clockwise until you hear it click into place.

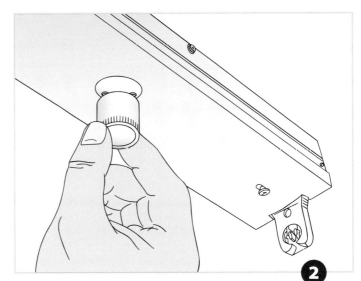

3. Installing a new tube

- For a straight tube, insert the pins vertically in the sockets (right) and twist the tube a quarter-turn to seat it. Replace the socket if the pins do not fit snugly (page 118).

- Install a circline tube by lining up the pins with the holes in the socket and pushing the socket onto the pins. Fit the tube between the fixture's retaining clips.

Ballasts and Sockets

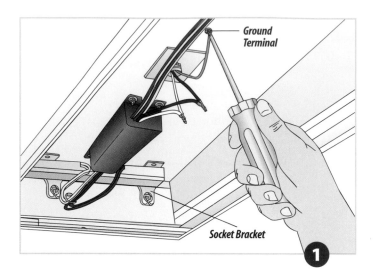

Ground Terminal

Socket Bracket

1. Testing for voltage and checking ground connections

- Flip off the switch and cut power to the circuit at the service panel (page 88). Remove the diffuser and tubes (page 117). Squeeze the cover plate to release it from the frame and expose the wiring.

- Unscrew the wire caps from the black, white, and ground-wire leads, taking care not to touch the bare wire ends.

- Set a multitester to 250 in the AC-voltage range (page 96), and check for the presence of power.

- Inspect the ground connection to the fixture. Tighten the screw if it's loose (left).

2. Replacing a socket

- With the power off, unscrew the socket bracket to expose the socket connections.

- If the socket has preattached leads (no push-in terminals or terminal screws), cut the wires close to the socket, leaving long leads (right). Disconnect a socket with push-in terminals by inserting a screwdriver tip into each terminal slot and pulling out the wire. For a socket with screw terminals, loosen the screws and remove the wires.

- Buy a replacement socket with screw terminals. Strip the wire back ½ inch on each lead, and connect the wires to the new socket. Either lead can go to either terminal.

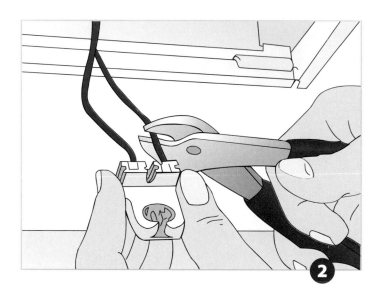

3. Replacing a ballast

Any of these symptoms may point to a faulty ballast: The fixture won't light; the tube flickers or is slow to light; or the fixture hums. The clearest sign is black resin dripping from the ballast.

- The ballast is the most expensive part of a fluorescent fixture, so you may choose to replace the fixture altogether.

- To replace a ballast, disconnect the wires, unscrew the ballast (left), and buy an exact replacement. Reattach all the wires in their original positions.

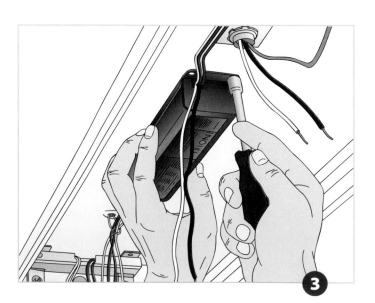

Replacing a Fluorescent Fixture

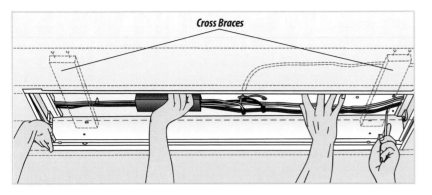

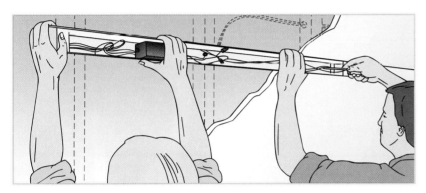

Dismounting the old, installing the new

- Flip on the switch and cut power to the fixture at the service panel (page 88).

- Remove the diffuser and tubes. Squeeze the cover plate to release it from the frame, exposing the sockets. Test for voltage to confirm that power is off (page 118).

- Twist the wire caps off the connections between the incoming cable and the ballast's black and white leads, then disconnect the cable ground wire from the fixture. Unscrew the locknut on the clamp that secures the power cable to the fixture.

- Have a helper support the fixture while you remove the fasteners. Fixtures recessed in drywall or plaster ceilings are usually screwed to cross braces between joists (top left). Surface-mount fixtures (middle left) are usually attached directly to the ceiling or wall. Fixtures recessed in a suspended ceiling (bottom left) are usually supported by the ceiling grid; safety chains, straps, or wire may hold them in place. Remove any ceiling tiles around the fixture for access.

- Have a helper support the fixture while you clamp the cable to the unit through the knockout in the housing.

- Mount the new fixture to the ceiling.

- Connect the black lead to the black house wire and the white lead to the white house wire. Secure the connections with wire caps.

- Connect the cable's bare copper ground wire to the grounding terminal on the fixture housing (page 116).

- Replace the cover plate, install the tubes and the diffuser, and then restore power.

Wall Switches

HOW THEY WORK

A single-pole switch (below) has two terminals. Inside a typical switch is a metal bar called a contact arm. It's hinged at the bottom, where it's always in contact with the lower terminal. When the switch is in the OFF position, as it is here, a spring holds the top of the bar away from the upper terminal. Flipping the toggle ON snaps the bar into contact with the upper terminal, completing the circuit.

Three-way switches (page 124) are designed to control lights from more than one location. Dimmer switches (page 126) offer infinite adjustability to control the intensity of light.

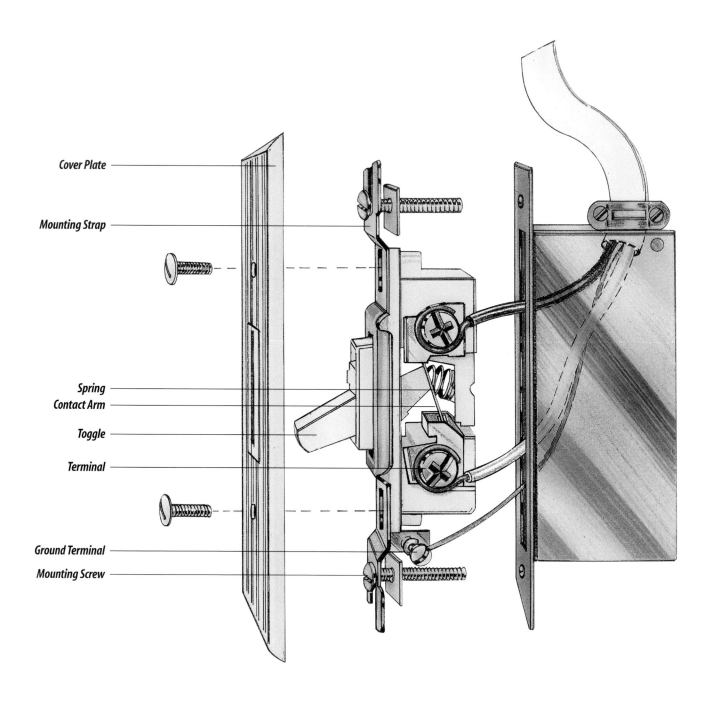

Cover Plate

Mounting Strap

Spring

Contact Arm

Toggle

Terminal

Ground Terminal

Mounting Screw

BEFORE YOU START

When a light controlled by a switch doesn't work, begin your investigation by replacing the bulb, resetting the circuit breaker, or changing the fuse. Or the difficulty may lie in the wiring connections to the switch; tighten them before replacing the switch.

Most wall switches last 20 years or longer; and when they finally wear out, it's the mechanism that goes, rather than their ability to conduct electricity. In some instances, you may choose to replace a switch in good working order with one of a different kind. Dimmer switches, for example, are handy in many parts of the house. Other switches can turn lights on and off automatically or even tell you when you've left the basement light on.

SAFETY FIRST

Before working on a switch, turn off power to the circuit by removing the fuse from the service panel or tripping the circuit breaker. Never restore power until you have returned the switch to its box.

If a switch-controlled light won't turn on
- Replace bulb; replace fuse or reset breaker **88**
- Test and replace switch **122–123**
- Check the light fixture **106–119**

If a fuse blows or breaker continually trips when you turn on a switch
- Adjust load on circuit **91**
- Check switch-wiring connections . . . **122**
- Check the light fixture **106–119**

If a light flickers, or the switch sparks or makes a crackling noise
- Check switch-wiring connections . . . **122**
- Test and replace switch **122–123**

If a toggle does not stay ON
- Replace switch **123**

If both 3-way switches must be flipped to turn on fixture
- Check switch-wiring connections . . . **122**
- Test switches and replace if faulty **124–125**

If a dimmer turns light on and off but will not dim
- Replace dimmer **126**

Testing and Replacing a Single-Pole Switch

1. Checking for voltage

- Cut power to the circuit at the service panel by switching off the circuit breaker or removing the fuse (page 88). Take out the two screws securing the cover plate (inset), and lift it off.

- Set a multitester to 250 in the AC-voltage range (page 96). If the wall box is metal, touch one tester probe to the box; for plastic boxes, touch the probe to a bare grounding wire. In both cases touch the other probe to each wire connected to the switch (right). The multitester should register 0 voltage in each case.

- If any reading is greater than 0, return to the service panel and turn off power to the circuit.

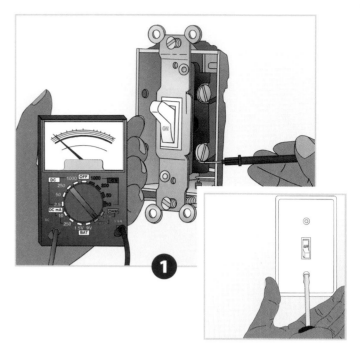

2. Freeing the switch

- Remove the mounting screws at the top and bottom of the mounting strap (left).

- Grasp the mounting strap, and pull the switch out from the box.

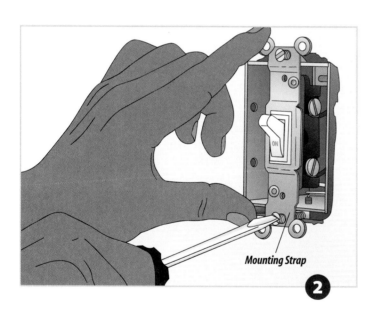

Mounting Strap

3. Checking terminal connections

- Use a screwdriver to tighten any loose connections.

- If the wire ends are burned or damaged, clip them off (right), restrip the ends (page 97), and form new hooks (page 123, sidebar).

- Reconnect the wires, return the switch to the box (Step 5), turn on the power, and flip on the switch. If it works, reattach the cover plate. If not, shut off power to the circuit again, then proceed to the next step.

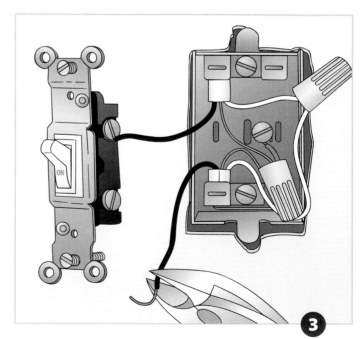

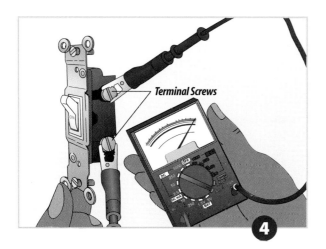

4. Testing the switch for continuity

- Loosen the terminal screws and disconnect the wires to free the switch.
- Set a multitester to RX1, turn on the switch, and clip one probe to each switch terminal (left). The meter should indicate continuity (page 96).
- Turn off the switch and repeat the test. The meter should indicate an open circuit.
- If your results differ, replace the switch.

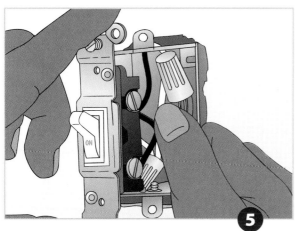

5. Connecting the new switch

- Hold the switch so the toggle points up when ON.
- Hook the wires around the terminal screws of the new switch just as they had been connected to the old one. Tighten the screws securely.
- Put the switch in the box, carefully folding the wires to make them fit (left).
- Screw the mounting strap to the box, making sure the switch is straight. Reattach the cover plate and turn on the power.

Making Perfect Connections

Poor connections can cause lights to flicker and dim, and electric motors to run hotter and die sooner. They have even been known to overheat wiring and start fires. A switch may have wire leads that are connected to the house wiring with wire caps (page 125), or wires may connect to the switch at screw terminals.

To create a hook for connecting a wire to a screw terminal, first strip about ½ inch of insulation from the wire end. Using long-nose pliers, make a right-angle bend (below left).

Move the pliers' jaw tips about halfway along the stripped wire end, and bend it about 45 degrees in the opposite direction (center). With the tips of the pliers, bend the wire to a C-shape, leaving the loop open to fit around the screw (above).

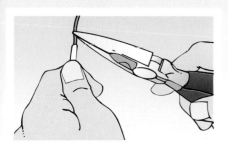

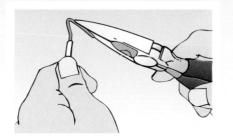

Troubleshooting a 3-Way Switch

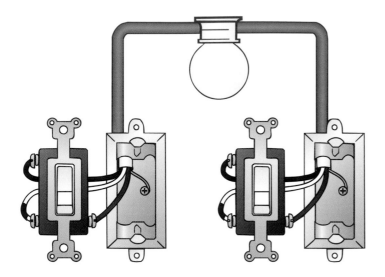

A 3-way circuit

Named for the number of terminals per switch, 3-way switches control a light from two locations. The illustration (left) shows one typical wiring scheme, in which black wires connect to switches' common terminals (black or copper), white wires are painted black or wrapped with black tape to indicate that they are hot, and red wires connect to the switches' brass terminals.

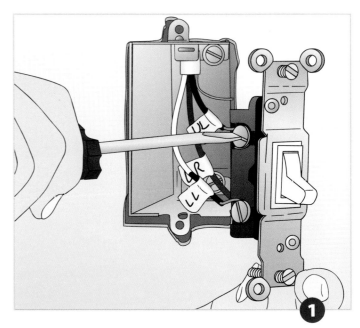

1. Removing the old switch

- Turn off power to the circuit at the main service panel (page 88).

- Remove the cover plate and, with a multitester, check for voltage at the switch terminals (page 122).

- Remove the mounting screws, and pull the switch from the box.

- Tag each wire with a label indicating the switch terminal to which it is connected. Loosen the terminal screws and pull off the wires (right).

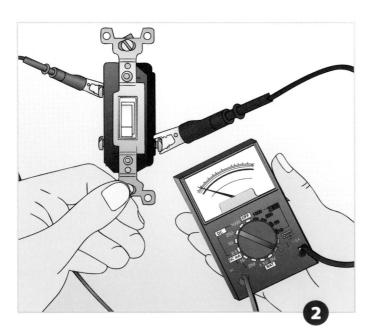

2. Testing a 3-way switch

- Set a multitester to RX1. Clip one probe to the black or copper terminal, and the other probe to either of the others (left).

- Flip the switch. If the switch is good, the meter will indicate continuity in one position and not the other (page 96).

- Flip the switch to the position in which the meter indicated continuity in the previous test, then clip the black probe to the terminal you haven't yet tested. The meter should indicate no continuity.

- Without moving the probes, flip the switch. The meter should indicate continuity.

- If the first switch passes, check the other one in the circuit. If either switch fails, replace it (Step 3).

3. Installing the new switch

- Connect the wires to the terminals of the new switch as they were connected to the old one, using the tags you attached to them as a guide (right). As a rule, the incoming hot wire (black) goes to the black or copper terminal on the switch. Other wires—white, white recoded as black, and red—are generally connected to the brass or silver terminals. If present, the bare copper or green wire should be connected to the green ground terminal.

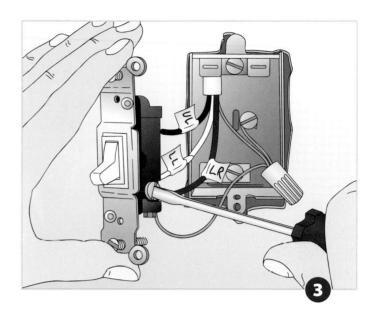

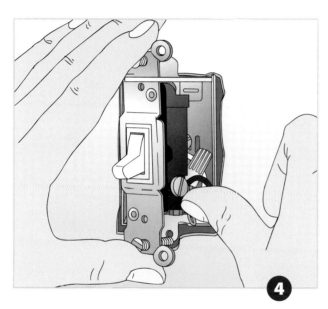

4. Remounting the switch

- Fold the wires into the switch box while pushing the switch into place (above).
- Tighten the mounting screws to fasten the switch to the box.
- Remount the switch plate, and turn on power to the circuit at the service panel.

Making Tight Splices

When splicing wires, strip off about 1 inch of insulation from the ends of the wires to be joined—more than actually seems necessary. Hold the wires side by side with one hand, grip the bare ends with a pair of lineman's pliers, and twist them together clockwise until the turns are tight and uniform (below left). Test the connection with a slight tug.

Clip about ½ to ¾ inch off the splice with diagonal-cutting pliers, snipping an angle to create a distinct point at the spliced wire ends (below middle). Tighten the cap (below right) clockwise until no copper shows. Wrap electrical tape around the base of the cap to make sure that everything stays put.

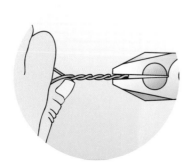

Replacing a Dimmer Switch

Checking for voltage

- Turn off power to the circuit at the service panel (page 88). Pull off the control knob, and unscrew the cover plate. Free the switch housing (page 122). Remove the wire caps joining the switch leads to the house wires.

- Set a multitester to 250 in the AC-voltage range. Touch one probe to the box if it's metal (or ground wire if it's plastic) and the other to each exposed splice in turn (right). Then test the wire connections against each other. If the meter shows voltage present, return to the service panel and cut power to the circuit before continuing.

- Check for loose connections, corrosion, and burned wires at the splices. Clean the wire ends or clip the wires back (page 136) as necessary. Then reinstall the dimmer and turn on the power.

- If the switch doesn't work after these efforts, replace it.

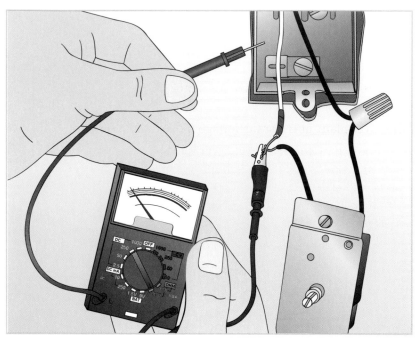

Connecting a dimmer

Single-pole dimmer switches have two leads. Get a replacement rated at the same wattage as the old switch.

- To install a single-pole dimmer, secure either lead to either wire in the electrical box with wire caps (right).

- Place the switch in the box, attach the cover plate and control knobs, and turn on the power at the service panel.

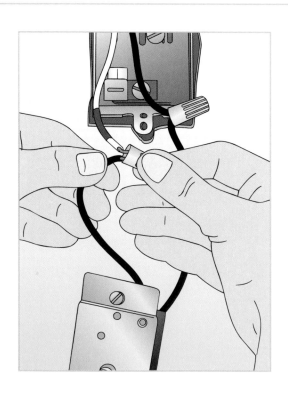

Servicing Ganged Switches

Multiple switches on the same circuit

- When two switches occupy one box, both are on the same circuit if one black wire is connected to both switches by jumpers (right).

- Shut off power to the circuit at the service panel (page 88).

- Remove the cover plate, and test for voltage (page 122).

- When you are sure that power to the circuit is off, unscrew the wire caps as necessary and inspect all connections (page 123). Clean terminals and the wires, clip off any burned ends, and restrip the wires; then reconnect them as you found them.

- Return the switches to the box, turn on the power, and flip the switch.

- If the fixture does not light, turn off the power, disconnect the switch, and test it for continuity (pages 96 and 123).

- If the switch fails the continuity test, replace it with a new one.

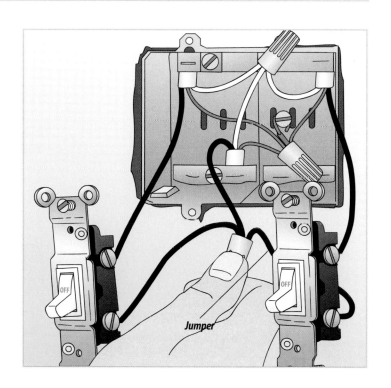

Jumper

Multiple switches on separate circuits

Two switches installed in a single box are on different circuits if none of the wires are connected to both switches by jumpers.

- Shut off power to both circuits at the service panel (page 88) and test for voltage (page 122).

- Disconnect the inoperative switch (right), and test it for continuity (page 123). If the switch fails the continuity test, replace it with a new one.

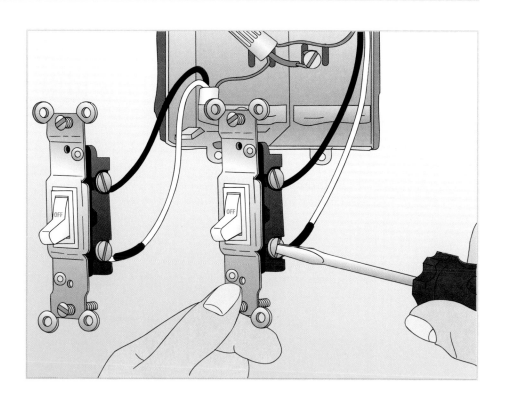

Grounding Switches and Switch Boxes

Grounding is an important safety precaution. If the cable in the box has a ground wire, any of the wiring plans shown here will result in good grounding.

Metal Box with One Cable

When the switch has no ground terminal, secure the cable ground wire to the screw at the back of the box. The screws holding the switch to the box complete the grounding circuit.

For a switch with a ground terminal, use a jumper and a wire cap to connect it to the cable ground wire and to a jumper from the ground screw in the box.

Metal Box with Two Cables

For a switch without a ground terminal, attach a jumper to the ground screw at the back of the box, twist it together with the bare ground wires from the two cables, and then secure them with a wire cap. If the switch has a ground terminal, attach a jumper wire and join it with both cable ground wires and a jumper to the box.

Plastic Boxes

Where the switch has a ground terminal and the box doesn't, secure a jumper to the cable ground wire and fasten it to the switch ground terminal. If only the box has a ground terminal, fasten the cable ground wire to it. Where two cables enter a plastic box, splice ground wires from both to a jumper and connect it to the ground terminal on the box or switch.

CAUTION: *Never pair a switch and a plastic box unless one of them has a ground terminal.*

METAL BOX WITH 1 CABLE

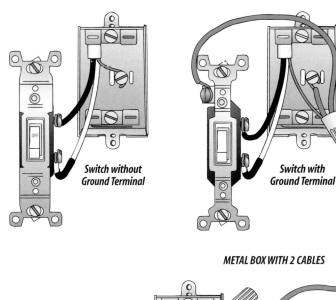

Switch without Ground Terminal

Switch with Ground Terminal

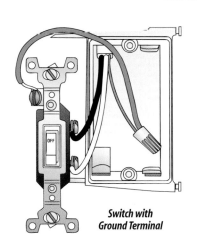

Switch with Ground Terminal

PLASTIC BOX WITH 1 CABLE

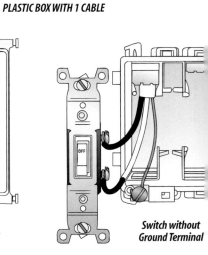

Switch without Ground Terminal

METAL BOX WITH 2 CABLES

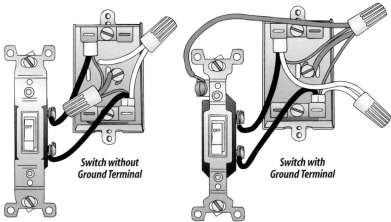

Switch without Ground Terminal

Switch with Ground Terminal

Troubleshooting a Switch-Outlet

When switch and outlet are independent

A switch-outlet combines a toggle switch with an outlet. The switch and outlet may work independently, or the switch may control the outlet. Shown (right) is the wiring for independent operation.

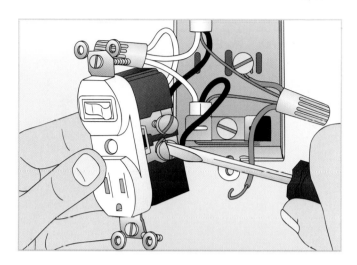

- Shut off power to the circuit at the main service panel (page 88). Remove the cover plate and test all connections for voltage (page 122), and free the switch from the box.

- Before loosening the terminals with a screwdriver (right), tag the black wire that leads to the brass terminal on the side of the switch with the connecting tab.

- Check and clean or repair the connections as necessary (page 123).

- Restore power to the circuit at the service panel. Flip on the switch to see whether the light that it controls gets power. Plug a lamp into the outlet to see whether it works. If one of these tests fails, turn off the power and test the switch for continuity (below).

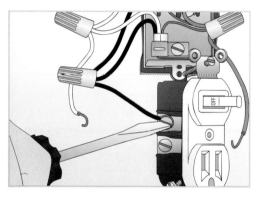

When the switch controls the outlet

This illustration shows the typical wiring for a combination switch-outlet where the switch controls the outlet. Follow the troubleshooting procedures described above; then, if necessary, perform continuity tests as described below. To reconnect or replace the unit, proceed as follows:

- Connect the black jumper wire to the upper terminal on the side with no connecting tab (left). Fasten the white jumper around the lower terminal on the same side. Attach the ground jumper to the ground terminal.

Testing for continuity

- After turning off the power and disconnecting the unit, set a multitester to RX1.

- Touch the probes to the two upper terminals, and toggle the switch. If the switch is good, the meter will indicate continuity in the ON position but not in the OFF position (page 96).

- If the unit fails the test, replace it, reattaching the wires as you found them.

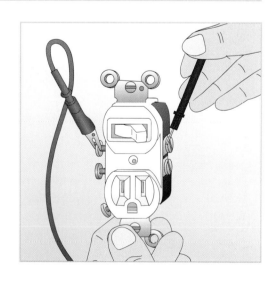

Doorbells and Chimes

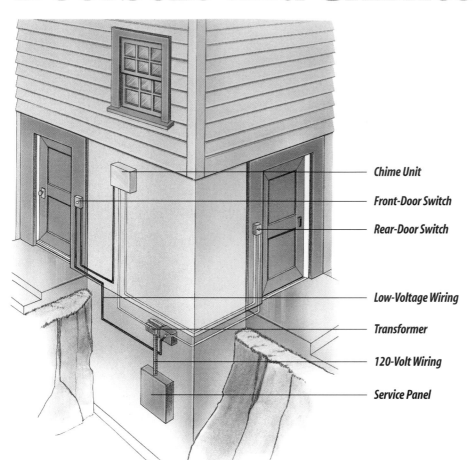

Chime Unit

Front-Door Switch

Rear-Door Switch

Low-Voltage Wiring

Transformer

120-Volt Wiring

Service Panel

HOW THEY WORK

In a typical doorbell system, standard 120-volt current coming from the service panel is fed to a transformer, which reduces voltage to meet the requirements of the bell or chime unit. Bells usually work on 10 to 20 volts, chimes on 16 volts. Low-voltage current flows from the transformer to the bell or chime unit by way of push-button switches mounted at the doors. Pressing the button closes contacts within the switch, completing the circuit to sound the chimes or bell. When working on a doorbell or chime, you don't have to shut off power, because low voltage is not dangerous.

Push-Button Repairs

1. Servicing the contacts

- Pry off or unscrew the push-button cover and set it aside.
- Use fine sandpaper to clean the metal contacts. Pry up the contacts with a screwdriver to improve the connection (right).
- If the bell rings or the chime unit hums continuously, you've bent the contacts too far; bend the contacts down slightly. If the bell doesn't ring at all, go to Step 2.

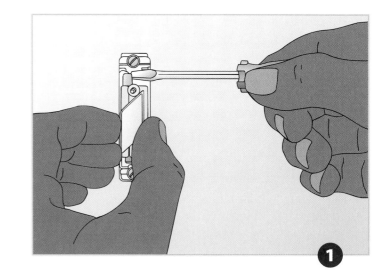

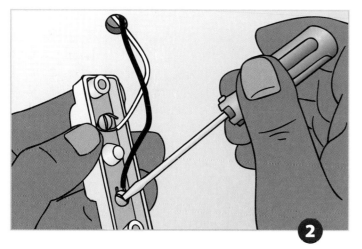

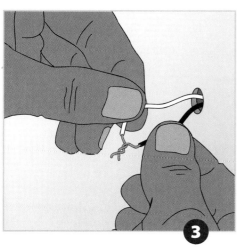

2. Remaking the connections

- Pry off or unscrew the push-button cover and set it aside.

- Loosen the screws securing the mounting plate to the door frame or siding. Pull the mounting plate forward to expose the wiring. Loosen the terminal screws and unhook the wires (left).

- Clip the exposed wire ends, strip back the insulation, and reattach the wires to the terminals.

- If the bell doesn't sound when you push the button, proceed to Step 3.

3. Isolating the problem

- Remove the wires and touch them together. If the bell now sounds, the push button is faulty. If the bell doesn't sound, test the transformer (page 132).

- To replace a faulty push-button switch, connect the wires to the terminal screws on the new mounting plate.

- Screw the mounting plate to the siding or door frame, snap on the cover, and test.

Fixes for Chimes and Bells

1. Servicing the unit

The illustrations here and on the next page show a mechanical chime, but the sounding device may instead be a bell, a buzzer, or an electronic chime.

- Remove any screws holding the cover in place, and pull it forward to reveal the sounding components.

- Locate the terminals labeled FRONT, TRANS, and REAR. Clean and tighten loose connections (right). Cut back any damaged wire ends, restrip them, and attach them to the terminals.

- On mechanical chimes, blow dirt away from the plungers and sounding bars. Clean the plungers with alcohol and a cotton swab. Test; if there's no sound, go to Step 2.

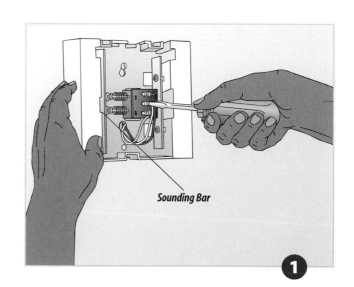

Sounding Bar

(CONTINUED)

Fixes for Chimes and Bells—continued

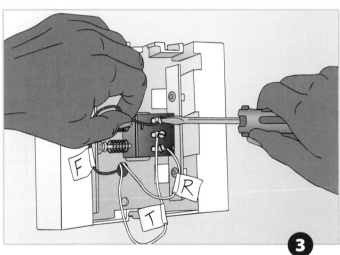

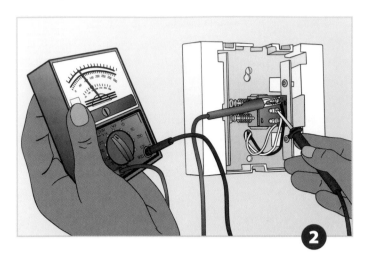

2. Testing the unit

- Locate the transformer and check the low-voltage output on the specification label. Set a multitester to 50 in the AC-voltage range.

- Holding the probes by their plastic covers, test a chime unit by clipping one probe on the TRANS terminal and touching the second probe to the FRONT terminal (left). Repeat the test with the REAR terminal, if present. (Test a bell unit by touching one probe to each bell terminal.)

- Readings within 2 volts of the transformer rating indicate sufficient voltage at the sounding unit; replace the unit if it doesn't ring. A reading of 0 volts indicates a break in the wiring; locate and replace faulty wires.

3. Replacing the unit

- Label the wires and disconnect them (left). Remove any mounting screws.

- Buy a replacement chime or bell that matches the transformer's voltage and amperage ratings. Mount it to the wall.

- Using labels on wires as a guide, attach the wires to the correct terminals of the new unit. Restore power and test.

Replacing a Faulty Transformer

1. Checking the low-voltage side

- Set a multitester to 50 in the AC-voltage range (page 96). Holding the probes by their plastic handles, touch one to each low-voltage terminal on the transformer (right). A reading that corresponds to the transformer rating indicates a faulty bell or chime. Go to Step 2 if there is no reading.

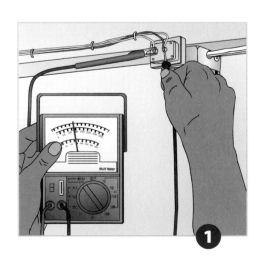

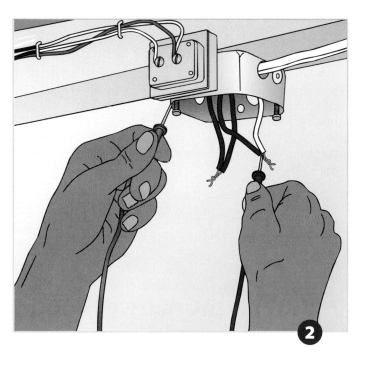

2. Servicing the 120-volt connections

- Turn off power to the circuit at the service panel (page 88). Unscrew the junction box cover to expose the 120-volt connections to the transformer.

- Unscrew the wire caps, taking care not to touch exposed wire ends. Set a multitester to 250 in the AC-voltage range. Touch one probe to the box if it's metal or to the ground screw if it's plastic; touch the other probe to each wire in turn (left). Next test between the two wire connections. If there's a voltage reading in any test, go the service panel and cut power to the correct circuit.

- Burnish wire ends or clip off damaged ones, strip back the insulation (page 96), and reattach them. Restore power and test. Install a new transformer if the bell or chime does not ring (Step 3).

3. Replacing the transformer

- Turn off power to the circuit at the service panel (page 88). Test for voltage at the junction box (Step 2) to be sure the circuit is dead.

- Label the wires connected to the terminal screws on the low-voltage side of the transformer, and detach them.

- Disconnect the wires inside the junction box and unscrew the transformer (right). Buy a replacement of the same voltage and amperage ratings.

- Thread the transformer leads through the side of the junction box, and fasten the transformer securely to the box.

- Twist one transformer lead to the black house wire and the other to the white house wire, securing each connection with a wire cap. Following their label instructions, attach the low-voltage wires to the transformer terminals, then restore power and test. Check the chime or bell unit if it does not ring (page 131).

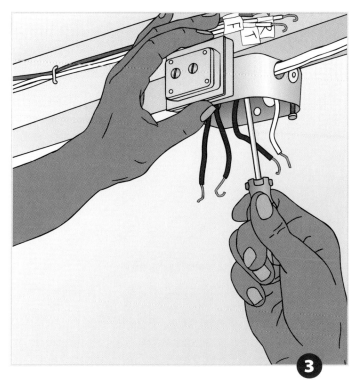

Wall Outlets

HOW THEY WORK

The illustration below shows a modern 120-volt, 15-amp duplex (two-receptacle) wall outlet. Each receptacle has three openings. One leads to the black (hot) wire, always connected to a brass terminal screw, that brings power from the service panel. A shorter slot beside it leads to the white, or neutral, wire (silver terminal).

The third, round slot leads to a grounding terminal.

A duplex outlet also has a connector tab that links the two receptacles electrically and assigns both to the same circuit. Breaking off the tab permits each receptacle to be on a different circuit or to have one receptacle but not the other controlled by a wall switch.

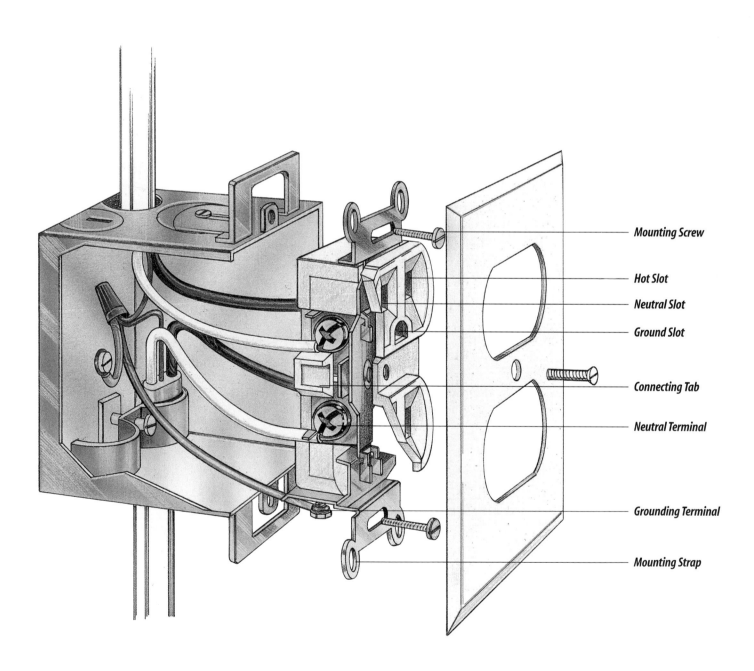

Mounting Screw

Hot Slot

Neutral Slot

Ground Slot

Connecting Tab

Neutral Terminal

Grounding Terminal

Mounting Strap

BEFORE YOU START

The most common problem with outlets that have been in service for many years is worn internal contacts—plugs feel loose when you insert them in the outlet. Replace the outlet if its contacts are worn.

Wires connected to outlets can work themselves loose with ordinary expansion and contraction or from vibration. This can cause sparking and a potential fire hazard. Always tighten terminal screws firmly on wires and avoid using the push-in terminals found on the back of many outlets.

An outlet equipped with a ground-fault circuit interrupter (GFCI) turns off power instantly when it detects potentially dangerous current leakage (page 141). And there are 240-volt outlets for larger appliances (page 143), which are supplied by two 120-volt hot conductors.

TIPS

- A white wire marked with black tape or paint serves as a hot wire; connect it to a brass terminal.
- If your house wiring has no grounding, you can provide this protection against fire and shock by installing a GFCI outlet on each circuit as the first outlet that the cable encounters after leaving the service panel.

If a plugged-in appliance does not work
- Check appliance
- Replace fuse or reset circuit breaker .. **88**
- Repair outlet connections or replace outlet **136–137**

If a fuse blows or breaker trips when appliance is turned on
- Move appliance to another circuit
- Service or replace appliance
- Look for a short in the wiring

If an appliance runs intermittently or lamp flickers
- Call technician to check appliance
- Repair lamp or cord **92–105**
- Check outlet connections **136**

If you see sparks or get a mild shock when plugging in appliance
- Turn appliance off before plugging it in
- Hold plug by insulation when plugging it in
- Service or replace appliance
- Check outlet connections **136**

If a switch-controlled outlet does not deliver power
- Test wall switch and replace **122**
- Check outlet connections **136**

If a GFCI trips repeatedly
- Service or replace appliances on the circuit
- Check outlet connections **136**
- Have an electrician locate the ground fault

If a GFCI does not trip off when test button is pushed
- Replace outlet **141**

If outlets are not connected to a grounded circuit
- Install a GFCI-equipped outlet in each ungrounded circuit **141**

Duplex Outlets

1. Testing a 120-volt outlet for voltage

• After removing the cover plate, confirm that the power is off by setting a multitester to 250 in the AC-voltage range (page 96).

• Holding the probes by their insulated grips, touch one probe to a brass terminal where a wire is attached, and the other to a silver terminal where a wire is connected (right). Then touch one probe to the grounding terminal, and the other to the brass and silver terminals in succession. The multitester should register 0 voltage.

• If any test indicates that voltage is present, return to the service panel and turn off power to the correct circuit.

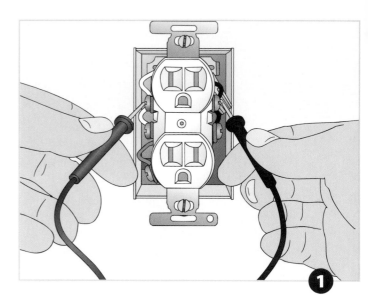

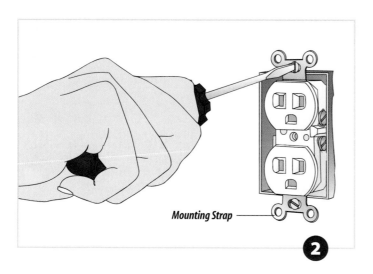

2. Freeing the outlet from the box

• Loosen the mounting screws (left).

• Grasp the mounting strap, and pull the outlet out of the box.

Mounting Strap

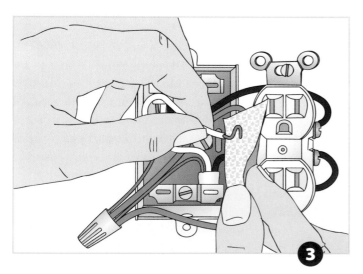

3. Checking and repairing the connections

• For a dirty or corroded connection, disconnect the wire, then burnish it with fine sandpaper (left).

• Clip off the end of a discolored wire with diagonal-cutting pliers, then use wire strippers to remove ¾ inch of insulation. Shape the wire end into a loop, and curl it around its terminal.

• If outlet terminals appear blackened or burned, replace the outlet (Step 4).

• Fasten the outlet in the box, put on the cover plate, and restore power to the circuit. Plug in a lamp to see whether the outlet is working; if not, replace the outlet.

4. Replacing the outlet

- Connect the wires as you found them connected to the old outlet: black wires to brass terminals, white wires to silver terminals, and the grounding jumper to the green grounding terminal. Tighten the terminal screws securely.

- Gently fold the wires into the box and set the outlet in place (right). Screw the mounting strap to the box, making sure that the outlet is vertical.

- Restore the cover plate and turn on the power.

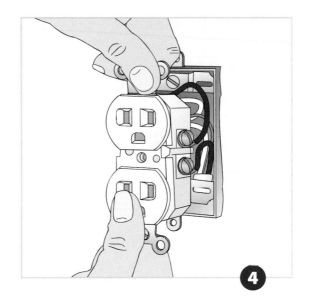

Identifying the Wiring

When you open an outlet, it can be useful to figure out the position of the outlet or switch in the circuit, as well as the function of each wire. This can help you pinpoint problems and connect wires to the correct terminals when making repairs.

If you can't find the source of a problem with an outlet, work from that point back to the service panel, troubleshooting each load on the circuit and its connections until you locate the fault.

End-of-run outlet

When there's only one cable entering an outlet box, it means the outlet is the last fixture on the circuit (near right). Power comes from the service panel along the black (hot) wire through other outlets, switches, and light fixtures on the circuit and begins its return to the source through the white (neutral) wire attached to this outlet. The black wire attaches to a brass terminal; the white wire, to a silver terminal.

Middle-of-run outlet

Two cables entering an outlet box means the outlet is not the last fixture on a circuit (right). One of

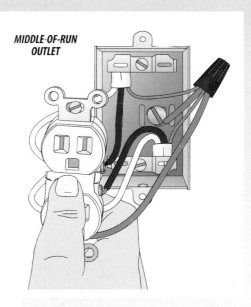

MIDDLE-OF-RUN OUTLET

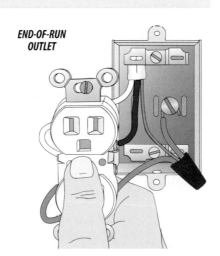

END-OF-RUN OUTLET

the black wires receives power from the service panel; the other sends it on to other loads on the circuit. The white wires allow current passing through the outlet and the other loads on the circuit to return to the panel.

Upgrading a 2-Slot Outlet

1. Testing a 2-slot outlet for ground

You can replace a 2-slot outlet with a 3-slot grounded outlet if the outlet box is grounded.

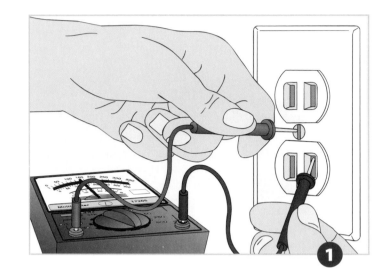

- Set a multitester to 250 in the AC-voltage range (page 96). Place one probe on the cover plate screw (scrape off paint as needed to uncover bare metal) and the other into one slot, then the other (right). The meter should indicate full voltage when the probe is in one slot, but not the other.

  CAUTION: *This is a live voltage test. Be sure to hold the multitester probes by their insulated handles.*

- A voltage reading of 0 at both slots means the box isn't grounded. Have an electrician extend a grounded circuit to it, or install a GFCI in the box (page 141).

- If the test shows that the outlet is grounded, turn off the power to the circuit at the service panel. Test for voltage (page 136) to make sure power is off, then proceed to Step 2.

How to Ground an Outlet

In a metal box (near right), the box itself as well as the outlet should be grounded. The best method is to use two jumper wires (green or bare copper), one connected to the receptacle and one to a screw at the back of the box. Or, the box's jumper wire may be connected to a clip attached to the side of the box.

If your system uses metal conduit or metal-sheathed cable (BX), there may be no grounding wire; the conduit or sheathing provides the path for grounding.

If the box is plastic (far right), only the receptacle is grounded.

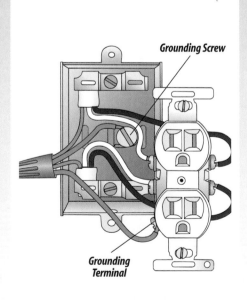

Grounding Screw

Grounding Terminal

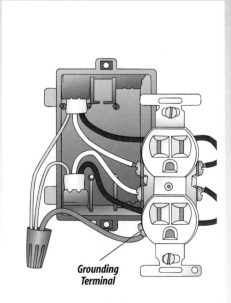

Grounding Terminal

2. Creating a grounding pigtail

Never join two wires to a single terminal; use a pigtail instead.

- Cut two lengths of wire—the same color and gauge as the wire in the box—about 6 inches long. Strip ¾ inch of insulation from all the ends (page 97).

- Form a loop at the end of one (page 123), and attach it to the grounding screw at the back of the box (right).

- Hold the two short pieces next to the grounding wire, and twist the three wire ends together in a clockwise direction using a pair of lineman's pliers (page 112). Snip off the end, and secure the splice with a wire cap.

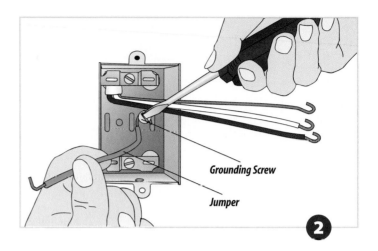

Grounding Screw

Jumper

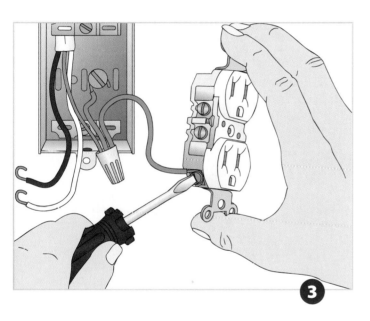

3. Connecting the grounded outlet

- Hook the free jumper from the 3-wire grounding pigtail around the green terminal on the outlet, and tighten the terminal screw securely (above).

- Hook the black wire around a brass terminal and the white wire around a silver terminal. Tighten the terminal screws.

(CONTINUED)

Using a Receptacle Analyzer

This inexpensive tool quickly tells you whether your receptacles are safely wired or not. If you have GFCI receptacles, buy an analyzer that can test them as well. Simply plug one into a receptacle. Three display lights indicate whether there is current to the receptacle, whether the hot and neutral wires are reversed, and whether the outlet is properly grounded. Always check both receptacles in an outlet. If the analyzer reveals a wiring fault, shut off power, remove the receptacle, and either rearrange the wiring or replace the receptacle.

Upgrading a 2-Slot Outlet—continued

4. Checking a 3-slot outlet for ground

• Restore power to the circuit at the service panel.

• With the multitester set to 250 volts in the AC-voltage range, insert one probe into the round grounding slot and the other probe into the other two slots in turn. This is a live test, so be sure to hold the multitester probes by their insulated handles.

• The meter should indicate voltage when the second probe is in the short slot (right) but not when it's in the longer slot.

• If the outlet fails the test, turn off the power and check the connections. Make sure the ground wires are tightly spliced and joined, that white wires are connected to silver terminals, and that black or colored wires are connected to brass-colored terminals.

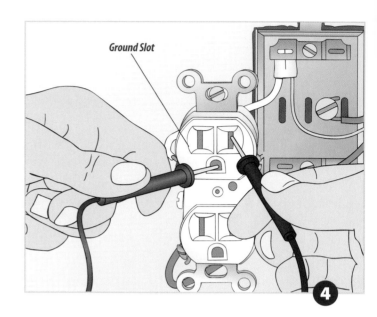

Ground Slot

4

When a Wire is Too Short

Sometimes a damaged wire may be too short for you to form a loop in the end and reconnect it directly to its terminal (below left). The solution is to attach a jumper wire to the terminal and splice it to the broken wire with a wire cap (below right).

To make the jumper, cut a 6-inch length of wire the same color and gauge as the wire in the box. With a wire stripper or multipurpose tool, remove ¾ inch of insulation from each end (page 97). Form a loop at one end with long-nose pliers (page 123). Strip the same amount of insulation off the end of the short wire in the box. With lineman's pliers, twist the two wire ends together, snip off the ends, and secure the connection with a wire cap. Hook the loop around the terminal screw and tighten it.

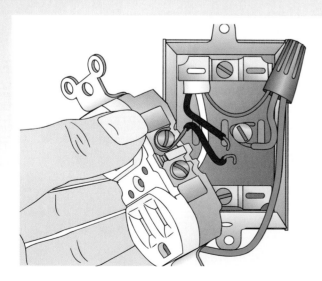

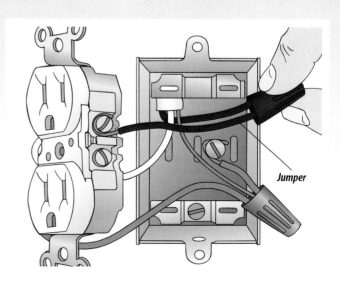

Jumper

GFCI Outlets

1. Testing the outlet

- For safety, a GFCI (ground-fault circuit interrupter) outlet shuts off power when it senses a difference in amperage between the hot and neutral wires caused by current leaking to ground or to an inappropriate conductor (such as a human body).

- Press the test button (left) once a month; if the reset button fails to pop out, replace the outlet.

- If a GFCI outlet trips repeatedly, call an electrician to find the fault on the circuit.

2. Replacing the outlet

- Turn off power to the circuit at the service panel (page 88). Remove the cover plate and test for voltage (page 136). If voltage is not 0, return to the service panel and turn off the correct circuit.

- Pull the outlet from the box. If two cables enter the box, tag the black and white wires connected to the terminals marked LINE on the back of the outlet, then disconnect all the wires (top right). (You need not tag wires in a 1-cable box.)

- When installing a GFCI outlet in a 2-cable box, connect the tagged black wire to the brass terminal marked LINE, and the tagged white wire to the corresponding silver terminal. Connect the remaining black and white wires to the other brass and silver terminals (LOAD).

- In a 1-cable box (bottom right), the black wire goes to the brass terminal marked LINE, and the white wire goes to the corresponding silver terminal.

- Connect the grounding wire to the green terminal.

- Reinstall the outlet, turn on the power, and press RESET.

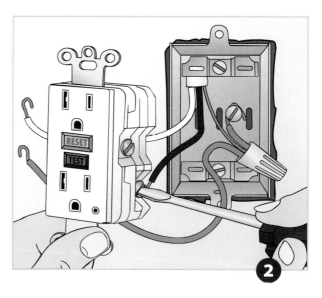

Split-Circuit Outlets

Removing the connecting tab and installing the new outlet

You can recognize a split-circuit outlet by the absence of a connecting tab linking the brass terminals. Separate hot wires attach to each brass terminal, so each receptacle is on a separate circuit.

- Turn off power to the circuits at the service panel (page 88). Usually, both circuits will be on a single 240-volt breaker, one hot wire per circuit. Remove the outlet cover and test all the wires to make sure power to both circuits is off (page 136).

- Buy a standard 120-volt receptacle, and break off the connecting tab between the two brass terminals by bending it back and forth with long-nose pliers (inset).

- Attach each hot wire (usually, one black and one red) to a brass terminal. Connect the white wire to either of the silver terminals, and the grounding jumper to the green grounding terminal. Fold the wires into the box, screw the outlet into place, replace the cover plate, and restore power.

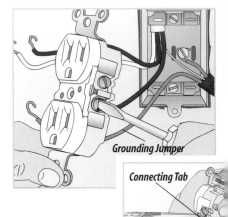
Grounding Jumper
Connecting Tab

Switch-Controlled Outlets

When the switch controls both receptacles

If a switch-controlled outlet does not work, first check the switch (page 122).

- Turn off power to the circuit at the service panel (page 88). Remove the outlet cover plate and test for power (page 136). If the power is off, pull the outlet from the box and detach the wires.

- If two cables enter the box, you are likely to find two white wires—one marked with black paint or tape—attached to the outlet. Attach the marked white wire to the brass terminal on the new outlet (below), and the other white wire to a silver terminal. Where there's only one cable, the black wire goes to a brass terminal and the white wire to a silver one. Reconnect the green jumper to the green terminal.

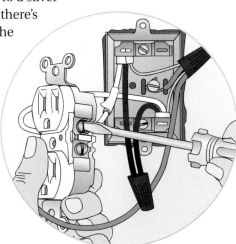

When the switch controls one receptacle

- Break off the connecting tab between the outlet's brass terminals (above).

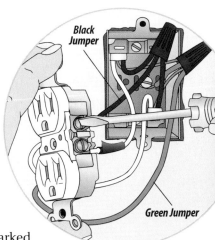
Black Jumper
Green Jumper

- For a 2-cable box (right), hook the marked white wire and the black jumper to the brass terminals. Connect the unmarked white wire to a silver terminal, and the grounding jumper to the green terminal.

- If there is one cable in the box, connect the black wire to one brass terminal, the red wire to the other brass terminal, and the white wire to a silver terminal. Attach the ground wire to the green terminal.

- Fasten the outlet to the box, screw on the cover plate, and then restore power.

240-Volt Outlets

THREE DIFFERENT TYPES

A 240-volt circuit has two hot wires; each feeds 120 volts of current to separate terminals of a 240-volt outlet. There are variations in the design and function of 240-volt outlets—the arrangement and shapes of the slots ensure that only the correct plug can be inserted. A 120/240-volt outlet is used for appliances like dryers and ranges that require 240 volts for the heating elements and 120 volts for motors, timers, and lights.

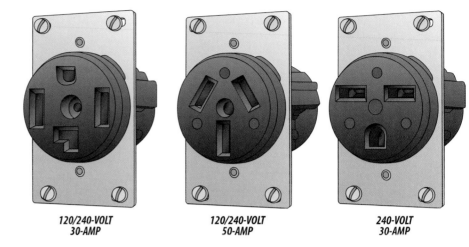

120/240-VOLT 30-AMP　　**120/240-VOLT 50-AMP**　　**240-VOLT 30-AMP**

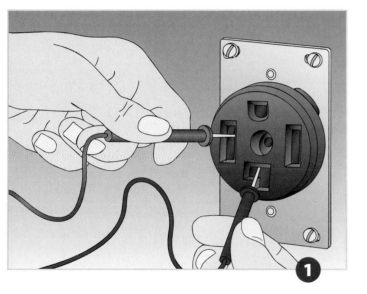

1. Checking for voltage

If an appliance seems to get no power, check the circuit breaker or fuse panel first (page 88).

- Set a multitester to 250 volts in the AC range (page 96). Insert one probe into the lower (neutral) slot, and the other into each of the upper slots, in turn (left). The meter should indicate around 120 volts for each. Then insert the probes in the two upper slots; the meter should indicate about 240 volts.

    CAUTION: *This is a live voltage test. Be sure to hold the probes by their insulated handles.*

- If you obtain different results, the outlet connections need attention or you need a new outlet. Turn off the power and test all the slots to see that power is off.

2. Checking the connections

- Remove the cover plate. Release the outlet from the box by removing the screws on the top and bottom of the mounting plate. Pull the outlet out.

- Loosen the terminal setscrews on the back of the outlet (right), and pull out each wire in turn. See that the wire ends are straight, not formed in loops. Clean any dirty or corroded connections. If necessary, clip and strip the wire ends (page 97).

- Reinsert the wires, and tighten the setscrews. Reinstall the outlet, and restore power. Test for power again (Step 1). If you get an incorrect reading for any test, turn off the power and replace the outlet, connecting wires to the new outlet as you found them on the old one.

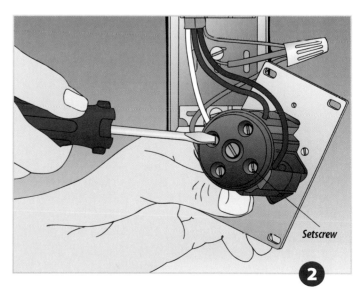

Setscrew

Heating & Cooling

Contents

INTRODUCTION

In this chapter you will learn to understand your heating and air-conditioning system and maybe save yourself a service call the next time you have a problem. Your heating and cooling system may seem too complicated for you to maintain and repair; but if you break it down into its components, there are many things you can do yourself to maintain and repair your system to keep it running trouble-free. Understanding and maintaining your system will save you money in the long run by preventing most major problems in your units from ever occuring.

Specifically, this chapter focuses on all of the major types of heating and cooling systems: forced air, electric, gas and oil furnaces, and heat pumps, as well as air-conditioning systems—both centrally located and portable window units. Your particular heating and cooling units may not exactly fit the components covered here, but you will be able to diagnose most any problem that may arise.

Questions you may have concerning your particular heating and cooling system can be answered by a heating and cooling supplier. Suppliers are usually happy to help you diagnose a problem or find the right replacement part you are looking for.

BEFORE YOU START

Locate the electrical and gas shutoffs for your unit(s). In water systems, you'll also need to know where the inlet valve to your boiler is located, as well as your system-drain valve. Know where they are and how to operate them. Call the gas or fuel-oil company if you are not sure, and a technician will help you locate them. Remember to shut off the gas or electrical supply when necessary for repairs.

System Controls

HOW THEY WORK

Your entire heating and cooling system is controlled centrally by a thermostat and can be augmented by a humidistat. A thermostat turns the entire heating or cooling system on when it senses a temperature change at its location. An automatic thermostat can be set to lower or raise the temperature in the home during preset times. A humidistat senses changes in the moisture of your home. The humidistat can change the humidity in your home by controlling a humidifier or dehumidifier in your heating and cooling system to keep the humidity at a comfortable level.

Thermostats come in various shapes and sizes, but the most common are round (below) or rectangular low-voltage thermostats, and line-voltage thermostats. A low-voltage thermostat has the voltage marked inside the unit. The line powering the heating and cooling system is stepped down by a transformer to the appropriate voltage for the thermostat. The thermostat works by signaling various relays to turn on or off the heating and cooling units in the system.

Most low-voltage thermostats use a temperature-sensitive bimetal coil that opens and closes a switch to turn the system on and off. The switch is commonly a mercury bulb-type. An encased ball of mercury rolls toward or away from electrical contacts as the bimetal coil changes shape due to temperature changes. It is imperative that these thermostats be installed perfectly level.

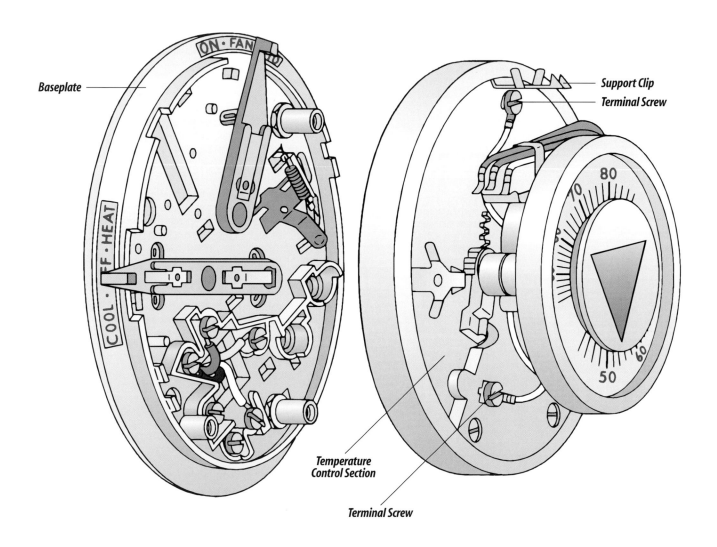

Baseplate

Support Clip
Terminal Screw

Temperature
Control Section

Terminal Screw

Troubleshooting

If you have no heat
- Replace fuse or reset circuit breaker **88–89**
- Clean thermostat **148**
- Test thermostat **152**

If heating exceeds or does not reach desired temperature
- Level thermostat **150**
- Adjust anticipator **148–149**
- Recalibrate low-voltage or line-voltage thermostat **150–151**
- Adjust range stops **151**
- Set thermostat higher or lower

If heating system short-cycles (turns on and off repeatedly)
- Clean thermostat **148**
- Adjust anticipator **148–149**

If heating system does not turn off
- Replace fuse or reset circuit breaker **88–89**
- Clean thermostat **148**
- Test thermostat **152**

If cooling system does not turn on
- Replace fuse or reset circuit breaker **88–89**
- Clean thermostat **148**
- Test thermostat **152**

If cooling exceeds or does not reach set temperature
- Recalibrate low-voltage or line-voltage thermostat **150–151**
- Level thermostat **150**

If humidifier does not turn on
- Replace fuse or reset circuit breaker **88–89**
- Test humidistat **153**

Cleaning Thermostat Switches

Cleaning the contacts and the bimetal coil

- Turn off the power to the heating and cooling system. Remove the thermostat cover and unscrew the temperature control section from the base.

- Dip a cotton swab in a solution of vinegar and water mixed 50/50. Rub the swab against contacts to clean them (right).

- Gently turn a round thermostat's dial or a rectangular thermostat's lever from the lowest to the highest setting to help dislodge stubborn particles.

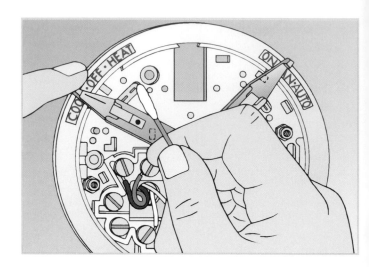

Adjusting the Anticipator

Checking and setting the anticipator

- You'll find a label listing the amperage setting for your thermostat circuit in your system's instruction manual, on an electric furnace's service panel, and on an oil- or gas-fired furnace or boiler's transformer or relay box.

- Turn off power to the heating system at your home's service panel, and remove the thermostat cover.

- Note the position of the anticipator indicator on its scale. On an air-distribution system, the indicator should point to the recommended amperage setting you found on the service panel. In a water-distribution system, the indicator should point to a number 1.4 times the amperage setting.

- If the anticipator is not set at the correct amperage setting, use a toothpick or a pencil to carefully shift the indicator— along a round thermostat's linear scale (right) or a rectangular thermostat's circular scale (inset).

- A two-stage thermostat has two adjustable anticipators; adjust each according to the recommended amperage setting for its heating unit.

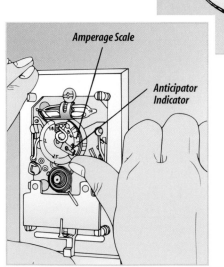

Amperage Scale

Anticipator Indicator

Thermostats with Automatic Temperature Adjustment

By maintaining the highest or lowest required temperatures for 4 or 5 hours a day instead of 24 hours, a programmable thermostat pays for itself, in energy saved, in 4 years.

Programmable thermostats use microprocessors and thermistor sensors. Most programmable thermostats store and repeat multiple daily settings, which you can manually override without affecting the rest of the daily or weekly program. They can store six or more temperature settings a day and adjust heating or air-conditioning turn-on times as the outside temperature changes. Most have a liquid crystal temperature display and use backup battery packs so there's no need to reprogram the time or clock after a power failure.

There are five basic types of automatic and programmable thermostats:

- Electromechanical (EM)
- Digital
- Hybrid
- Occupancy
- Light-sensing

Most range from $30 to $100, except for occupancy and light-sensing thermostats, which cost around $200.

Electromechanical (EM) thermostats, usually the easiest to operate, typically have manual controls such as movable tabs to set a rotary timer and sliding levers for night and day temperature settings. These work with most conventional heating and cooling systems, except heat pumps. EM controls have limited flexibility and can store only the same settings for each day, although at least one

manufacturer has a model with separate settings for each day of the week. EM thermostats are best suited for people with regular schedules.

Digital thermostats are identified by their LED or LCD digital readouts and data entry pads or buttons. They offer the widest range of features and flexibility, and can be used with most heating and cooling systems. They provide precise temperature control, and they permit custom scheduling. Programming some models can be complicated. Have a dealer or salesperson show you how to program the models you are interested in so you can determine what level of features and complexity you want.

Hybrid systems combine the technology of digital controls with manual slides and knobs to simplify use and maintain flexibility. Hybrid models are available for most systems, including heat pumps.

Occupancy thermostats maintain the setback temperature until someone presses a button to call for heating or cooling. They do not rely on the time of day. The ensuing preset "comfort period" lasts from 30 minutes to 12 hours, depending on how you've set the thermostat. Then, the temperature returns to the setback level. These units offer the ultimate in simplicity but lack flexibility. They are best suited for spaces that remain unoccupied for long periods.

Light-sensing thermostats, designed for offices and stores, are set to trip on or off when the room's lights are turned on or off

Before you buy a programmable

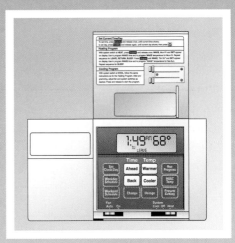

thermostat, keep track of your daily schedule for a week so you can determine exactly when you want your system to come on and off each day. This will help you decide what type of thermostat will best serve your needs.

Some modern heating and cooling systems require special controls. Heat pumps, for instance, usually require special setback thermostats, which typically use algorithms to minimize the use of backup electric-resistance heat systems. Electric-resistance systems, such as electric baseboard heating, also require thermostats capable of directly controlling 120-volt or 240-volt line-voltage circuits.

When a heat pump is in its heating mode, setting back a conventional heat pump thermostat can cause the unit to operate inefficiently, canceling out any savings achieved by lowering the temperature setting. Maintaining a moderate setting is the most cost-effective. Recently, however, some companies have begun selling specially designed setback thermostats for heat pumps, which make setting back the thermostat cost-effective.

Leveling a Low-Voltage Thermostat

Checking the level of the thermostat

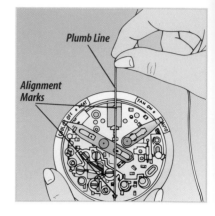

Plumb Line

Alignment Marks

- First, turn off the power to your heating system at your home's main service panel (pages 88–89).

- Remove the thermostat cover.

- To check the level of a round thermostat, use a short length of string and a nut as a plumb line (right). Suspend the string in front of the thermostat base.

- Note the alignment marks on the thermostat base, and set the top of the plumb line at this mark. The bottom of your plumb line should line up perfectly with the alignment mark on the bottom. If these are out of alignment, loosen the screws that hold the thermostat to the wall and adjust the thermostat so that it is level.

- Check the level of a rectangular thermostat by placing a carpenter's level on the top of the thermostat housing. If it is out of level, loosen the screws that hold the thermostat housing to the wall and adjust so that the housing is level.

Recalibrating a Low-Voltage Thermostat

Setting the thermostat to room temperature

- First, turn off the power to the heating system at your home's main service panel (pages 88–89).

- Remove the thermostat cover and check the calibration by setting the thermostat at the actual room temperature. Check the room temperature of the thermostat against the temperature reading of a household thermometer. If this is the exact setting where the mercury bulb shifts from one end of the bulb to the other, the thermostat is properly calibrated.

- To recalibrate the thermostat, set the temperature to 5 degrees above the actual room temperature.

- Find the recalibration nut under the bimetal coil. Set a calibration wrench (available at any heating and cooling supply house) on the calibration nut.

- Holding the thermostat dial steady, and being careful not to touch or breathe on the bimetal coil, slowly rotate the nut clockwise just until the mercury shifts to the right of the contacts (inset).

- Now set the temperature on the thermostat 10 degrees lower and wait about 5 minutes.

- Now set the thermostat dial to match the room temperature.

- Holding the thermostat dial firmly, turn the calibration nut in the opposite direction until the mercury shifts on the contacts.

- Allow the recalibrated thermostat to stabilize at the new setting for about 30 minutes.

- Again, check whether the room temperature matches the set temperature on the thermostat. If it does, you have successfully recalibrated your thermostat. If not, recalibrate again.

- Install the cover and turn the power back on.

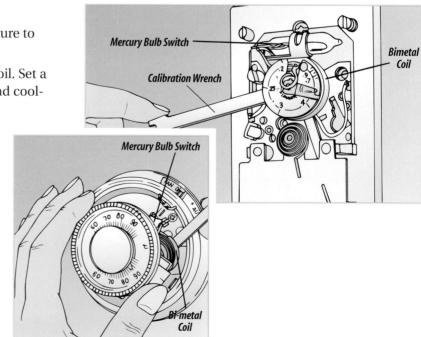

Mercury Bulb Switch

Calibration Wrench

Bimetal Coil

Mercury Bulb Switch

Bi-metal Coil

Recalibrating a Line-Voltage Thermostat

Testing and recalibrating the thermostat

- A line-voltage thermostat is recalibrated with the power to the unit on. Turn the dial on the thermostat up until you hear the unit turn on.

- If the setting matches the room temperature on the thermostat and your household thermometer, the thermostat is calibrated. If not, note the temperature of the room and the temperature reading of your thermostat.

- Now turn off the power to the unit at the main service panel (pages 88–89).

- Rotate the thermostat dial to its highest setting, and remove the thermostat knob and cover.

- Fit a calibration wrench onto the calibration screw behind the setting dial (right).

- Check the temperature readings you recorded earlier. If the setting on the thermostat was higher than the room temperature you recorded, turn the calibration screw one-eighth turn clockwise for each degree Fahrenheit that the thermostat is out of calibration. If the temperature reading was higher, rotate the calibra-

tion screw one-eighth turn counterclockwise for each degree the thermostat is out of calibration.

- Replace the cover and set the dial to the normal room temperature setting. Wait 10 minutes, then restore power to the unit and check the calibration.

- If the room temperature and the dial setting match after about half an hour, you have successfully calibrated the thermostat. If not, recalibrate. You may have to recalibrate a line-voltage thermostat a couple of times to get it just right.

- Once you are satisfied with the calibration, you might want to remove the thermostat knob and cover and apply just a dab of fingernail polish to the calibration screw threads to help hold the screw in place.

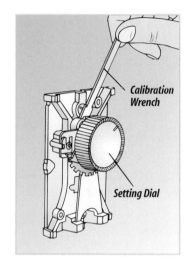

Calibration Wrench

Setting Dial

Setting the Range Stops for a Line-Voltage Thermostat

Testing and setting the range stops

- Your line-voltage thermostat may have range stops that restrict the high and low limits of your heater. These can be adjusted.

- To test the range stops, first turn the setting dial clockwise as far as it will go. The high-range stop is properly adjusted if the indicator stops at the highest desired setting.

- Now turn the dial as far as it will go counterclockwise. The range stop is properly set if the dial stops at the lowest desired setting.

- To adjust the high- and low-range stops, first turn off power to the system at the main service panel (pages 88–89).

- Remove the thermostat cover.

- Using a slotted calibration wrench (right) or a pair of

needlenose pliers, carefully bend down the misadjusted high- or low-range stop tab.

- To set a new high-range stop, first reinstall the cover and move the setting dial to the highest desired temperature setting. Then remove the cover and bend the range stop tab up just to the left of the indicator.

- To adjust the low-range stop, move the setting dial to the lowest desired temperature setting, then remove the cover and bend up the range stop tab just to the right of the indicator.

- Reinstall the cover and restore power to the heating system.

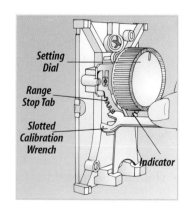

Setting Dial

Range Stop Tab

Slotted Calibration Wrench

Indicator

Testing and Replacing a Low-Voltage Thermostat

1. Testing the thermostat

- To test a low-voltage thermostat, first turn off the power at the main service panel (pages 88–89).

- Set the thermostat to AUTO and HEAT.

- Remove a round thermostat's cover and body. Unscrew a rectangular thermostat's base from the wall.

- Using a jumper cable (below), attach the alligator clips to the terminals marked R and W connected to the red wire and a white wire from the wall. These terminals can be found on the front of a round thermostat or the back of a rectangular thermostat.

- Turn on the power. If the furnace does not turn on, the thermostat tests okay.

- Turn off the power and reassemble the thermostat.

- If the furnace or boiler

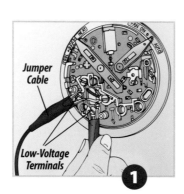

Jumper Cable

Low-Voltage Terminals

1

now turns on, the thermostat is faulty; turn off the power and install a new thermostat.

2. Installing a new thermostat

- To install a new thermostat, first make sure the power to the thermostat is off.

- Disconnect the wires from their terminals on the base (right), but be careful not to let them slip back into the wall cavity. Feed the wires through the opening in a new round thermostat's base, and connect them. On a rectangular model, connect the wires to the terminals on its back.

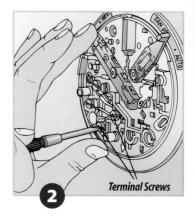

Terminal Screws

2

- Level the thermostat, and screw the new thermostat in place. Install the body on a round style. Snap the cover in place and turn the power back on.

Testing and Replacing a Line-Voltage Thermostat

1. Removing the thermostat (not shown)

- Turn off the power to the heating system at the main service panel (pages 88–89).

- Unscrew the thermostat and gently pull it out of the wall box to expose the wires. Label all of the wires with tape.

- Use a voltage tester to ensure that power is disconnected to the thermostat: Touch one end of the wire tester to each wire while touching the other end of the tester to the metal box. If at any time the tester lights up, you still have power to the thermostat—find the correct circuit breaker and turn it off.

2. Testing the thermostat

- Rotate the setting dial from the lowest to the highest setting, and listen for a click at the room temperature setting. If the setting dial does not click, set a multitester to RX1K to test for continuity.

- Turn the setting dial to the lowest setting, and touch a multitester probe to each thermostat lead (below). The multitester should not show continuity.

- Next, turn the dial past room temperature and test again. The tester should show continuity. If the thermostat tests okay, reconnect the leads, reassemble the thermostat, and turn on the power.

- If the thermostat fails either test or does not click, replace it with a new thermostat. Make sure the replacement thermostat has an equal or greater amperage rating.

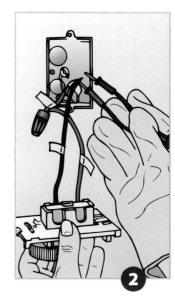

2

Testing and Replacing a Humidistat

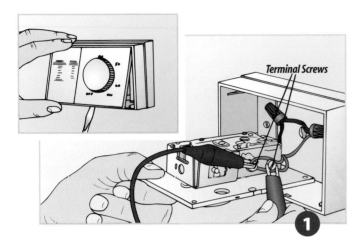

Terminal Screws

1. Testing the humidistat

- The humidity inside the room needs to be lower than the humidistat setting for you to test your humidistat accurately.

- Turn off the power to heating system at the main service panel (pages 88–89).

- With the power off, open the humidistat body (inset). You'll find two wires running to the humidistat. Using a jumper cable, attach a clip to each terminal screw that the wires are attached to (left).

- Turn on the power to the heating system. If the humidifier drum is operating, your humidistat is faulty.

2. Replacing the humidistat

- Turn off the power, and use tape to label the wires.

- Disconnect the humidistat from the wiring (left), and replace the humidistat with an identical unit. You should be able to match your old humidistat with one available from any heating supplier.

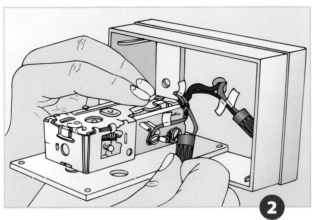

Insulate Thermostat Holes

Your thermostat's placement in the home can greatly affect the efficiency at which your system cools and heats your home. You need to read the instructions that come with your thermostat to make sure you locate your thermostat in an area of the home that will prevent "ghost" readings or unnecessary cycling of your furnace or air conditioner. Make sure your thermostat is not placed in an area of direct sunlight, drafts, exterior doorways, or windows.

If your thermostat is located on an exterior wall or on a wall adjoining a room that is not controlled by your heating and cooling system—a garage, for example—you need to be sure the wall cavity behind the thermostat is well insulated. If it isn't, the cold or hot area behind the thermostat can affect the thermostat readings and settings. You can also pack the hole around the wires with loose insulation

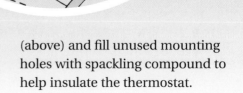

(above) and fill unused mounting holes with spackling compound to help insulate the thermostat.

Forced-Air Systems

HOW THEY WORK

A forced-air heating system circulates heated or cooled air throughout your home to create an ideal climate. The air is drawn through a return by a blower and directed through your furnace, where the air is heated or cooled. The air is then distributed through air ducts to every room in the home. The airflow is regulated by adjustable dampers in the air ducts or at the registers. Your thermostat should be located near your return on the ground floor of the home. Gas- and oil-fired furnaces use a fan-and-limit control on the plenum (below) to switch the blower on and off in response to plenum temperature. Electric furnaces and central air conditioners separate blower relays or fan centers to switch the blower in direct response to the thermostat.

A humidifier mounted directly on the supply duct responds to a humidistat and runs only when the furnace operates. Most models pull the air through a wet pad from which the moisture evaporates to increase the amount of water vapor in the air inside your home. The evaporating tray is fed through a water supply connected to a cold-water line in your home. The water level in the tray is regulated by an adjustable float.

Every month during the heating or cooling season, you should check the air filter and clean or replace it if necessary. Annually, you should clean the blower blades, lubricate the blower motor, and inspect the belt.

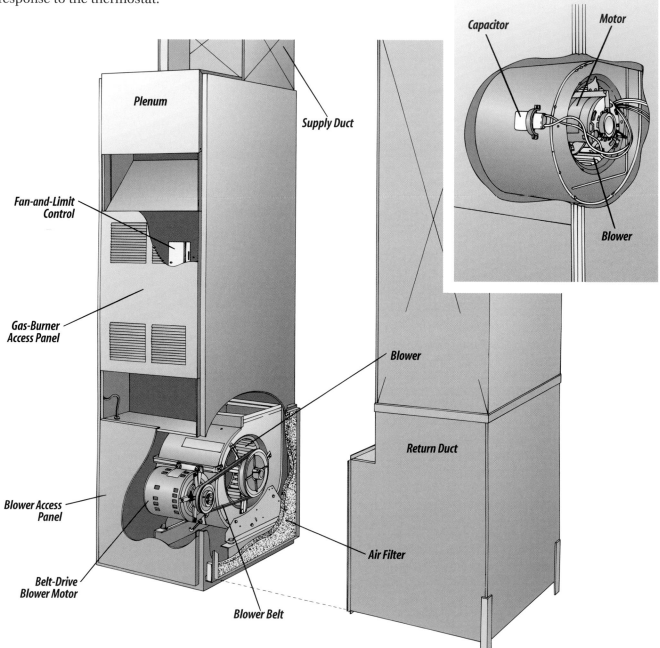

Capacitor

Motor

Plenum

Supply Duct

Blower

Fan-and-Limit Control

Gas-Burner Access Panel

Blower

Blower Access Panel

Return Duct

Belt-Drive Blower Motor

Air Filter

Blower Belt

Troubleshooting

If your heating and air conditioning are not running at all

- Reset circuit breaker or replace fuse **88–89**

If your system runs with no airflow

- Inspect and adjust the blower belt tension and pulley alignment . . **157–158**
- Replace belt **157**
- Test fan-and-limit control, and replace if necessary **160–161**
- Test blower relay and replace if necessary **159**

If the blower motor does not work

- Inspect blower motor **162–163**
- Discharge, test, and replace capacitor **192–193**
- Have the belt-drive blower motor or direct-drive blower motor replaced if necessary **162–163**

If heating or cooling is insufficient in part of the house

- Inspect filter and replace if necessary **156**
- Inspect register and open or unclog
- Clean blower blades **158**
- Check duct connections and damper position

If heating or cooling are insufficient throughout the entire home

- Inspect air filter and clean or replace **156**
- Oil the blower motor and bearings **156–157**
- Adjust blower speed
- Adjust blower belt tension and blower pulley alignment
- Clean blower blades **157–158**
- Lubricate bearings
- Replace bearings **157**

- Adjust duct dampers

If airflow is noisy

- Lower the blower speed

If joints are loose at duct corners

- Tighten joints and adjust duct hangers, or call for service to build new duct joints

If blower noise is excessive

- Lubricate motor and bearings . . **156–157**
- Tighten mounting hardware

If the blower belt slips or squeals

- Adjust belt tension or replace belt . . . **157**
- Align blower pulleys **158**

HUMIDIFIER
If the air is too dry

- Wash or replace evaporator pad **164–165**
- Test humidistat **153**
- Test humidifier motor and have it replaced if necessary
- Test transformer and have it replaced if necessary
- Adjust water-level float to raise water level **165**

If water overflows or is leaking

- Adjust water-level float to lower water level **165**

Servicing Filters

Accessing the filter

- Your filter should be accessible outside the furnace in a built-in slot between the return duct and the blower (inset). The filter is usually located just before the blower. If you cannot locate your filter compartment easily, it may be housed inside the furnace and you may have to unscrew an access panel.

- Before disassembling any part of your furnace, disconnect the power at the main service panel (pages 88–89).

- There are a variety of filters you can buy for your furnace. The important issue is to inspect your filters monthly and, if needed, change them. Hold your filter up to the light to inspect it.

- Reusable filters (top right and near right) can be washed with a high-pressure hose and drip-dried before replacing.

- Pleated paper and fiberglass filters are simply discarded and replaced.

- Make sure that your filter is sized correctly for the furnace. The filter should fit tightly in the slot without any large gaps around the filter.

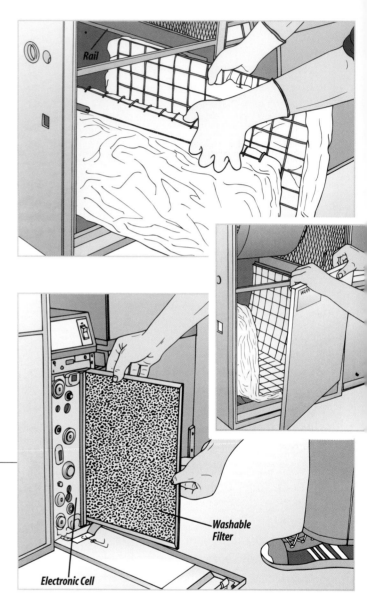

Rail

Washable Filter

Electronic Cell

Lubricating the Motor and Blower

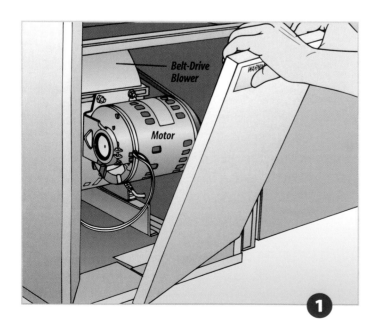

Belt-Drive Blower

Motor

1

1. Accessing the blower

- First, turn off power to the furnace at the main service panel (pages 88–89) and make sure the power is off at the furnace.

- The blower should be located in the bottom of your furnace near your filter. Remove the access panel to get at the blower motor (left).

- Most blower motors with lubrication ports should be lubricated once a year (Step 2).

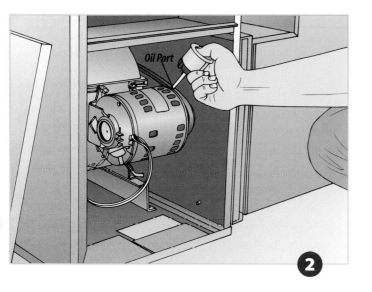

2. Lubricating the bearings

- Usually only the motor needs oiling, because most belt-drive blowers turn on sealed bearings. Direct-drive blowers turn on the motor's bearings. Follow the maintenance instructions for your furnace to determine what type of oil and how much to use when lubricating.

- Locate the motor-bearing oil ports at each end of the motor casing (left). If the ports are capped, use the blade of a screwdriver to pry up the caps.

- Squirt about five drops of SAE-30 motor oil into each port. Do not over-oil.

- If there are ports at the bearings where the blower shaft is mounted, oil them in the same manner.

Adjusting the Blower-Belt Tension

Accessing and adjusting the belt

- To check the belt tension between the blower and the motor, first turn off the power to the furnace (pages 88–89). Make sure the power is off at the furnace switch.

- Remove the access panel and inspect the belt for any cracks or signs of wear.

- Test the tension of the belt by pushing down on the belt midway between the pulleys until it is taught (inset). It should slacken about 1 inch. If is slackens more than this, it should be tightened or replaced. If the belt slackens less than 1 inch, it needs to be loosened.

- To adjust the belt tension, first turn off the power to the furnace at the main service panel (pages 88–89) and the unit-disconnect.

- Locate the locknut on the blower-belt adjustment bolt, and loosen it with an open-ended wrench.

- Next, turn the adjustment bolt by hand clockwise to tighten the belt or counterclockwise to loosen it

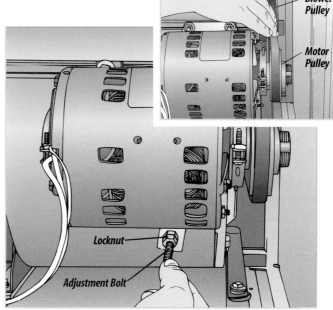

(above). Check the belt tension, and when you are satisfied with the tension, tighten the locknut.

- Reinstall the access panel and restore power to the furnace.

Cleaning the Blower Blades

Accessing and cleaning the blower blades

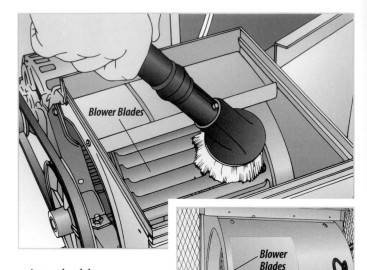

- Blower blades need to be cleaned only if the filter-changing schedule has been neglected and the fan blades are dirty. Accumulated dirt can affect the efficiency of the blower.

- To clean the blades, first turn off the power to the furnace and the motor (pages 88–89).

- Remove the entire blower assembly from the furnace to access the blower blades.

- Vacuum the blades, using a strong vacuum with a brush attachment (right).

- If necessary, remove the belt and blower pulley to insert a small brush inside to loosen dirt. An auto parts cleaning brush or a toothbrush works great for this. Tap the blower casing to dislodge the dirt.

- Replace the blower assembly and reassemble the unit. Restore power to the furnace.

- To clean direct-drive blower blades, turn off the power to the furnace at the main service panel and make sure power is off to the motor (pages 88–89).

- Remove the access panels covering the blower. Reach into the blower cavity with a toothbrush to clean the inside and outside surfaces of each blade (inset).

- If a vacuum nozzle will fit, use the vacuum to dislodge the dirt. If the blades are inaccessible, remove the direct-drive blower for cleaning.

- After cleaning the blades, reassemble the unit and restore the power.

Aligning the Blower and Motor Pulleys

Aligning and adjusting the motor and blower pulleys

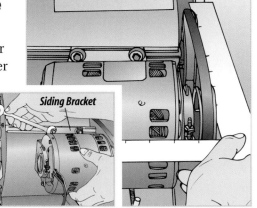

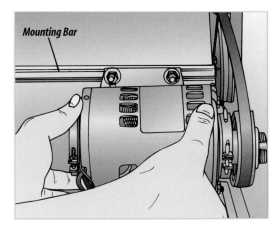

- To align the blower and motor pulleys, first turn off the power to the furnace at the service panel (pages 88–89).

- Remove the pulley motor's access panels.

- Using a carpenter's square, check the alignment of the pulleys (right). They should be in a straight line, and the edge of the square should rest squarely across each pulley.

- If they are out of alignment, use a wrench to loosen the nuts securing the sliding bracket to the mounting bar (inset). This will let you shift the location of the motor from left to right. Shift it until the pulleys are aligned (above), and tighten the mounting bolts.

- Check the belt tension and replace the access panels.

- Restore power to the unit, and check that the belt runs smoothly and quietly.

Testing and Replacing the Blower Motor Relay

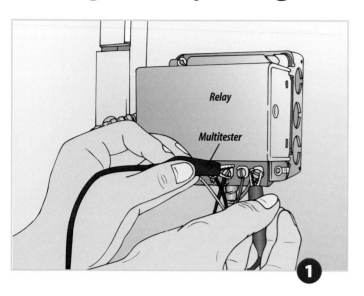

2. Testing the relay for continuity

* First make sure the power to the system is off (pages 88–89).

* Set a multitester to test continuity. Touch one probe to the G terminal and the other to the C terminal (right).

* There should be continuity; if there is not, replace the relay.

* If there is continuity through the relay but the blower will not run, the blower motor may be faulty (see page 162).

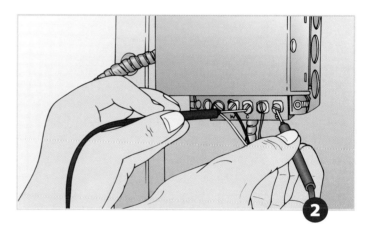

1. Testing the thermostat circuit

* Turn off the power to the furnace and air conditioning system at the main service panel (pages 88–89) and the unit-disconnect switch.

* Set a multitester to the ACV setting, 50-volt range, to test the voltage.

* Attach one clip to the G terminal, and the other clip to the C, T, or V terminal (left).

* Without touching the clips or terminals, have someone turn on the power and turn the thermostat fan switch to ON. The tester should read about 24 volts, and the blower should click on. If not, the thermostat circuit is faulty. If the reading is 24 volts, turn off the power and test the relay for continuity (Step 2).

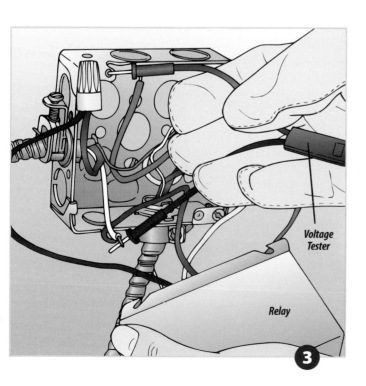

3. Testing the blower leads and replacing the relay

* To access the blower leads, make sure the power to the unit is off (pages 88–89) and remove the retaining screws that hold the relay to the junction box.

* Now pull the relay off the junction box. Taking care not to touch the bare wires, remove the wire nuts on the black and white leads in the relay box.

* Hold one probe of a voltage tester to the black wire ends and the other to the surface of the junction box (left). Turn on the power to the unit and see whether the voltage tester lights up.

* Now test between the white wires and the box. Then test between the black and white wires. The tester should not light up. If it does, turn off power and retest.

* Label all wires, and replace the relay with an identical new one. Reconnect the wires, reassemble the relay to the junction box, and restore power.

Testing the Fan-and-Limit Control

1. Accessing the control box and testing the blower motor

The fan-and-limit control used on gas and oil furnaces consists of a fan (blower) switch and a limit (shutoff) switch. On gas furnaces, the box is mounted near other controls: behind the access panel and against the plenum.

- Lift off the access panel (right) and set it aside.

- An oil furnace fan-and-limit control is usually mounted directly on the plenum. Look on the limit control box for a push/pull or toggle switch marked manual/automatic or summer/winter (inset), or a switch mounted separately on an exterior panel.

- Set the button/toggle to manual or summer.

- If the blower runs, the blower motor is okay. If the blower does not run, test the fan switch (Step 2).

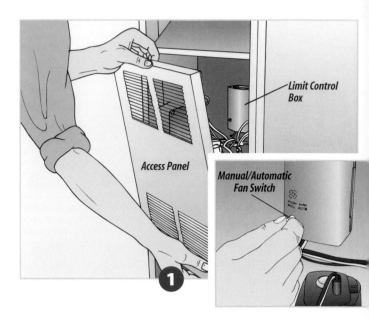

2. Testing the fan switch

- Turn off the power at the service panel (pages 88–89) and turn off the unit-disconnect switch.

- Pull off the control cover, and disconnect the fan wire from its terminal.

- Set a multitester to test continuity. With the switch on manual, touch one probe to the fan contact slot and the other probe to the common contact slot (left).

- If there is continuity, the fan switch is okay; go to Step 3. If there is no continuity, replace the fan-and-limit control.

3. Testing the limit switch

- To test the limit switch, set a multitester to the RX1K setting to test continuity. Disconnect the limit-switch wire from its terminal. Touch one tester probe to the limit-switch contact slot and the other probe to the common contact slot (right).

- If there is no continuity, the limit control is faulty; replace it. Otherwise, reassemble the fan-and-limit control (opposite page).

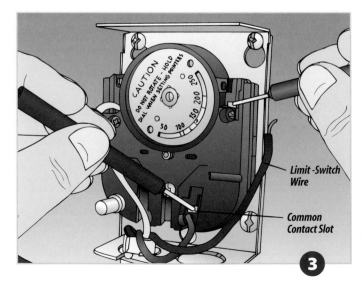

Replacing the Fan-and-Limit Control Box

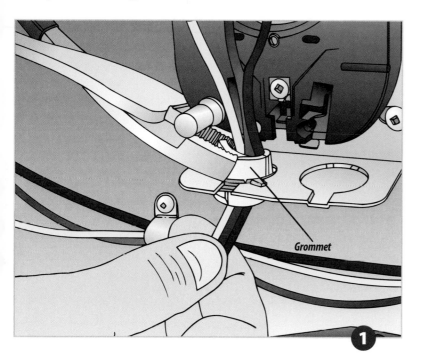

Grommet

1. Removing the wiring

- Turn off the power to the furnace at the main service panel (pages 88–89) and at the unit-disconnect switch.

- Pinch the inside rim of the wire grommet with pliers, and push it out through the wiring access hole in the bottom of the fan-and-limit control box (left).

2. Removing a fan-and-limit control

- To unfasten a fan-and-limit control, first label the wires and disconnect them.

- Use a screwdriver to remove the screws holding the fan-and-limit control on the plenum (inset). Pull the control out of the furnace (right).

- Install an identical new replacement, reversing these steps.

- Reassemble the furnace and restore power to the system.

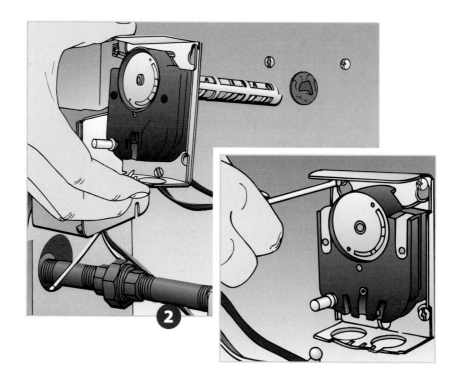

Testing and Replacing a Direct-Drive Blower Motor

1. Accessing the motor

- First turn off the power at the main service panel (pages 88–89) and unit-disconnect switch.

- Remove access panels to the blower.

- Locate the point at which the motor's wire leads can be disconnected: at the motor, at the relay and switch terminals, or—on an electric furnace—at the control box. Label the wires and then use long needlenose pliers to disconnect them (right).

- Discharge and disconnect the capacitor (page 163).

- Use a socket wrench to remove the retaining bolts from the mounting bracket. (The weight of the blower is held by the slide rails; it will not fall.)

- If the motor is mounted on the bottom of the furnace, unbolt it from its slide rails.

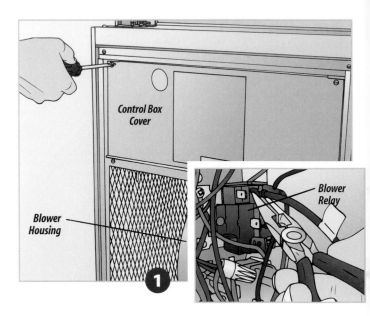

2. Testing the motor

- To test the motor, first try turning the motor shaft. If it moves stiffly, lubricate the motor. If it will not turn at all, the motor has seized; replace the motor.

- A direct-drive blower and motor weigh 25 to 50 pounds. Have a helper remove it with you. Crouching down, support the blower housing firmly and slide it out until it clears the slide rails (right).

- Place the assembly motor-side up on the floor.

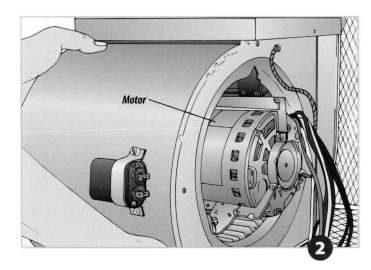

3. Replacing the motor

- To replace the motor, first disconnect the ground wire from the motor.

- Turn the blower on its side and, using a hex wrench, loosen the setscrew to release the motor shaft from the blower fan.

- Turn the blower upright and, using a socket wrench, unbolt the motor bracket from the blower housing (right). Pull the motor out of the blower and place it on the floor. Unscrew the bracket collar bolts, using a screwdriver and open-ended wrench (inset).

- Purchase an identical replacement from a motor supplier or from the manufacturer, and install it by reversing these instructions.

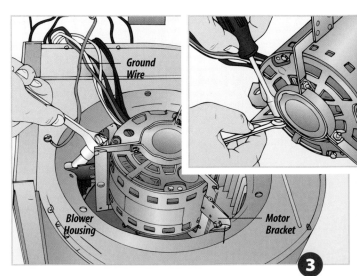

Discharging and Testing a Blower Motor Capacitor

1. Discharging a capacitor

It is dangerous to attempt to test a capacitor without discharging it first. You will need to make your own capacitor-discharging tool (below).

- At an electronics supply store, buy two jumper cable with alligator clips on each end and a 20,000-ohm 2-watt resistor. Turn off the power to the motor or condenser you are working on (pages 88–89), clip one end of each jumper to the leads of the resistor, and then clip one jumper to the blade of a screwdriver with a rubber handle (right).

- Make sure the power to the unit is off at the main service panel and the unit-disconnect switch.

- Remove the control box cover to access the capacitor.

- Clip the free jumper to the common terminal of the capacitor. Hold the screwdriver handle in one hand and put the other behind you. Touch the end of the screwdriver to each capacitor for 5 seconds (top right).

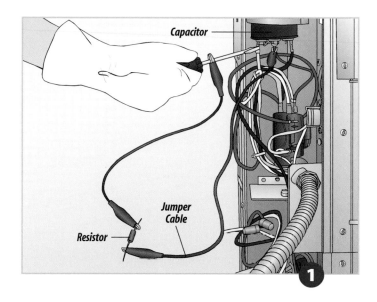

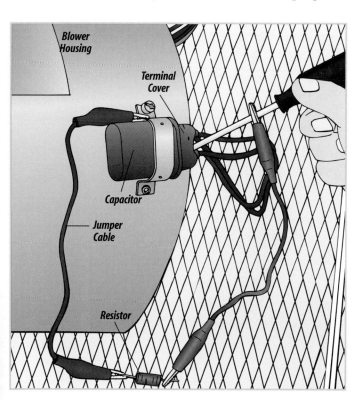

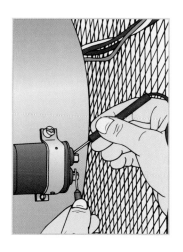
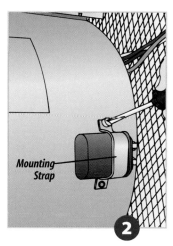

2. Testing the capacitor

- With the power off and the capacitor discharged, set a multitester to the RX1K scale to measure resistance.

- Slip the terminal cover off the capacitor. Label the wires, and use long-nose pliers to pull the connectors off the terminals.

- Touch one multitester probe to each capacitor terminal (above right). The multitester needle should swing to the right and then sweep back.

- If the multitester needle does not move, or if it moves and does not sweep back, replace the capacitor: Loosen the screws on its mounting strap (above left) and slide out the capacitor. Replace it with an identically rated capacitor, reconnect the wires, and restore the power.

Maintaining a Humidifier

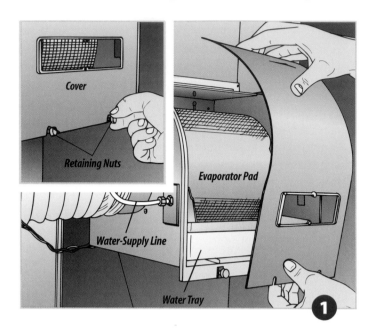

Cover

Retaining Nuts

Evaporator Pad

Water-Supply Line

Water Tray

1. Accessing the pad and tray

Your humidifier's evaporator pad should be changed every year at the end of the heating season.

- First turn the power off to the heating and cooling system at the main service panel and unit-disconnect switch (pages 88–89).

- Loosen the retaining nuts along the bottom lip of the humidifier cover (inset) and lift off the cover to access the evaporator pad and water tray (left).

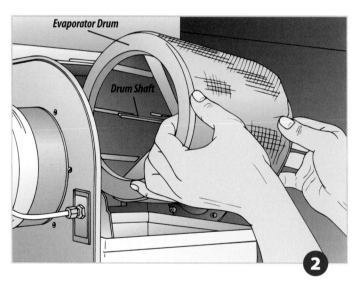

Evaporator Drum

Drum Shaft

2. Removing the evaporator drum

- Grasp both ends of the evaporator drum and lift the shaft out of its slots (left).

- Water mineral content varies, and you should visually check the pad monthly during the heating season to identify how often you need to clean the pad. When the pad becomes hard, remove it and clean it or replace it (Step 3).

3. Cleaning or replacing the pad

- To clean or replace the evaporator pad, first pinch the drum shaft retaining clip and pull it off the drum shaft (inset). Pull apart the two sections of the drum to release the pad (right).

- If the pad is slightly hardened, soak it in a solution of 3 parts vinegar to 1 part water until it softens, then squeeze the solution through to wash it out.

- If the pad does not soften or has deteriorated, replace it with an identical new one, available from a hardware store or a heating and cooling supply store.

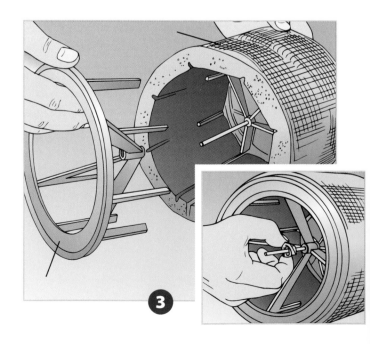

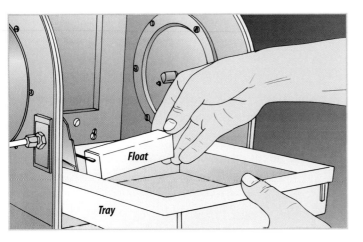

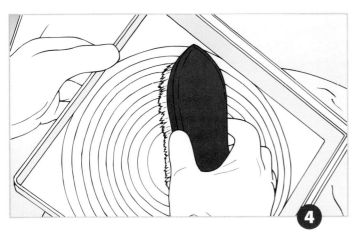

4. Cleaning the tray

- To clean the tray, first turn off the water supply to the humidifier.

- Lift the float and pull out the tray (top left).

- To dislodge scale deposits, wash the tray using a stiff brush and a vinegar-and-water solution or a humidifier descaler available from a hardware store (bottom left).

- Rinse the tray well.

- Add water treatment tablets or liquid—also available from a hardware store—to inhibit mineral buildup and bacteria; follow the instructions on the package.

- Reassemble the humidifier and turn on the water valve; restore the power.

Adjusting the Humidifier Tray Water Level

Checking and adjusting the water level in the tray

- With the power to the heating and cooling system shut off at the main service panel and at the unit-disconnect switch (pages 88–89), remove the cover panel and check the depth of water in the tray. The water level should be about 1½ inches deep, enough to soak the evaporator pad as it turns.

- To adjust the water level, loosen the float-assembly locknut on the water supply line with an open-ended wrench. Then move the float up to raise the water level, or down to lower the water level.

- Retighten the locknut securely against the retainer plate.

- Check the new water level.

- Reinstall the humidifier cover, and restore the power to the unit.

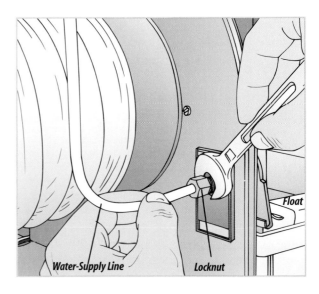

Hot-Water and Steam Systems

HOW THEY WORK

Prior to forced-air furnaces, it was common to install water-distribution heating systems in the home. Most of these systems were installed prior to 1950, yet these can provide an effective heating system if maintained properly. They use a thermostat to control a boiler that heats water, which is then forced through pipes and radiators or convectors throughout the home. Water is distributed through the system at about 15 to 20 pounds per square inch (psi), depending on the distance of the radiators or convectors from the pump and boiler. An expansion tank allows the heated water to expand safely.

Proper maintenance of a water-distribution system includes annual bleeding of radiators or convectors. Check the pressure-reducing valve before you start up the furnace each year, test the aquastats, and oil the pump and motor.

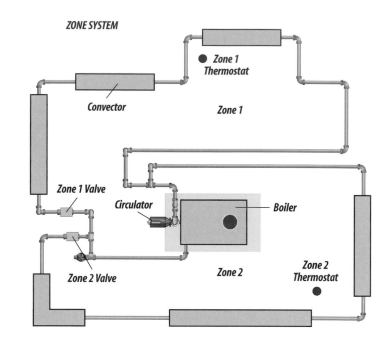

ZONE SYSTEM

- Zone 1 Thermostat
- Convector
- Zone 1
- Zone 1 Valve
- Circulator
- Boiler
- Zone 2 Valve
- Zone 2
- Zone 2 Thermostat

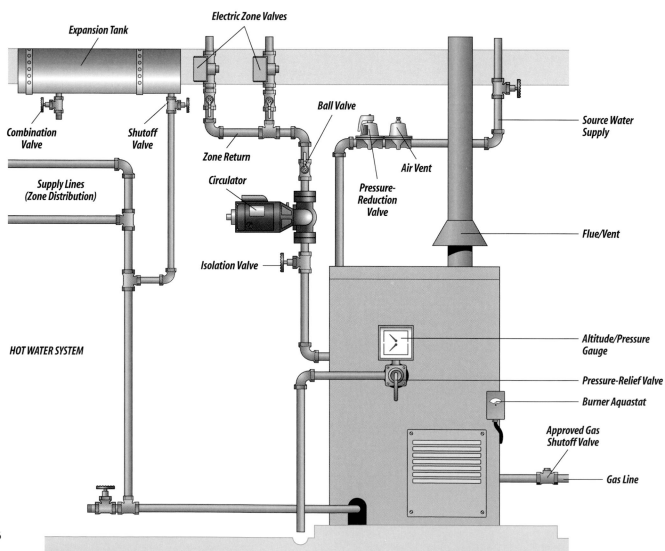

Expansion Tank

Electric Zone Valves

Ball Valve

Source Water Supply

Combination Valve

Shutoff Valve

Air Vent

Supply Lines (Zone Distribution)

Zone Return

Circulator

Pressure-Reduction Valve

Flue/Vent

Isolation Valve

HOT WATER SYSTEM

Altitude/Pressure Gauge

Pressure-Relief Valve

Burner Aquastat

Approved Gas Shutoff Valve

Gas Line

Troubleshooting

If you have no heat
- Replace fuse or reset circuit breaker **88–89**
- Test aquastats and replace if necessary **170–171**
- Bleed radiators **168**
- Replace coupler **173–175**
- Have circulator pump replaced

If you have no heat; motor is hot and smells like it is burning
- Test windings and replace circulator motor **173–175**

If you hear gurgling sounds in pipes
- Bleed radiators **168**

If you have too much heat; burner does not turn off
- Test burner aquastat and replace if necessary **170–171**

If your heat is uneven throughout home
- Bleed radiators **168**
- Replace coupler **173–175**
- Have circulator pump replaced
- Have pressure-reducing valve reset higher

If your radiator is cold; hammering noise in pipes
- Level sloping radiator with wood shims, raising the leg below the bleed valve

If you do not have enough heat; convector is lukewarm
- Vacuum convector fins and straighten them with pliers
- Bleed convectors **168**
- Have circulator pump checked and replaced if necessary

If you do not have enough heat; radiators are lukewarm (water pressure may be too low)
- Have pressure gauge checked
- Tighten pipe joints or have them checked

- Check pressure-reducing valve and have it replaced if necessary
- Drain and refill system, adding a rust inhibitor
- Have circulator pump checked and replaced if necessary

If your radiators are lukewarm (water pressure exceeds 30 psi soon after burner turns on, and safety valve discharges)
- Recharge old-style expansion tank . . **172**
- If old-style expansion tank is leaking, have it checked
- Replace diaphragm-type expansion tank if leaking **172**

If your radiators above boiler are lukewarm; others are cold
- Test and replace pump aquastat **170–171**
- Test windings and replace circulator motor **173–175**
- Have circulator pump checked and replaced

If your circulator motor is noisy
- Lubricate pump and motor **173–175**

If your circulator motor sounds like chain is being dragged through system
- Replace coupler **173**

If water spills from safety discharge valve
- Recharge old-style expansion tank . . **172**
- If leaking, have it checked
- Replace diaphragm-type expansion tank **172**

If your circulator pump leaks
- Have pump seal and impeller checked

If your inlet valve leaks
- Replace valve packing **169**

If your bleed valve drips constantly or will not turn
- Replace bleed valve **168**

Bleeding a Radiator

Testing the release valve and bleeding the radiator

- At the beginning of each heating season, bleed the valve on each radiator, beginning on the top floor at the farthest radiator away from the system and working your way to the radiator closest to the system.

- Have a rag handy: When the air is released from the radiator, water will also escape from the valve.

- On models with a bleed valve knob, turn the knob 180 degrees counterclockwise to purge the radiator or convector of air (inset).

- On models without a bleed valve knob, use a screwdriver (right) or radiator-venting key, as appropriate.

- Automatic bleed valves are supposed to bleed themselves, but impurities in the water can build up and clog them. If a radiator with an automatic bleed valve is not heating up, bleed the valve by taking off the cap, turning it upside down, and pushing it into the air valve, just like bleeding air from a bicycle tire.

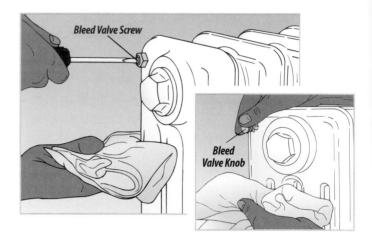

Bleed Valve Screw

Bleed Valve Knob

- On all bleed valves, when you notice water escaping in a steady stream, the air has been bled and you can close the valve.

Caution: *The water inside your system can be very oxidized and rusty or black and can stain rugs, carpet, or furniture located around the radiator when you bleed it. Be careful and have rags handy for this procedure.*

Removing and Replacing a Bleed Valve

Replacing a conventional valve

If a valve is dripping constantly or will not bleed at all, replace it. This simple and inexpensive procedure will save time and frustration during annual bleeding.

- Buy a new bleed valve to fit your radiator.

- Turn off the power to the boiler at the main service panel and unit-disconnect switch (pages 88–89); allow the boiler to cool.

- Drain the system just until water stops leaking from the bleed valve.

- Loosen the old bleed valve from its fitting, and unscrew the valve. Be careful here: Some valves may not want to come off easily. Be careful not to break off the valve body from the threads.

- Screw the new valve in place, using Teflon plumber's tape on the threads and taking care not to cross-thread the fitting (below left).

- Refill the system, then restore power. If the new valve is leaking, try tightening the fitting. If it still leaks, call for service.

Make it adjustable

One-pipe steam radiators are either on or off, hot or cold. To fine-tune the temperature, replace the existing valve with an adjustable air-vent valve.

- Turn the heat off, and wait until the radiator feels cool. Remove the existing valve with a pipe wrench.

- Take the old valve to a plumbing or heating supplier. Buy an adjustable replacement, plus joint compound designed for steam radiators.

- At home, apply the joint compound to the threads, and screw the new valve into place, tightening with a wrench. Adjust the heat by adjusting the vent, usually by turning a screw somewhere on the valve.

Repairing a Leaky Inlet Valve

1. Unscrewing the handle

- If your inlet valve is leaking, you can try to tighten the packing nut just under the handle a quarter-turn.

- If this doesn't work, remove the handle screw and pull the handle off the valve stem (inset). When you loosen the packing nut, the leaking may increase, so wrap rags around the valve area first.

- Use two wrenches, one to hold the valve steady and one to loosen the packing nut; turn the packing nut counterclockwise to loosen it (right).

- Unscrew the packing nut all the way, and slip it off the valve stem.

- If excessive water is leaking, reinstall the nut and drain the system.

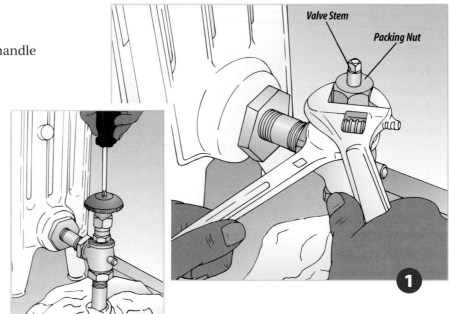

Valve Stem
Packing Nut

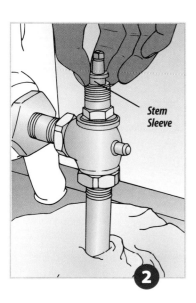

2. Dismantling the valve

- With the packing nut removed, pull the washer, if any, off the stem.
- Use the blade of a flat-tipped screwdriver to pry up the stem sleeve, if any.
- Once loosened, slip it off the stem by hand (left).

Stem Sleeve

3. Repacking the valve

- To repack the valve, leave the old packing in place and add Teflon pipe tape (right) or new packing string. Wrap the tape or string several times around the old packing. Stretch the tape or string and press it down as you go.

- Replace the stem sleeve and washer, and reinstall the packing nut.

- Use a wrench to tighten the packing nut until it stops leaking.

- Screw on the valve handle.

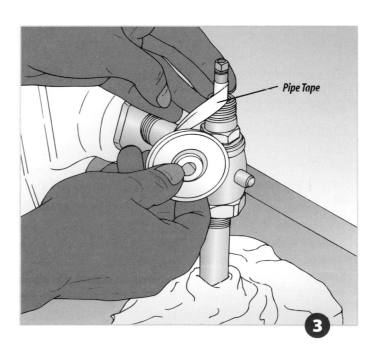

Pipe Tape

Aquastat Types

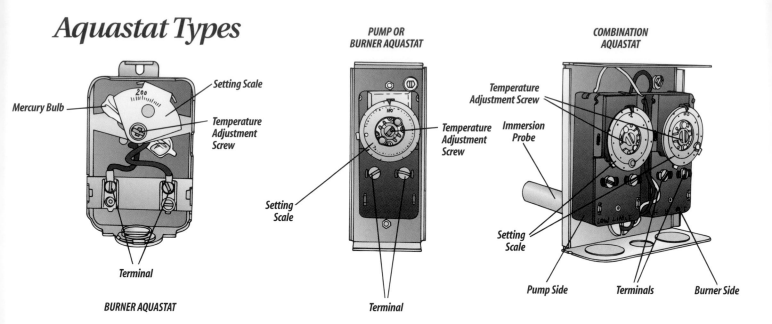

PUMP OR BURNER AQUASTAT

COMBINATION AQUASTAT

Setting Scale

Mercury Bulb

200

Temperature Adjustment Screw

Temperature Adjustment Screw

Immersion Probe

Temperature Adjustment Screw

Setting Scale

Setting Scale

Terminal

Terminal

Setting Scale

Pump Side

Terminals

Burner Side

BURNER AQUASTAT

THREE TYPES OF AQUASTATS

An aquastat senses the temperature of the water in your system and responds by turning the burner or circulator pump on or off, as appropriate. All systems have at least one aquastat; some systems have as many as three. An aquastat may be surface-mounted—located on a pipe; or the immersion type—with a probe inserted into a well in the boiler. All boilers have a burner aquastat (left) that acts as a safety switch, turning off the burner if the water temperature rises above a safe level, usually around 200°F. A second aquastat, the pump aquastat (middle), turns on the circulator pump when the temperature of the water is high enough to heat the house (usually around 110°F). When the water cools down, it turns off the pump. On some systems, a combination aquastat serves both as pump and burner aquastat (right).

Testing and Replacing an Aquastat

1. Testing an aquastat (not shown)

- To test an aquastat, raise the thermostat to 80°F; the burner should go on. Then locate the temperature-adjustment screw on the cover of the aquastat.

- On a burner aquastat, note the temperature setting, then use a screwdriver to lower the setting below 100°F; the burner should turn off. Raise the setting to its orignal position; after a slight delay (up to 10 minutes on an oil burner with a stack-mounted relay), the burner should turn on.

- On a pump aquastat, note the temperature setting, then use a screwdriver to raise the setting above 100°F; the pump should turn on. Then lower the setting below 100°F; the pump should turn off. If the aquastat fails either test, it is faulty; replace it.

2. Removing the cover

- First turn off power to the boiler at the main service panel (pages 88–89) and the unit-disconnect switch, and let the boiler cool.

- On either a surface-mounted aquastat (as shown) or an immersion type, use a screwdriver to loosen the cover-retaining screw.

- Pull off the cover to expose the terminal screw connections (right).

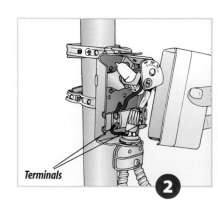

Terminals

2

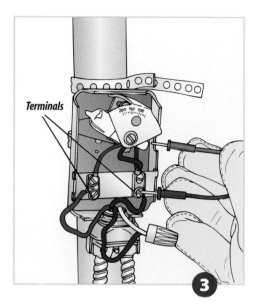

Terminals

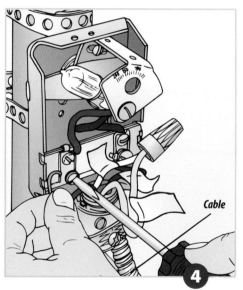

Cable

3. Testing to ensure that power is off

- Confirm that the power is off by using a voltage tester before disconnecting any aquastat wires.

- Working with one hand only, touch one tester probe to each of the aquastat line-voltage terminal screws.

- Then test between each terminal screw and the grounded aquastat box (left).

- Next, unscrew the wire nut connecting the white line-voltage wires and touch one tester probe to the bare wire ends and the other probe to one terminal screw, then the other.

- Finally, test between the bare wire ends and the grounded aquastat box.

- The tester should not glow in any test. If it does, this means that power to the boiler is still on; turn off power to the proper circuit and test again to make sure the power is off.

4. Replacing the aquastat

- To replace a surface-mounted aquastat, make sure the power is off, and label the wires inside the aquastat box for correct reconnection.

- Unscrew the terminals (left) and remove the wire nuts.

- Remove the fastener holding the line-voltage cable in place.

- Unscrew the aquastat from the metal straps holding it to the pipe.

- Connect an exact replacement aquastat—set on the same setting as the old one—to the pipe with the metal straps.

- Reconnect the wires, screw on the aquastat cover, and restore power to the boiler.

- Test the new aquastat to make sure it works properly.

5. Replacing an immersion aquastat

- To replace an immersion aquastat, make sure the power to the boiler is off (pages 88–89) and label the wires inside the aquastat box for correct reconnection.

- Unscrew the terminals and remove the wire nuts.

- Remove the fastener holding the line-voltage cable in place.

- Loosen the screws holding the aquastat to the well, and slide the aquastat probe out of the well; use pliers to gently twist the probe if necessary (right).

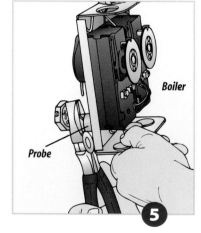

Boiler

Probe

- Slide an exact replacement aquastat—set on the same setting as the old one—into place in the well.

- Reconnect the wires, screw on the aquastat cover, and restore power to the boiler.

- Test the new aquastat to make sure it works properly.

Replacing a Diaphragm-Type Expansion Tank

Replacing the tank

- First disconnect power to the boiler at the main service panel (pages 88–89) and at the unit-disconnect switch, and let the boiler cool.

- Close the expansion-tank valve.

- Use a pipe wrench to grip the fitting connecting the expansion tank to the pipe (right).

- Use another wrench to loosen the tank just until water starts to drip; wait until the water stops dripping.

Caution: *The tank is full of water and will be heavy. Have a helper hold it for safety.*

- Twist the tank off the pipe fitting by hand.

- Purchase a new expansion tank from a heating supplies dealer.

- Wrap Teflon tape around the threads.

- Install the tank, reversing these instructions.

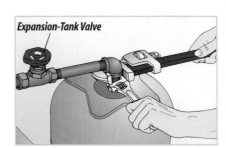

- Open the expansion-tank valve slowly, then restore power to the boiler.

Servicing an Old-Style Expansion Tank

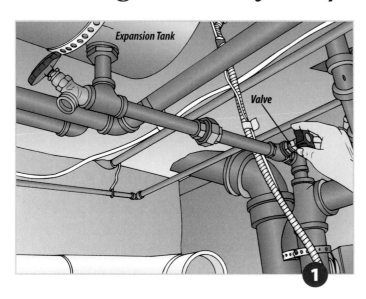

1. Testing the tank

- First, shut off the water to the tank.

- If the pressure gauge reading rises to 30 psi or above and the safety valve spouts water, the expansion tank may be waterlogged and must be recharged.

- Turn off the power to the boiler at the main service panel (pages 88–89) and at the unit-disconnect switch, and allow the boiler to cool.

- Close the expansion-tank valve (above left).

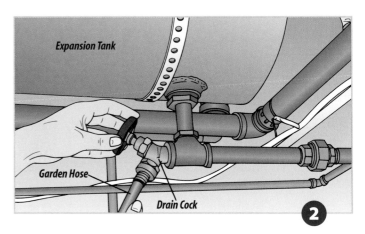

2. Recharging the tank

- To drain and refill the tank, connect a garden hose to the drain cock on the bottom of the expansion tank (above right).

- Open the air-release valve on the side of the tank.

- When the tank has drained completely, tighten the air-release valve, close the drain cock, and partially open the tank's shutoff valve. You will hear water slowly entering the tank; after the sound stops, open the valve completely.

- When the pressure gauge reads about 15 psi, restore power to the boiler.

- When the radiators or convectors are warm, bleed all of them (page 168), beginning on the top floor.

Maintaining a Circulating Pump

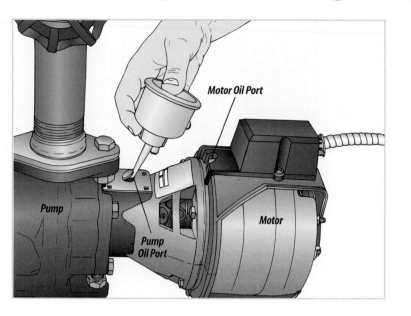

Lubricating the pump

- The pump or motor should be lubricated annually. Be sure to check the pump and motor label plates and any maintenance instructions that came with the pump or motor.

- Locate the oil ports, usually three, on the top of the circulator pump and motor; use a screwdriver blade to pry up the port caps.

- Squirt SAE-30 nondetergent motor oil into the ports (left). Newer models, such as the one shown, generally require about 30 drops of oil in the pump oil port and about 15 drops of oil in the motor oil port; older models usually require fewer drops, applied more frequently.

- Do not force oil into the ports.

Testing and Replacing a Motor and Coupler

1. Accessing the wires

- Make sure that the power is off to the boiler at the main service panel (pages 88–89) and unit-disconnect switch. If your system has a pump aquastat, test at the aquastat to make sure power is indeed off (page 171).

- Unscrew the screws holding the junction box cover to the top of the circulator motor (right) and take off the cover.

- Locate the wire nuts connecting the circulator motor to the line-voltage wires.

- Taking care not to touch any exposed wire ends, unscrew the wire nuts (inset).

(CONTINUED)

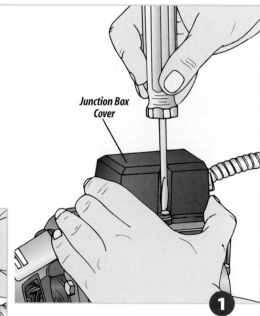

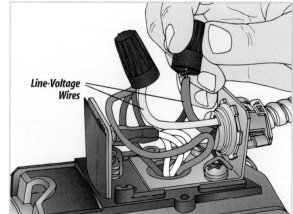

Testing and Replacing a Motor and Coupler—continued

2. Testing for power

- As a safety precaution, use a voltage tester to confirm that power to the circulator motor is indeed off.

- Touch one tester probe to the grounded junction box on the motor and the other probe to each exposed wire pair, in turn (right).

- Then test between the two wire ends.

- The voltage tester should not glow in any test. If it does, find the correct circuit and turn off power to the unit. Test again to make sure the power is off before proceeding.

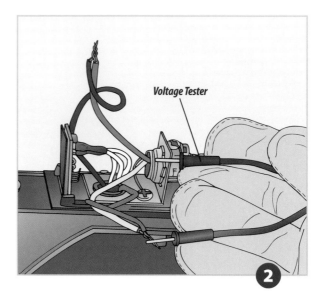

Voltage Tester

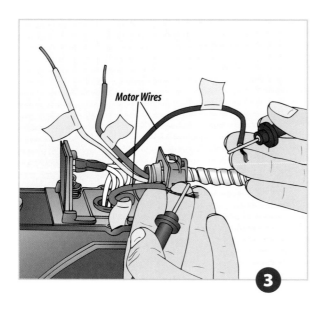

Motor Wires

3. Testing the motor

- Set a multitester to the RX1K setting to test continuity.

- Locate the two motor wires that were connected to the line-voltage wires with wire nuts.

- Label the wires for correct reconnection, and separate the wire ends.

- Touch a multitester probe to each motor wire (left).

- If the tester shows continuity, the motor is okay; if there is not continuity, replace the coupler and motor or take the motor for professional service.

4. Locating the coupler

If the pump or motor jams, the coupler—a spring-loaded connector between the pump shaft and motor shaft—will come apart, preventing the motor from overheating.

- Reach into the housing and rotate the motor with the end of a hex wrench until you can see the coupler's motor-shaft setscrew.

- Use the hex wrench to loosen the setscrew holding the coupler to the motor shaft (right).

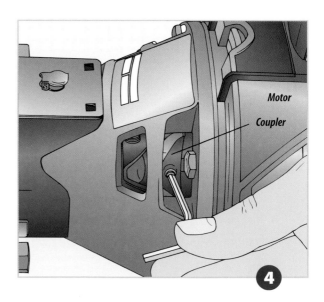

Motor

Coupler

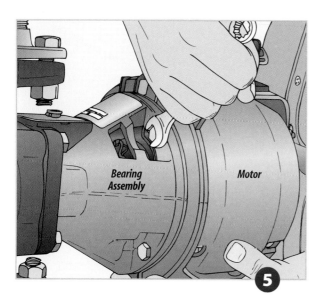

5. Removing the motor

- Use a wrench to remove the bolts holding the motor to the bearing assembly (left).

- Pull the motor free of the bearing assembly, and pry the coupler off the motor shaft with a screwdriver if it sticks.

- If the coupler is broken, replace it; if you suspect that the motor is faulty, test it (Step 3).

6. Replacing the coupler

- Use a hex wrench to loosen the setscrew holding the coupler to the pump shaft (right).

- Once the coupler is loosened, work it off the shaft by twisting it. If necessary, carefully pry it off with a screwdriver.

- Replace the entire coupler with an identical model; do not attempt to replace the springs.

- Line up the new coupler setscrew with the setscrew hole on the pump shaft, and then use a hex wrench to tighten the setscrew.

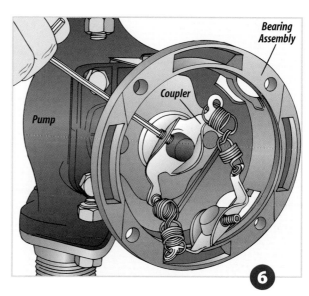

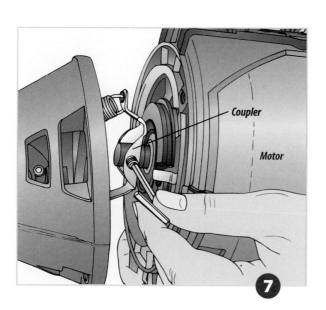

7. Reinstalling the motor

- Hold the motor in one hand, and slide the coupler over the motor shaft.

- Line up the setscrew with the setscrew hole, and use a hex wrench to tighten the setscrew (left).

- Reinstall the bolts securing the motor to the bearing assembly in a crisscross sequence: first, the bolt in the 12 o'clock position, then 6 o'clock, then 3 o'clock, then 9 o'clock.

- Reconnect the wiring, and screw on the junction box cover.

- Restore power to the boiler and allow the system to warm up to 110°F before judging whether or not the new motor works.

Oil Burners

HOW THEY WORK

A pump supplies pressurized oil to the system. The oil is forced through a tiny opening in a nozzle, creating a fine mist that burns quickly and completely. To ignite the oil, an ignition transformer raises the current to about 10,000 volts.

An oil furnace needs maintenance prior to each heating season. Cleaning and adjusting the components will allow your system to run efficiently and cut your fuel bills.

BEFORE SERVICING YOUR OIL BURNER

Working on an oil burner can be a messy job. Before servicing your unit, set out newspapers to protect the floor, a pan of sand or cat litter to catch drips, and a bucket to dispose of sludge and excess oil. Turn off the burner's master switch and cut power to the circuit that powers the burner at the main service panel (pages 88–89). Locate the oil shutoff valve, and stop the supply of oil between the filter and the storage tank. Your oil line may have a special fire safety valve at the pump. If it does, turn the handle clockwise to push the stem down. The valve is closed when the handle slips off the stem. To seat the valve completely, give the stem a light tap with a wrench.

When you are finished servicing the oil burner, reopen the oil line before restoring power to the burner. This prevents air pockets from entering the oil supply.

REPAIRING THE FURNACE

An air leak, a dirty heat exchanger, soot in the flue and chimney, or a crumbling combustion chamber can affect burner efficiency. You can seal leaks with furnace cement.

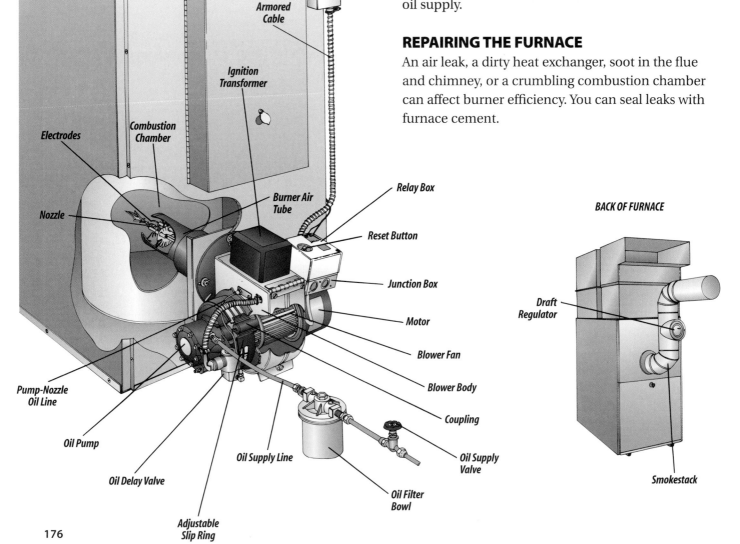

Armored Cable

Ignition Transformer

Combustion Chamber

Electrodes

Nozzle

Burner Air Tube

Relay Box

Reset Button

Junction Box

Motor

Blower Fan

Blower Body

Coupling

Pump-Nozzle Oil Line

Oil Pump

Oil Delay Valve

Oil Supply Line

Oil Supply Valve

Oil Filter Bowl

Adjustable Slip Ring

BACK OF FURNACE

Draft Regulator

Smokestack

If you have no heat or insufficient heat

- Check fuel tank gauge; refill tank if necessary
- Replace fuse or reset circuit breaker **88–89**
- Press relay or stack heat sensor reset button no more than twice; if the system does not start, call for service
- Tighten pump fittings if oil leaking; if no improvement, have pump replaced
- Check electrodes and adjust if necessary **180–181**
- Replace nozzle **180–181**
- Clean photoelectric cell and replace if necessary **179**
- Clean soot buildup out of stack heat sensor
- Test pump pressure; take pump for service or replace if necessary
- Press reset button on motor; if motor is silent or hums but does not turn, check and replace motor **179**
- Replace oil filter **178**
- Clean oil strainer **178**

If you have intermittent heat

- Check fuel tank gauge; have tank refilled if necessary
- Replace oil filter **178**
- Clean oil strainer and replace if necessary **178**
- Test pump pressure to see whether too high; take pump for service or replace if necessary
- Press reset button on motor; if motor is silent or hums but does not turn, check and replace motor
- Test pump pressure; take pump for service or replace if necessary
- Replace nozzle **180–181**
- Clean or replace photoelectric cell . . **179**
- Clean soot buildup out of stack heat sensor

If your fuel consumption is high

- Replace nozzle **180–181**
- Test pump pressure; take pump for service or replace if necessary

If your burner system is noisy

- Lubricate motor bearings **179**
- Test pump pressure; take pump for service or replace if necessary
- Test draft regulator and adjust counterweight
- Test stack temperature, and call for service if necessary

If you smell diesel fuel odor from burner system

- Adjust counterweight to close draft regulator
- Test stack temperature; call for service to have stack heat exchanger cleaned
- Replace pump
- Replace nozzle **180–181**
- Check electrodes and adjust if necessary **180–181**
- Call for service if stack is damaged

If you smell electrical insulation odor from burner system

- Test ignition transformer and replace if necessary
- Replace motor

Unclogging a Dirty Filter

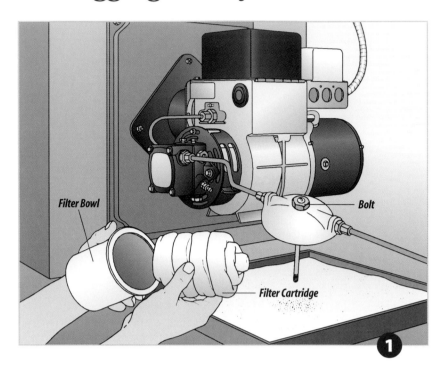

Filter Bowl

Bolt

Filter Cartridge

1. Replacing the oil filter

- Make sure the power is off at the main service panel (pages 88–89).

- Switch off the burner and close the supply valve. Set a disposable pan filled with cat litter or sand under the oil filter.

- Unscrew the bolt on the cover above the filter bowl (left). Remove the bowl and upend it into the pan, letting the filter cartridge inside fall out.

- Use a rag to wipe the inside of the bowl clean and peel off the old gasket.

- Insert a new cartridge and place a new gasket on the lip of the filter bowl, then reattach the bowl to the cover.

2. Cleaning out the pump strainer

- Unbolt the pump cover and set it aside without disconnecting the oil line.

- Discard the thin gasket around the cover rim.

- Remove the screen strainer (right). Inspect it for tears or dents.

- Replace a torn or bent strainer. Soak a dirty strainer in solvent such as paint thinner and use a toothbrush to clean any dirt or debris out of the strainer.

- Reinstall the clean strainer with a new gasket, reversing the above instructions.

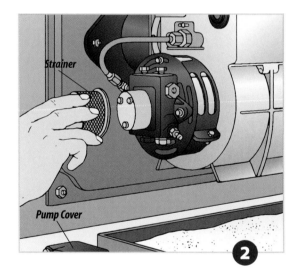

Strainer

Pump Cover

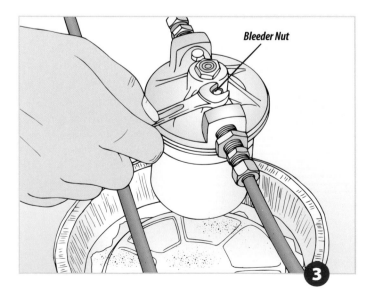

Bleeder Nut

3. Bleeding air from the filter bowl

- Locate the bleeder valve nut in the lid of the filter bowl (left). Use an open-ended wrench to turn the nut counterclockwise, which will open the bleeder.

- Now open the oil supply valve.

- The filter bowl should fill with oil, forcing air out of the filter bowl through the bleeder valve.

- When oil begins to escape from the bleeder valve, close it. The bowl should now be full of oil.

- Restore power to the burner.

Cleaning the Fan and Lubricating the Motor

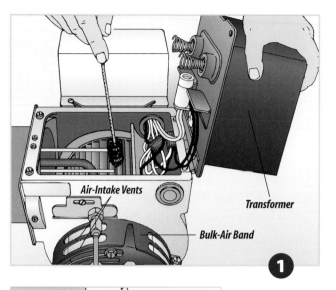

You should clean the fan and air-intake vents on the fan housing prior to each heating season. During the season, visually check them for dirt and debris and clean if necessary. This will help to maintain high efficiency of the fan and burner.

1. Cleaning the fan

- Brush off the air-intake vents on the fan housing with a long narrow brush.
- Unscrew the transformer located on top of the burner, and move it out of the way to expose the fan.
- Using a brush and a shop vac, brush off the fan blades. Wipe the interior of the fan housing clean with a rag.
- On an old-style burner, mark the position of the slotted bulk-air band that surrounds the housing. Loosen the screw holding the band, and slide the band back.
- Clean the fan and then reposition the band in its original position and tighten the screw.

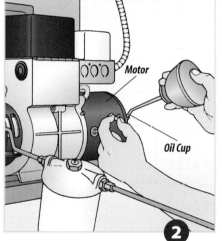

2. Lubricating the motor

- Some burner motors have small oil ports at each end. If your burner motor does not have oil ports, it is a permanently sealed motor and does not need oiling. A motor with oil ports should be lubricated every 2 months or at intervals specified by the motor manufacturer.
- To lubricate your motor, lift the caps on the oil ports, lubricate with five drops of SAE-10 nondetergent electric-motor oil in each port, and replace the lid.

Cleaning the Flame Sensor

The light-detecting cell

The photoelectric cell or flame sensor must be kept clean. The flame sensor shuts off the motor when ignition fails, and it cannot sense ignition failure if it is dirty. The sensor is located on the underside of the transformer or is attached to the burner housing near the end of the air tube.

- Wipe dirt from the photoelectric cell with a clean dry cloth, then screw the transformer back in place.

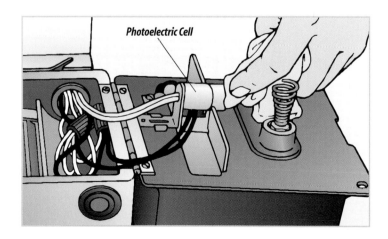

Maintaining the Firing Assembly

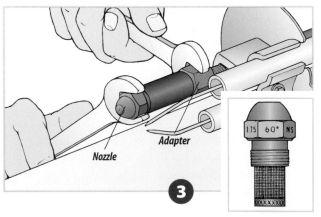

1. Removing the firing assembly

- Shut off power to the oil burner at the main service panel (pages 88–89). Access the electrodes and nozzle oil line by moving the transformer out of the way.

- Mark the position of the oil line in the air tube.

- Disconnect the nozzle oil line from the pump oil line by loosening the flare nut first, and then the locknut.

- Carefully pull the entire firing assembly out of the air tube (left). You may have to give the assembly a slight twist as you pull it out, but be careful not to bump the electrodes or nozzle against the burner housing as you remove the assembly.

- Clean the air tube with a clean cloth and a toothbrush.

- If there is a flame-retention device—a circular metal piece with fins or vanes—at the end of the tube, clean it, too.

2. Cleaning the ignition system

- With a clean cloth dipped in solvent, wipe the soot off the electrodes, insulators, electrode extension rods, and transformer terminals (right).

- Inspect insulators for cracks and cables for fraying. If you find either, take the assembly to a heating supplier for repair or replacement.

- Measure the spacing of the electrode tips. The distance should match the manufacturer's specifications, usually about ⅛ inch apart. They should be set no more than ½ inch above the center of the nozzle tip and no more than ⅛ inch beyond the front of the nozzle (inset). If the electrodes need adjustment, loosen the screw on the electrode holder and gently move the electrodes into place. If you are not sure of the correct spacing, take the entire assembly to a heating supplier.

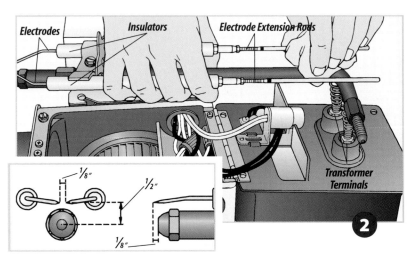

3. Removing the nozzle

- Place one open-ended wrench on the hexagonal adapter at the end of the nozzle oil line to act as a brace to hold the oil line steady (left). Use another to remove the nozzle. Be careful not to twist the oil line or move the position of the electrodes.

- Examine the tip of the nozzle (inset): The stamped specifications show the firing rate in gallons of oil per hour, or gph (1.75 as shown), and the angle of spray (60 degrees as shown). Letters on the nozzle usually indicate the type of spray pattern.

- If the nozzle has a firing rate of 1.50 gph or less, replace it with an identical nozzle. If the nozzle has a higher rate, you can clean and reuse it.

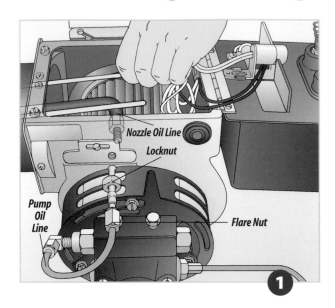

4. Disassembling the nozzle

- Unscrew the strainer from the back of the nozzle. Now access the distributor inside the nozzle tip by unscrewing it from the back of the nozzle (right). Slide the locknut and distributor out of the nozzle body.

- Soak all of the nozzle parts in solvent and scrub all debris off with a toothbrush. Clean the distributor slots with a piece of stiff paper, and clean the nozzle orifice with a toothbrush. Never try to clean the orifice with any wire or metal brush: You can adversely affect the spray pattern.

- Flush all of the clean parts with hot water and leave them to dry.

- Reassemble the dry parts, using clean tools. Screw the nozzle on the adapter finger-tight, then snug it a quarter-turn with the wrenches.

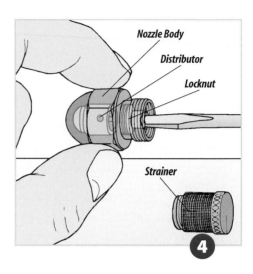

Nozzle Body
Distributor
Locknut
Strainer

4

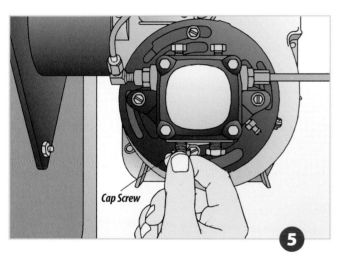

Cap Screw

5

5. Opening the oil line

(Skip this step if your storage tank is below the oil burner.)

- Loosen the cap screw on the unused intake port of the underside of the pump cover (left).

- Place a pan of sand under the oil pump, and open the supply valve.

- When oil begins to flow from the intake port, let it run into the pan for about 15 seconds before tightening the cap screw.

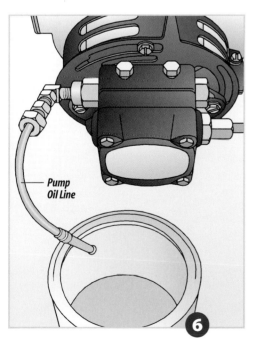

Pump Oil Line

6

6. Priming the pump

- Get an old bucket or cleaned-out can for oil to run into. Loosen the pump oil line at the pump to feed the unattached end into the bucket (right). (For safety, temporarily swing the transformer down or, on an old-style burner, screw on the rear plate.)

- Set the house thermostat to a high temperature, and restore power at the service panel. Hold the bucket and have a helper throw the master switch.

- Oil will gush from the line with great force. Let the pump run for about 10 seconds, then have your helper turn off power at the master switch and the service panel. Lift the transformer (or remove the rear plate).

- Guided by the marks made in Step 1, install the firing assembly. Connect the pump and nozzle oil lines by tightening the locknuts first by hand, then giving them a quarter-turn with a wrench. Screw down the transformer. Restore power.

- To expel air from the oil line, turn on the burner at the master switch. Run the burner for 10 seconds and shut it off. Repeat five times, or until the burner shuts down smoothly and instantaneously.

Gas Burners

HOW THEY WORK

Gas furnaces are very reliable yet require some annual maintenance and occasional repairs. While some repairs are best left to professionals, you can save money by doing the repairs shown here.

As a part of annual maintenance, check the temperature rise—the difference between the air temperatures in the supply and return ducts. Too high a difference may crack the heat exchanger; which transfers furnace heat to the air; condensation may corrode the system if the difference is too low.

Pilot Light

Older furnaces use a standing-pilot ignition, similar to a water heater. Maintenance involves turning off the pilot each spring and lighting the furnace each fall. The thermocouple that senses whether the pilot is lit can need replacement, and the pilot and burner may need adjustment.

Electronic Ignition

Newer gas furnaces use an electric spark to light the gas. If a newer furnace fails to spark, call for service. However, you can test and replace a hot-surface igniter that does not glow when the system starts.

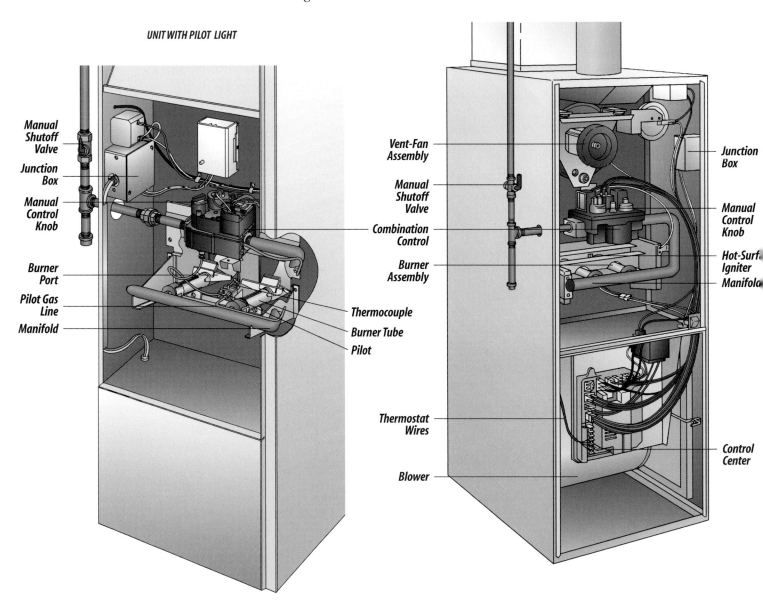

UNIT WITH ELECTRONIC IGNITION

UNIT WITH PILOT LIGHT

Manual Shutoff Valve

Junction Box

Manual Control Knob

Burner Port

Pilot Gas Line

Manifold

Thermocouple

Burner Tube

Pilot

Vent-Fan Assembly

Manual Shutoff Valve

Combination Control

Burner Assembly

Thermostat Wires

Blower

Junction Box

Manual Control Knob

Hot-Surf. Igniter

Manifold

Control Center

Troubleshooting

No heat

- Replace fuse or reset circuit breaker **88–89**
- Relight pilot light **184**
- Call for service of combination control

Insufficient heat

- Adjust burner air shutter **186**
- Clean burner ports
- Call for service if gas pressure is too low

Excessive fuel consumption

- Adjust pilot to lower setting **186**
- Call for service if gas pressure is too high

Pilot does not light or does not stay lit

- Clean pilot orifice **186–187**
- Test thermocouple and replace if necessary **185**
- Call for service if electric pilot is faulty
- Call for service if combination control is faulty

Pilot lights, but burner does not ignite

- Call for service

Pilot flame flickers

- Adjust pilot flame **186**

Exploding sound when burner ignites

- Adjust pilot to higher setting **186**
- Clean pilot orifice **187**
- Call for service if gas pressure is too low or too high or if pilot light is not positioned correctly
- Clean burner ports

Burner takes more than a few seconds to ignite

- Clean pilot orifice **187**
- Adjust pilot **186**

Burner flame is uneven

- Clean burner ports

Burner flame too yellow

- Clean burner **186–187**
- Provide air from outside by opening vents in furnace room; if problem persists, call for service
- Adjust burner air shutter **186**
- Call for service of faulty burners

Noisy furnace: Rumbling when burners off

- Clean burner **186–187**
- Adjust burner air shutter **186**

Lighting a Pilot

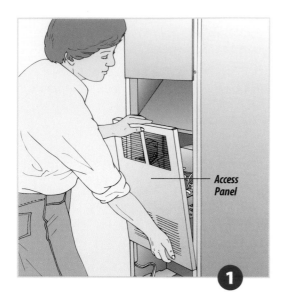

Access Panel

1. Accessing the control knob

- To remove the front access panel, look for any screws holding it in place and remove them.

- Firmly grasp the top and bottom of the panel and slide it up and out toward you (left). If the front panel will not budge, try tapping it lightly around the edges to loosen it.

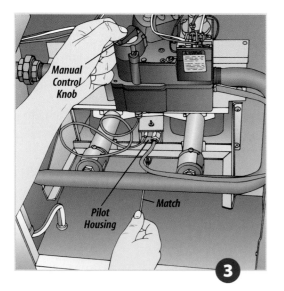

Combination Control

2. Turning off the gas

- Make sure the power to the unit is off at the main service panel (pages 88–89) and at the unit-disconnect switch. Set the control knob on the furnace to the OFF position (left), and wait 10 minutes to let any gas dissipate.

- If you continue to smell gas, do not attempt to light the pilot. Shut off gas to the furnace (page 186) and call for service.

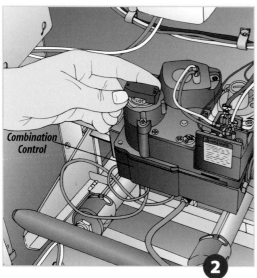

Manual Control Knob

Pilot Housing

Match

3. Relighting the pilot

You will probably find the lighting instructions near the control. If you find instructions to light your pilot, follow them. If not, follow this general procedure.

- Turn on the gas by setting the control knob to the PILOT position. Strike a long match and hold it just under the pilot gas port (left).

- Depress the control knob, and the pilot should light. Remove the match while continuing to hold down on the control knob for 30 seconds. Let the knob up, and turn the control to the ON position.

- If the pilot goes out when you release pressure on the control knob, relight the pilot. Wait one minute this time to see whether the pilot stays lit. If it goes out after one minute, the thermocouple may be faulty. Service the thermocouple (opposite page).

Adjusting and Replacing a Thermocouple

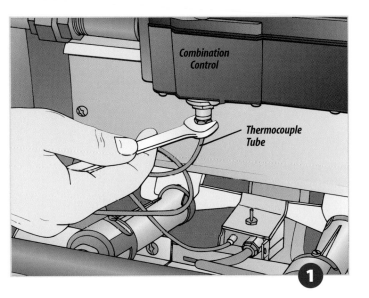

1. Removing the thermocouple tube

- To test the thermocouple, the pilot must be lit. Turn the control knob to PILOT. You need a helper to hold down the control while you test the thermocouple.

- While holding down the control knob, detach the thermocouple tube by unscrewing the fitting with an open-ended wrench (left).

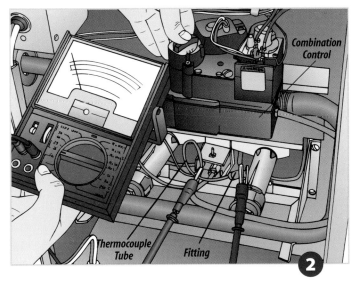

2. Testing the thermocouple

If a pilot does not stay lit (Step 3, opposite page), the termocouple probaby needs to be replaced. To make sure, test it.

- Set a multitester to the DCV scale, lowest volt range.

- With the control knob depressed, clip one multitester lead to the end of the thermocouple tube nearest the pilot and the other multitester lead to the fitting on the other end of the tube (left).

- If the multitester shows a reading, the thermocouple is generating sufficient voltage; put back the thermocouple tube. If there is no reading, release the control knob and go to Step 3.

3. Removing and replacing the thermocouple

- Shut off the main gas valve, located on the gas-supply pipe that leads into the burner (page 186). Also shut off power to the burner at the main service panel (pages 88–89).

- Slide the defective thermocouple out of the bracket that holds it in place next to the pilot (right).

- Use a cloth to clean the fitting on the combination control, and screw a new thermocouple tube into the fitting. After tightening it by hand, turn it a quarter-turn with an open-ended wrench.

- Insert the thermocouple into the pilot bracket, being careful not to crimp the tubing.

- Retstore power and relight the pilot (opposite page).

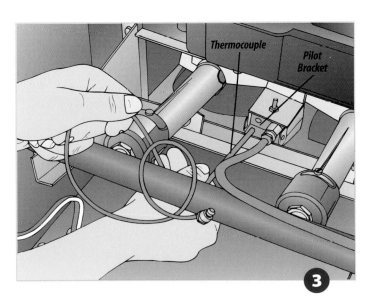

Adjusting the Burner Flame

Rotating the air shutter

- The burners in most furnaces have an adjustable shutter that is held in place by a short sheet-metal screw, or lock screw. Fixed shutters must be repaired by a professional.

- If your furnace has an adjustable shutter, turn the thermostat to its highest setting to start the burner and keep it running. Wait for the furnace to ignite and heat up, then remove the burner access panel and loosen the lock screw (inset).

- Slowly rotate the shutter open (right) until the blue base of the flame appears to lift slightly from the burner port surface. Then close the shutter until the flame reseats itself on the surface and looks correct (below center).

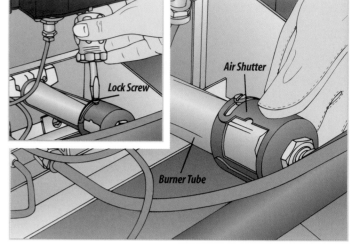

Lock Screw
Air Shutter
Burner Tube

TOO LITTLE AIR
Yellow tip with
green inner flame

CORRECT FLAME
Blue flame with soft blue-
green inner flame.
Occasional yellow streaking.

TOO MUCH AIR
Blue with hard
blue inner flame

Replacing the Igniter

1. Shutting off the gas to the furnace

- Turn off the gas to the furnace by closing the manual shutoff, located on the gas line coming into the control box.

- The valve is closed when the handle (right) is perpendicular to the valve body and the pipe. It is open when it is parallel, or in line with the fitting and pipe.

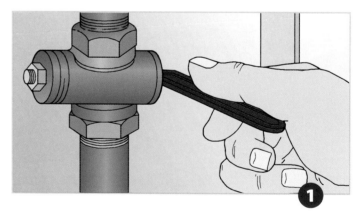

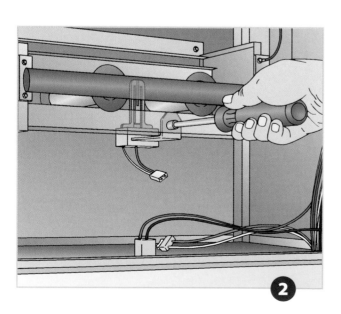

2. Replacing the igniter

- Remove the burner access panel and unplug the igniter.

- Test the igniter with a mulitester set to RX1. Attach an alligator clip to each prong in the igniter's plug. If the multi-tester registers between 45 and 90 ohms, replace the control center (left). Otherwise, install a new igniter.

- Unscrew or unclip the defective igniter and remove it. The hot-surface igniter is fragile and should be handled with care.

- Screw or clip the new igniter in place and plug it in. Remount the access panel, and restore power and gas to the furnace.

Cleaning the Pilot

1. Disassembling the pilot

- Shut off the gas to the furnace (opposite page). Turn off the power to the furnace at the main service panel (pages 88–89) or at the unit-disconnect switch. If the furnace has been running, wait 30 minutes to allow metal parts to cool.

- Disconnect and remove the thermocouple tube. With a pair of pliers, steady the gas line connecting the pilot to the combination control; be careful not to bend or damage the line.

- With an open-ended wrench in your other hand, loosen the nut attaching the pilot gas line (right).

- Unscrew and remove the bracket holding the pilot's thermocouple assembly in place. Carefully unscrew the pilot nozzle from the bracket and then pull the two apart (inset).

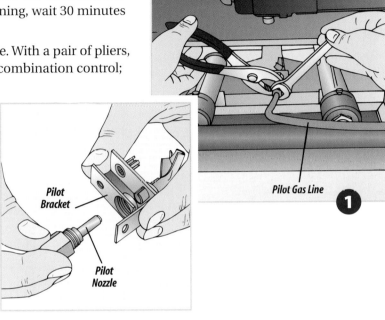

Pilot Gas Line

Pilot Bracket

Pilot Nozzle

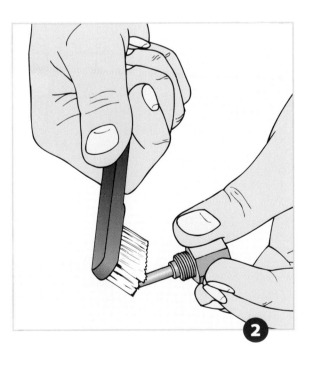

2. Cleaning the pilot nozzle

- Brush the surface dirt off the pilot nozzle with a toothbrush. Use a soft wire or a toothbrush to dislodge deposits from inside the pilot (left), being careful not to damage or chip it.

- Reassemble the pilot assembly and reinstall it in the burner. Turn on the gas and power to the burner and relight the pilot.

Heat Pumps and Central Air

HOW THEY WORK

Air conditioners and heat pumps work on the same principles, only in reverse. This is why they share the same equipment. Repairs involving the air conditioning refrigerant should be performed only by a licensed professional. In some areas, it is against the law to work with refrigerant without a license.

There are two main parts to the heat pump and air conditioning system: the outside condenser unit, and the evaporator coil, located inside the home. In the summer, liquid refrigerant in the condenser coils is sent indoors by the compressor to evaporator coils in the home. The heat from warm air circulating over the coils is absorbed by the cold evaporator coils. This absorption transforms the liquid refrigerant to gas. The refrigerant in gas form returns outside to the condenser. Heat absorbed indoors is released outside, as the refrigerant becomes a liquid again.

In the winter, a heat pump reverses this process. Refrigerant in the outdoor coil absorbs heat from the air, the compressor pumps the vaporized refrigerant to the indoor coil, and the blower circulates indoor air over the heated coil, warming the air. As the hot vapor cools, it becomes liquid again and returns to the outdoor coil. Check to see that your condenser is level to ensure its proper operation. Once a year, clean the condenser coils and straighten any bent fins (page 191). Lubricate the fan motor if necessary, and inspect the fan for loose or deformed blades that can ruin the motor.

The air conditioner coils inside the home condense moisture from the outside air that collects in a drain pan under the coils. Annually, pour a 50/50 solution of water and chlorine bleach into the pan to prevent algae growth.

Heat pumps have a reversing valve that changes the direction for refrigerant flow to switch from cooling to heating and back. If your heat pump produces hot air in summer or the condenser coils do not de-ice in winter, check the reversing valve solenoid coil and replace it if it is defective (page 196).

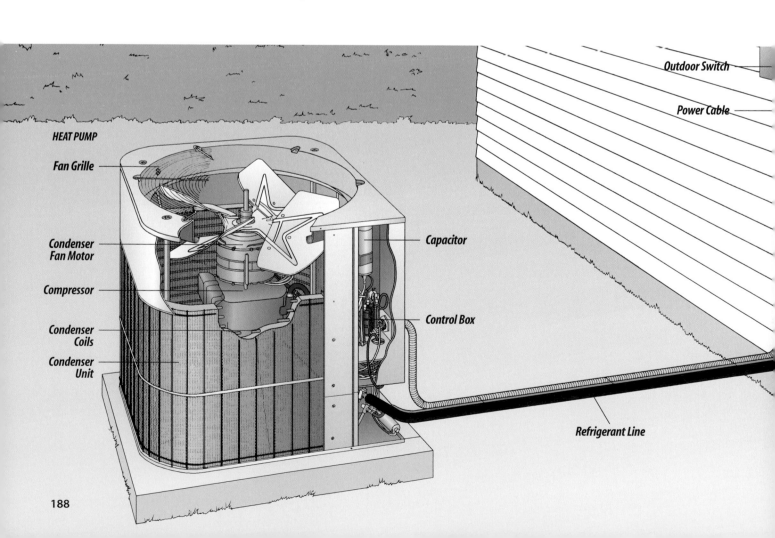

HEAT PUMP

Fan Grille

Condenser Fan Motor

Compressor

Condenser Coils

Condenser Unit

Capacitor

Control Box

Outdoor Switch

Power Cable

Refrigerant Line

BEFORE YOU START

Before beginning any repair, turn off the power at the main service panel (pages 88–89) and at the outside switch near the condenser. Leave the unit off for at least five minutes before turning it back on, to prevent excess refrigerant pressure from overloading the compressor.

If your condenser unit does not turn on

- Turn on outdoor switch; replace fuse or reset circuit breaker **88–89**
- Lower thermostat setting
- Discharge capacitors **162–163**
- Test capacitors and replace if necessary **193**
- Test fan and motor and replace if necessary **190**

If your condenser unit does not turn off

- Clean contactor; test and replace if necessary **194–195**

If your condenser unit is noisy when running

- Tighten fan-grille screws or coil-guard screws
- Adjust fan blades
- Lubricate fan motor, and test and replace if necessary **190**

If your air conditioning does not cool

- Set thermostat higher
- Clean coils **197**
- Test fan motor and replace if necessary **190**

If water is leaking inside the furnace

- Clean drain pan **197**
- Inspect and clean the drain trap

If your heat pump produces hot air in summer and does not de-ice in winter

- Test solenoid coil and replace if necessary **196**

CENTRAL AIR CONDITIONER

A-Shaped Evaperator Coils

Plenum

Condensate Drainpipe

V-Shaped Evaporator Coils

Drain Pan

Maintaining the Fan and Motor

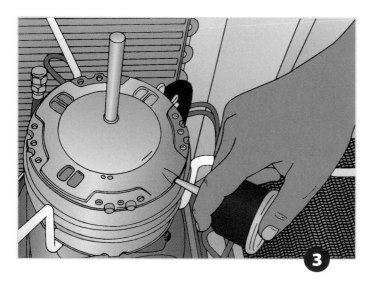

Fan Grille

1. Removing the fan grille

- Turn off the power at the main service panel (pages 88–89) and the unit-disconnect switch located outside near the condenser. Remove the screws holding the fan grille to the top of the unit, and lift off the grille (above).

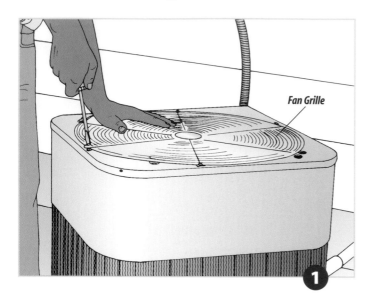

3. Oiling the fan motor

- Locate the oil ports on the motor housing. The ports may be sealed by plastic plugs. Remove the plugs with a screwdriver, and inject two to three drops of non-detergent light machine oil into each port (above). Do not over-oil.

- Replace the plugs. Replace the fan grille, and restore power to the unit.

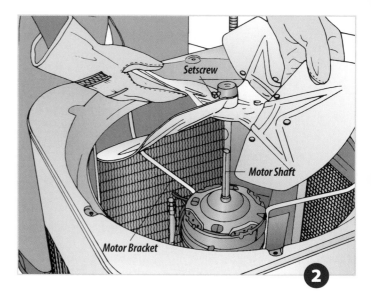

Setscrew

Motor Shaft

Motor Bracket

2. Replacing the fan blades

- Using gloves, turn the fan blades, looking for any wobbling or loose points.

- Loosen the setscrew that attaches the fan blades to the motor shaft, and remove the blades (above).

- Wipe the blades clean and visually inspect the blades to see that they are all in alignment. If the blades are badly bent or rusted, or if the blade coupling that holds the blade to the motor shaft is worn or cracked, replace the fan blades with an identical set, available from a heating equipment supplier.

- Slide the fan blades onto the motor shaft, aligning the setscrew on the fan blade coupling with the flat area on the motor shaft. Leave about 1 inch of clearance between the fan blades and the motor. Make sure that the setscrew that attaches the fan blades to the motor is tight.

Flushing the Condenser Coils

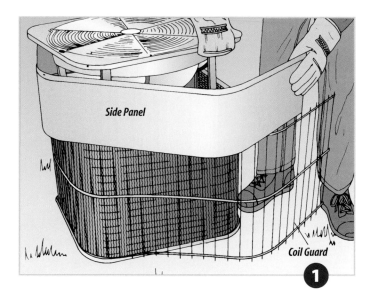

(1)

1. Removing the coil guard

- Turn off the power to the condenser at the main service panel (pages 88–89) and the unit-disconnect switch located outside near the condenser.

- Remove the screws that connect the side panel to the condenser unit top panel and frame. You may also have to remove the screws that secure the top of the unit to support rods inside.

- Work the side panel and coil guard loose without bending them (above). Unwrap them from the condenser unit frame.

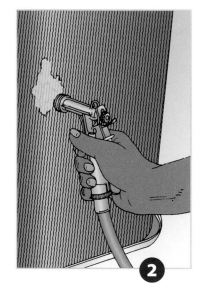

(2)

2. Cleaning and straightening the condenser fins

- Spray water through the fins from the inside out, and outside in, until they are clean (above). Avoid spraying the condenser motor directly. Extremely dirty coils can be cleaned with a fin-cleaning solvent that you spray on and wash off.

- Straighten fins with a fin comb (page 197).

3. Reinstalling the panels

- Attach with a screw the end you removed last when you took off the side panel. Then wrap the coil guard around the condenser and carefully work it in place. Replace the coil guard, replacing the screws you took out earlier as you go. Reach into the unit and hold each top-panel support rod in position (left).

- Reattach the grille if you had to remove it.

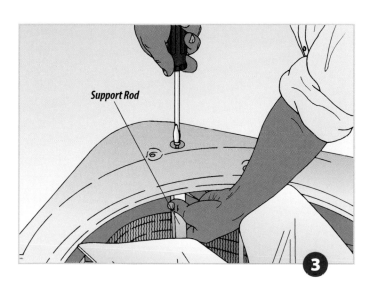

(3)

Locating and Discharging a Capacitor

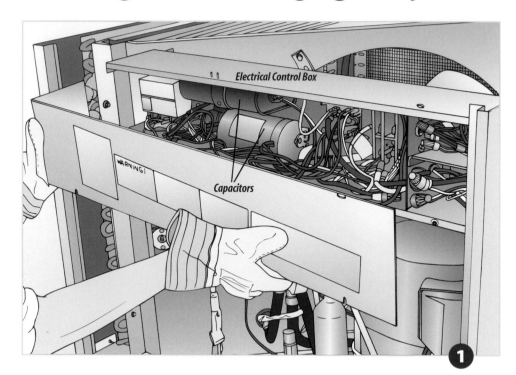

1. Accessing the capacitor

- Remove the electrical control box panel by removing the hex-head screws with a socket wrench or nut driver. Wearing work gloves, pull off the panel (left).

2. Discharging the capacitor

- It is dangerous to attempt to test a capacitor without discharging it first. You will need to make your own capacitor-discharging tool (pages 162–163). At an electronics supply store, buy two jumper cables with alligator clips on each end and a 20,000-ohm, 2-watt resistor.

- Turn off the power to the motor or condenser you are working on (pages 88–89).

- Clip one end of each jumper to the leads of the resistor, then clip one jumper to the blade of a rubber-handled screwdriver (right). Make sure the power to the unit is off at the main service panel and the unit-disconnect switch.

- Remove the control box cover to access the capacitor.

- Clip the free jumper to the common terminal of the capacitor. Hold the screwdriver handle in one hand, and put your other hand behind you. Touch the end of the screwdriver to each capacitor for 5 seconds.

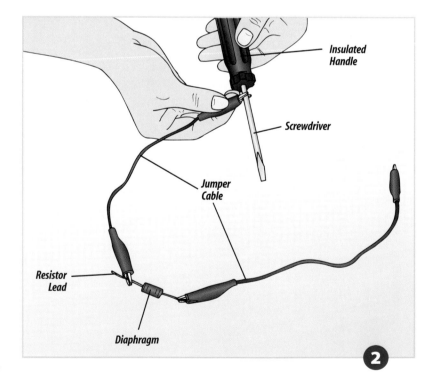

Testing, Removing, and Replacing a Discharged Capacitor

1. Testing the discharged capacitor

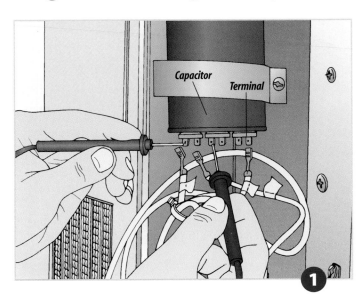

- Turn off the power to the condenser at the main service panel (pages 88–89) and the unit-disconnect switch.

- Discharge the capacitor (opposite page). To test a three-pronged capacitor, label and disconnect its wires. Set a multitester to RX1K to measure resistance, and touch the multitester probes together and set the needle to 0 with the ohms-adjust dial. Touch one probe to one of the connectors on the common terminal, marked C, and touch the other probe to both of the other terminals in turn (right). In each case, watch for the multitester needle to swing toward 0 resistance, then slowly move across the scale toward infinity.

- A correct response in both tests indicates a serviceable capacitor. If for either test the needle swings to 0 and stays there—or if it does not move at all—replace the capacitor.

- If the condenser has multiple, two-terminal capacitors, discharge them both, then test them individually by touching the multitester probes to both terminals of each.

2. Replacing the capacitor

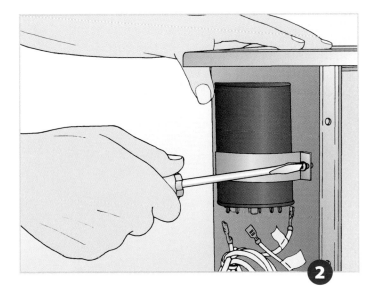

- Loosen the bracket (right) and slide out the old capacitor.

- Replace it with an identical one, available from a heating supplies dealer. Slide in the new capacitor and tighten the bracket. Reconnect the wires to the correct terminals, and restore power.

- You should have the heating supplies dealer dispose of the old capacitor.

Maintaining the Contactor

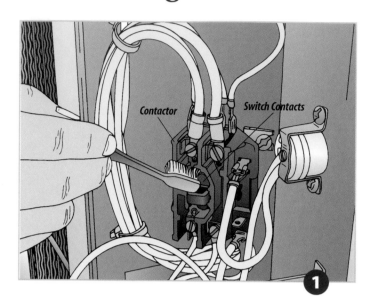

1. Cleaning the contacts

- Shut off the power at the main service panel (pages 88–89) and the outside unit-disconnect switch.

- Discharge the capacitor (pages 162–163).

- Locate the contactor and visually inspect the reed-style switch contacts. If they are stuck together or if the spring is missing, replace the contactor (page 195).

- Clean the contacts with a small toothbrush moistened with contact cleaner (left).

2. Disconnecting the wires

- Label the wires, including the wires for the solenoid coil behind the contactor, and disconnect them (right).

- Pull wires from space connectors with needlenose pliers. If you need to, unscrew the contactor and remove it from the control box for easier access to the contacts.

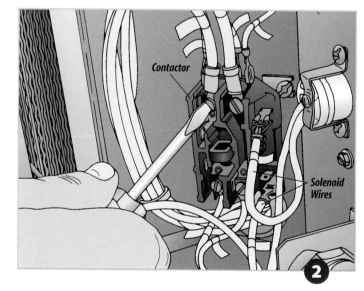

3. Cleaning the terminals

- If the terminals are dirty or corroded, you can clean them up with an emery board (left). Gently rub them to brighten the metal.

- Now examine the female connectors attached to the wires you removed in Step 2. If any of the connections are loose or badly corroded from the wire to the female connector, replace the connectors. Cut them off and strip away ⅜ inch of insulation and crimp a new, identical-sized solderless female connector to the bare wire with the appropriate notch of a wire stripper.

- Reconnect each wire in turn, crimping the connector onto the terminal.

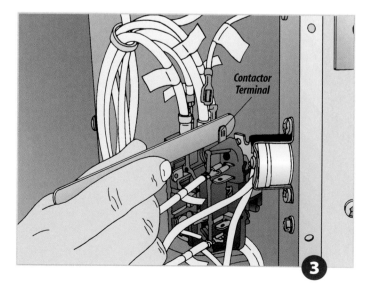

Testing and Replacing a Contactor

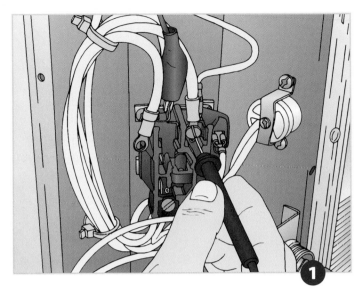

1. Contacts-open test

- With the power to the unit off and the capacitors discharged (pages 162–163), set a multitester to the RX1K setting.
- Disconnect the wires from one upper screw terminal.
- Clip one end of the multitester to one of the upper terminals, and touch the other lead's probe to the adjacent screw terminal (left). Check that the multitester needle points to infinity.
- Now disconnect the wires from one of the lower terminals and test the lower pair the same way.
- If the needle points to infinity in both tests, proceed to Step 2. If not, replace the capacitor.

2. Contacts-closed test

- Gently hold the upper switch contacts closed (right) and repeat the test from Step 1. Check that the multitester needle points to 0.
- Test the lower pair of switch contacts the same way.
- Replace the contactor if the multitest needle does not point to 0 in either test.
- If the contacts are okay, you need to test the solenoid coil. To test the coil, disconnect the upper and lower wires from the coil terminals. Set a multitester to RX1K and touch the probes to the terminals. If there is no continuity, replace the contactor.

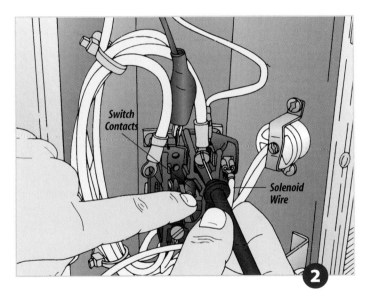

Switch Contacts

Solenoid Wire

3. Replacing the contactor

- Remove the mounting screws holding the contactor to the control box wall (left), and take out the contactor.
- Replace the contactor with an identical replacement. Screw the new contactor in place, and reconnect the labeled wires.
- Restore power to the unit.

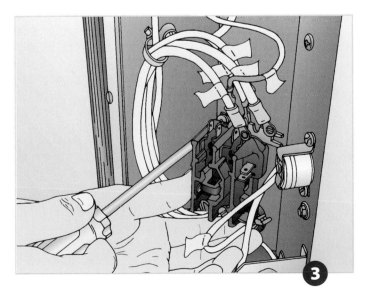

Servicing a Heat Pump Reversing Valve

1. Testing the solenoid coil

- Remove the rear access panel and find the solenoid coil attached to the reversing valve, a cylindrical device with one refrigerant pipe extending from the top and three from the bottom.

- Gently disconnect the plug from the solenoid coil.

- Set a multitester to RX1K. Reaching under the solenoid bracket cover, touch probes to the solenoid coil terminals (right). Check that the meter registers a value other than 0 or infinity. If the coil fails this test, replace it.

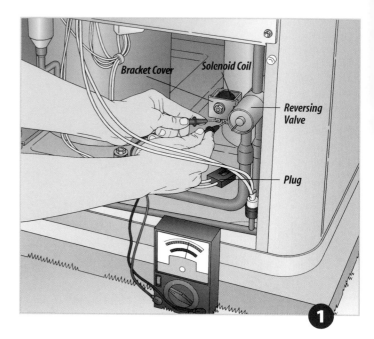

Bracket Cover · Solenoid Coil · Reversing Valve · Plug · ①

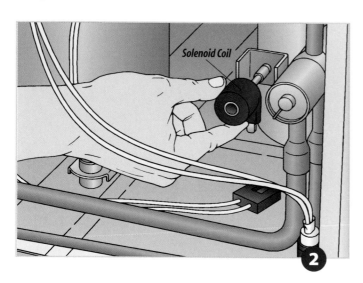

Solenoid Coil · ②

2. Replacing the solenoid coil

- Using an open-ended wrench, remove the nut that holds the solenoid bracket cover and coil in place.

- Pull the metal bracket cover away from the coil assembly, and slide the old coil off the shaft (left) and replace it with an identical new one.

- Reinstall the access panel.

Checking the Defrosting System

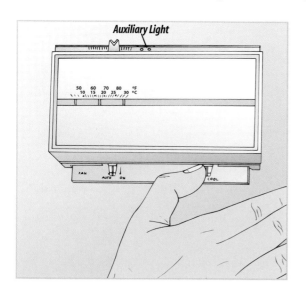

Auxiliary Light

50 60 70 80 °F
10 15 20 25 30 °C

FAN · AUTO · ON · COOL

Troubleshooting the defrosting system

- The auxiliary light on the thermostat indicates that the heat pump is in defrost mode or that the outside temperature is low enough to activate the auxiliary heating system. If the light remains continuously lit and you notice ice buildup on the outside coils, set the indoor thermostat to COOL (left). This should deliver warm refrigerant from the indoor coils to the outdoor coils that will thaw the ice.

- Wait at least 30 minutes, and inspect the outdoor coils. If the ice has thawed, the reversing valve may have been stuck. Reset the thermostat to HEAT.

- If the problem recurs, either the defrost sensing system or the reversing valve is faulty. You need to call a professional.

- If the coils remain iced, the reversing valve solenoid may be defective. Service the reversing valve (above).

Maintaining the Evaporator

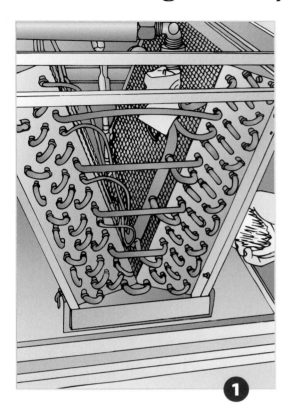

1. Accessing and cleaning the evaporator coils

- Turn off the power at the main service panel (pages 88–89) and the outdoor unit-disconnect switch.

- In most furnaces, the evaporator coils are top-mounted and hard if not impossible to access. You may be able to have a service technician install an access panel on the plenum. If the evaporator coils are bottom-mounted, you can access them as shown here and service them. Remove the blower panel and then the coil panel.

- Dirt can get to the evaporator coils if the filter is loaded up or not maintained. Clean the coils by gently running a soft brush along the coils and along the fins (left). Have a shop vac handy to vacuum off the dirt.

- Pay special attention to the air intake area of the coils. If the dirt is sticking, you can use a mild soap-and-water solution to loosen it.

- If the coils are top-mounted, be careful not to let water drip on the heat exchanger or on the heating elements.

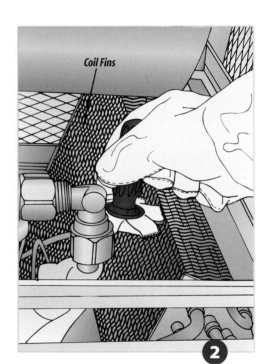

Coil Fins

2. Straightening the fins

- To straighten bent fins, fit the teeth of a fin comb into the fins and pull the comb through to straighten them (right).

3. Cleaning the drain pan

- Algae and sediment can collect in the drain pan. This can lead to corrosion, which can eventually cause your drain pan to leak. You should periodically check and clean your drain pan if necessary.

- Wipe the pan out with a sponge, then flush out the pan and drain tube using a hose or a pitcher of water (left).

- To help curb algae formation, add ½ cup bleach to the water in the drain pan. You can also use an algaecide manufactured specifically for drain pans.

Drain Pan

Window Air Conditioners

HOW THEY WORK

Pressurized refrigerant flows through an air conditioner, alternately in gas and liquid form. When the air conditioner is switched on, the condenser sucks in refrigerant gas and pressurizes it, raising its temperature. The heated high-pressure gas travels to the condenser coils outdoors, where the fins give off heat to the surrounding cooler air as the gas condenses into a liquid. This liquid refigerant travels indoors to the evaporator coils where, under reduced pressure, it vaporizes into a gas, absorb-

ing heat from the room. The blower pulls room air through the air filter and across the evaporator coils, where it is cooled, then blown back into the room.

Window air conditioners can be effective in cooling a room or an entire floor if they are sized appropriately for area to be cooled. Depending on the size of the unit, they may run on 120- or 240-volt current. They are easy to maintain and, with proper maintenance, should last many years. Clean the grille and the drain system annually. Use a shop vac to clean the evaporator coils and the condenser coils. At the same time, check the coil fins. Clean or replace your filter once a month during summer use. When moving the air conditioner, be careful not to move the coils or refrigerant lines; these carry high-pressure refrigerant and should be serviced only by a professional.

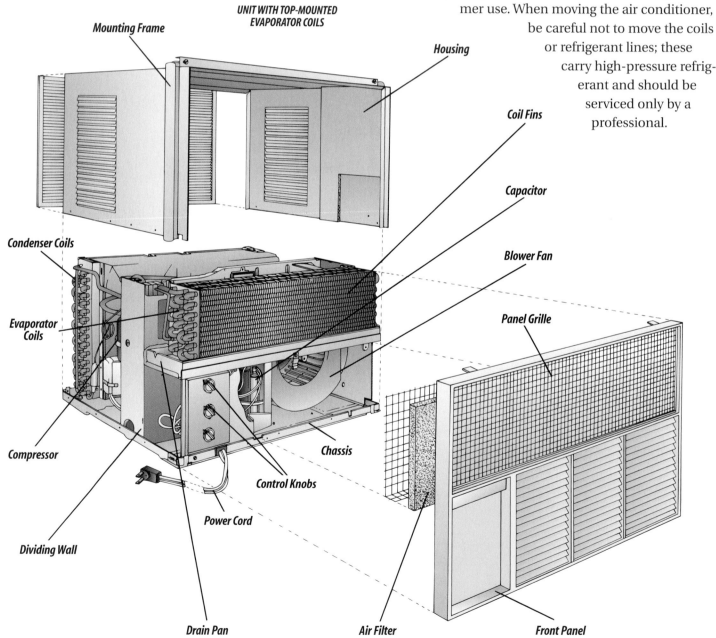

UNIT WITH TOP-MOUNTED EVAPORATOR COILS

Mounting Frame

Housing

Coil Fins

Capacitor

Blower Fan

Panel Grille

Condenser Coils

Evaporator Coils

Compressor

Chassis

Control Knobs

Power Cord

Dividing Wall

Drain Pan

Air Filter

Front Panel

Troubleshooting

If your air conditioner does not run at all

- Replace fuse or reset circuit breaker **88–89**
- Wash or replace filter **201**

If your air conditioner repeatedly trips circuit breaker

- Clean coils and straighten fins **202**

If the fan runs but conditioner does not cool

- Set thermostat below room temperature

If your air conditioner short-cycles (turns on and off repeatedly)

- Remove obstruction in condenser
- Clean coils and straighten fins **202**

If your air conditioner does not cool sufficiently

- Lower thermostat
- Clean or replace filter **201**

If your air conditioner is noisy when running

- Tighten housing screws and ensure that clips are in place
- Lubricate fan-motor bearings **202**

If your air conditioner drips water inside

- Check drain system and flush if necessary **203**

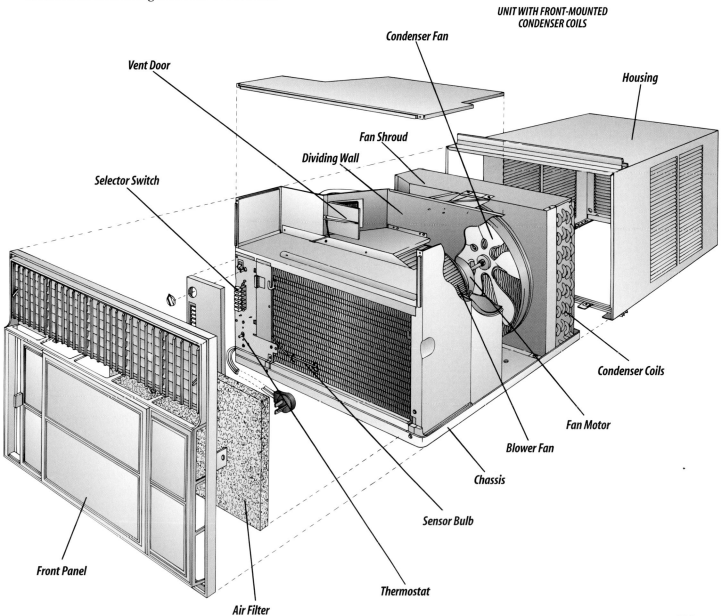

UNIT WITH FRONT-MOUNTED CONDENSER COILS

Condenser Fan

Vent Door

Housing

Fan Shroud

Dividing Wall

Selector Switch

Condenser Coils

Fan Motor

Blower Fan

Chassis

Sensor Bulb

Front Panel

Thermostat

Air Filter

Accessing the Components

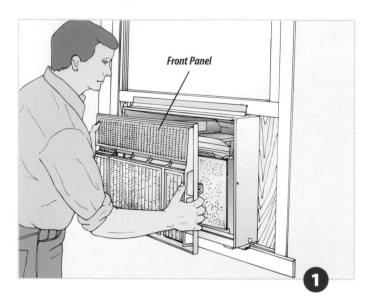

Front Panel

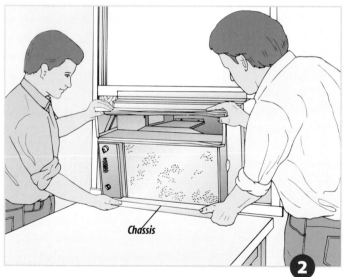

Chassis

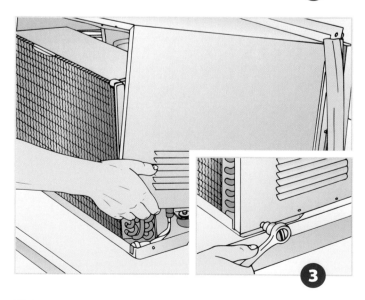

1. Removing the front panel

- Unplug the air conditioner. If you are just changing the filter, you do not need to take the air conditioner out of the housing; you can access the filter by removing the front cover of the air conditioner. For most other repairs, you will need to remove the entire air conditioner from the window and remove the housing.

- To remove the front panel, look for and remove any screws or clips that hold it to the air conditioner. Remove them and gently pull off the front cover (left).

2. Taking the air conditioner out of the window

- Most larger, heavier air conditioners have a slide-out chassis that fits into the housing bolted permanently to the window frame. Many small air conditioners have sliding panels at the sides and may or may not be supported by a bracket outside the window. To remove a small air conditioner, have a helper support it while you carefully open the window.

    Caution: *The air conditioner is very heavy and can easily tip backward (and fall out the window).*

- Collapse the side panels. Place a sturdy table you can use to work on the air conditioner next to the window under the air conditioner, and work with a helper to remove it. Keeping your back straight and your knees bent to avoid muscle strain, slide the chassis—or the entire unit—out of the window onto the table. If the air conditioner has a wraparound housing, remove it.

3. Removing the housing

- Most window air conditioners have a back panel secured to the chassis with bolts or sheet-metal screws. Some are attached with screws and clips under the front panel top.

- Remove these bolts or screws, as well as those on the top and sides of the housing (inset). If they are stuck or hard to remove, use a few drops of penetrating oil to help loosen them.

- Firmly grasp the housing and remove it (left). Set it aside.

Maintaining the Filter and Grille

1. Removing the air filter

- Unplug the air conditioner and remove the front cover.
- The filter should be located in front of the evaporator coils or attached to the back of the front panel. Remove any clips holding the filter in place, and take off the filter (right), being careful not to rip it.

2. Washing or replacing the filter

- During the cooling season, you should clean the filter once a month. If the filter is not washable, or is torn, replace it with an identical filter.
- If the filter is washable, vacuum off the heavy dirt and then place the filter in a bucket of a light detergent and water solution. Wring it out a few times to remove the dirt, and then rinse it with warm water (left).
- Wring it out and let it dry before reinstalling it.

3. Cleaning and replacing the front panel

- Use a shop vac with a brush attachment to loosen the heavy dirt from the cover and grilles. You can spray the cover with a light detergent-and-water solution and rinse it with clean water.
- Wipe the surface clean with a damp cloth (right). Reattach the dry cover.

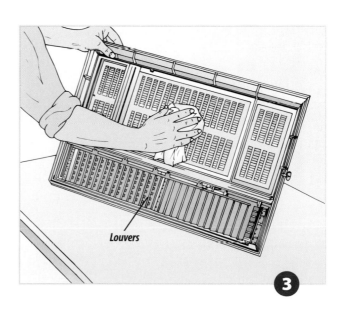

Maintaining the Coils

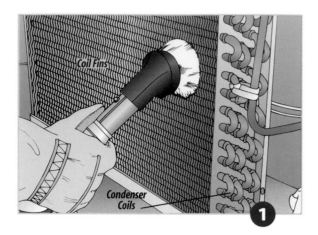

Coil Fins

Condenser Coils

1

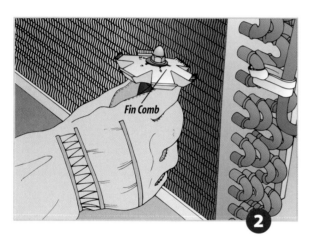

Fin Comb

2

1. Vacuuming the coil fins

- Unplug the air conditioner, and remove the air conditioner from the window. Take off the wraparound housing if necessary.

- Using a shop vac with a brush attachment, vacuum the coils and evaporator coil fins (left). If the coils are greasy or very dirty, have them steam-cleaned by a professional.

2. Straightening the coil fins

- With the air conditioner unplugged, use a fin comb to straighten bent coil fins (left). Determine which head of the comb corresponds to the spacing of the fins on the coils. The comb teeth should fit between the fins.

- Wearing gloves, gently fit the fin comb teeth between the coil fins into an undamaged section above the area to be straightened. Pull the fin comb down, sliding it through the damaged area. At the same time, comb out any debris between the fins.

- Never use anything but a fin comb to straighten fins—otherwise, you can damage the coil.

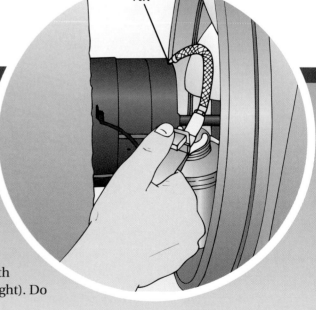

Port

Fan Motor Lubrication

Your window air conditioner motor may have oil ports, which need to be lubricated each season. You should also lubricate the motor shaft if it squeaks when you manually rotate the fan blades.

- Unplug the air conditioner and remove it from the window. Access the motor by removing the cover.

- Look for oil ports on the motor housing; if you can't find any, your motor may be permanently sealed and does not need lubrication.

- Pry the caps off of the ports. Insert three drops of SAE-10 nondetergent oil into each port. If the ports are difficult to reach, use an oil can with a long, flexible spout (right). Do not over-lubricate.

- If the motor shaft squeaks when you manually turn the shaft, insert two drops of SAE-10 nondetergent oil along the shaft where it meets the motor housing and the fan.

- Manually turn the fan to work the oil into the motor.

- Reassemble and reinstall the air conditioner.

Maintaining the Drain System

1. Clearing the drain tube

- Unplug the air conditioner and remove the front cover. Take the air conditioner out of the window.

- If your model has an evaporator drain pan and a condenser drain pan, locate the drain tube connecting them. Pull out the tube from under the compressor base, and run a wire through it to loosen any obstruction (right).

- Flush the tube with ½ cup chlorine bleach in ½ cup water to prevent algae formation.

- If the air conditioner does not have a drain tube, use a cloth to wipe clean the drain channels molded into the drain pan.

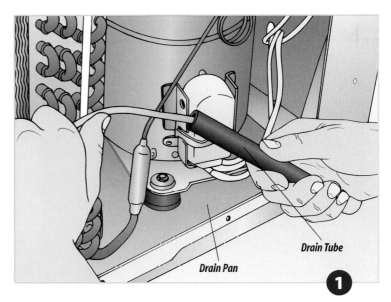

Drain Tube

Drain Pan

2. Clearing the drain hole

- Find the drain hole on the rear bottom of the housing (left). Clean any obstructions covering the hole.

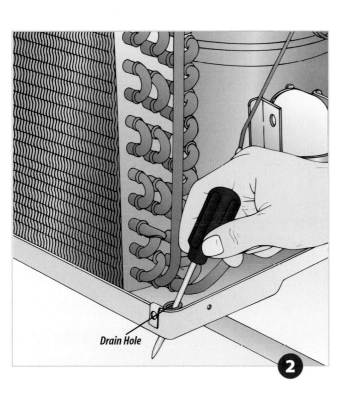

Drain Hole

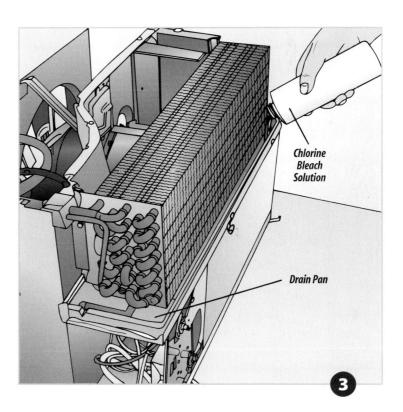

Chlorine Bleach Solution

Drain Pan

3. Cleaning the drain pan

- Place a bucket under the drain hole to catch overflow. Use a solution of 1 cup chlorine bleach and 1 cup water to prevent algae formation in the pan (right). Flush out each pan with the bleach solution, and then rinse with water.

Walls, Ceilings, Floors & Stairs

Contents

INTRODUCTION

This chapter deals with the visible interior surfaces of your home—the first things people notice about your house. Most of the repairs are cosmetic rather than structural, so make some decorating decisions before beginning a repair.

Matching Wall and Ceiling Surfaces

Some homes have walls and ceilings that are perfectly smooth; others were given a textured surface; and many older homes have generally imperfect surfaces. Learn how to match your surface so the repair will not look out of place.

If your surfaces are textured, it may be surprisingly difficult to get a patch to blend in. If possible, find out the materials and techniques used on the original wall. You may need to rent a texture sprayer, which spatters the wall with joint compound; after spraying, either leave it alone or scrape it gently with a very large taping knife for an "orange peel" surface. Years ago, workmen used hand tools only, or even their hands. Practice on a scrap piece of drywall until you get the look you are after.

It takes a good deal of time to make a wall truly smooth and flat. Don't be surprised if you have to apply joint compound, allow to dry, and sand the same spot three or four times before you remove all the indentations and high spots. Do not expect paint to cover up imperfections; often, it may actually accentuate them. The glossier the paint, the less forgiving it is. High-gloss paint will show every little problem, while ceiling paint—which is actually flatter than flat wall paint—can hide minor flaws.

Walls and Ceilings

HOW WALLS ARE CONSTRUCTED

The interior walls of most homes built during and after the 1950s are covered with drywall (also known as Sheetrock or wallboard). Most homes built earlier have lath-and-plaster walls.

Framing

Beneath the drywall or plaster and lath, walls are framed with vertical members, called studs, and horizontal members, the top plates and sole plates—all usually cut from 2×4 lumber. Studs are usually spaced 16 inches apart, but not always; older homes especially may have odd spacings.

Some homes also have firestops, short horizontal 2×4s spanning from stud to stud about halfway up the wall. Horizontal headers, made of laminated 2-by lumber, span across the tops of doors and windows (page 250). Larger boards called joists support ceilings and floors.

Drywall

This is relatively easy to install and cheap. Though not as strong as plaster, it actually resists cracking better than plaster.

Most residential drywall is ½ inch thick, but ⅝-inch drywall may be used for extra strength and resistance to fire. Drywall is attached directly to studs and joists with

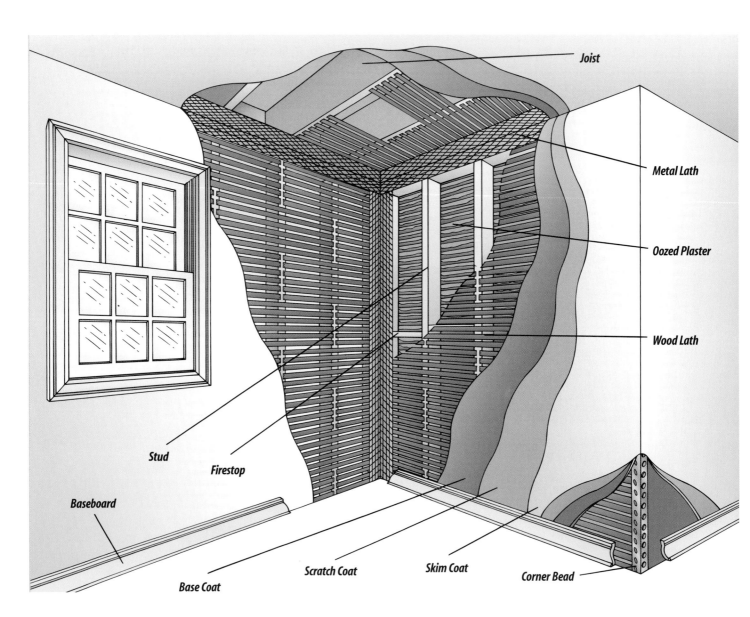

Joist

Metal Lath

Oozed Plaster

Wood Lath

Stud

Firestop

Baseboard

Base Coat

Scratch Coat

Skim Coat

Corner Bead

nails or screws. The joints between drywall pieces are covered with paper or fiberglass-mesh tape, and sealed with several coats of joint compound, which is sanded to produce a smooth, even surface.

Plaster

In a typical plaster wall, rough wood strips called lath, generally ⅜ inch thick and 1½ inches wide, are nailed across studs and joists. The strips are spaced about ¼ inch apart so that the plaster can ooze between them for a good grip. At corners, lath is sometimes strengthened with a 4- to 6-inch-wide strip of metal lath, a sort of rough mesh.

Plaster is applied in two or three coats. The rough coat uses sandy-textured plaster; the finish coat is smooth and hard. Plaster can vary in thickness even on a single wall, anywhere from ¼ inch to ¾ inch.

BEFORE YOU START

When working on walls, it is often important to know where the studs and joists are. One way is to tap the wall or ceiling and listen for a less-hollow sound; then drive small nails to make sure you have found a structural member. However, this is a hit-or-miss proposition, and you may end up with lots of unsightly holes. Purchase an electronic stud finder, which can find studs or joists even below plaster lath or wood flooring.

When assessing damage to a wall or ceiling, press on the surrounding surface with the heel of your hand. If drywall pushes in and springs back, it may need reattaching to the wood underneath; use drywall screws. If plaster feels bouncy, it may be coming loose from the lath. This problem will only grow over time. Remove all loose plaster and install drywall.

Drywall that has gotten soaked with water will become crumbly and weak; tear it out and replace it. If water has been leaking into a spot for a long time, the studs or joists may be rotten; inspect by poking the wood with a screwdriver.

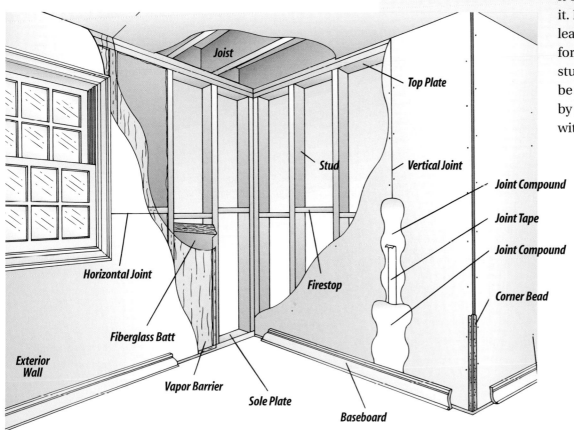

Joist

Top Plate

Stud

Vertical Joint

Joint Compound

Joint Tape

Joint Compound

Horizontal Joint

Firestop

Corner Bead

Fiberglass Batt

Exterior Wall

Vapor Barrier

Sole Plate

Baseboard

Repairing Loose Nails and Damaged Corners

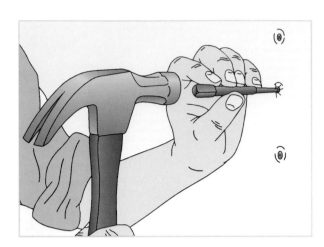

Hiding a popped nail

- Drive 1¼-inch drywall screws 2 inches above and below the popped nail, dimpling the surface without tearing it.
- With a nail set and hammer, sink the nail about ¹⁄₁₆ inch below the drywall surface (left).
- To check that the nail- and screwheads are countersunk properly, run a putty knife over them; a clicking sound indicates that they need to be driven in farther.
- Cover the nail and the screws with joint compound; let it dry.
- Apply a second coat of compound over a slightly larger area, let it dry, then sand with fine-grit sandpaper on a sanding block.

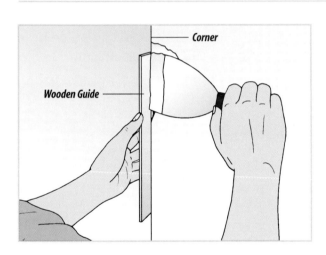

Rebuilding a corner

- If the metal corner bead has been damaged, reseat it with 1⅝-inch drywall screws and flatten any protruding bends with a metal file.
- Run a taping knife along the surface to make sure no portion of the corner bead protrudes; knock down any high spots.
- Holding a flat piece of wood against one side of the corner, apply joint compound to the other (left). Reverse sides and repeat, taking care not to dent the fresh joint compound.
- Scrape off excess compound, and let the area dry completely.
- Repeat, let dry, and sand smooth.

Choosing Patching Compound

For small patches, use vinyl spackling compound, which dries quickly. On larger areas, use joint compound. There are two options:

Ready-mixed joint compound comes in 1- or 5-gallon buckets. Just pop the lid and dig in. Be sure to keep the lid on whenever possible so that it will not dry out. Ready-mix is fine for most jobs, but it dries slowly and is not particularly strong.

Dry-mix joint compound comes in 25-pound bags; mix it with water before using. Use it whenever you need strength or a fast drying time. Usually, three types are available: "20," "45," and "90." The numbers tell you roughly how many minutes before the product sets. Once it starts to set, throw the excess away; you cannot remix it. Dry-mix is much stronger than ready-mix but more difficult to sand. For both strength and sandability, use dry-mix compound for the first coat, then ready-mix for the second and third coats.

Keep the compound clean. Even tiny crumbs of hardened material will produce annoying streaks.

Repairing a Dent or Gouge in Drywall

1. Preparing the damaged surface

- Use a utility knife to trim off any loose, frayed, or bunched paper around the damaged area of drywall. Keep your free hand away from the blade or, if you must use both hands, wear work gloves for protection.

- To ensure a firm grip for the filler, roughen the inside edges of the damaged drywall with coarse sandpaper (right). Any surface paper in the damaged area should be well scuffed. Brush away loose particles.

2. Filling the damaged area

- Dampen the sanded area with a moist sponge to limit shrinkage of the patching material.

- Pack spackling or joint compound into the damaged area with a putty knife (right), working from the center to the outside edges, until the patch is a little higher than the undamaged surface. Then use a larger knife—one that spans the repair area—to scrape across the undamaged surface in broad, smooth passes, scraping off excess compound.

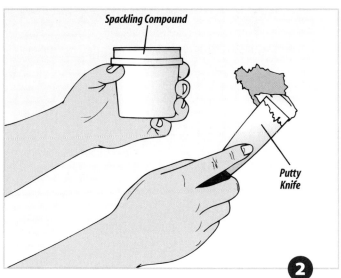

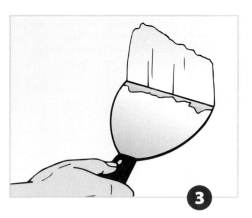

3. Finishing the surface

- Most fillers shrink as they dry, leaving cracks or depressions that require a second coat. To help this next application adhere, lightly score the surface of the first coat before it dries, using the tip of the knife blade. Let the repair dry overnight.

- Apply a second coat, again using a knife with a blade wide enough to cover the repair in one pass (left). It may take several coats to get the patch perfectly smooth and level with the surrounding surface. Once the final coat is dry, smooth the patch with medium-grit sandpaper on a sanding block and then brush off the dust. Seal the repair with primer.

Fixing Small Holes in Drywall

1. Installing a backing

- Pull out loose pieces of drywall, and cut away torn surface paper with a utility knife.

- Roughen the edges of the hole with coarse sandpaper, and brush away the dust.

- Cut a piece of wire screening slightly larger than the hole, and loop a string through the center. Tie a pencil to it, with 4 to 6 inches of slack (inset).

- Wearing rubber gloves, coat the edges of the screen backing with joint compound, roll the backing, and work it into the hole, maintaining a grip on the pencil (right).

- Reach into the hole to dampen the edges of the drywall, and then coat them with joint compound.

- Carefully pull the backing flat against the hole.

- Wrap the string around the pencil, then twist it against the wall to hold the backing in place.

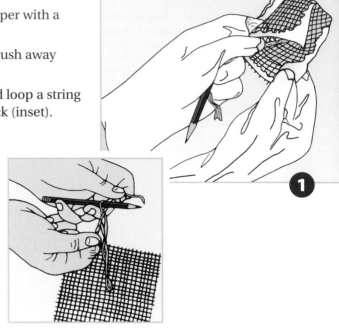

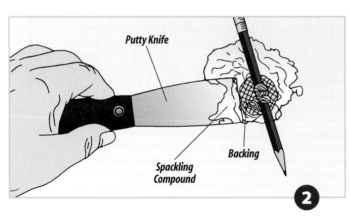

Putty Knife

Spackling Compound

Backing

2. Applying the first coat

- Using a putty knife, gently fill the hole nearly flush with the drywall surface, leaving a gap around the string (above). Let the compound set until it hardens (it doesn't have to dry).

- Cut the string as close to the screen as possible, freeing the pencil.

- Dampen the edges of the center gap, then fill it with fresh joint compound. Fill the hole flush with the dry-wall surface, and allow the patch to dry.

- Spread joint compound or spackling compound over the patch with a wide-blade putty knife. Make this top layer wider than the underlying patch.

- After the compound has dried for 24 hours, sand it with a fine-grit paper on a sanding block, feathering the patch's edges.

Aerosol Crack Sealer

Hairline cracks in plaster or drywall present a problem: Do you go through all the work of applying tape, followed by several coats of joint compound, all of which have to dry? Or do you just paint over it and hope it doesn't reappear?

Aerosol crack sealer may be the solution. Simply spray it on shortly before painting (read the instructions on the can). It forms a flexible membrane, so the crack won't come back.

This is not a structural solution, of course. If the crack grows larger (as sometimes happens when a house settles) or if the crack is wider than $\frac{1}{16}$ inch, this product will probably not help.

Patching a Medium-Sized Hole

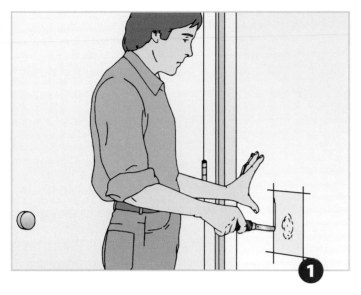

1. Cutting out the damage

- With a carpenter's square, pencil a rectangle around the damaged area. Cut the pencil line with a knife, deep enough to slice through the paper.

- Use a drywall saw to cut along the inside of the knife cut (left). Start the cut by forcing the pointed tip of the saw blade through the drywall. Do not let the cutout drop behind the wall.

- Use the cutout as a pattern for a patch that is made from drywall of the same thickness.

- From a 1×3, a 1×4, or a strip of plywood, cut two braces for the patch, each about 5 inches longer than the height of the opening.

2. Installing the braces

- Hold a brace behind the wall so that it extends equally above and below the opening and is half hidden by the side of the opening.

- Drive a 1¼-inch drywall screw through the wall and into the brace, positioning the screw in line with the side of the hole and about 1 inch above it (right). Sink the head below the surface of the drywall, but do not tear the drywall paper. Drive a second screw below the opening.

- For holes taller than 8 inches, drive an additional drywall screw along the side.

- Install the second brace on the opposite side of the opening the same way.

- Slip the drywall patch into the opening, and screw it to the braces in the four corners and opposite any screws along the sides.

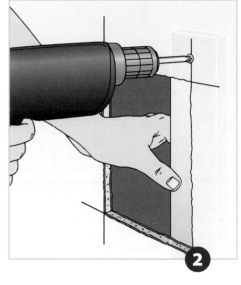

3. Taping the edges of the hole

- Cut pieces of mesh drywall tape to cover the edges of the patch, and press them into place.

- Using a 6- or 8-inch drywall knife, spread joint compound over the tape, just thick enough to cover the tape. Take care not to wrinkle the tape.

- Allow the patch to dry for 24 hours, then apply a second coat, feathering the edges.

- Once the patch has dried, smooth it with fine-grit sandpaper on a sanding block, feathering the edges. It may take a third or even fourth coat to get a perfectly smooth patch.

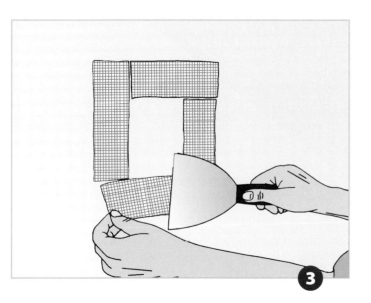

Repairing Failing Joints

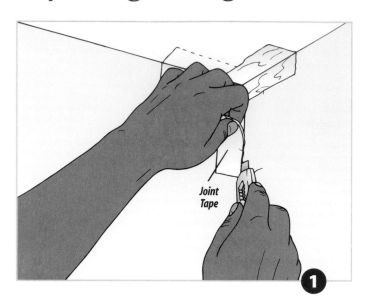

Joint
Tape

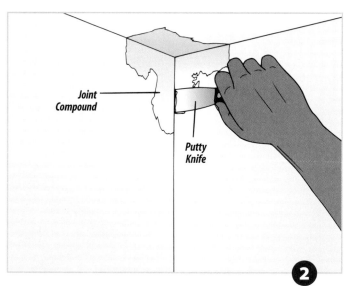

Joint
Compound

Putty
Knife

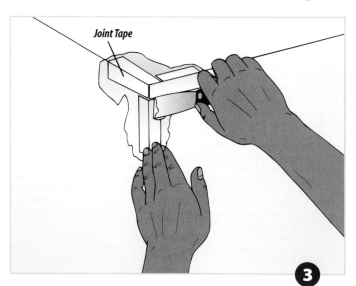

Joint Tape

1. Stripping off the damaged tape

A failing joint between drywall panels may occur at an inside corner—the meeting of two walls, a wall and a ceiling, or two walls and a ceiling, as shown here. It may also be found at a flat joint on a ceiling or a wall. The repair is similar for both.

- Score through the damaged tape along its center and cut across it at both ends, using a straightedge as a scoring guide if needed. At the junction of two walls and ceiling, cut through the tape at all three joints.

- Use a utility knife to pry up a corner of the damaged tape at one cut end. Strip off the tape carefully (left), working ahead with the utility knife to free up problem spots and avoiding tears in the drywall surface paper.

- Rarely will the damaged tape strip off easily in one piece. Continue to pry and tug until it is all removed.

- Sand away remaining joint compound to expose the drywall. Smooth rough edges, and brush off dust.

2. Applying joint compound

- Use a flexible putty knife to cover the joint with a thin bed of compound.

- Apply a 2- to 3-inch width of compound on one wall at a time.

3. Setting the tape

- For a joint at an inside corner, use paper drywall tape, which is scored to fold easily down its center. For a flat joint, use mesh tape.

- Cut lengths of paper tape to cover the joints without overlapping their ends.

- Crease a length of paper tape and use a flexible putty knife to sink the tape into the compound, forcing the crease into the corner (left). Work along the tape one side at a time, starting with the ceiling joints.

- Use a putty knife or 4-inch taping knife to smooth out ripples or puckers in the tape as it swells with compound. If necessary, lift the tape out of the compound and resink it, wetting the knife first for added moisture.

4. Finishing the patch

- Cover the tape with a thin coat of compound; at an inside corner, work perpendicular to the joint, one side at a time, using a flexible 4- or 6-inch knife.

- Smooth the joint with a wetted corner trowel if desired. Scrape off excess compound and allow 24 hours for the patch to dry thoroughly.

- Use medium-grit sandpaper on a sanding block to smooth the repair surface; brush clean and dampen.

- Cover with a thin finishing coat of compound. At an inside corner, apply a 3- to 4-inch width on each surface using a 4- or 6-inch knife (right), smoothing with a corner trowel if desired.

- Feather the edges and let the compound dry 24 hours. Repeat this step with a flexible 6- or 8-inch knife.

- Apply primer, then paint.

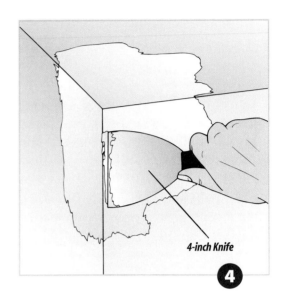

4-inch Knife

4

Surgery for Large Holes in Drywall

1. Cutting between studs or joists

- Locate the position of the nearest stud or joist on each side of the hole.

- Using a carpenter's square, mark an opening with 90-degree corners to be cut around the hole. Draw along the inside edges of the two studs or joists that flank the hole, and along any framing members between them.

- If a stud frames a window or door, as shown (right), continue the marks to the next stud: Doing so avoids a joint in line with the opening, which would otherwise be subject to cracking from repeated opening and closing. Where a hole lies within 8 inches of an inside corner, draw to the end of the panel to avoid forming a new joint too close to the corner.

- Cut out sections of drywall between framing members with a drywall saw or a keyhole saw (right).

- Clean the edges of the cuts with a utility knife.

(CONTINUED)

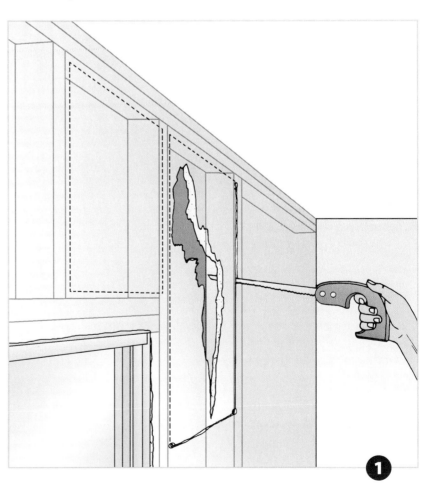

1

Surgery for Large Holes in Drywall—continued

2. Making the patch

- Measure each side of the opening as well as the sizes and positions of any electrical boxes, door frames, or window frames within it.

- Transfer the measurements to a drywall sheet of the same thickness as the damaged drywall, using a carpenter's square to ensure 90-degree corners (right). Do not use the panel's tapered edges for the patch's edges unless an edge of the opening falls at an inside corner.

- Cut out the patch, positioning the saw blade on the outline's inner edge; for an opening within the patch, cut just outside the line. This will ensure an easy fit.

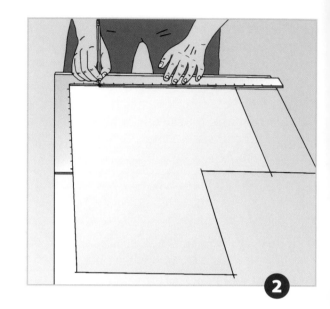

3. Adding cleats

- For fastening the patch, cut 2×4 or 2×2 cleats to fit alongside the joists or studs at the edges of the opening. Where possible, cut the cleats 2 to 3 inches longer than the opening.

- Secure the cleats flush with the studs or joists by driving 3-inch screws every 4 to 6 inches along the cleat (right).

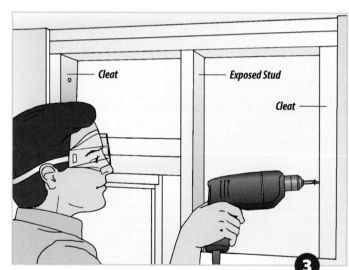

4. Installing the patch

- Before positioning the patch, mark the location of any exposed stud or joist on the wall or ceiling near the opening.

- Fit the patch in the opening and drive 1⅝-inch drywall screws through the patch about every 6 inches into each cleat, stud, or joist, starting at the middle and working to the edges (right).

- Finish the repair as described on page 211.

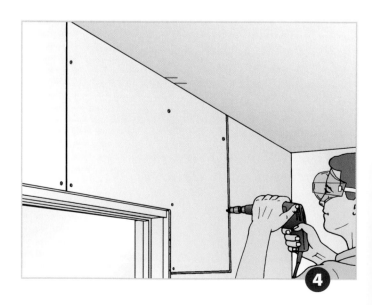

Filling Cracks in Plaster

1. Preparing the crack

For a very narrow crack, apply mesh tape and spread joint compound over it (Step 3). Or use aerosol crack sealer (page 210). Follow this and the next step if the crack is wider than ⅛ inch, or if it has grown over the years.

- To help lock the patching material in place, scrape some of the plaster from behind the edges; a pry-type can opener works well (right). Make the crack wider at the base than at the surface.

- Brush out dust and loose plaster, then dampen the interior surfaces of the crack.

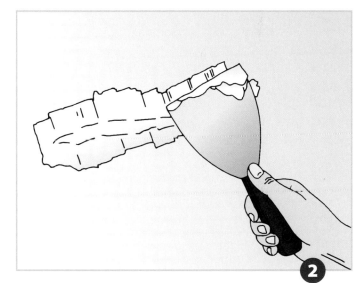

2. Filling the crack

- Using a 6-inch drywall knife, pack joint compound into the crack, working it behind the undercut edges.

- Stroke the knife back and forth across the crack (right) until it is completely filled, then draw the knife along the crack to bring the patch surface flush with the wall.

- Allow the patch to dry thoroughly.

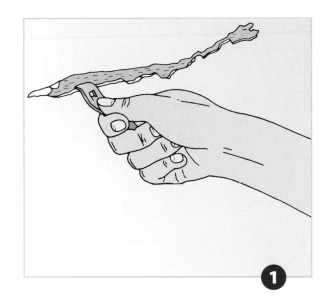

3. Reinforcing the patch with tape

- Cut a piece of fiberglass tape 2 inches longer than the crack, and press it into place over the crack.

- Spread a wide layer of joint compound over the tape (right), feathering the edges.

- Allow the area to dry, then apply a second coat, feathering the edges.

- After the patch dries, sand it smooth.

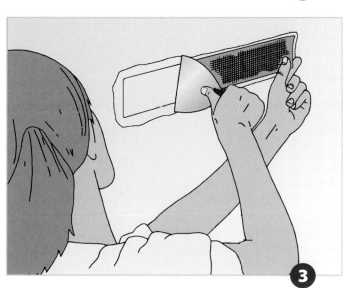

Drywall Repairs in Plaster

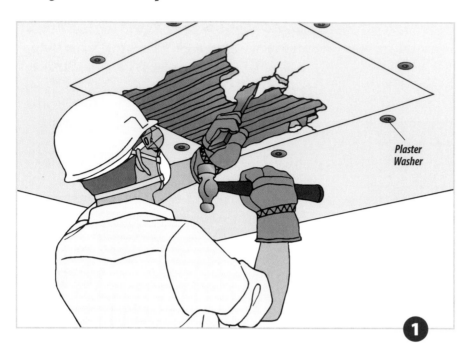

1. Removing the plaster

- Draw a line to form a rectangle that encompasses the damage.

- To protect sound plaster from damage while clearing deteriorated plaster from the rectangle, screw plaster washers just outside the drawn lines.

- Score the plaster along the lines with a utility knife; then, with a hammer and cold chisel, remove the damaged plaster within the rectangle (left), chiseling gently to avoid loosening plaster outside the rectangle.

2. Attaching plywood strips

If the drywall you will use for the patch is thick enough to come flush with the surrounding ceiling surface, skip this step.

- Cut strips of ¼-inch plywood, 1 inch wide.

- Edge the opening with the strips, loosely fastened with 1⅝-inch drywall screws driven partway into the lath.

- Shim the strips to position a scrap of drywall flush with the plaster (right). Tighten the screws.

- Trim the protruding shims with a keyhole saw.

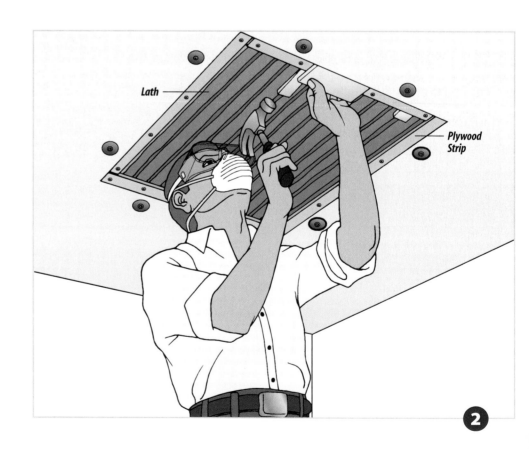

③

3. Installing the patch

- Cut a piece of drywall to fit the rectangle. Depending on the thickness of the plaster, you may use ¼-, ⅜-, ½-, or ⅝-inch drywall.

- Apply a bead of construction adhesive to each plywood strip, then press the drywall against the adhesive.

- Fasten the drywall to the plywood strips with 1-inch drywall screws 6 inches apart, starting at the corners (left).

- Tape the joints as described on page 211.

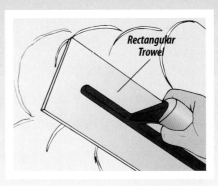

Stippling Brush

Restoring a Textured Surface

Finishing a repair in textured plaster takes a light touch and a bit of artistry. To fill nail holes and hairline cracks, use your finger to work a bit of spackling compound or caulk into tiny crevices. For larger repairs, a wide range of effects can be created by brushes, sponges, trowels, and putty knives. Repair damaged plaster as shown in this chapter. Reproduce the wall texture using a final layer of joint compound. (Some wall finishers add a handful of sand to a bucket of joint compound.)

Experiment before you begin—a scrap of drywall or a thick, heavy piece of cardboard makes a good surface on which to practice. Achieve a stucco effect (right) by dabbing at the wet compound with a small margin trowel, placing the blade flat against the surface and then pulling it away to form peaks. To recreate a stippled effect, use a stippling brush (above right), a whisk broom, or a wire brush to strike the surface of the wet compound. A rectangular trowel

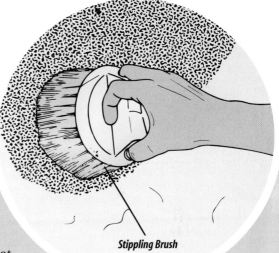

Rectangular Trowel

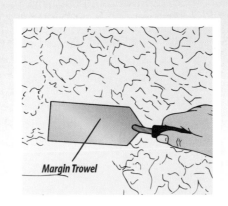

Margin Trowel

handled with a semicircular motion creates a ridged adobe effect (above). Perhaps soften the peaks of the new texture with fine sandpaper after it dries.

217

Floors and Stairs

HOW FLOORS ARE CONSTRUCTED

Floors are supported by joists, which are usually spaced 16 inches apart. Bridging adds a bit of strength to the joists and keeps them from warping if their undersides are not covered with drywall or plaster.

The longer the distance a joist must span, the wider the joist needs to be. Modern building codes are strict about this, ensuring that the joists will be strong enough to support the floor without sagging. Older homes, however, sometimes have undersized joists, and sagging floors may be the result. If your floors sag or feel bouncy, call in a professional carpenter to see whether the structure needs to be supported.

In newer homes that are designed with wall-to-wall carpeting in mind, floor construction is simple: One or two layers of plywood are attached to floor joists.

A hardwood floor is constructed in layers. In older homes, the subfloor is made of wide planks or tongue-and-groove boards, laid diagonally for extra stability (right). Newer homes use sheets of ¾-inch plywood instead; the plywood is sometimes glued as well as nailed to the joists. A moistureproof and sound-deadening underlayment of heavy roofing felt or building paper is stapled to the subfloor.

The finish flooring, most commonly strips of oak ¾ inch thick and 2¼ inches wide, has interlocking tongues and grooves on the sides and ends. They are attached by driving and setting 3-inch flooring nails at an angle above the tongues, where the nails will be concealed by the upper lips of the adjoining grooves. In some older homes, the tongue-and-groove flooring is set on top of sleepers, pieces of 1×3 laid perpendicular to the flooring and spaced about 12 inches apart. For details on stair construction, see page 232.

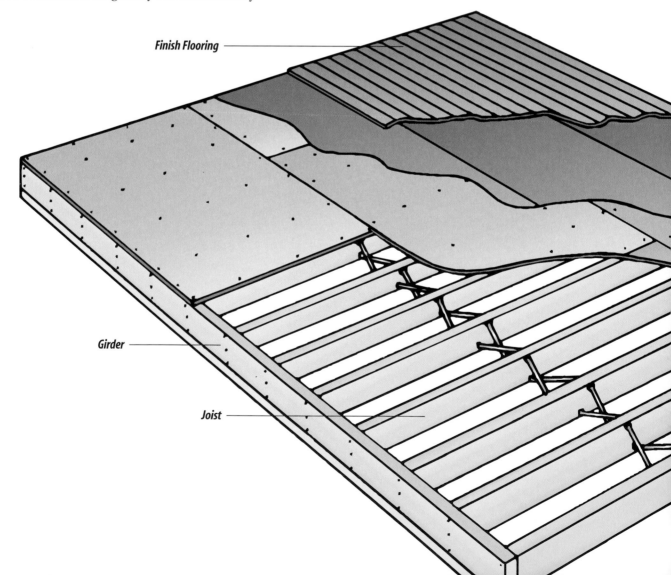

Finish Flooring

Girder

Joist

Plank Subflooring

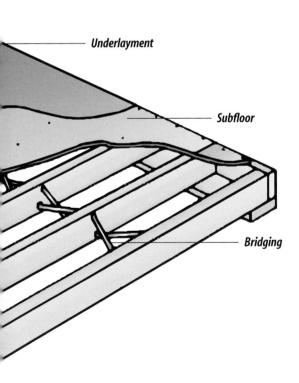

Underlayment

Subfloor

Bridging

BEFORE YOU START

Squeaks are usually caused by subflooring that is no longer firmly attached to the joists, or by the rubbing of finish floorboards that have worked loose from the subfloor. To retighten either, see page 220.

If cracks develop between flooring boards, force colored wood putty into the crevices with a putty knife. To get a very close color match, sand some flooring boards in a corner of a closet, and gather up the sawdust; mix 4 parts sawdust and 1 part penetrating sealer into a thick paste, and immediately trowel it into the cracks.

Stains and burns, if not too deep, can be erased by sanding. Go over the blemished area with a paint scraper. If the defect starts to lift out, the board can be saved by sanding and refinishing; otherwise, you will have to replace it.

Replace ruined boards in the winter if possible; dry furnace heat will shrink the wood and ease the job of fitting in new pieces. Inspect for decay and termite damage in the subfloor if you see any sign of rot in the floorboards: Poke the wood with a screwdriver. If it feels spongy or cracks across the grain, rot has set in. Treat lightly decayed subfloors with a preservative. Replace any boards that have extensive rot.

Most termite damage occurs inside boards; by the time you see anything, the board may be mostly eaten up. If you suspect termites, call in an exterminator.

Eliminating Squeaks

Shimming the subfloor

- If the subfloor is accessible from below, have someone walk on the floor while you look for movement in the subfloor over a joist.
- To eliminate movement, apply a bead of construction adhesive to both sides of a wood shingle and wedge it between the joist and the loose subfloor (left).
- Do not force the subfloor upward, or you may cause boards in the finish floor to separate.

Securing inaccessible subfloors

- If the ceiling beneath the floor is finished, refasten the loose section of subfloor to the nearest joist through the finish floor above.
- Use a stud finder to locate the joist. Then drill pairs of pilot holes angled toward each other, and drive 3-inch finishing nails or trim-head screws into the subfloor and joist below (right).
- Set the nailheads or countersink the screws, and cover them with wood putty that has been tinted to match the color of the boards.

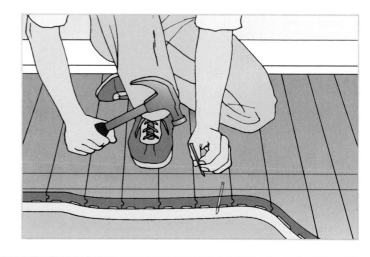

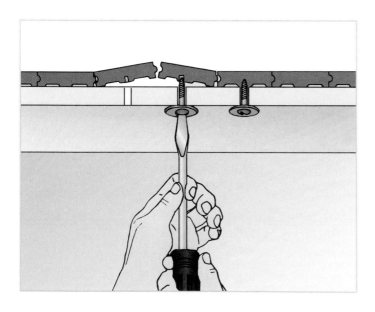

Anchoring floorboards from below

- Select screws that will reach to no higher than ¼ inch below the surface of the finish floor.
- Drill pilot holes through the subfloor, using a bit with a diameter at least as large as that of the screw shanks so that the screws will turn freely. To avoid penetrating into the finish floor, mark the subfloor's thickness on the drill bit with a piece of tape.
- Drill pilot holes into the finish floor with a bit slightly narrower than the screws.
- Fit the screws with large washers, apply a bit of candle wax to the threads to ease installation, and drive them into the pilot holes (left). The screw threads will bite into the finish floorboards, pulling them tight to the subfloor.

Cutting Out a Damaged Area

1. Making end cuts

You will need a very sharp chisel for this job; you may need to sharpen it halfway through the project.

- Plan to remove boards in a staggered pattern, with adjacent end joints at least 6 inches apart. At the end of a damaged board, make a vertical cut with a sharp 1-inch wood chisel, keeping its bevel side toward the portion of the board to be removed (right).

- Working back toward the vertical cut, angle the blade and drive the chisel at about 30 degrees along the board.

- Repeat this sequence until you have cut all the way through the board. Repeat at the other end.

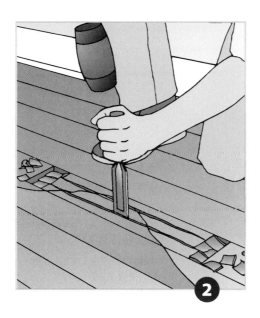

2. Splitting the board

- With the chisel, make two parallel incisions a little less than an inch apart along the middle of the board from one end to the other (left).

- Use the chisel to pry up the board between the incisions just enough to split the wood.

3. Prying the boards out

- Working on a board at the center of the damaged area, insert a prybar into the lengthwise crack created with the chisel (right). Pry the middle strip out, then the groove side of the board, and finally the tongue side.

- Remove the adjacent boards in the same way, working toward the edge of the damaged area and taking care not to harm any good boards. Remove exposed nails or drive them down with a nail set.

- Take a sample of the flooring to a lumberyard to get matching replacement boards.

Patching the Hole

Replacement Board

Hammering Block

1. Inserting a new board sideways

- Cut a replacement board to fill the outermost space on the tongued side of the damaged area.

- Using a scrap of flooring with a groove that fits the tongue of the replacement piece as a hammering block, wedge the new board securely into place.

2. Blind-nailing a board

- Drive and set 3-inch flooring nails at a 45-degree angle through the corner of the tongue of the replacement piece. Pilot holes are not essential but may be helpful.

- If existing boards around the repair have separated slightly, try to match their spacing by inserting thin shims such as metal washers between the new board and the old one while driving the nails.

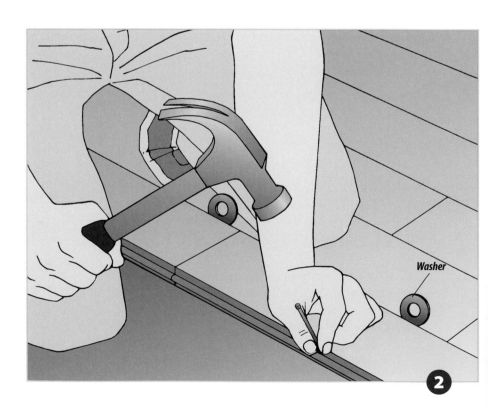

Washer

3. Inserting a new board lengthwise

- To slide a replacement between two boards, lay it flat on the subfloor and work the tips of its tongue and groove into those of the existing pieces.

- Using a scrap hammering block, tap it all the way in.

4. Inserting a new board from above

- For the last few spaces where you cannot slide the pieces into place, lay a replacement board upside down on a piece of scrap wood and chisel off the lower lip of the groove as indicated by the blue line on the board at right.

- Turn the board face-up and gently tap it into place from above.

5. Face-nailing

- To fasten the last replacement boards, which offer no access for blind-nailing, drill angled pilot holes every 12 inches about ½ inch from the edges of the face. Drive 3-inch finishing nails or trim-head screws into the holes.

- Set the nails or countersink the screws, and cover them with wood putty that has been tinted to match the color of the boards.

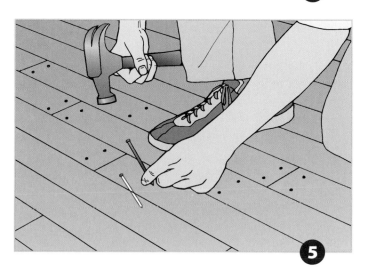

Repairing Loose Resilient Flooring

Securing a loose tile

- Lift the loose portion of the tile, and spread a thin coat of latex adhesive on the underside of it with a putty knife. If only a corner of the tile has come unstuck, loosen more of it until you can turn the tile back far enough to spread the adhesive.

- Press the tile into place so that it is level with those tiles that surround it. Hold it down with a 20-pound weight for at least an hour.

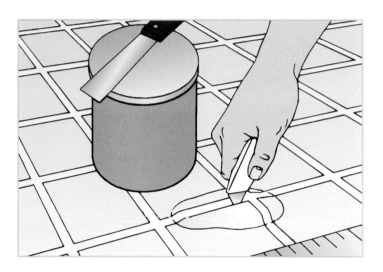

Deflating a blister

- Following a line in the flooring pattern if possible, score then slice along the length of a blister with a utility knife (left). Extend the cut ½ inch beyond the blister at both ends.

- With a putty knife, slip a thin layer of flooring adhesive through the slit onto the underside of the flooring.

- Press the vinyl down; if one edge overlaps because the flooring has stretched, use it as a guide to trim the edge beneath. Remove the trimmed-off scrap, then press the edges together and put a 20-pound weight on the repaired area for at least 1 hour.

Replacing a Damaged Vinyl Tile

1. Removing a tile

- Lay a towel on the tile, and warm it with an iron at medium heat until the adhesive softens and you can lift one corner with a putty knife.

- Pull up the corner and slice at the adhesive underneath with the putty knife, reheating the tile with the iron if necessary, until you can take out the entire tile.

- Scrape the remaining adhesive from the subfloor.

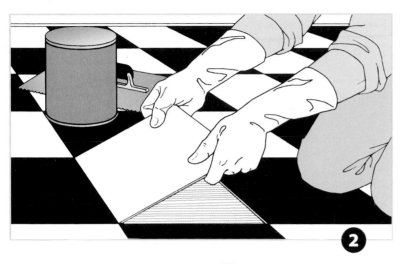

2. Installing a replacement

- Spread a thin layer of adhesive—not more than half the thickness of your tile—on the subfloor with a notched trowel, then butt one edge of the new tile against the edge of an adjoining tile, aligning the pattern.

- Ease the tile into place. Make sure it is level with surrounding tiles. If it is too high, press it down and quickly wipe away excess adhesive before it dries; if the tile is too low, gently pry it out with a putty knife and add more adhesive beneath it. Rest a 20-pound weight on it for the length of time specified by the adhesive manufacturer.

Patching Sheet Flooring

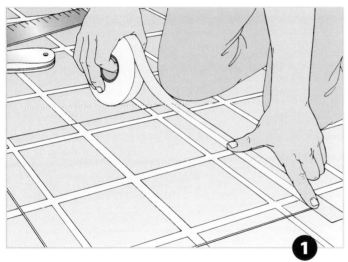

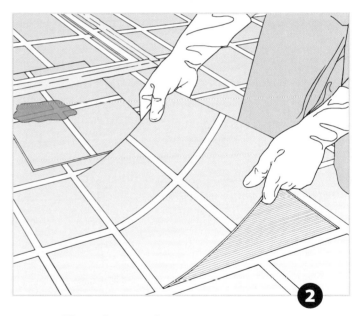

1. Cutting the patch

- Place over the damaged spot a spare piece of matching flooring larger than the area to be patched, aligning the design of the replacement piece with that of the floor. Secure it in position with tape (above).

- With a straightedge and a utility knife, score the top piece, following lines in the pattern where possible. Guided by the scored line, cut through the replacement piece and the flooring underneath. Keep slicing along the same lines until you have cut through both sheets.

- Set the replacement piece aside and loosen the adhesive under the section you are replacing as shown in Step 1 on page 224. Remove the damaged section and the old adhesive.

2. Installing the patch

- Spread adhesive over the exposed subfloor with a notched trowel, and set the replacement patch in position as you would a tile (above).

- Hide the outline of the patch by a careful application of heat: Cover the edges of the patch with heavy aluminum foil, dull side down, and press the foil several times with a very hot iron. This will partly melt the cut edges of the flooring so they form a solid and almost undetectable bond.

Replacing Ceramic Tile

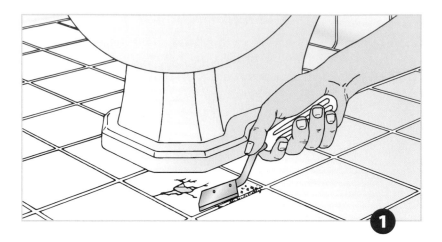

1. Removing the grout

To replace an unobstructed tile, use a grout saw to remove the grout on all sides. Try prying the tile out using a flat bar; place a thin piece of wood under it to prevent damaging the adjacent tile.

- Run a grout saw along the joints bordering the damaged tile, applying firm pressure as you move the saw back and forth.
- Clean fine debris and dust from grooves with a brush or shop vacuum.

2. Taking out the tile

- For ceramic tile that sits partly under a fixture, score an X on the damaged piece with a glass cutter and straightedge, then score along the base of the fixture (right).
- Drill a hole through the center of the X with a ¼-inch masonry bit. Hammer a cold chisel into the hole and, working toward the edges, break the tile into small pieces. Remove the tile fragments, and scrape off the old adhesive beneath them with a putty knife.
- On marble or slate tile, mark an X with a grease pencil. With a masonry bit, drill ¾-inch holes every ½ inch along the X and the fixture's base. Break out the tile with a hammer and chisel.

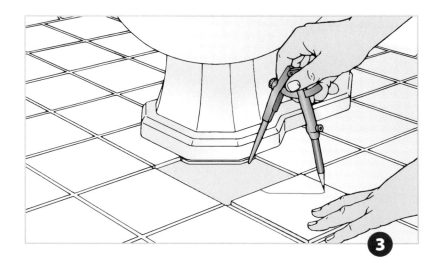

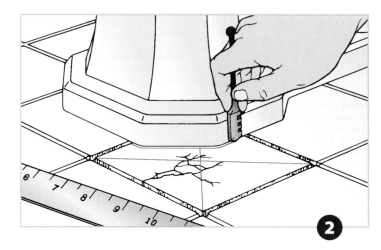

3. Marking the new tile

- Lay a new tile over the tile adjacent to the space you have cleared.
- Replace the pencil in a school compass or scribe with a grease pencil, and open the compass to the width of a tile.
- Set the pencil at the edge of the new tile and the point of the compass or scribe at the corresponding point on the base of the fixture.
- Holding the new tile securely, move the compass slowly along the base of the fixture to mark the shape of the base on the new tile.

4. Cutting the tile

- Score the fixture outline with a glass cutter, then score a crisscross pattern in the area to be cut away (left).

- Using only the corners of the nipper blades, nibble ⅛-inch pieces of tile away from the scored area with tile nippers. Check the tile for fit, and smooth the edges with sandpaper. To replace tile around a pipe, mark the pipe diameter on adjacent edges of the tile, draw lines across the tile, and use a carbide-tipped hole saw to drill a hole at the center of the square thus formed. Using a glass cutter, score the tile through the center of the hole, then set the tile on a pencil and break the tile by pressing on both sides at the same time.

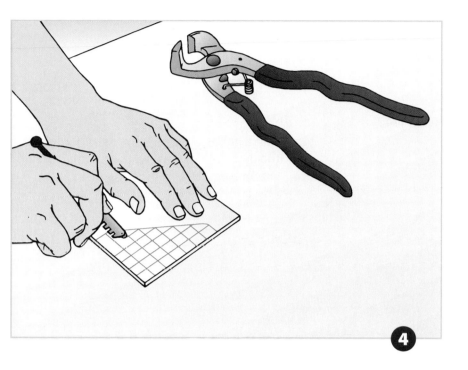

5. Setting the tile in place

- With a notched trowel, apply adhesive to the subfloor or mortar bed. If the new tile has tabs on its back, also add a thin coat of adhesive to the tile bottom.

- Apply enough adhesive to raise the tile slightly higher than the ones around it. Use toothpicks or coins set on edge as spacers to keep the joints between ceramic tiles open and even.

- Lay a 2×4 across the tile, and tap it down with a mallet or hammer.

- Let the adhesive set for 24 hours, remove the spacers, and fill the joints with latex-reinforced grout.

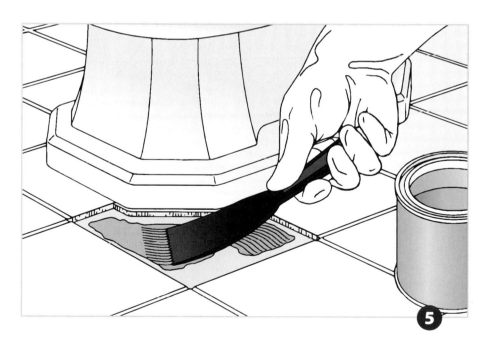

Durable Patches for Concrete

1. Preparing the area

- Break up the damaged concrete with a sledge-hammer or a rented electric jackhammer. Cut reinforcing wire in the broken concrete with wire cutters or lineman's pliers, and clear away the debris.

- Using a cold chisel and a hammer, slope the edge of the hole toward the center. Then dislodge loose particles of concrete with a wire brush and remove them.

- Dig out the top 4 inches of dirt from the hole, and tamp the bottom firm with the end of a 2×4. Fill the hole to the bottom of the slab with clean ¾-inch gravel.

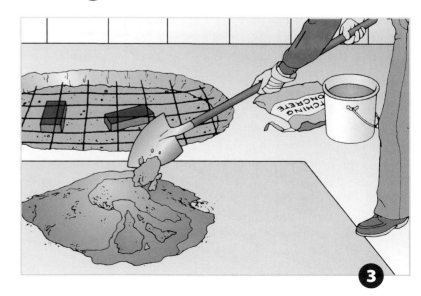

2. Reinforcing the patch

- Unroll wire reinforcing mesh over the hole, and cut it with wire cutters so that the ends of the wires rest on the sloped edge of the hole. You might have to bend it into a backwards roll first to get it to lie flat.

- Place the mesh in the hole, and raise it slightly off the ground with scraps of concrete or bricks.

3. Pouring the patch

- Form a cone of premixed patching concrete on a piece of plywood or in a mortar pan. Hollow out the top, add water, and mix.

- Coat the edges of the hole with an epoxy bonding agent. Shovel the concrete into the hole. Jab with the shovel tip to force the mix against the sides of the hole and through the reinforcing mesh.

- Fill the hole to the level of the slab, then add a few extra shovelfuls to allow for settling.

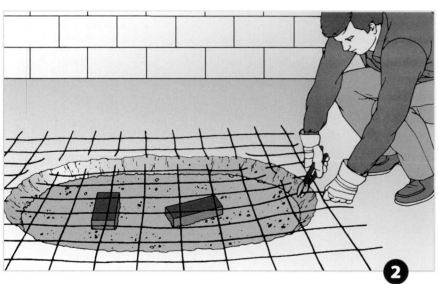

4. Finishing the patch

- With a helper, work a straight 2×4 across the surface of the patch with a back-and-forth motion. Fill surface depressions with concrete, and smooth the patch again.

- A thin film of water will soon appear on the surface. When it evaporates and the surface sheen disappears, smooth the patch with a metal trowel.

- When the concrete hardens, sprinkle it with water and cover it with plastic sheeting. Let the patch cure for 3 to 7 days, checking it daily and sprinkling it as needed to keep the surface damp. (The slower the concrete cures, the stronger it will be.)

Spot-Refinishing a Floor

1. Removing the damaged finish

- Remove any molding in the way. If the surface is waxed, strip off the wax.

- For a small or superficially damaged surface, wear rubber gloves and use a fine steel wool pad moistened with mineral spirits. Scrub along the wood grain until the visible damage is removed, then feather out around the scrubbed spot with light strokes. Use a clean cloth to wipe the spot dry.

- For a large or deeply damaged surface, use an orbital sander or a hand sanding block fitted with fine sandpaper; sand back and forth along the surface in long, smooth, overlapping strokes (above right). Work carefully to remove only the damaged finish; avoid sanding off any penetrating stain applied to the wood to color it.

- Vacuum sanding particles off the surface, and wipe it with a damp cloth.

2. Touching up the finish

- Choose a finish to match the original. Use a paintbrush to apply a thin, even coat of finish on the surface, brushing along the wood grain in smooth strokes (right) and feathering the edges. At the end of each stroke, lap back over the surface just coated. Smooth any unevenness immediately.

- Allow the finish to dry, then smooth the surface with fine sandpaper and apply another coat.

- Continue to smooth and apply finish until the surface is uniform, feathering the edges slightly farther each time to disguise the repair.

Replacing a Stretch-In Carpet Section

1. Preparing to remove the damaged section

- Find a matching carpet remnant for a replacement section.

- Use a knee-kicker (opposite page) to slacken the tension of the carpet on each side of the damaged section. Position the knee-kicker on the carpet 8 inches from one side of the damaged section. Thrust it to slide the carpet forward toward the damaged section.

- Holding the knee-kicker steady with your knee, lay a carpet scrap upside down just ahead of it; nail through the carpet scrap to temporarily hold the slackened carpet. Repeat the procedure on the other sides of the damaged section.

- Mark a square-cornered outline around the damaged section; use the tip of an old screwdriver to work along each side of the damaged section between two rows of

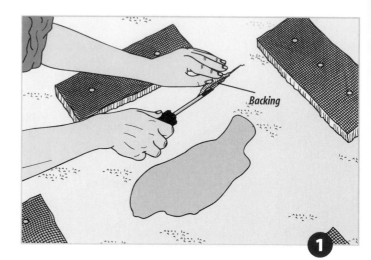

pile tufts, separating them to expose the line of backing under them (above).

2. Removing the damaged section

- Lay a carpenter's square on the carpet, aligning it with two adjacent marked lines of the outline around the damaged section.

- Pressing down on the square, part the tufts of pile along the inside edges of it and use a utility knife to score repeatedly along them (left), cutting through the carpet backing along two adjacent edges of the damaged section.

- Use the same procedure to cut along the other two adjacent marked lines, then pull out the damaged section. Remove the padding.

- Fit a replacement section of matching padding in the opening and staple it in place every 3 inches along each edge with a ⅜-inch staple.

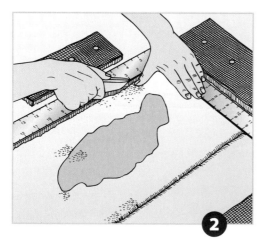

3. Preparing to install the replacement section

- Make a template of the opening out of cardboard, trace it onto the back of the carpet remnant, and then cut the replacement section to size with a utility knife.

- Apply a bead of latex seam adhesive to the base of the pile along each edge of the replacement section and the opening, then let it dry.

- Fit a strip of 2-inch cloth binding along each edge of the opening, centering it under the undamaged carpet; buy cloth carpet binding and cut it to size.

- Wearing rubber gloves, use a putty knife to apply latex multipurpose adhesive on each binding strip. Lift each edge of the undamaged carpet in turn to coat the binding strip under it, then press the undamaged carpet into place and coat the binding strip exposed in the opening (left).

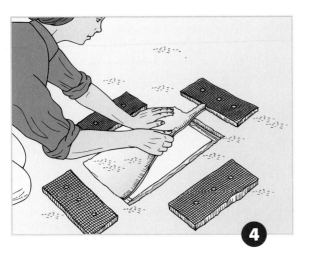

4. Installing the replacement section

- Press the replacement section carefully into place, its pile aligned with the surrounding carpet (left). If any pile catches, free it using the tip of an old screwdriver or an awl. Blot any extruded adhesive with a clean cloth.

- Place a weight on the replacement section, and let the adhesive set for the time specified by the manufacturer—usually 12 hours.

- Remove the weight, and pry off the carpet scraps nailed along each edge of the replacement section; then gently rub any flattened pile to raise it.

Raising Flattened Carpet Pile

If a section of pile is flattened, try using a coin to raise it. Making short, brisk strokes, scrape the coin against the pile of the flattened section to lift it upright. Or try raising the pile using an old hair comb, brushing it the same way.

If you cannot raise the pile with a coin or a hair comb, use a steam iron set to its lowest steam setting. Lay a clean cloth on the flattened section of pile, then hold the steam iron a few inches above it and depress the steam button a few times, releasing short bursts of steam (above).

CAUTION: *Do not place a hot iron directly onto the carpet.*

After steaming, set aside the iron and cloth, then use the coin or comb to try raising the pile again. If necessary, use the cloth and steam iron again, repeating the same procedure as necessary until the flattened section of pile is raised.

Using a Knee-Kicker

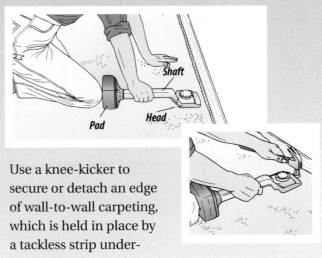

Use a knee-kicker to secure or detach an edge of wall-to-wall carpeting, which is held in place by a tackless strip underneath. Test the tooth depth on a scrap piece of carpet. The teeth should grab firmly but not poke through.

To secure a carpet edge to a carpet strip, lay it a few inches from the edge. Holding the shaft firmly with one hand, thrust your knee against the pad (above) to bite the carpet and push the carpet edge forward. Repeat if necessary.

Keeping your knee against the knee-kicker pad to hold it steady, run the face of a hammer along the carpet edge (inset) to secure it to the tackless strip underneath.

To detach a carpet from a tackless strip, push the carpet forward in the same way, and use a flat pry bar to pull the loosened edge free.

CHAPTER 1

Two Types of Stairs

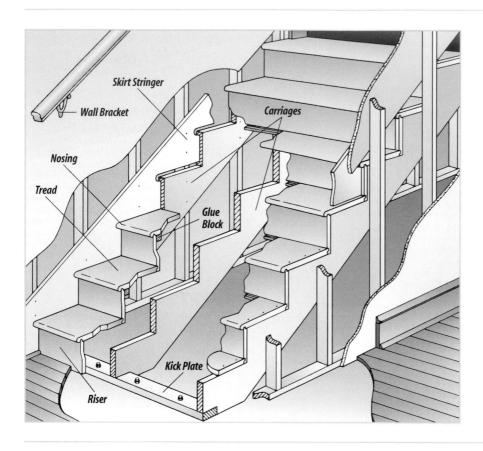

A carriage-supported stairway

In most older stairways and in a few newer ones, thick sawtooth-notched boards called carriages (left) support the treads and provide surfaces for nailing the risers, the vertical boards between treads.

At the bottom, the carriages fit over a kick plate nailed to the floor to keep them from sliding. Each tread has a tongue on its back edge that fits into a groove in the riser behind it and a groove under the front edge that drops over a tongue on the riser below. The treads are also nailed to the carriages. Each tread projects beyond the riser beneath it and ends in a rounded edge called a nosing. Glue blocks are used to reinforce the joints between the treads and risers, and nails through the back of the riser into the tread strengthen that joint.

A prefabricated stairway

In the modern prefabricated stairway, the functions of the carriages and the skirt stringer are combined in one board, called a housed stringer. Wedges are tapped in to clamp the ends of the treads and risers in V-shaped notches, which are routed into the side of the housed stringer. The treads and risers usually meet in rabbet joints and are glue-blocked and nailed.

A walled stairway uses housed stringers on both sides, but an open-sided stairway like this one (right) supports the outer ends of the treads on an open stringer cut like a carriage. Since it is too light to serve as a true carriage, the studding of the wall beneath it must be used to provide extra support.

The vertical cuts on the open stringer are mitered to match a miter at the end of the riser, concealing the end grain. The end of each tread has a return nosing nailed on, also hiding end grain. A return molding at the end and a scotia molding at the front complete the tread trim.

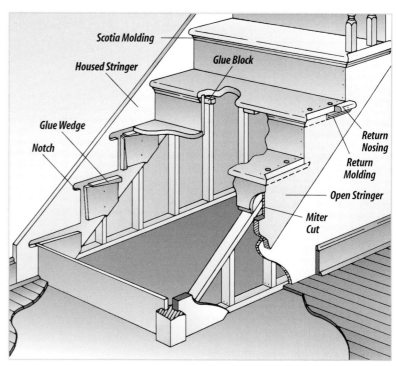

Stopping Stair Squeaks

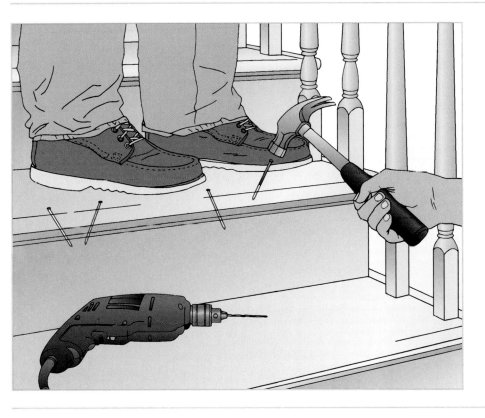

Nailing a tread down

- With a helper standing on the tread, drill ³⁄₃₂-inch pilot holes angled through the tread and into the riser at the point of movement. If the squeak comes from the ends of the tread, angle the holes in the carriage.

- Drive 2½-inch finishing nails into the holes, sink the heads with a nail set, and fill with wood putty.

- If the tread spring is too great for nails to close, drill pilot holes as above and secure the tread with 2½-inch trim-head screws. Apply paraffin wax to the threads to make the screws turn easily in the hardwood. Countersink the heads and fill the holes with wood putty.

Wedging treads tight

- Remove the scotia molding under the tread nose, and insert a knife into the tread joints in order to discover the kind of joints that were used. With butt joints, the knife will slip vertically into the joint behind the tread and horizontally under the tread; with rabbet or tongue-and-groove joints, the knife-entry directions are reversed.

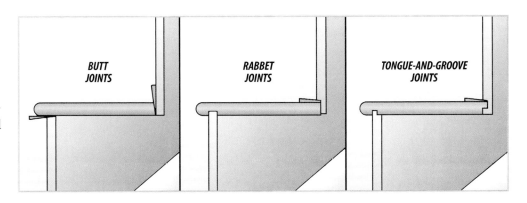

- Drive sharply tapered hardwood wedges coated with wood glue into the cracks as far as possible, depending on your type of joint.

- Cut off the wedges' protruding ends with a utility knife; replace the scotia molding. Use shoe molding to cover joints at the back of the treads.

(CONTINUED)

CHAPTER FIVE

Stopping Stair Squeaks—continued

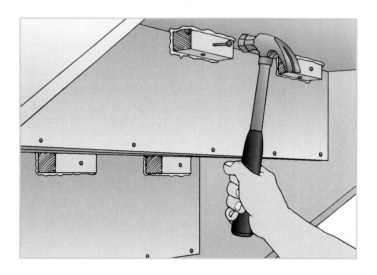

Installing glue blocks

- If the joint has old blocks underneath that have come partly unstuck, pry them off with a screwdriver or putty knife and scrape the dried glue off the tread and riser.

- Spread glue on two sides of a 2×2 block of wood that is about 3 inches long. Press the block into the joint between the tread and the riser, and slide it back and forth a little to strengthen the glue bond.

- Drill pilot holes and drive nails in each direction.

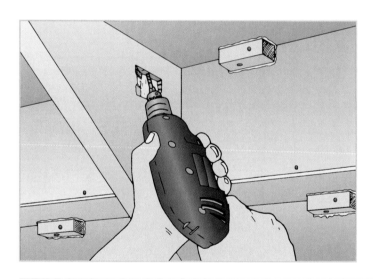

Drilling through a carriage

- About 2 inches below the tread, chisel a shallow notch into the carriage. With a helper standing on the tread, drill a ⅛-inch pilot hole angled at about 30 degrees through the notch and ¾ inch into the tread (left). Then use a ¼-inch bit to enlarge the hole through the carriage only.

- With the helper off the tread, spread a bead of construction adhesive along both sides of the joint between the tread and the carriage, and work it into the joint with a putty knife.

- Have the helper stand on the tread again, and drive a 3-inch-long #12 wood screw.

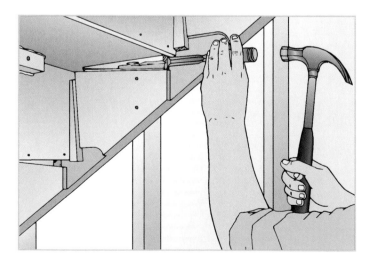

Replacing loose wedges on a prefab stairway

- Split out the old wedge with a chisel (left), and pare dried glue and splinters from the notch.

- Plane a new wedge from a piece of hardwood to fit within an inch of the riser. Coat the notch, the bottom of the tread, and the top and bottom of the wedge with glue.

- Hammer the wedge snugly into the notch, tap it along the side to force it against the notch face, then hit the end a few more times to jam the wedge tightly under the tread.

Tightening a Shaky Post

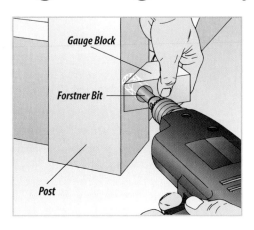

Gauge Block

Forstner Bit

Post

Installing a lag screw

- With a ¾-inch bit, drill a hole ¾ inch deep in the post (left). Extend the hole through the post with a ⁵⁄₁₆-inch bit and into the carriage with a ⁷⁄₃₂-inch bit.

- With a socket wrench, drive a ⁵⁄₁₆-inch lag screw 4 inches long fitted with a washer. Plug the hole with a dowel, then cut the dowel flush.

- To steady a post set in a bullnose tread, drive two nails through the flooring near the post. From beneath, measure from the nails to locate the center of the newel post. Drill shank and pilot holes, and install a 3-inch-long ⁵⁄₁₆-inch lag screw. Pull the nails and putty the holes.

Replacing a Doweled Baluster

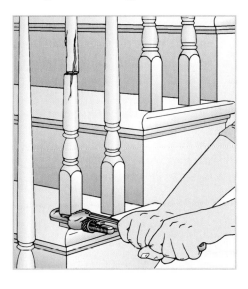

Removing the damaged baluster

- Saw the baluster in two, and sharply twist the bottom piece with a pipe wrench to break the glue joint at the base (left). Then remove the top piece; if it is stuck, use the wrench.

- If the joints do not break, saw the baluster flush, using cardboard on the tread to guard it from the saw. Then drill out the dowel ends.

- On the new baluster, trim the bottom dowel to a ³⁄₁₆-inch stub. Measure from the high edge of the dowel hole in the railing to the tread; add ⁷⁄₁₆ inch. Cut off the top dowel to shorten the new baluster to this length.

- Smear glue in the tread hole, angle the top dowel into the railing hole, and pull the bottom of the baluster across the tread and into the hole. You will lift the railing about ¼ inch in the process. Seat the bottom dowel in the tread hole.

Dealing with a Dovetailed Baluster

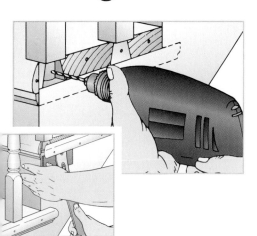

Removing the return nosing and securing the new baluster

- While protecting the stringer with a pry block, insert a pry bar and remove the return molding and return nosing (inset).

- Saw through the old baluster and hammer it out of the dovetail.

- Insert the top of a cut-to-length doweled baluster into the railing hole, and set its base in the tread dovetail. Shim behind the dowel, if necessary, to align it with its neighbors.

- Drill a ¹⁄₁₆-inch pilot hole through the dowel into the tread (left), and drive a 1½-inch finishing nail through the hole into the tread.

Windows & Doors

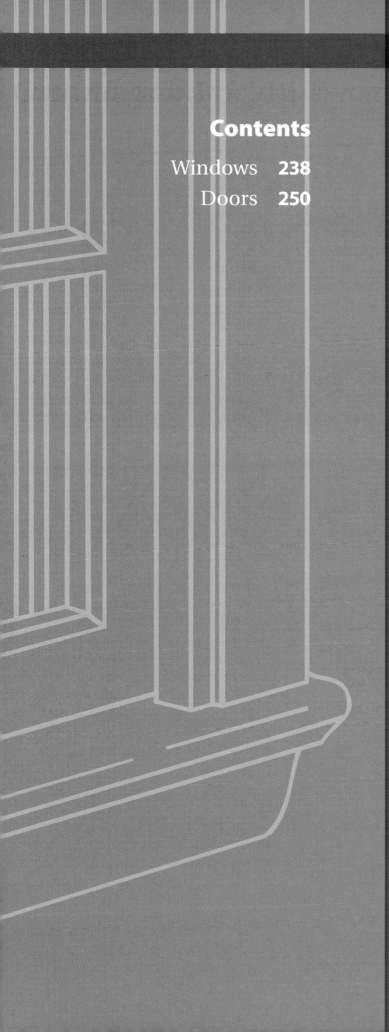

Contents

INTRODUCTION

Movable parts wear out quickly, so it's not surprising that windows and doors require regular maintenance. Windows and exterior doors should open easily and smoothly to let air in when you want, and they should close with a tight seal to keep hot or cold weather out.

Regular Maintenance

Inspect your windows and doors twice a year, just before cold or hot weather sets in. Check for gaps that let in air and cost you money.

Regular cleaning helps ensure smooth opening and closing. Windows have narrow channels where dust and debris collect and gum up the works. Vacuum first, then use a damp cloth to get up all the stuff.

If your windows or doors are made of wood, keep them well protected. Paint that has blistered or cracked will let in moisture and permit rot to develop in a hurry. An hour or so with a paint brush and/or caulk gun can save you plenty of work and money down the road. Mechanical parts can rust or corrode, so keep them as dry as possible, and oil them regularly.

Replacing Windows or Doors

Often, worn or damaged windows and doors can be repaired so they are nearly good as new. But if major parts are broken or warped, it may not be possible to make them seal tightly and operate smoothly. And many older windows and doors were never able to insulate well.

If a window or door looks good but doesn't seal well, you can probably save energy costs by having storm-and-screen windows or doors installed. However, take care: Many units are cheaply made and easily damaged. Get guarantees and inspect the work closely before you write the final check to the installer.

Windows

HOW THEY WORK

All four of these window types have a glazed window or sash, and a frame and stops to hold the window in place. The difference is how they open. Double-hung windows open up and down, while casement and awning windows open out. Sliding windows open side to side. Each type may be made of wood, vinyl, or aluminum.

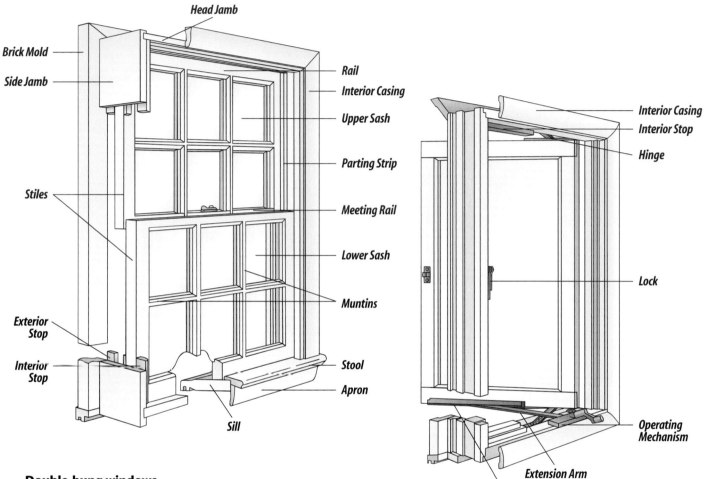

Head Jamb
Brick Mold
Side Jamb
Stiles
Exterior Stop
Interior Stop
Sill
Rail
Interior Casing
Upper Sash
Parting Strip
Meeting Rail
Lower Sash
Muntins
Stool
Apron

Interior Casing
Interior Stop
Hinge
Lock
Operating Mechanism
Extension Arm
Extension-Arm Track

Double-hung windows

The frame of a double hung window consists of two side jambs, a head jamb, and a two-piece bottom that has a sill outside and a stool inside. The inside stool and outside sill are usually trimmed with an apron. The upper and lower sashes are held in place by stops on the inside and outside and have a parting strip between them. Each sash is made up of two horizontal rails and two vertical stiles. The glass fits into a rabbet on the inside and is held in place by glazing points inside and glazing compound on the outside.

Casement windows

These have hinges on one side that allow the window to swing out. A mechanism, usually a crank, moves the window out and in. The window does not have exterior stops because the mechanism holds it in place. In some older casement windows, the sash is pushed out and pulled in by hand or with a rod. Casement windows often do not have a stool or apron. Instead, a bottom stop and a fourth piece of interior casing complete the window frame.

BEFORE YOU START

Most window problems have simple solutions. When a window is stuck, first clean any tracks or channels. Then try lubricating with paraffin, or spray with a silicone lubricant. Soak rollers, glides, and other small parts in mineral spirits; then apply grease or spray with a silicone lubricant. If the problem persists, consult the following pages.

On a double-hung window, identify the balance system. If a cord or chain disappears into the side jamb on either side, it is a weight-and-pulley system. If a small tube runs the length of the sash channel, it is a spiral balance; and if a steel tape runs along the sash channel, it is a clockspring balance.

Most parts on casement, awning, and sliding windows can be repaired or replaced. Swingers—casement and awning windows—break more often than other windows because they have more moving parts.

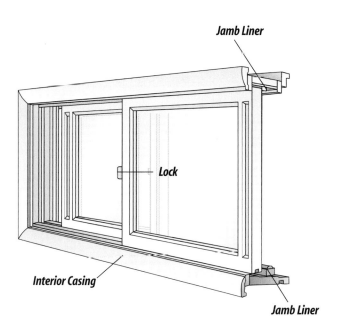

Sliding windows

Sliders move from side to side on metal or plastic rollers. The rollers sit in channels along the top and bottom of the window frame. A latch and lock are mounted on the meeting stiles. With most models, you can remove a sash simply by lifting the window and tilting the bottom out of the channel. The bottom of the window usually is trimmed with casing rather than an apron and stool.

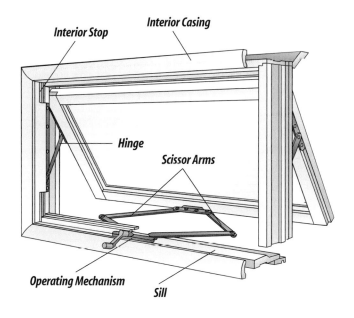

Awning windows

Here the sash is hinged near the top of the stile and swings out at the bottom to ventilate a room while blocking rain. The mechanism has two scissor arms that fold against the sill when the window is closed. Like a casement window, an awning window often has interior casing on the bottom instead of an apron and stool.

Repairing a Broken Window Pane

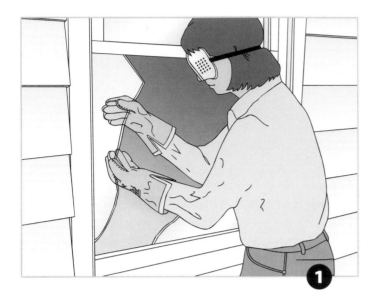

1. Removing the glass fragments

- Wearing heavy work gloves and safety goggles, start at the top of the window to remove shards of glass. Pull each shard straight out of the sash (left). Gently wiggle stubborn fragments free.

  CAUTION: *Remove glass from muntins—strips that divide the panes of a window—with care. Muntins are delicate, and replacing them requires a carpenter's skills.*

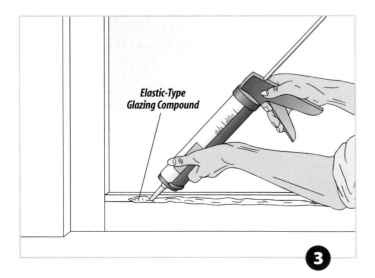

Glazing Compound

2. Removing old glazing compound

- If the compound has hardened, coat it with linseed oil and let it soak into the compound for 30 minutes. If the compound is painted, soften it with a soldering iron or a heat gun designed for stripping paint.
- Pry old glazing compound out with an old chisel (left).
- Pull the glazier's points from the window frame with long-nose pliers and clean the channel with a wire brush.

  CAUTION: *When using a soldering iron, be careful not to burn adjacent wood.*

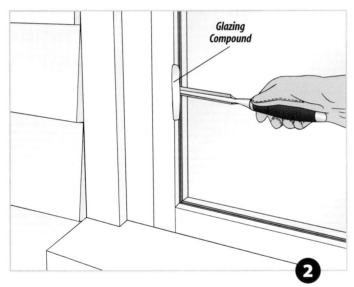

Elastic-Type Glazing Compound

3. Preparing the "bed"

There are two common glazing compounds used to form a "bed" for the glass: an elastic type that comes in a caulking tube, and glazing putty that comes in a tub.

- Depending on the compound you choose, you may first need to prime the channel. If so, follow the manufacturer's instructions.
- To apply the elastic type, squeeze a uniform ⅜-inch bead into the channel (left).
- For glazing putty, roll it into a snakelike shape; then press it into the channel.

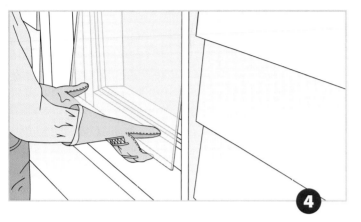

4. Installing the glass

- Set the pane into the bed of glazing compound, centering the pane in the opening (left).

- With a stiff putty knife, press glazier's points halfway into the sash and flush against the glass. Position a glazier's point every 6 inches or so, but use at least two points on each side of the pane. Push the points into the wood using a putty knife.

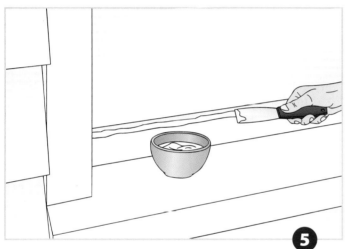

5. Covering the glazier's points

- Apply glazing compound to the joint between the pane and frame as in Step 3, but apply a thicker bead. Cover all the glazing points.

- Dip a putty knife in water and draw it over the bead to create a bevel at approximately 45 degrees (left). Check that the putty will not be visible from inside the house. If the surface is rough, run your finger along the bead in the opposite direction.

- Seal corners and trim excess compound inside and out.

- When the compound is dry—it no longer shows a thumbprint—paint it.

Patching Screens

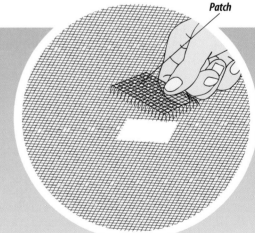

Patch

Repair tiny holes in a fiberglass screen by applying a few drops of "super" glue.

To repair a larger hole (below right), make a patch from leftover screening that is large enough to cover the hole. Coat the edges of the patch and the area around the hole with a thin coat of glue, then press the patch over the hole.

Seal tiny holes in an aluminum screen with a few drops of waterproof glue, such as epoxy. To repair a larger hole, first cut the hole square with

scissors. Then cut a patch of matching screening about 2 inches wider and longer than the hole.

Pull several strands of wire out of

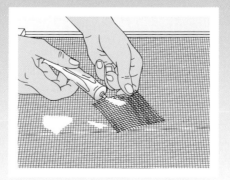

each edge and bend the remaining wires down over the sides (above). Position the patch evenly over the hole and work the wires through the screening. Turn the screen over, pull the patch tight, and bend the wires down against the screen.

Unbinding a Wood Sash

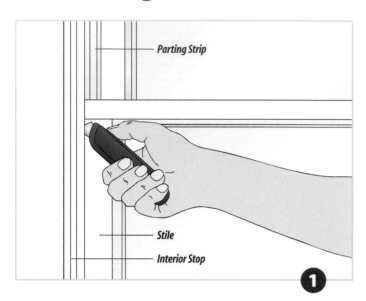

Parting Strip

Stile

Interior Stop

1

1. Breaking a paint bond

- Slice through the paint bond with a utility knife (left), taking care not to gouge either the stop or the sash.

- Cut the paint wherever the sash makes contact with a stop, a parting strip, the windowsill, or the other sash.

- If the window still won't open, continue to Steps 2 and 3. If it opens with difficulty, scrape or strip the paint from the jamb where the sash slides against it.

2. Separating stop from sash

- Wedge a pair of putty knives between the stop and the stile, and drive them apart with a cold chisel and a hammer (right). Repeat the procedure up and down the window.

- If the window doesn't open, use a knife or chisel to separate the sash from the parting strips.

- For windows that still will not open, go to Step 3.

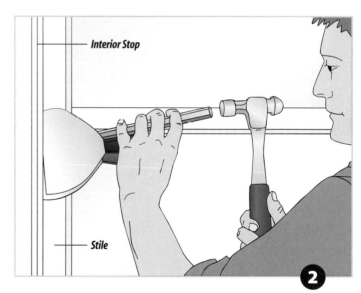

Interior Stop

Stile

2

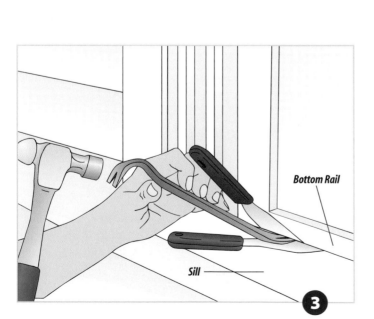

Bottom Rail

Sill

3

3. Forcing up the sash

- From the outside, wedge two putty knives between the sill and the sash's bottom rail near a corner. Drive the knives apart with a prybar and a hammer (left). Alternate working on each corner to free the sash.

- If this fails, remove the sash (opposite page). If it binds because it is too wide, plane the sash.

CAUTION: *Hammer gently. Too much force may separate the sash joints.*

Removing Upper and Lower Sashes

1. Prying off an interior stop

- If the window has a spiral balance (page 246), unscrew its tube from the top of the jamb and its mounting bracket from the bottom rail before prying off the stops.

- Break any paint bond between the stop and jamb (opposite page). Push two putty knives between the stop and the jamb, and drive them apart with a cold chisel and hammer (right). Start at the middle of the stop and work up and down.

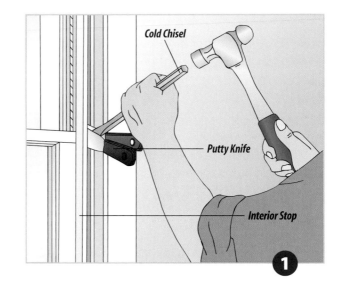

2. Removing the lower sash

- Pull the sash out of the frame on the side where you removed the stop.

- Remove any screws or nails securing the sash cord to the sash (above). Push a nail through the cord to prevent it from slipping past the pulley.

- Lift out the other side of the window and remove the cord in the same way.

- If the balance is a clockspring (page 245), unhook the tape from the sash and feed it back to the drum.

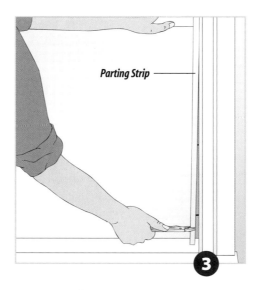

3. Removing the upper sash

- If the window has a spiral balance (page 246), support the sash with a board, then disengage the balance.

- Remove the parting strip from the side where you removed the interior stop.

- Pull the bottom of the strip out of its groove in the jamb, using locking pliers padded by wood shims (above). Lower the upper sash and remove it as you did the lower sash in Step 2.

- After completing the repair, reassemble by reversing the disassembly steps. To allow the sash to move freely when reinstalling the stops, insert playing cards as temporary spacers between the stop and the sash.

Replacing a Broken Sash Chain

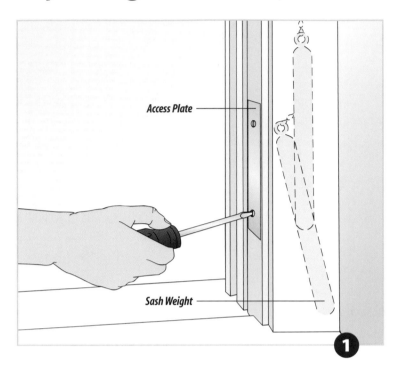

Access Plate

Sash Weight

1

1. Removing the access plate

- To determine how long a replacement chain needs to be—these instructions also apply to replacing a sash cord—measure from the top of the pulley to the stool and add 6 inches.

- Unscrew the access plate in the sash channel on the side of the broken chain (left). If screws aren't visible, the plate may be nailed shut. Pry the nail out with a screwdriver. If there is no plate, remove the window trim to expose the weights and cord.

Replacement Chain

String

2

2. Feeding the chain or cord

- Remove the weight and detach the chain or cord.

- Tie a nail or screw to a piece of string to serve as a weight. Feed the weighted end of the string over the pulley and down into the pocket.

- Tie the unweighted end of the string to one end of the new chain, and push a nail through the other end to prevent the chain from slipping past the pulley.

- Pull the string through the access opening until the chain appears (right).

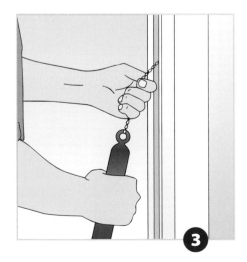

3

3. Connecting the chain or cord

- Untie the string from the chain, secure it to the weight, and put the weight back in place (left).

- Pull the free end of the chain until the weight hits the pulley. Run a nail through the chain and rest it across the pulley hole.

- Rest the sash on the sill, feed the free end of the chain into the sash groove, and secure it with nails or screws.

- Remove the nail in the chain. Raise and hold the sash in place. Adjust the chain's length as needed for the weight to hang 3 inches above the sill. Reinstall the access plate.

Replacing a Clockspring Balance

1. Removing a clockspring balance

- Take out the sash (page 243) and unhook the balance tape from its bracket on the sash (inset).
- Remove the screws securing the clockspring plate to the jamb (right) and pull the clockspring drum free of its pocket.
- Take the drum to a window specialist and buy an exact replacement.

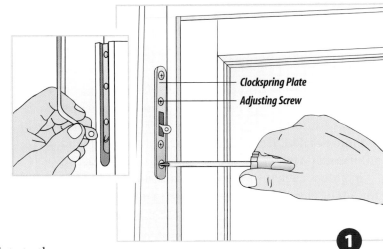

Clockspring Plate
Adjusting Screw

2. Replacing the clockspring

- Position the new drum in its pocket and screw the plate to the jamb (right).
- Place the sash on the sill, angled out slightly on the side of the new balance.
- With one hand holding the sash, pull down the balance tape clip with the other hand and attach it to the bracket on the side of the sash. Reinstall the sash.
- Although the new balance is weight-specific, it can be adjusted plus or minus 2 pounds. To increase the balance tension, turn the adjusting screws (Step 1) clockwise; turn counterclockwise to decrease tension.

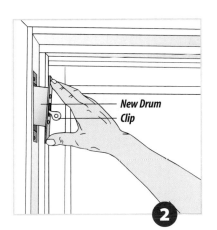

New Drum Clip

Reinforcing the Joints of a Wood Sash

Remove the sash (page 243) and clamp it to a work table so the weak joint extends over the edge.

With a drill and a ¼-inch bit, bore a hole through the tenon (right).

Cut a ¼-inch dowel slightly longer than the thickness of the sash.

Apply glue to the dowel and drive it into the hole with a hammer.

When the glue is dry, sand the dowel flush.

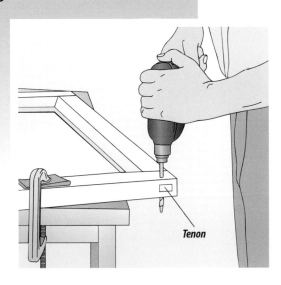

Tenon

Adjusting and Replacing a Spiral Balance

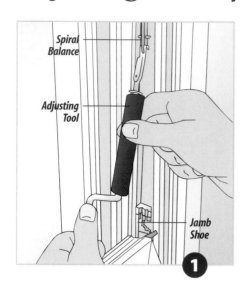

1. Adjusting a spiral balance

When a window with spiral balances misbehaves, try adjusting the balances. This will be easy if you purchase a special spiral balancing tool from the window manufacturer.

- Release the slide catches on the sash and tilt the sash indoors. Unhook the balance from the jamb shoe with a spiral-balance adjusting tool (left).

- For windows that are hard to open or close, decrease tension by rotating the tool counterclockwise a few turns. If the window won't stay open, turn clockwise.

- If the problem persists, one or both balances may need replacing (Step 3).

2. Removing the sashes and jamb liner

To remove a broken balance, you'll first need to remove the sashes.

- Tilt the sash until it is level, then raise one side of the sash to free the corner pivot from the shoe (right). Lift out the other side and store the sash in a safe place. Lower the upper sash and remove it the same way.

- Unhook the broken balance from the jamb shoe using the spiral-balance adjusting tool.

- To remove a broken spiral balance on a tilt-in sash, first take off the jamb liner if you find one. To do so, slip a screwdriver under one end of the liner and pry it up so you can grasp the liner and pull it free (inset).

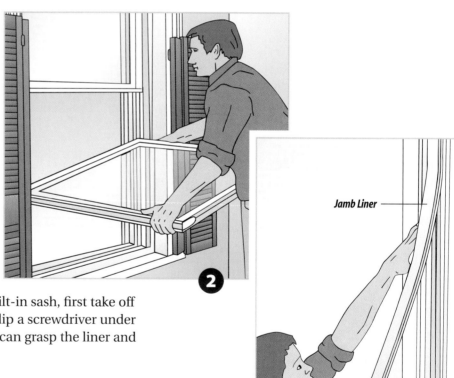

3. Replacing the spiral balance

- Remove the screw at the top of the spiral balance that secures the tube end to the jamb, and lift out the balance (left).

- Screw an exact replacement to the jamb.

- Rehook the spiral end of the balance into the slot in the shoe with the adjusting tool. Adjust the balance as described in Step 1.

Casement Windows

1. Freeing the operating mechanism

If the mechanism is broken or requires a thorough cleaning, remove it.

- Open the window halfway, then remove the screws holding the operating mechanism to the frame (right). If your window has a lever instead of a crank, take out the screws that attach the pivot mount to the sill.

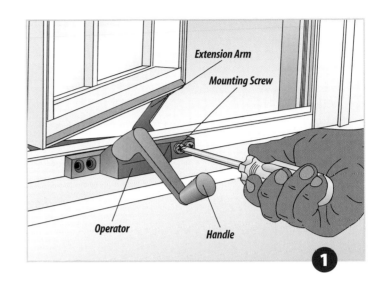

2. Removing the extension-arm shoe

- To disengage the extension arm from the sash, slide it along the sash until the extension-arm shoe reaches the access slot.

- Push the extension arm down and pull the shoe through the slot (right). If there is no slot, free the arm by sliding it off the end of the track. If the window is lever-operated, unscrew the pivot plate that secures the lever to the sash.

3. Replacing the mechanism

- Pull the operating mechanism free of its slot in the window frame (right). Loosen the handle setscrew and remove the handle.

- Examine the interlocking teeth of the handle and operating mechanism. If they or the teeth at the base of the extension arm are rounded or broken, consult a window specialist for replacements.

- To reinstall the operator, reverse the steps taken for removal.

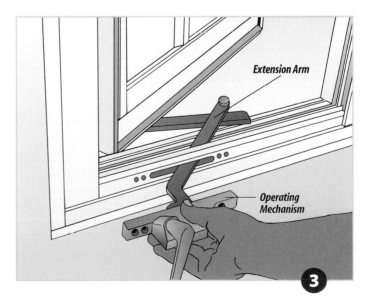

Jalousie Windows

Replacing a broken pane

- Wearing heavy work gloves, pull down the lip of the jalousie clip and slide out the cracked or broken glass (left).

- Measure one of the unbroken panes and order a replacement pane cut to size. Have the exposed edges of the new glass rounded for safety.

  CAUTION: *Do not bend the lip of the clip more than necessary. It may break.*

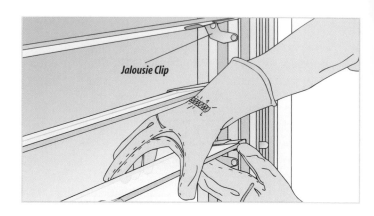

Jalousie Clip

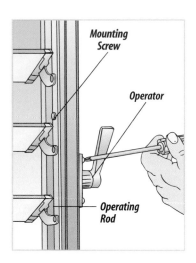

Mounting Screw

Operator

Operating Rod

Removing the operating mechanism

- To remove either a lever operator or a crank operator from a jalousie window, take out its mounting screw.

- Then remove the mounting screw from the operating rod and pull out the mechanism. If you find a stud and a snap-on fastener instead of a screw, pry off the fastener with a screwdriver and pull out the stud.

- To install the operating mechanism, hold it in place with one hand and reinstall the screw that connects the mechanism rod to the operator. Then secure the mechanism to the frame with its mounting screws (left).

Servicing an Awning Window

Open the window as wide as possible. Remove the mounting screws that secure the operating mechanism to the window frame.

Reach under the sash and unhook the scissor arms from their clips on the sash. If the scissor arms are secured to the sash, remove the screws. If the window has extension arms that slide along a track on the sash, spread the arms and slide their shoes off each end of the track.

Straighten the scissor arms and pull them clear of the window frame (right).

Clean and lubricate the operating mechanism. If gears are worn or broken, replace the operating mechanism.

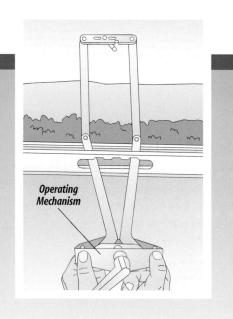

Operating Mechanism

Sliding Windows

Fixing a sash that rattles

- To replace faulty insulation that can cause rattling, lift up the sash, swing the bottom out, and remove it. Then twist out the liner of the top jamb that holds in the foam.

- Replace the old foam with the same type, but ½ inch thicker (right), and then snap the liner into place to secure it.

- Set the sash in the top channel, swing in the bottom, and then set it into the lower channel.

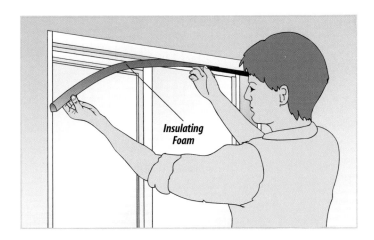

Insulating Foam

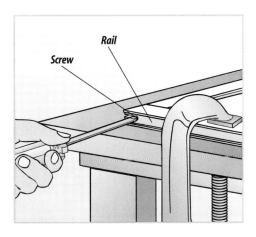

Rail

Screw

Replacing the window glides

- To replace a glide, remove the sash (see Step above).

- Clamp the sash down and remove the screws that secure the stiles to the rails (above). Then knock the bottom rail free with a hammer and a block of wood.

- Insert a screwdriver into the channel in the rail and force out the glide.

- Tap the new glide into the rail with a hammer, and screw the rail to the stile.

Burglar-Proofing a Sliding Window

It's all too easy for an intruder to pry apart the sections of a sliding window or door and shove it open. To prevent this, secure sliding windows and doors with a dowel, old broomstick, or other piece of wood cut to fit the interior channel (below).

Measure the length of the channel with the window or door closed and locked. With a saw, cut the wood to fit snugly into this space, making sure it lies flat in the channel.

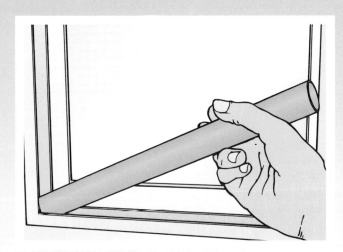

Doors

HOW THEY WORK

Most older interior and exterior doors are made of solid wood frame-and-panel construction. Many newer exterior doors have solid composite interiors and are wrapped outside with a wood, vinyl, or fiberglass veneer. Inexpensive hollow-core interior doors are found in most newer homes.

Openings for both interior and exterior doors are framed much alike (below). A header spans the opening, supported by a pair of jack studs. These in turn attach to king studs, which are part of the wall structure. A jamb, shimmed so it is perfectly plumb on both sides, lines this rough opening. Door hinges on one side, and a strike plate on the other, attach to the jamb. Casing trim covers the space between the jamb and the wall.

A panel door like the one shown below uses solid pieces of wood that fit together with a series of mortise-and-tenon

joints. This arrangement allows the door to expand and contract during changes of weather without cracking. A solid-core door typically has a layer of wood veneer covering a slab of particle board. An inexpensive hollow-core door, designed for interior use only, has only strips of cardboard sandwiched between pieces of wood veneer. Steel doors, often filled with foam for added insulation, are stronger and more fire-resistant than wood doors.

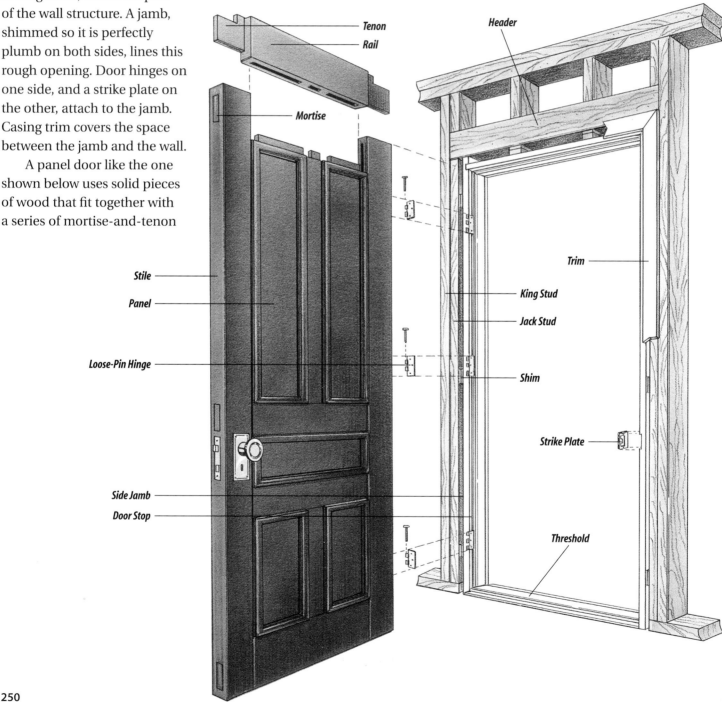

250

BEFORE YOU START

Tackle door closing problems by checking the hinges first, then the door itself, and finally the jamb and frame.

COMMON PROBLEMS

If a door sticks or binds, open the door and pull on it while looking at the hinges. If one is loose, remove the screws one at a time, insert toothpicks (page 254), and redrive them. If that's not the problem, shut the door just enough so it starts to bind, and find out where the sticking points are by sliding a playing card between the door and the jamb. Plane the door as needed; you may have to remove the door first.

TIPS

Before you dismount a door, make sure you have something solid to lean it against so it will not wobble while you work on it.

To keep from losing hinge pins, slip them back into the jamb hinge leaves after you have removed a door.

If your door hinges are squeaky
- Remove, clean, and oil hinge pins

If the door won't close properly
- Clean dirt or paint buildup around latch and lubricate latch **252**
- Replace latch or latch spring **252**
- Shim hinges that are set too deep . . . **254**
- Adjust strike plate **253**
- Reposition door stop **255**
- Plane a portion of the door that rubs against the jamb **256**

If the door rattles
- Adjust strike plate **253**
- Weatherstrip door to compensate for house settling or a door that has shrunk **308–311**
- Shim hinges or strike plate **253–254**

If the door sticks or binds
- Firmly attach loose hinge **254**
- Plane door **256**

If a top-hung slider door is jammed
- Restore rollers to correct position on the track **259**
- Adjust bottom guide **259**

If a folding door's corner is broken
- Repair corner and reseat pivot pin . . **258**

Old-Style Knob-and-Latch Assemblies

1. Removing a lock case

- Paint buildup is often the cause of a sticking latch. With a utility knife, break the paint seal around the latch and scrape paint off its surface.

- Unscrew one of the doorknobs and pull it off its shaft. You may need to unscrew the knob itself, and/or a small setscrew holding the knob on the shaft. Then withdraw the shaft from the door by pulling on the other knob.

- With a utility knife, scrape away paint that fills the screw slots at the top and bottom of the lock case edge plate. Remove the screws and carefully pry out the case (right).

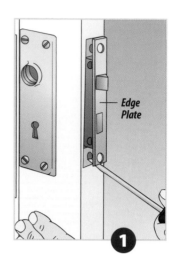

2. Servicing the lock case

If you cannot locate replacement parts for an old latch, you may be able to find a similar latch and scavenge parts from it. Otherwise, replace the entire latch.

- With the lock case on a flat surface, unscrew the cover plate and remove it (right). Sketch the interior layout for reference, then spray the works with a silicone lubricant.

- If either the latch spring or deadbolt tension strip is damaged, replace it.

- Check the action on both the latch and the bolt. If either will not budge, enlarge the openings in the lock case with a file.

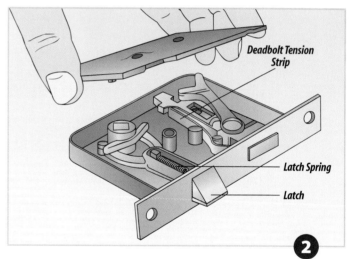

Modern Knob-and-Latch Assemblies

Removing the latch

- Take out the mounting plate screws and edge plate screws. Then pull gently on the remaining knob as you wiggle the latch and edge plate free (right). Buy an exact duplicate for the broken latch.

- To reassemble, insert the latch assembly and slide the knob in, wiggling it to engage the latch. Secure the edge and mounting plates with screws. When adding the escutcheon, turn it until it catches. Then set the doorknob on the shank, aligning the catch with the slot, and slide it into place.

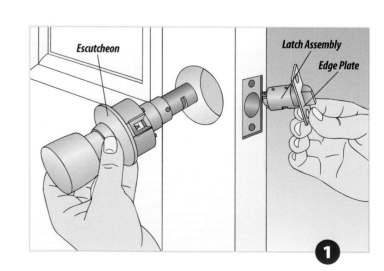

Moving a Strike Plate

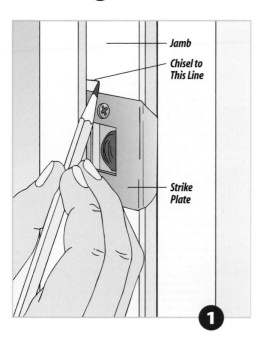

Jamb

Chisel to This Line

Strike Plate

1

1. Marking the jamb and extending the mortise

- To pinpoint problems with the strike plate, mortise, or latch hole, rub a crayon on the latch edge and close the door (right). Open the door and examine the smudge on the strike plate.

- Mark the distance on the jamb (left).

- Remove the strike plate and chisel the mortise up to the new line.

2. Enlarging the strike hole

- To increase the diameter or depth of a strike hole, chip away wood up to the new strike hole outline with a chisel and a hammer (right). Several light cuts will produce a cleaner hole than a few heavy cuts.

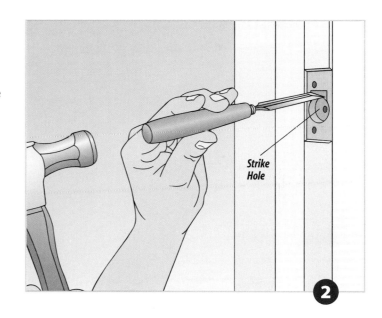

Strike Hole

2

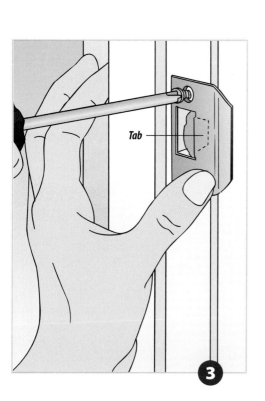

Tab

3

3. Repositioning the strike plate

- Place the strike plate in position and mark the screw locations. Drill a pilot hole for the top screw, stuffing the old hole with toothpicks if necessary (page 254). Position the plate and drive the screw (left).

- Next, close the door to make sure the latch slides easily into the hole. If it does, add the bottom screw. If not, adjust the mortise, strike hole, or strike plate.

- Fill the gap at the strike plate end with wood putty or spackling compound.

- To silence a rattling door, pry the tab outward with a screwdriver. Push it in slightly if the latch sticks.

Causes of Binding

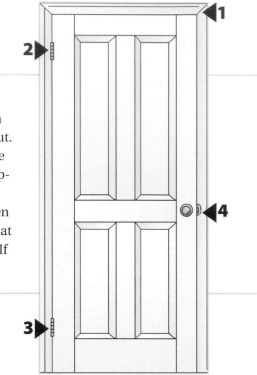

Correcting a binding door

When rubbing occurs all along the length of a door's latch edge, tighten any loose hinge screws or deepen hinge mortises if the hinge leaves stick out. Otherwise, plane the hinge side of the door rather than the latch side, or the latch may not fit afterward. If the latch edge rubs only near the top (1), deepen the mortise of the corresponding hinge (2) or plane the door without removing it. If the top edge binds, plane it or shim the same hinge or deepen the mortise of the lowest hinge (3). The same technique works for a door that rubs near the bottom, though you will have to remove the door to plane it. If binding occurs at the latch area (4), deepen the strike plate mortise.

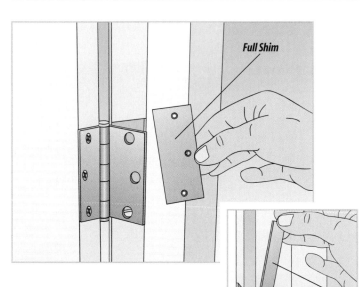

Shimming hinges

Every hinge leaf should be flush with the surrounding surface—either the jamb or the door edge. If the hinge is raised above the surrounding area, remove it and chisel the area beneath it.

- If the hinge is set too deep, remove the screws on the hinge leaf that needs shimming. Cut a piece of cardboard to fit into the mortise (above left). If only part of the hinge leaf was set too deep, cut a narrow piece and put it in that spot (inset).

- Insert the shim, and drive the screws back in. If the screw holes are too large, pack them with toothpicks (right).

Tightening Screws with Toothpicks

Often a door will bind simply because its hinges are loose. Over time, the weight and daily use of the door combine to pull the screws out of the jamb. In some cases, a longer screw will save the day. Or, you can give the old screws something to grip—for instance, a few round toothpicks. Push a few toothpicks into the hole, and snap them off flush (below). No glue is needed. Reinstalling the screws will wedge the toothpicks tight. This technique is also useful when you need to shift a screw hole slightly, such as when repositioning a strike plate.

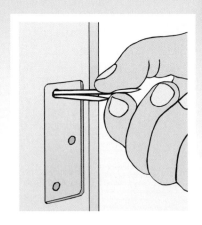

Repositioning the Door Stop

1. Removing the stop

If a door rattles or the latch doesn't quite make it to the hole, you may need to move the stop.

- Score any paint sealing the stop to the jamb with a utility knife. Starting at the top of the doorway, insert a putty knife between the stop and the jamb. Tap the knife gently to open a crack between the stop and the jamb.

- Slip a utility bar into the crack, pivoting it on the blade to protect the wood (right). Exert gentle pressure, lifting the stop out about ¼ inch at each nail.

- Slip the utility bar behind the stop and use both hands to pull the stop free. Remove the nails from the stop and the jamb.

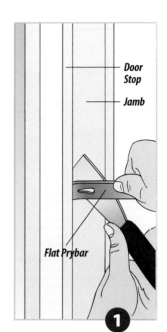

Door Stop

Jamb

Flat Prybar

1

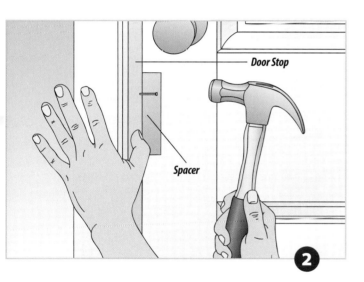

Door Stop

Spacer

2

2. Repositioning/ securing the stop

- Close the door, and position the stop and a thin cardboard spacer against it near the latch.

- Lightly press the stop against the cardboard and drive a finishing nail most of the way in (left). Continue driving nails, using spacers next to each nail. Doing so forces the stop to conform to the door.

- Test the door, then drive the nails slightly below the surface with a nail set. Fill the holes with wood putty.

Dismounting a Door

Removing the door

- Wedge the door open with shims.

- Scrape off any paint that may be binding the hinge pins to the hinge knuckles.

- Beginning with the lowest hinge, tap the hinge pin out with a nail set and a hammer (right) until about ½ inch of the pin is exposed. Then pull the pin out by hand.

- If it will not budge, knock it free with a screwdriver and a hammer.

- Then free the middle hinge (if there is one), and the top hinge. Pull the door out.

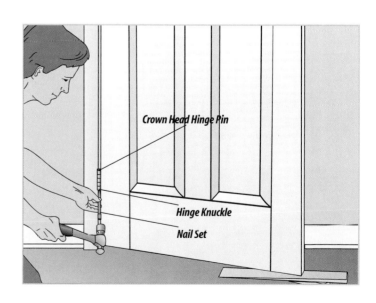

Crown Head Hinge Pin

Hinge Knuckle

Nail Set

Planing a Door to Shape

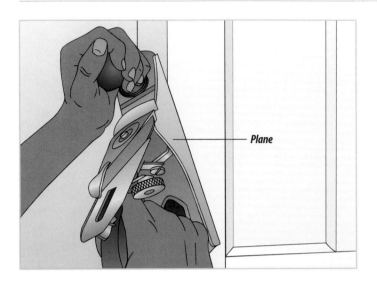

Spot-planing a door

- To spot-plane, first wedge the door open with shims at the floor.
- Set a plane's blade for a light cut, and test it on a scrap of wood.
- Take off just enough wood so the edge will not catch on the jamb as the door is closed (left).
- The latch edge of a door is beveled so it can swing closed. If you smooth off the bevel, reshape it with the plane or with sandpaper.

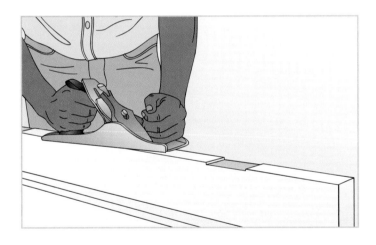

Planing the entire edge

- Remove the door and its hinges and prop it securely, latch side down.
- With a bench plane set for a light cut, plane the entire length of the door (left). The long base of the plane will help you produce a straight, flat surface.
- If you shave so much wood from the hinge side that a hinge mortise becomes too shallow, use a hammer and chisel to deepen the mortise so the hinge leaf will be flush with the surrounding wood.

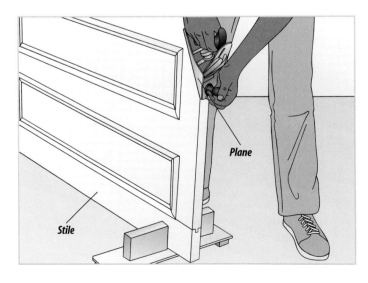

Planing door tops and bottoms

If more than ¼ inch of the door end needs to be removed, cut it (opposite page) rather than planing it.

- You may be able to spot-plane the top of a door with the door still hung. To plane a door bottom, remove it and prop it securely.
- Set the plane for a light cut and plane the door, making sure to go in the direction of the grain (left). To avoid splintering, lift the plane before you reach the end grain of the stiles.
- Plane the end grain of the stiles carefully, to avoid splintering. Use a very sharp blade and plane toward the middle of the door, not toward the edge.

Trimming a Solid Door

Cutting the door

- Draw a line along a carpenter's square to shorten the door as required. Extend the line across the door. Score the line with a knife.

- Adjust the cutting depth of a circular saw blade to ¼ inch deeper than the thickness of the door.

- Clamp a piece of wood to the door to serve as a guide for the base plate of the saw; this will help ensure a straight cut. Wearing protective eyewear, cut on the waste side of the knife score to minimize splintering (right).

- After cutting, smooth any roughness or splinters with sandpaper wrapped around a sanding block.

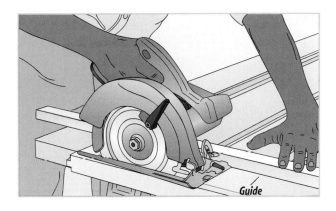

Guide

- Hang the door. If necessary, make any minor adjustments with a plane (opposite page).

Cutting a Hollow-Core Door

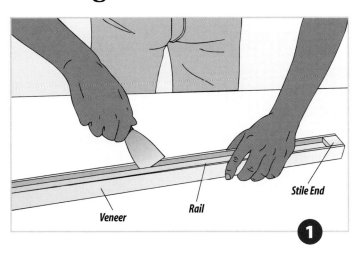

Veneer   *Rail*   *Stile End*

1

1. Freeing the rail

- Cut as you would a solid-core door (above). On the cut-off piece, run the blade of a putty knife between the rail and the veneer to break the glue seal (left). Snap off the stile ends and scrape away splintered veneer and dried adhesive with a putty knife or paint scraper.

- Drive a short finishing nail partway into the rail near either end to aid in repositioning (Step 2).

- Push back any support material inside the door that might interfere with insertion of the rail.

2. Clamping the rail

- Apply a thin bead of carpenter's glue to both veneer panels, just inside the opening. Allow the glue to set for a few minutes, until it becomes tacky.

- Lightly tap the rail into position. If you accidentally tap either end in too far, pull on the finishing nails to adjust it.

- Using C-clamps and strips of wood to protect the veneer, clamp the veneer against the rail (left).

- When the glue is dry, remove the clamps and pull out the nails. Hang the door.

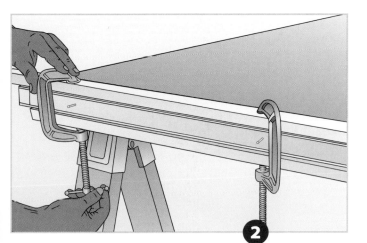

2

Folding Doors

Spring-Pivot Pin

Correcting a dragging door

- Fold the door open and lift it out of the floor bracket, then pull it down and out of the slider and top corner bracket (left).

- To prevent the door from dragging—on newly installed carpeting, for example—raise the floor bracket. To do so, unscrew it and trace its outline on a scrap of wood no thicker than the distance between the top of the door and the slider.

- Cut out the shape and insert it as a shim under the floor bracket. Reinstall the bracket using longer screws.

- To rehang the door, fit the top corner pin into its bracket, then lift the door and set the pin on the bottom of the door into the floor bracket.

- Next, depress the spring-pivot pin on top of the door, slip it into the slider, then release it (right).

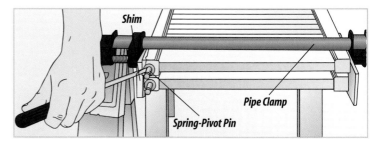

Shim

Pipe Clamp

Spring-Pivot Pin

Repairing a broken corner

- Remove the door (left) and place it on sawhorses.

- Apply a small amount of glue to the broken piece, fit it in place, and secure it with a pipe clamp padded with wooden shims.

- Before the glue sets, tap the pin in place with a screwdriver and a mallet (above). Remove the clamps after the glue has dried.

Top-Hung Sliding Doors

Retracking a top-hung door

- To fix a door that has jumped its track at the top of the doorway, first remove the bottom guide from the floor.
- Check inside the closet to see whether the track has access slots to permit reinsertion of the rollers.
- Swing the door out and lift it upward (left). If the track has access slots, fit the rollers through the slots and into the track. For a door without access slots, set the rollers on top of the track.

Adjusting the bottom guide

- Sliding doors also jam because the bottom guide becomes askew. If this happens, loosen the screws in the guide, align it, and retighten the screws.
- If a door slips out of the guide, it may be necessary to fit a wood shim under the guide to raise it (right).

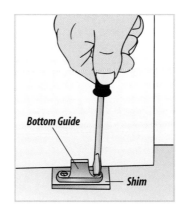

Bottom Guide

Shim

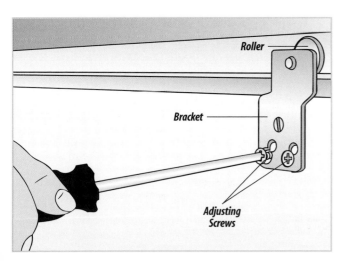

Roller

Bracket

Adjusting Screws

Correcting a dragging door

- Some sliding doors have adjustable roller brackets that allow you to raise the door, say, to accommodate new carpeting. To increase door height, loosen the adjusting screws (left), raise the door, and retighten the screws.
- If the door needs to be raised more than the adjustment allows, or if your door isn't adjustable, remove the door and cut or plane the bottom (pages 256–257). To compensate for raising the door, add shims under the bottom guide (above).

Gutters, Roofs & Siding

Contents

INTRODUCTION

Repairs to a house's exterior often call for heavier and more dangerous physical work than interior repairs. Even if you decide to hire professionals to handle this strenuous work, this chapter will help you understand when repairs are needed and how they are performed so you can avoid getting gouged by a contractor.

Work Safely

Homeowners often injure themselves working on roofs, gutters, and exteriors, usually because they do not use a ladder properly. Read pages 262–265 for ladder safety tips.

Avoid working in awkward positions. Take the time to move a ladder or to install a roof jack, rather than trying to get the job done quickly by reaching way over to the side. Often, taking a safety measure will lead to a better repair, since you will be working comfortably and from the best vantage point.

Repairing Underlying Lumber

If your finish materials fail, water can seep into the wood beneath and do serious damage. You may need to replace boards that are rotten.

Find out what lies under your roof shingles. In most new homes, there will be a layer of $1/2$-inch plywood with roofing felt (tar paper) stapled onto it. Older homes will have planks, often 1×6s. A home built with cedar shakes will have planks with spaces between them.

When replacing a section of planks on an older home, it is usually best to use $3/4$-inch plywood. If you suspect that the wood may get moist from time to time, use pressure-treated lumber or plywood.

Using a Stepladder

Setting up a stepladder

- To work safely and comfortably up to 10 feet from the ground, set up a stepladder that is at least 2 feet longer than the height at which you need to stand.

- Do not use a stepladder if a foot is worn, a step is loose, or a spreader brace does not open fully. Read the safety instruction label, usually located on a side rail.

- Set the stepladder on firm, level ground, and open its legs completely, locking its spreader brace(s). If the

Spreader Brace

ground is soft or uneven, place boards under the front and back feet. Never use an unanchored object such as a stone to prop it up.

- Wearing footgear with a well-defined heel, face the stepladder to climb up or down it, using both hands to grasp the steps rather than the side rails.

- While working from the stepladder, lean into it and keep your hips between the side rails (left); do not stand higher than the third step from the top.

- Never overreach or straddle the space between the stepladder and the house; instead, climb down from the stepladder and reposition it.

Using an Extension Ladder

1. Positioning and raising the ladder

- To work safely more than 10 feet from the ground or on the roof, use an extension ladder. Do not use the ladder if a shoe is worn or missing, a rung is loose, or a rung lock or the rope-and-pulley system is faulty.

Fly Section

Side Rail

Shoe

1

- Place the unextended ladder on the ground, perpendicular to the wall where it will be used, with its fly section (the part that slides) on the bottom and its feet out from the wall ¼ of the height to which it will be raised.

- With a helper bracing the bottom of the ladder with his or her feet, use both hands to raise the top of it above your head (above). Walk under the ladder toward the bottom of it, moving your hands along the side rails, until it is upright.

2. Extending the fly section

- With your helper supporting the ladder, stand slightly to one side of it, bracing the bottom of it with one foot,

Fly Section

Stabilizer

Rung Lock

2

and pull on the rope to disengage the rung locks and raise the fly section (above).

- When the fly section is extended to the height desired, gently release pressure on the rope to engage the rung locks. If your ladder does not have a rope-and-pulley system, keep both feet on the ground against the bottom of the side rails to push the fly section up with your hands; never stand on the ladder to raise the fly section.

- Check that the bottom of the ladder is out from the wall by ¼ the height of the ladder. To protect the gutter, install standoff stabilizers on the ladder, making sure they rest properly against the siding (inset). Or, use a piece of 2×4 (Step 4).

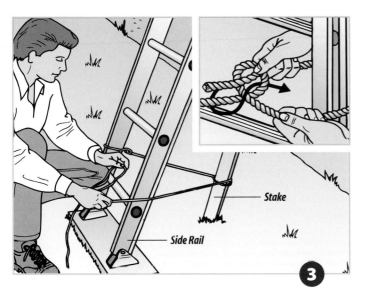

Stake

Side Rail

3. Stabilizing the bottom of the ladder

- Stand on the first rung of the ladder to test its stability. If the ladder does not stand steady on firm, level ground, place a board under the feet. If necessary, dig up the soil with a spade to level it.

- To stabilize the bottom of the ladder, drive a wooden stake into the ground between it and the wall, and use rope to tie each side rail to the stake (left), using a slip-proof knot such as the bowline (inset).

4. Stabilizing the top of the ladder

- If you are working at the eave or plan to get off the ladder onto the roof, stabilize the top of the ladder. If the ladder rests against a gutter, first fit a 2×4 inside the gutter to keep it from crushing under the weight of the ladder. Then install an eye screw or drive a 3-inch nail into the fascia near each side rail, just above or below the gutter. Using ⅜-inch-diameter nylon rope, tie each side rail of the ladder to the eye screw (right) or nail.

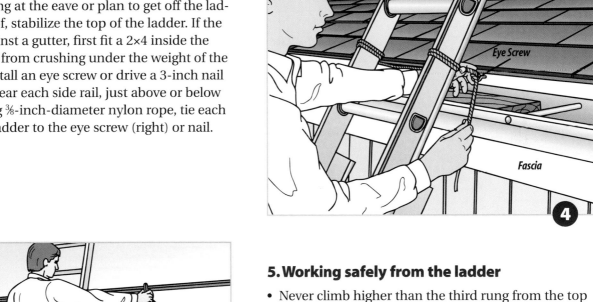

Eye Screw

Fascia

5. Working safely from the ladder

- Never climb higher than the third rung from the top of the ladder. While working from the ladder, hold onto a rung with one hand, if possible (left). Lean against the ladder and keep your hips between the side rails. Spread your legs slightly, keeping your feet against the side rails.

- Never overreach or straddle the space between the ladder and the siding; instead, climb down from the ladder and reposition it. Keep other people away from the ladder while you are working from it.

Getting On and Off the Roof

1. Getting onto the roof from the ladder

- Never go up onto the roof in wet, cold, or windy weather.

- Climb the ladder until your feet are on the rung that's level with or just below the eave.

- Holding firmly onto the top of the side rails with your hands, keep your left foot on the rung of the ladder and carefully step onto the roof with your right foot (right), without leaning forward onto the top of the ladder.

- Grasp the right side rail with your left hand, then remove your right hand from the top of it and carefully step onto the roof with your left foot (inset).

2. Getting onto the ladder from the roof

- To get off the roof onto the ladder, stand to the left of the ladder, facing it, and grasp the top of the side rail closest to you with your right hand. At the same time, swing your left foot onto the center of the rung at the eave and grasp the top of the other side rail with your left hand, pivoting on your right foot.

- Then, swing your right foot onto the center of the rung below your left foot, still grasping the side rails with your hands (left).

- Finally, step down one rung with your left foot and spread your legs slightly, keeping your feet against the side rails.

- Remove the eye screws or nails and apply a sealant to the holes in the fascia; use wood putty for wood or a sealant of a matching color for aluminum or vinyl.

Working on the Roof

Gutter

Transporting tools and materials

- To raise tools and materials up to the roof, use a bucket and a ⅜-inch-diameter nylon rope long enough to reach the roof with about 10 feet to spare. Tie one end of the rope to the bucket handle, place the tools and materials in the bucket, and tie the other end of the rope to your belt loop; do not overload the bucket.

- Climb up the ladder (page 263) and get onto the roof (opposite page). Sitting on the roof next to the ladder with your feet planted flat for stability, pull up on the rope to raise the bucket (left). When the bucket reaches the eave, carefully pull it over the gutter or roof overhang and onto the roof; hold onto the ladder for stability.

- Reverse the procedure to lower tools and materials to the ground. Then, get off the roof onto the ladder (opposite page).

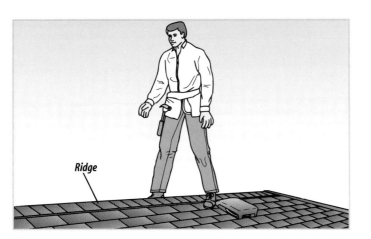

Ridge

Traversing the roof

- While working on the roof, avoid walking along the eave or rake. If the roof is so steep that you feel uncomfortable on it, hire a pro to do the work.

- Do not walk diagonally up the slope. Instead, walk carefully straight up from the ladder at the eave to the ridge, bending your knees slightly to maintain a low center of gravity. When you reach the ridge, stand straddling it and walk along it (above), keeping your legs spread and one foot on each side of it, as shown.

- When you reach the area of the roof desired, carefully walk straight down the slope to it.

- Reverse the procedure to walk back to the ladder. Then, transport tools and materials to the ground and get off the roof onto the ladder.

Roof Jack

When working on a steep roof, don't run the risk of sliding down and off. Roof jacks provide peace of mind for a small cost and only a little effort.

Install two jacks, spaced about 4 feet apart. Carefully lift up a shingle and start driving a nail in a location that will be covered by a shingle when you are done. Slip a ladder jack onto the nail, and finish driving the nail. Install the other jack the same way,  and lay a piece of 2×6 on top of the jacks. You now have a firm foothold for working.

To remove a jack, tap it with a hammer up toward the ridge, and slide it out. Slip a flat pry bar under a shingle and on top of the nail, and drive the nail down with a hammer.

Gutters and Downspouts

HOW THEY WORK

Gutters collect runoff water from the roof and channel it to downspouts that carry it safely past the siding and away from the foundation, where it might otherwise pool and leak into the basement or damage the lawn and garden.

Water must always have a clear and smooth path into the gutters and down through the downspouts. That means that roofing must overhang the gutters, and gutters must be tightly attached to the fascia, so that water will not flow behind the gutter and damage the fascia. Downspout sections fit together with a narrow end inserted into a wide end so water does not seep out.

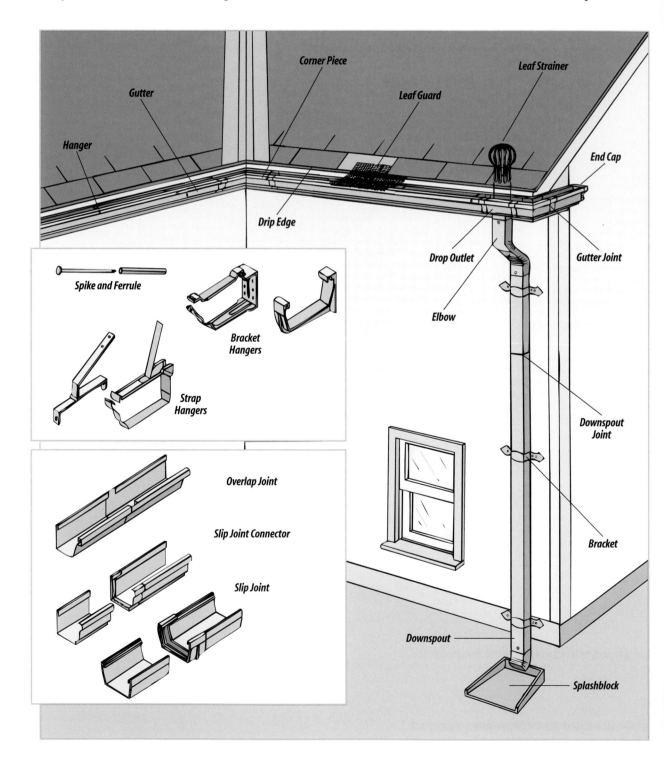

Corner Piece

Gutter

Hanger

Leaf Strainer

Leaf Guard

End Cap

Drip Edge

Gutter Joint

Spike and Ferrule

Bracket Hangers

Drop Outlet

Elbow

Strap Hangers

Downspout Joint

Overlap Joint

Slip Joint Connector

Slip Joint

Bracket

Downspout

Splashblock

BEFORE YOU START

Most gutter and downspout systems today are made of metal—galvanized steel or aluminum—or vinyl. Proper maintenance prolongs the life of gutters and downspouts and helps prevent problems such as blockages and sags that can lead to water damage inside and outside your home. Clean gutters and downspouts (page 268) every fall and spring. Install leaf guards and strainers to prevent blockages (page 269). You may need to scrape and paint a metal system every few years to slow its deterioration; a vinyl system needs no paint.

A damaged gutter or downspout section can be easily replaced, but working at the eaves can be intimidating. Before undertaking a repair, properly set up any ladder or scaffolding required (pages 262–265).

Some gutters are strong enough that you can lean a ladder against them. But many are easily damaged. To be safe, use a ladder stabilizer (page 262), or place a 2×4 inside the gutter to keep it stable (page 263).

Most repairs to a metal system call for simple tools such as a hacksaw, tin snips, and a flat file; repairs to a vinyl system require few tools since its components usually are snap-fit.

When shopping for a replacement part, bring along a piece of your system to be sure you get a part that fits exactly.

Troubleshooting

Cleaning a Gutter

Flushing a gutter

- Prepare to work safely with a ladder (pages 262–265). Wearing rubber gloves, handpick and bag any leaves, twigs, and other debris at the roof edge or in leaf guards, open gutters, and leaf strainers. Work from one end of the gutter to the other end.

- To flush dirt and grit out of the gutter, start at the end without a downspout, or at the center if there is a downspout at each end. If the gutter has a leaf guard, remove it.

- Have a helper pass up a garden hose and turn on the water. Wash dirt and grit off the gutter, brushing it ahead toward the downspout with a whisk broom

(below). Use a small putty knife, if necessary, to carefully dislodge material adhering to the gutter.

- Continue until you reach the downspout, inspecting the gutter as you go.

Cleaning a Downspout

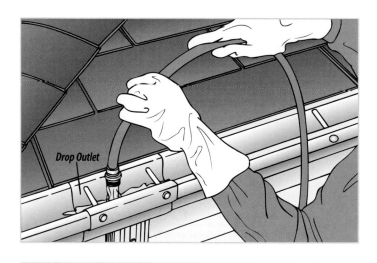

Drop Outlet

Flushing a downspout

- Wearing rubber gloves, reach down the drop outlet and pull out as much debris as possible.

- Have a helper pass up a garden hose. Aim the hose into the drop outlet (left), and flush debris through the elbow and out the bottom of the downspout.

- If the downspout is not cleared by flushing, unclog it (next step). To prevent a blockage in the future, install a leaf strainer in the downspout or a leaf guard in the gutter (opposite page).

Unclogging a downspout

- If a hose does not clear things up, use a drain auger (plumber's snake).

- Wearing rubber gloves, push the auger coil into the drop outlet, as far as possible through the elbow, and then lock the handle. Slowly turn the handle clockwise (right). When the handle moves easily, stop turning it, feed in more coil, and repeat the procedure.

- Continue until the downspout is unclogged, then remove the coil and flush the downspout (previous step).

- If necessary, work from the bottom of the downspout to unclog it. To prevent a blockage in the future, install a leaf strainer in the downspout or a leaf guard in the gutter (opposite page).

Auger

Elbow

Screening Gutters and Downspouts

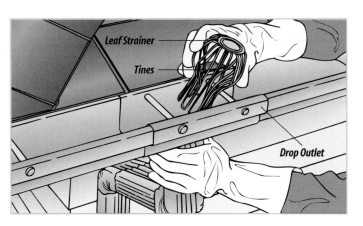

Installing a leaf strainer or leaf guard

- Prepare to work safely with a ladder (pages 262–265). In a moderately wooded area, prevent blockages by installing a leaf strainer in each downspout.

- Buy leaf strainers at a building supply center. Wear rubber gloves and insert one into the drop outlet (left). If the strainer is too large for the opening, squeeze the tines together. If it is too loose, bend the tines apart. Adjust the tines until the strainer fits snugly in the drop outlet.

Installing a leaf guard

In a heavily wooded area, prevent blockages by installing a wide-mesh plastic leaf guard in the gutter.

- Buy a roll of leaf guard designed to fit your type and size of gutter. Use scissors to cut off a strip of leaf guard as long as the gutter. At a corner, or if more than one strip is necessary, overlap the ends by at least 1 inch.

- To install each strip, fit one side between the roofing material and the building paper along the roof edge, pushing until the other side is aligned along the outside gutter edge.

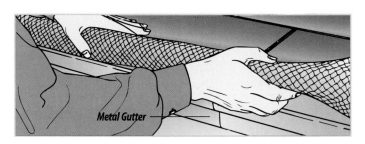

- If the roofing material cannot be lifted, roll the leaf guard and seat it in the gutter (above), notching it to fit over the hangers.

- To install a snap-on leaf guard along a vinyl gutter, press it into place under the hanger edges.

Patching a Metal Gutter

Using fiberglass mesh

- Prepare to work safely with a ladder (pages 262–265). Work on the gutter when it is dry.

- Remove grit and loose paint around the hole inside the gutter using a wire brush or a small putty knife. Use coarse-grit sandpaper to remove rust spots and smooth the surface; then wipe it with a clean, dry rag.

- Cut a piece of fiberglass mesh at least 1 inch longer and wider than the hole, using scissors. With a small putty knife, spread roofing cement around the hole edges. Center the tape over the hole and press it firmly into place, embedding it in the cement.

- Use the putty knife to apply a coat of roofing cement on the patch (right), saturating it completely. Feather the edges of the patch so that water can run smoothly over it.

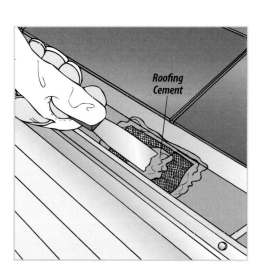

Correcting Sag with a Gutter Hanger

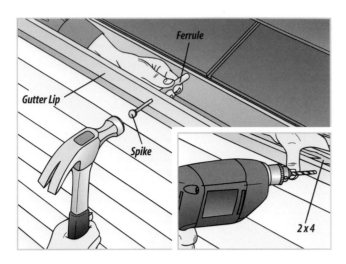

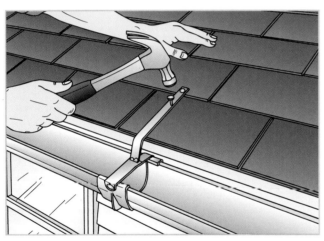

Installing a spike and ferrule

- Prepare to work safely with a ladder (pages 262–265). Remove as many spikes and ferrules as necessary. Use a level to see that the gutter slopes evenly.

- For each additional spike and ferrule to be installed, drill a hole in the gutter lip (inset), placing a 2×4 as a brace inside the gutter. If possible, position the hole at a rafter, usually located every 12 or 16 inches behind the fascia.

- To install a spike and ferrule, fit the ferrule inside the gutter over the hole and tap the spike into it. Hold the ferrule steady, position the gutter, and drive the spike through it (left), into the fascia and rafter behind it. There should be at least one spike and ferrule every 24 or 32 inches.

Installing a strap hanger

- If a sagging gutter uses strap or bracket hangers, remove as many hangers as necessary. Use a level to see that the gutter slopes evenly.

- Install strap hangers of a type that fits the gutter, following the manufacturer's instructions. Snap the clips onto the gutter edges. Position the strap on or under the edge of the roofing material, adjusting it until the gutter is in position, and drive roofing nails into it (left).

- Apply roofing cement on each nailhead. Use the same procedure to install at least one strap hanger every 24 or 32 inches.

Installing a Drip Edge

Install a drip edge if the roofing material does not overhang the roof edge by at least 1 inch, in which case water may seep behind the gutter.

Prepare to work safely with a ladder (pages 262–265). Buy drip edge equal to the length of the roof edge. If necessary, cut the drip edge to length using a hacksaw or tin snips, or assemble it in sections following the manufacturer's instructions. The

sections of the vinyl drip edge shown are spliced to interlock.

Remove burrs from any cut metal edges, and smooth rough spots on any cut vinyl edges with a flat file. To install the drip edge, fit one side between the roofing material and the building paper along the roof edge. Push until the other side is aligned along the inside gutter edge, overhanging it by at least 1 inch.

Carefully lift up the starter shingles and then drive a roofing nail every few feet to hold the drip edge in place.

Replacing a Metal Downspout Section

1. Removing the damaged section

- Prepare to work safely with a ladder (pages 262–265).

- To remove an entire downspout assembly, have a helper steady the bottom. Wearing work gloves, unscrew the elbow from the drop outlet (right) and then the brackets from the siding. Pull the elbow off the drop outlet, and lower the downspout assembly to the ground.

- To remove a damaged section, remove it and any downspout assembly below it in the same way. Then unscrew the parts.

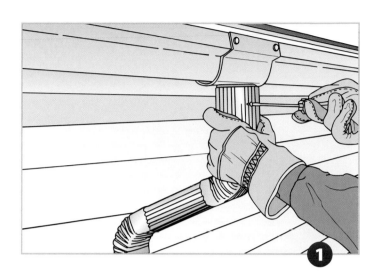

2. Preparing a replacement section

- Buy a replacement section of the same material, style, and size.

- Wearing work gloves and safety goggles, cut the replacement section to length using a hacksaw, and remove any burrs from the cut edges with a flat file, if necessary.

- Fit the narrow end of the replacement section into the wide end of the downspout assembly that you removed (right), pushing it in tightly. Drill a hole through the overlap of the ends, and drive a sheet metal screw (inset).

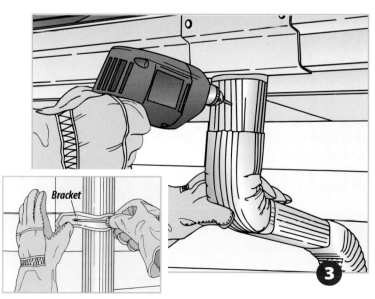

3. Installing the replacement section

- Install the downspout assembly with its wide end at the top. Have a helper steady the bottom while you fit the top of it onto the bottom of the downspout. Push the ends together tightly. If the top is a replacement section, drill a hole through the overlap of the ends (right) and drive in a sheet metal screw.

- Fit each bracket back into position around the downspout assembly. Screw them onto the siding (inset), installing one at the top and bottom of the downspout assembly, every 10 feet.

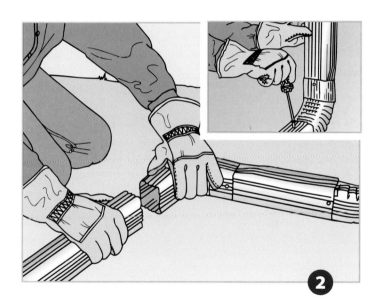

Bracket

Maintaining Fascias

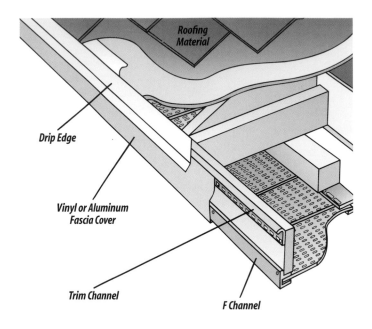

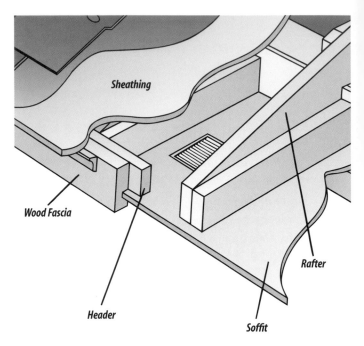

Fascia and soffit basics

Fascia is vulnerable to warping and rot. To keep it dry and maintenance-free, make sure water flows through the gutter only. You may need to install a drip edge or rehang the gutter (page 270). Soffits are less exposed and are usually trouble-free.

Replacing a fascia or a fascia cover is not too difficult, but working at heights can be intimidating. Prepare to work safely with a ladder (pages 262–265). Call for a professional evaluation if you find that wood beneath the fascia is damaged.

Most repairs require only basic tools, such as a pry bar, a hammer, a saw, and tin snips. For repairs to a vinyl fascia cover, you may also need a snaplock punch.

Replacing a Fascia

1. Inspecting the fascia

- Prepare to work safely with a ladder (pages 262–265). Remove any gutter section from the fascia. If there is a vinyl or an aluminum fascia cover, remove it, too. There also may be a piece of molding (right).

- Test the fascia for rot by poking it with a screwdriver: If the screwdriver tip penetrates easily, rot is present. Patch minor damage by removing the rotted spot and applying epoxy patching compound. If the damage is extensive, replace the fascia.

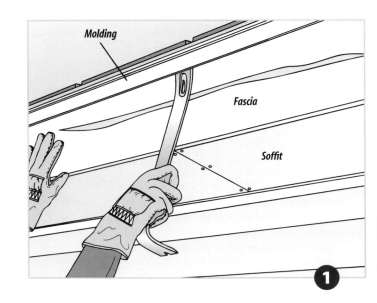

2. Removing damaged fascia

- Loosen the nails in the fascia by working a pry bar under it and along its bottom edge, if possible. With a helper holding the board steady, pull out the nails and lower it to the ground (right).

- If there is a header behind the fascia, test it for rot and patch minor damage. If the damage is extensive, remove the header as you did the fascia, also pulling out any nails driven through the soffit and into it. If the rafter ends are damaged, call for a professional evaluation.

3. Preparing a new fascia

- Buy replacement lumber of the same dimensions as the fascia, header, and molding. Use pressure-treated lumber, which ensures against rot. If the old fascia is grooved to hold the soffit, have a lumberyard cut a groove to match.

- Measure the length of the old fascia, and mark the new fascia for cutting. Wearing safety goggles, cut the new fascia to length with a circular saw. Bevel the end at a corner, if necessary (left).

- Use the same procedure to mark and cut any new header and molding.

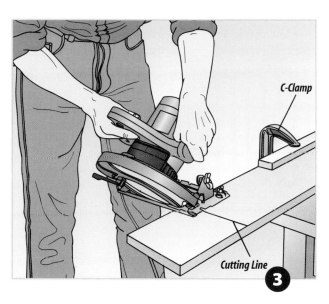

4. Installing the new fascia

- Install any new header first, as you would the new fascia.

- To install the new fascia, raise it into position with your helper steadying it; if it is grooved to hold the soffit, make sure it fits snugly. Drive nails into the new fascia (left), using the nailing pattern of the old fascia.

- Reinstall any vinyl or aluminum fascia cover that you removed. Install any molding at the top of the new fascia the same way.

- If necessary, refinish the repaired surfaces. Apply sealant along the joint between the new fascia and the soffit. Reinstall any gutter section you removed. Install a drip edge (page 270) to protect the new fascia, if necessary.

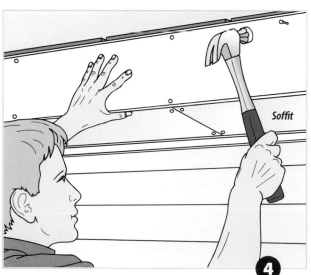

Roofs

HOW A ROOF IS CONSTRUCTED

In newer homes, the most common roof arrangement is ½-inch plywood on top of roof rafters that are 16 inches apart; if the rafters are 24 inches apart, the plywood will be thicker. A layer of roofing felt (tar paper) overlays the plywood sheathing, covered with asphalt or fiberglass shingles.

Older homes may have 1-by planks instead of plywood for sheathing. If the roofing is cedar shakes, the planks may have spaces between them to allow for air circulation.

Metal flashing is used around chimneys, in valleys, and wherever the roof meets a vertical surface. Flashing can be tricky: It must be installed so that water will run off of it and onto the top of shingles, and this can get surprisingly complicated, especially around a chimney or a skylight.

Diagnosing a Roof Problem

If a leak develops, it may take some detective work to find the source, since water may travel along the inside of the roof line before it starts dripping. If possible, go into your attic with a bright work light while it is raining, and look closely for the place where water is entering your home. Once you have found the spot, measure over from two reference points—for instance, the roof peak and a chimney—so you can locate the spot on top of the roof.

Often, the trouble will be with flashing rather than roofing. If the flashing has a hole, or has come loose from a chimney, you can attempt the repair (pages 282–283). If it is not clear why the flashing is leaking, call in a pro.

Sometimes only a small portion of a roof is damaged, and it makes sense to replace only a few shingles or shakes. Often, however, if one place is leaking, it means that the whole roof will need to be reroofed within a year or so.

Asphalt shingles that are wearing out may be faded in color and will have lost much of their protective granular surface. The shingles may start to curl or buckle, making the roof look a bit lumpy or wavy. High-quality asphalt shingles are guaranteed to last 20 years, but cheaper shingles may last only half as long.

Obtaining the Right Materials

There are many possible roofing materials, including clay tiles, metal, and slate. In this chapter, we cover repairs to the most common types—roofs made of asphalt (or fiberglass) shingles and cedar shakes. In most cases, you are well advised to call in professionals to repair the other types.

Often, roofers will leave a few leftover shingles or shakes at the job site when they are done. Check your garage or basement to see whether you have some replacement pieces lying around. If you need to patch a portion of an asphalt shingle roof, you may need to bring an old shingle to your supplier to get an exact color replacement.

Hiring a Roofer

Professionals can install a new roof very quickly. Roofers understand flashing, and they can often get a better price on materials than you can. So it usually makes sense to hire a contractor rather than installing a new roof yourself.

Check out a contractor's references, and get a solid guarantee in writing. See that all flashing will be replaced.

A major consideration: Can the new roof be simply laid on top of the old one, or does the old roof need to be removed? A "tear-off job" will raise the price dramatically. In most cases, you can have no more than three layers of roofing, or the total weight may damage the sheathing and framing.

If you do need a tear-off job, be clear with the contractor where the dumpster will be placed, and how much damage to your yard will result. Your contract should state that you will not pay in full until all the debris is cleared away.

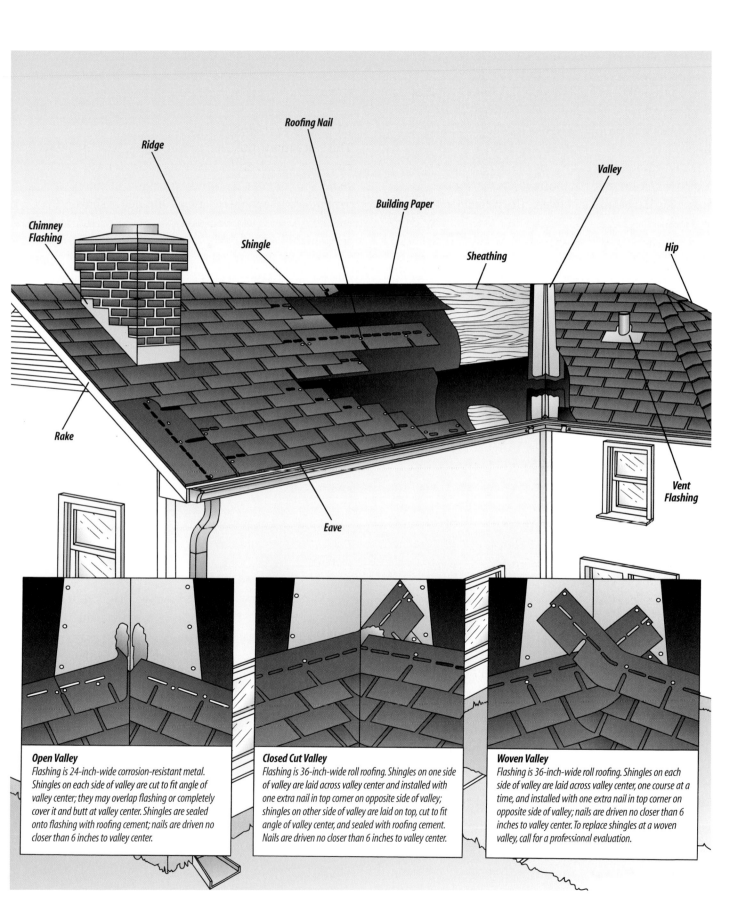

Roofing Nail

Ridge

Building Paper

Valley

Chimney Flashing

Shingle

Sheathing

Hip

Rake

Vent Flashing

Eave

Open Valley

Flashing is 24-inch-wide corrosion-resistant metal. Shingles on each side of valley are cut to fit angle of valley center; they may overlap flashing or completely cover it and butt at valley center. Shingles are sealed onto flashing with roofing cement; nails are driven no closer than 6 inches to valley center.

Closed Cut Valley

Flashing is 36-inch-wide roll roofing. Shingles on one side of valley are laid across valley center and installed with one extra nail in top corner on opposite side of valley; shingles on other side of valley are laid on top, cut to fit angle of valley center, and sealed with roofing cement. Nails are driven no closer than 6 inches to valley center.

Woven Valley

Flashing is 36-inch-wide roll roofing. Shingles on each side of valley are laid across valley center, one course at a time, and installed with one extra nail in top corner on opposite side of valley; nails are driven no closer than 6 inches to valley center. To replace shingles at a woven valley, call for a professional evaluation.

Repairing a Shingle Tab

Sealing a crack, tear, or hole

- Prepare to work safely on the roof (pages 262–265). Lift the tab high enough to expose the damage on the bottom of it. If it is sealed down, gently work a putty knife or a trowel under it and along its edges to loosen it.
- Use the putty knife or trowel to apply roofing cement on the bottom of the tab over the damage (left) and about 2 inches from the edges at each corner. Press the tab down firmly to seal it.
- Apply roofing cement on top of the tab over the damage. Scrape off excess roofing cement, and smooth the edges.

Sealing a lifted or curled edge

- To seal a lifted or curled edge, lift the tab high enough to reach under it. If it is partly sealed down, gently work a putty knife or a trowel under it and along its edges to loosen it.
- Hold up the tab, and use the putty knife or trowel to apply roofing cement on the bottom of it about 2 inches from the edges at each corner (right). Press the tab down firmly to seal it.
- Lay a brick on top of the tab to help the bonding of the roofing cement, and remove it when the roofing cement has set.

Replacing a Shingle

1. Removing the damaged shingle

- To locate the nails holding the damaged shingle, lift the tabs two courses (rows) above it and then the adjacent tabs one course above it. If a tab is sealed down, gently work a putty knife or a trowel under it and along its edges to loosen it.
- To pull out a nail, first fit a flat pry bar under the tab and around the nail shaft, and pry. Remove the pry bar and fit it around the raised nailhead on top of the tab, and pry the nail out. Continue until all the nails holding the damaged shingle are removed. Pull out the damaged shingle.

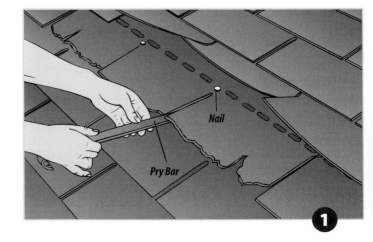

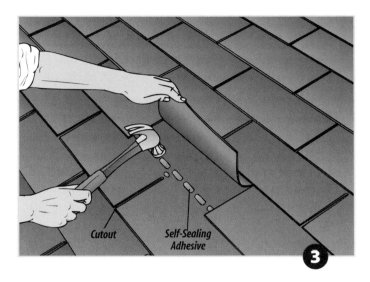

Cutout · **Self-Sealing Adhesive**

3. Nailing the replacement shingle

- Hold up in turn the adjacent tabs one course above the new shingle, and drive a roofing nail into the new shingle just below the self-sealing adhesive and about 1 inch from each side.

- Also nail at intervals specified by the manufacturer: for a three-tab shingle, at each cutout (above); for a one-tab shingle, 12 inches from each side (below left); for a two-tab shingle, 5 inches from each side of the cutout (below right).

- Use a putty knife or a trowel to apply roofing cement on the bottom of the adjacent tabs one course above the new shingle, so the cement covers each nail. Press each tab down firmly to seal it onto the roofing cement.

- Using the same procedure, nail the adjacent tabs one course above the new shingle about 1 inch to the side of each sealed hole. Then, seal the tab two courses above each tab of the new shingle with roofing cement.

2. Fitting a replacement shingle

- Slide the new shingle into position under the tabs one course above it (above) and aligned with the tabs on each side. If necessary, trim the replacement shingle with tin snips.

- Use a putty knife or a trowel to apply roofing cement on the bottom of the new shingle about 2 inches from the edges of the corners of each tab. Press each tab down firmly to seal it.

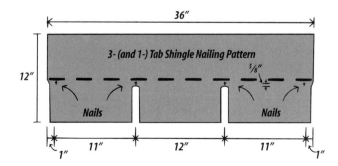

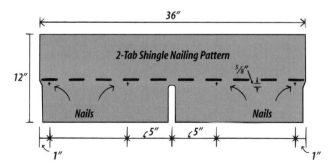

Replacing a Starter Shingle at an Eave

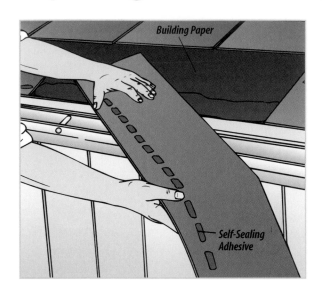

Building Paper

Self-Sealing Adhesive

Installing a replacement starter shingle

- Remove the damaged shingle with a flat pry bar.

- To make a standard shingle into a starter shingle, cut off the tabs just below the self-sealing adhesive with tin snips or a knife.

- Use a putty knife or a trowel to apply a line of roofing cement 3 inches wide along the building paper at the eave. Position the starter shingle with the cut edge along the eave (left) and overhanging it by ¼ to ⅜ inch.

- Press the starter shingle down firmly to seal it onto the roofing cement. Drive four roofing nails into the starter shingle, 3 to 4 inches from the eave and about 1 inch and 12 inches from each side.

- Install the replacement section of shingles on top of the starter shingle.

Replacing a Shingle at a Chimney

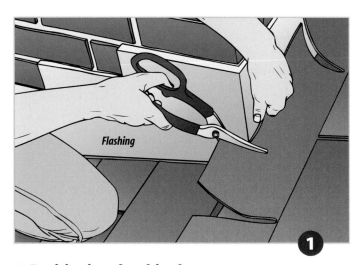

Flashing

1

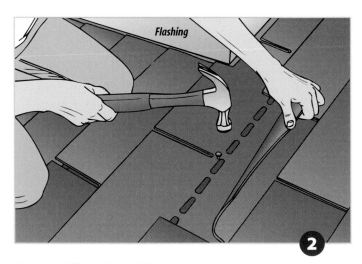

Flashing

2

1. Positioning the shingle

- Prepare to work safely on the roof (pages 262–265). If a damaged shingle is sealed under flashing, call in a pro; you don't want to disturb the flashing.

- If a damaged shingle sits on top of flashing, remove the shingle (pages 276–277).

- Slide a replacement shingle into position under the tabs of the shingle above it. Use tin snips or a knife to trim it to size.

2. Installing the shingle

- Use a putty knife or a trowel to apply a thick band of roofing cement wherever water might seep under flashing.

- Apply roofing cement on the bottom of the new shingle, about 2 inches from the edges at the unsealed corners of each tab. Press each tab down firmly to seal it.

- Hold up in turn the tabs of the shingle one course above, and drive a roofing nail into the new shingle just below the self-sealing adhesive and about 1 inch from each side. Cover the nailheads with roofing cement.

Replacing a Shingle at a Ridge or Hip

1. Fitting a replacement shingle

- Prepare to work safely on the roof (pages 262–265). To remove the nails holding the damaged shingle, work from it to the shingle two courses above it; see pages 276–277.

- To make a shingle for the ridge or hip, use tin snips or a knife to cut off a tab 12 inches square. Then cut a taper on each side (right).

- Slide the new shingle into position under the shingle one course above it, overlapping the taper. If you are at the end of a hip over the eave, trim the shingle to fit, using the edge of the shingles on each side of the corner as a guide (inset).

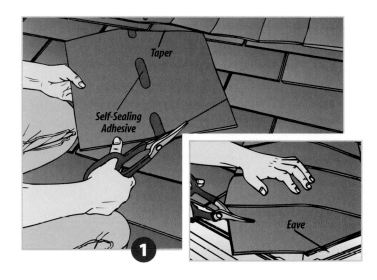

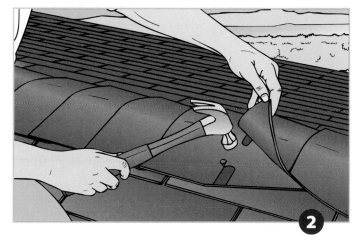

2. Installing the replacement shingle

- Holding up the shingle one course above the new shingle, drive a roofing nail into the new shingle just below the self-sealing adhesive and about 1 inch from each side (above).

- Use a putty knife or a trowel to apply roofing cement on the bottom of the shingle one course above the new shingle over each nail hole and about 2 inches from the edges at each corner. Press the shingle down firmly to seal it.

- Using the same procedure, nail the shingle one course above the new shingle about 1 inch to the side of each sealed hole. Then, seal the shingle two courses above the new shingle with roofing cement.

Choosing Roofing Nails and Cement

Roofing nails range in length from 1¼ inches to 2 inches. The size you choose depends on how many layers of roofing are on your roof. Use the shortest nails to attach a shingle directly to plywood, and the longest if you are applying a third layer of shingles. You should feel the nail bite into wood.

Test by pulling up a nail. If it comes up easily, a windstorm could rip shingles off your roof; use longer nails.

The most common and useful type of roofing cement has a fibrous consistency so that it will not flow. Some types can be applied even when the roof is wet; but wipe away most of the moisture first, to ensure a strong seal.

Use roofing cement both to seal and to adhere. When you apply it in a place where it will be exposed, feather out the edges so water can flow easily over it.

Maintaining a Cedar Shake Roof

Spray-cleaning cedar shakes

- If a stain is localized, hand-clean the surface. If the roofing is stained extensively, prepare to work safely on it (pages 262–265).

- Place the ladder at one end of the roof. Brush off debris and remove any peeling or lifting finish. Cover nearby branches with plastic sheeting.

- Rent or purchase a pump-up sprayer. Wearing rubber gloves, safety goggles, and long sleeves, mix enough cleaner to fill the canister.

- Start at the end of the roof farthest from the ladder, and work from ridge to eave in successive 5-foot-wide sections (above). Always stand on dry roofing, and do not point the wand into chimney flues or vents. Once you're done, rinse the surface thoroughly with clean water, again working in 5-foot sections.

Applying a preservative or finish

Fungus and moss may grow on a cedar shake roof. This is a cosmetic problem at first, but it can cause damage to the shakes if not treated. Start by cleaning the roof (previous step).

If a cedar shake roof is dried out, causing it to crack and curl, applying a coat of sealer can restore it and save you the expense of a new roof.

Purchase a sealer/finish recommended for use in your area; you may need one with a mildewcide, for instance.

Apply it with a pump sprayer (above), working in the same way as you would for washing a roof (previous step), except that you also should wear a respirator and a safety belt.

Replacing a Shake

1. Removing the damaged shake

- Prepare to work safely on the roof (pages 262–265). Lift the butt edge of the shake and pull it out (right), working it from side to side to break it off hidden nails. Avoid damaging any building paper.

- If the shake is difficult to remove, split it lengthwise with a hammer and chisel, and pull out the pieces.

- Fit a hacksaw blade behind the course above the shake removed, and cut off hidden nails that held it. These are usually about 2 inches above the butt line.

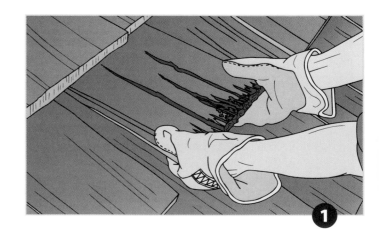

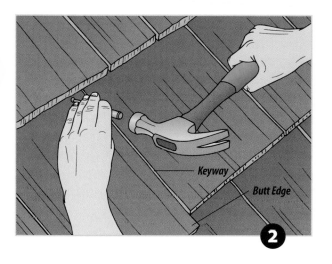

2. Fitting and installing a new shake

- Cut or choose a shake about 1 inch narrower than the opening. Slide the shake into place, with a ½-inch keyway on each side.

- Position the shake with its butt edge about 1 inch below the butt line of its course, and drill two pilot holes, at the butt line of the course above and at a 45-degree angle toward it, ¾ inch from opposite sides.

- Drive a nail into each hole. Set the heads with a nail set and a hammer (left).

- Hold a wood block under the butt edge of the shake, and tap it with a hammer until the butt edge is even with the butt line of its course.

Replacing Shingles or Shakes at a Ridge or a Hip

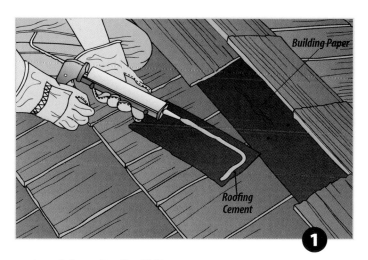

1. Patching the building paper

- Prepare to work safely on the roof (pages 262–265). See Step 1 above for removing the shake.

- If the building paper is damaged, remove as many shakes as necessary to cover the entire damaged area with a patch.

- Using a utility knife, cut a sheet of building paper for the patch at least 1 inch longer and wider than the damaged area. Wearing work gloves, apply roofing cement on the bottom of the patch with a caulking gun (above). Turn over the patch, position it, and press it into place.

2. Installing a new shingle or shake

- Cut a new shake to fit. Slide it into place, but leave its butt edge about 1 inch below the butt line of its course.

- Drill two pilot holes, at the butt line of the course above the shake and at a 45-degree angle toward it, ¾ inch from opposite sides.

- Drive a nail into each hole, using a hammer (above). Set its head with a nail set and the hammer. Hold a wood block under the butt edge of the shake, and tap it with a hammer until the butt edge is even with the butt line of its course.

Repairing Flashing

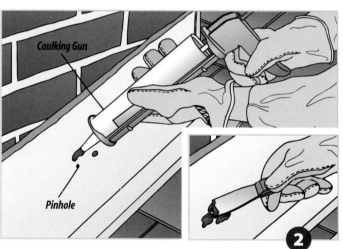

Caulking Gun

Pinhole

1. Preparing the surface

- Prepare to work safely on the roof (pages 262–265). If the flashing is extensively corroded or damaged, or if it leaks and you cannot see why, call for a professional evaluation.

- Restore flashing that is rusted slightly in spots. Use a wire brush to remove loose rust, dirt, and old finish (left). Then wipe the surface with a clean, moist rag.

- Using medium-grit sandpaper, remove any remaining rust, then wipe off the surface with a clean, dry rag. You might choose to paint the flashing.

2. Cementing the surface

- If the flashing has small holes, use a caulking gun loaded with a cartridge of roofing cement to fill the holes (left).

- Then use a putty knife to smooth the cement onto the flashing around the hole (inset). After filling each hole, or if the flashing is pitted, apply an even coat of roofing cement to the damaged surface.

- This repair may last a long time or may be short-lived, depending on weather conditions.

Repairing Flashing Joints

Sealing flashing joints

- Prepare to work safely on the roof (pages 262–265). If joints between overlapping pieces of flashing or between flashing and asphalt shingles are open, seal them.

- Use a putty knife to carefully scrape out any remaining old sealant (inset). Use a wire brush to remove debris, grit, and any old finish. Use medium-grit sandpaper to remove any remaining rust, then wipe off the surface with a clean, dry rag.

- Load a caulking gun with silicone caulk and apply a continuous bead along the length of the joint (right). If necessary, use a putty knife to press the sealant into the joint. Run a finger along the joint to smooth and shape it.

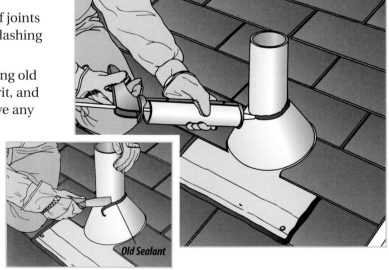

Old Sealant

Reattaching flashing to a mortar joint

- Wearing work gloves, carefully pull the flashing away from the mortar joint, freeing its edge, which may be bent to fit into a mortar joint.

- Taking care not to damage the flashing, use an old screwdriver or cold chisel to scrape any large pieces of loose mortar out of the joint. Then use a wire brush to remove any remaining bits of mortar and grit.

- Using a caulking gun loaded with roofing cement, fill the joint (right). Then push the flanged edge of the flashing back into the joint, setting it firmly in the roofing cement.

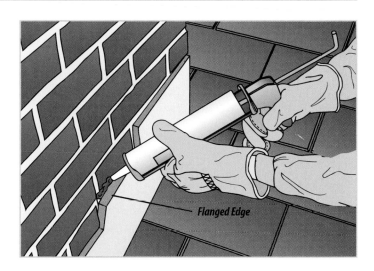

Flanged Edge

Masonry Nail

Reattaching flashing to a masonry surface

- Carefully pull the flashing away from the masonry surface. Use a putty knife to scrape any old sealant out of the joint, then clean the joint with a wire brush.

- Using a caulking gun loaded with roofing cement, fill the gap between the flashing and the masonry surface. Press the flashing firmly against the masonry surface to bond it to the roofing cement.

- If the flashing is bent and does not sit flush, secure it with masonry nails (left). Drive nails into mortar joints if possible.

Sealing flashing against brick

- Use a putty knife to cover each nailhead with a dab of roofing cement. Then, apply a 2-inch band of roofing cement along the edge of the flashing (left), covering the joint.

- On a brick wall, also pack roofing cement into the mortar joints along the edge of the flashing so that water will flow smoothly down onto the flashing.

Siding

HOW SIDING IS INSTALLED

Wood siding is sometimes nailed directly to wall studs or to horizontal furring strips, which are nailed to studs. Most buildings have some sort of sheathing between the studs and the siding. Sheathing may be made of plywood, fibrous or foam sheets, or (in older homes) 1-by planks. Building paper usually wraps the sheathing, and the siding is installed over the paper.

Vinyl and aluminum siding is often installed over existing wood siding. Various types of channels—starter strips, inside and outside corner posts, and trim channel—are installed first, and the siding is then cut to fit into the channels.

Maintaining Siding

To protect siding from lingering moisture, which can damage it, trim bushes and trees back so all portions of

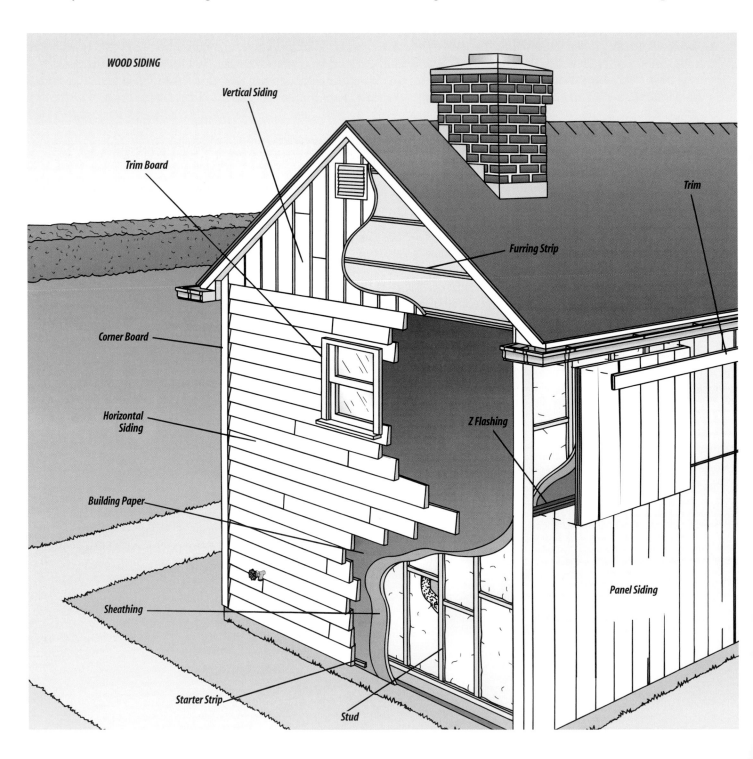

WOOD SIDING

Vertical Siding

Trim Board

Trim

Furring Strip

Corner Board

Horizontal Siding

Z Flashing

Building Paper

Panel Siding

Sheathing

Starter Strip

Stud

the exterior walls can dry out. Water can harm not only the siding, but also the underlying sheathing and perhaps even framing.

Keep wood siding well covered with paint; once a finish cracks or peels, wood can suffer damage quickly. Once a year, check all the joints where moisture could get in, especially around windows and doors and at corners. If the caulk has separated, scrape it off and apply new caulk (pages 306–307).

Vinyl and aluminum siding usually require less care. Wash the surface once a year with a mild soap solution. You may need to touch up the paint on aluminum siding once in a while.

Choosing Materials

There are many types of siding. Horizontal beveled siding (with its bottom edge thicker than the top) may be made of wood, pressed wood (Masonite), aluminum, or vinyl. If the lines run vertically, you may have large siding sheets (often called T1-11) or "shiplapped" pieces of solid wood, with the edge of one piece overlapping the edge of the other.

Older siding was often made of cedar, which has wonderful insulating qualities and natural beauty but is expensive. If you will be painting, you may choose to use replacement pieces made of less-expensive wood.

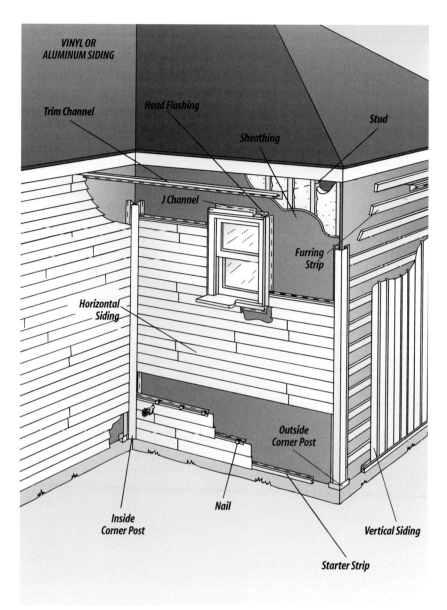

Exterior Painting

If your siding is covered with paint that looks smooth and is not cracking or peeling, you may be able to simply paint over it. If the paint is loose or ugly, however, painting will not reduce the appearance of alligator-skin, nor will it prevent peeling. To achieve a finished look, you may have to spend long tedious hours scraping and sanding. Experiment on a section that is usually out of view, to get an idea how much work you may be in for.

Nowadays, high-quality latex exterior paint actually lasts longer than oil-based paint on siding and trim. If

the surface will be walked on—a porch, for instance—oil-based paint is still the best choice.

It is very important to be sure that your paint will stick. If the existing paint is oil-based, you could get into real trouble if you simply paint over it with latex paint: It may all start to peel off within a year! Take a chip of the old paint to a paint dealer to find out whether it is latex or oil-based. If you are not sure that it is latex, apply a coat of primer before painting with latex. A good paint store will tint the primer so that it is close to your finish color.

Refinishing Wood Siding

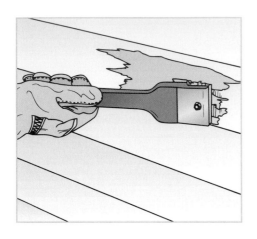

Removing the old finish

- If paint is loose or peeling, wear work gloves and safety goggles, and use a paint scraper to remove it (left). Use long, sweeping strokes to avoid digging into the wood.

- To loosen thick layers of paint or reach tight corners, it sometimes helps to rub with a wire brush before or after scraping.

- Brush off debris with a whisk broom, and use a putty knife to clean debris out of cracks.

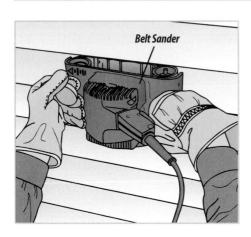

Sanding the surface

- Wearing work gloves and a dust mask, sand along the grain to smooth the surface. Use a belt sander on a large, flat area (left).

- Start with coarse sandpaper if the surface is rough or heavily coated. Start with medium sandpaper if it is scratched or moderately coated. You may want to use fine sandpaper for final smoothing.

Filling Small Holes and Cracks

Patching a small hole or crack

- Buy exterior-grade wood putty or spackle.

- Use a putty knife to pack putty into the hole or crack, overfilling it slightly. Scrape off the excess putty, leveling it with the surrounding surface.

- To fill a hole in the bottom edge of horizontal lapped siding, hold a wood block up against the bottom edge (right), and use it as a guide.

- Allow the wood putty to cure, then prime and paint.

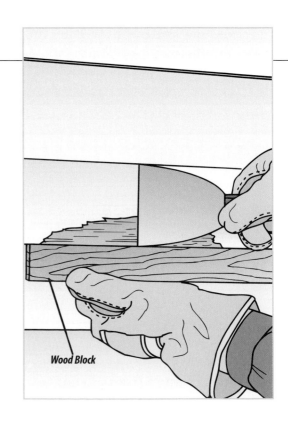

Repairing a Horizontal Lapped Board (Clapboard)

1. Cutting off the damaged section

- Using a framing square as a guide, mark each end of the damaged section by scoring with a knife.

- Pry the board above out ½ inch or so, and slip in a piece of shim just above the cutting line. Pry the damaged board out and shim it in the same way.

- Using a backsaw, saw off each end of the damaged section along the cutting line as far as possible (right). Work carefully to avoid damaging the board one course above and below it.

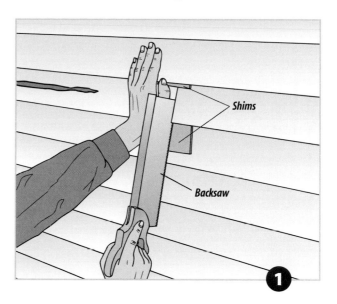

2. Finishing the cut

- Shift the top shim to one side of the cutting line. Pull out the bottom shim, and fit it beside the top shim on the other side of the cutting line.

- Have a helper support the damaged section if it is longer than 4 feet. Use a keyhole saw to complete the saw cut at each end (left), or use a chisel and a hammer to cut off each end.

- Remove the shims and pull out the damaged section. If it is stubborn, use a pry bar to pull any nails holding it out of the board one course above. Repair any damaged building paper.

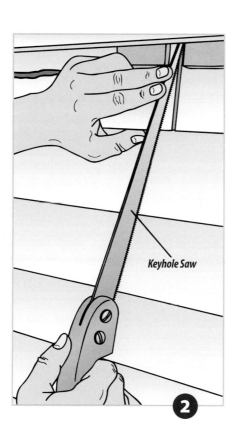

3. Fitting and installing a replacement section

- Buy a replacement board and cut it to the length of the opening. Apply a preservative, taking care that the ends are especially well coated.

- Slide the new board into the opening under the board one course above it. Use a mallet or a hammer and block of wood to tap it into place (right), if necessary.

- Drive nails into the new board and into any unnailed end of a board adjacent to it. Also replace any nails pulled out of the board one course above.

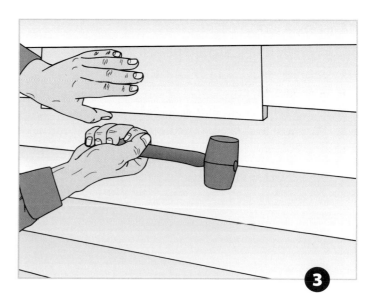

Repairing a Blistered Plywood Panel

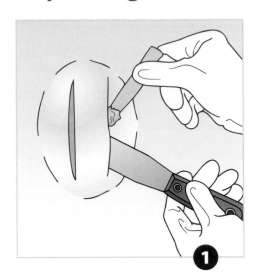

1. Applying glue

- If the blister is larger than 10 inches square or there is more than one blister, replace the panel.

- Otherwise, use a utility knife to slice through the blister from the top to the bottom every inch or so.

- If the wood is damp, allow it to dry out for several days.

- Gently pry up the blister with a putty knife, and work exterior-grade glue inside the blister (left).

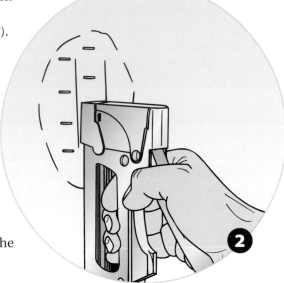

2. Stapling the surface

- Press down on the blister and use a clean, damp cloth to wipe off excess glue.

- Drive staples into the blister, spaced about 1 inch apart (right). Wipe off any extruded glue.

- After the glue has cured for about a week, pull out the staples with a small screwdriver. Fill the holes with wood putty, and paint the area.

Replacing a panel

- If a sheet of plywood siding is badly damaged, replace it. Use a hammer and flat pry bar to remove the old panel, and use it as a template for marking the new panel for cutting.

- Apply preservative or paint to the ends and cut edges of the replacement sheet.

- With a helper, slide the panel into position. It will probably slip under the sheet on one side and over the sheet on the other side.

- Drive siding nails every 8 inches or so into the furring strips or plywood sheathing. If necessary, prime and paint it.

Repairing a Dent in Aluminum

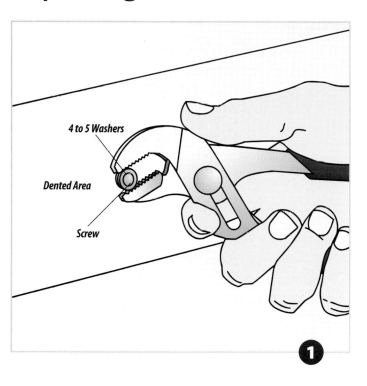

4 to 5 Washers

Dented Area

Screw

1. Drilling holes and pulling with screws

- If the dent is smaller than 2 inches in diameter, simply apply filler and paint it (Steps 2 and 3).

- For a larger dent, drill several ⅛-inch holes in the middle.

- For each hole, slide 4 to 5 washers onto a sheet-metal screw. Drive the screws into the holes, and pull them outward with pliers. Don't pull too far, or you'll create a bulge.

2. Applying auto-body filler (Bondo)

- Remove the screws. To make sure that you didn't pull out too far, run a scraper that is wider than the hole over it. Tap in any high spots.

- Mix the two parts of auto-body filler together according to manufacturer's directions. Apply it with the plastic scraper provided with the can so that it is slightly higher than the surrounding surface.

3. Smoothing and painting

- Before the filler completely hardens, scrape it smooth with a paint scraper. Or wait for it to dry, and sand it smooth.

- Apply primer, then paint.

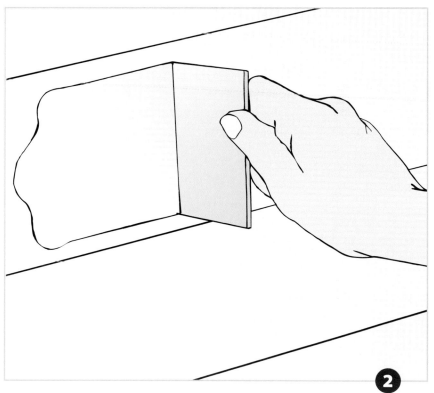

Replacing an Aluminum Siding Panel

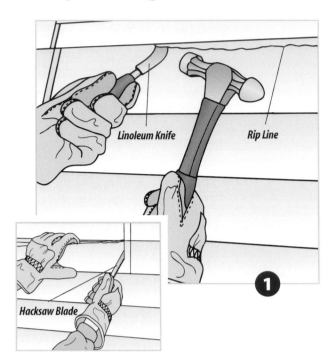

Linoleum Knife   Rip Line

Hacksaw Blade

1. Removing the damaged panel

- Wearing work gloves, use a utility knife to score repeatedly and heavily along a cutting line on each side of the damaged area.

- Drill a hole at the center of the panel and fit the tip of a linoleum knife into it. Hit the blade of the knife with a hammer to rip the panel along its length (left).

- Cut along the scored lines at the ends using a fine-toothed hacksaw blade (inset).

- To remove the ripped half of the panel, lift out its edge and bend it back and forth along the scored line to snap it off. To remove the other ripped half of the panel, push on it to unlock it from the panel or starter strip that it overlaps, then slide it out.

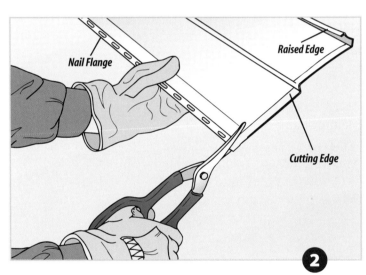

Nail Flange   Raised Edge

Cutting Edge

2. Cutting a replacement panel

- Buy a replacement panel of the same type. Using tin snips, cut it to length (right), 6 inches longer than the opening.

- To cut it to width, score it repeatedly with a utility knife, then bend it back and forth along the scored line until it snaps.

Sealant

3. Installing the replacement panel

- Apply roofing cement around the edges of the cutout. Working with a helper, position the new panel (left) so that there is an overlap of 3 inches at each end.

- Press firmly on the new panel to lock it onto the panel or starter strip that it overlaps and to bond it to the roofing cement. For a snug fit, hold a wood block against its lip and tap with a hammer.

- Use a soft cloth to wipe off any extruded cement.

Replacing an Aluminum Corner Cap

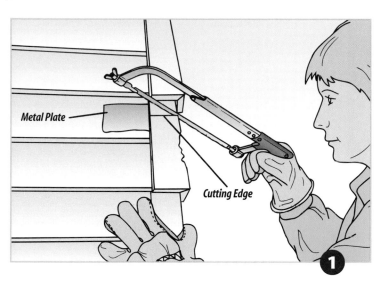

Metal Plate

Cutting Edge

1. Removing the damaged corner cap

- Slide a thin metal plate behind the top of a damaged corner cap on each side, to protect the siding.

- Use a carpenter's square to mark a cutting line across each side of the damaged corner cap, 2½ inches below the corner cap above it.

- Cut through the damaged corner cap along the cutting line with a hacksaw (left). Work carefully to avoid damaging the siding. Pull out the damaged corner cap, working it off the corner cap below it.

- Use a hammer and block of wood to flatten any protruding section of the remaining damaged corner post. Trim any ragged edges with tin snips.

2. Installing a replacement corner cap

- Use tin snips to cut the new corner cap 1 inch longer than the opening (½ inch more at each side); cut the excess off the top of it.

- Apply roofing cement or silicone caulk along each edge of the remaining damaged corner cap.

- Slide the new corner cap into place (right), fitting it onto the panel on each side of the corner. To fit it snugly, hold a wood block against its lip and tap with a hammer. Wipe off any extruded sealant with a soft cloth.

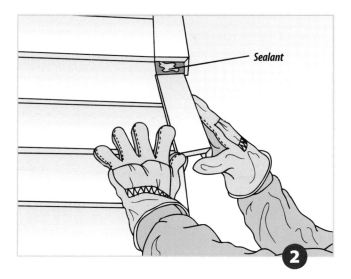

Sealant

Repointing Brick and Block Joints

1. Removing the old mortar

After a few decades, even the best-laid mortar may start to crumble and chip. Repointing, also called tuckpointing, is the solution. If a large area needs repointing, call in a professional.

- To tackle a small area, wear work gloves and goggles. Use a cold chisel and a hammer or small sledgehammer to cut back the joints ½ to ¾ inch (right). For large areas, rent a grinding tool.

- Brush away the dust and crumbs with a stiff brush.

- To prevent the bricks or blocks from leaching moisture out of the fresh mortar, apply enough water to penetrate the joints completely, using the fine spray of a garden hose or working water into the joints with a large paintbrush (inset).

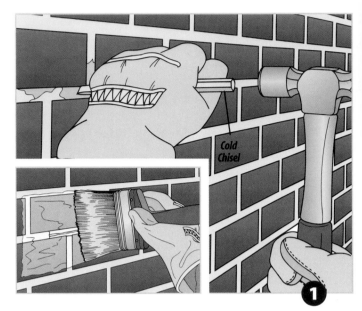

2. Repointing the joints

- Mix a small test batch of mortar and let it dry, to make sure you will get a color to match. You may need to add colorant.

- Wearing work gloves, mix a batch of mortar on a mason's hawk or a small board.

- Hold the hawk or board just below the joints to catch any mortar that is accidentally dropped. Use a pointing trowel to work mortar into the joints. Fill the joints completely, packing them as tightly as possible with mortar (left).

- Scrape off excess mortar with the trowel edge.

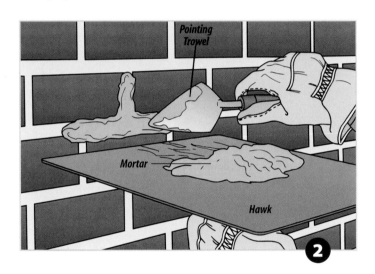

3. Striking the joints

- Wait 30 minutes or until the mortar has set just enough to hold a thumbprint.

- Using a jointer with a shape that matches the original joints, "strike" the joints: Press them to form a watertight seal. Strike the vertical joints first, then the horizontal joints. Wet the jointer with clean water and drag it smoothly, leaving a concave impression (right).

- Use a trowel edge to scrape off excess mortar.

- Using a rough cloth, wipe mortar off the brick or block faces. Allow the new mortar to cure, keeping it damp for at least 3 days: Mist the surface occasionally with a garden hose or, in hot weather, use duct tape to hang a wet cloth on the surface and moisten the cloth periodically.

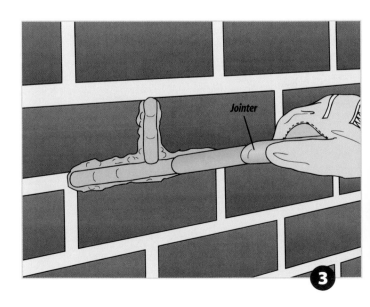

Replacing a Damaged Brick

1. Chipping out a brick

- Chip the brick out of the wall using a cold chisel and a small sledgehammer (left) or a ball-peen hammer.
- First, break the mortar around the brick, then break the brick into pieces small enough to be removed with a pry bar or the end of the chisel.
- Buy a replacement brick at a masonry supply center. If necessary, take a piece of the old brick to find a match.

2. Spreading new mortar

- Chip away any old mortar. Wet the cavity thoroughly.
- Mix a batch of mortar, and use a pointing trowel to spread a ¾-inch layer on the bottom and sides of the opening (right).
- Also "butter" the top of the brick with a ¾-inch-thick layer of mortar (inset).

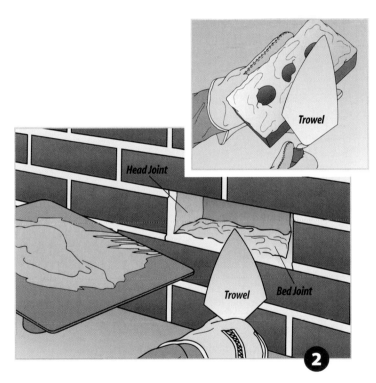

3. Inserting the brick into the cavity

- Place the brick on a mason's hawk or the back of a trowel, and slide it into the opening until the brick face is flush with the surrounding surface.
- If necessary, tap the brick in with the handle of a trowel.
- If mortar does not squeeze out from around the brick, the joint is too thin; remove the brick, add mortar, and reinsert it.
- Scrape away excess mortar with the edge of the trowel. Strike and smooth the joints (Step 3 on opposite page).

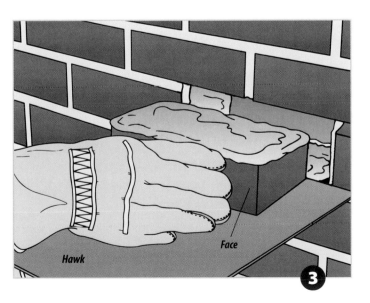

Plugging a Leaking Crack in a Masonry Wall

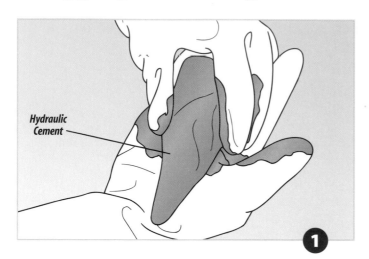

Hydraulic Cement

1

1. Making the plug

- Chisel out the crack to remove any loose material. "Key" it so that the bottom is wider than the face of the crack. Flush it with clean water.
- Buy quick-set hydraulic cement, made for patching leaks. Run a hose outside, so that water starts to leak through the crack.
- Wearing rubber gloves, mix the cement and work it into a plug with your hands (left), adding just enough water to give it the consistency of putty.

Plug

2

2. Inserting the plug

- Begin at the top of the crack and work downward, pressing the cement into the crack with your fingers (left).
- Keep pushing until the leak stops. If the cement starts to harden without stopping the leak, pry it out and try again.
- Use a trowel to smooth the patch flush with the wall.

Cleaning Weep Holes

Opening clogged weep holes

A weep hole in a wall allows condensed moisture to exit the wall. Clogged weep holes can cause water damage, especially around basement windows.

- Ream out the hole, using a power drill with a carbide-tipped masonry bit that is ¹⁄₁₆ inch narrower than the hole and long enough to reach the wall cavity behind the bricks. Usually a bit at least 4 inches long is required.
- Remember that a weep hole is designed to channel water out of the wall; it is angled and often backed by flashing. Follow the hole angle, and drill slowly to avoid damaging any flashing.

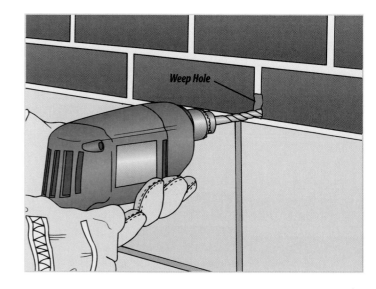

Weep Hole

Repairing a Chimney Cap

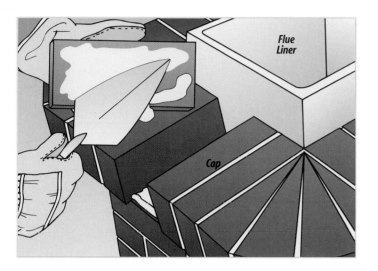

Replacing a damaged cap brick

- Prepare to work safely on the roof (pages 262–265). Chip away mortar, using a cold chisel and a small sledgehammer, and remove the brick.

- Chisel the mortar off the cavity bed and sides. Brush off particles using a stiff-fiber brush. Buy a replacement brick; if necessary, have it cut to size.

- Mix a batch of mortar. Soak the new brick and wet the cavity. Use a mason's trowel to apply a ¾-inch layer of mortar on the brick sides (left) and cavity bed. Position the brick and tap it into place with the trowel handle. Finish the joints (page 292).

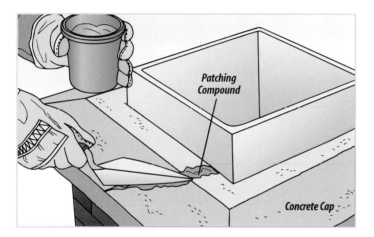

Patching a concrete cap

- Use a cold chisel and a small sledgehammer to enlarge and undercut the edges of a crack. Clean out the crack with a stiff-fiber brush.

- Mix a small amount of concrete patching compound, following the label instructions. Dampen the crack with a cloth or a paintbrush dipped in clean water, and use a pointing trowel to apply the compound (above).

- Smooth the patch surface with the trowel edge. Duct-tape a sheet of plastic over the patch so that the patch will take a week or so to cure. Do not use the fireplace until the plastic is removed. If the chimney also serves the furnace, do the work in the summer, and don't run the furnance until you've removed the plastic.

Adding a Flue Cap

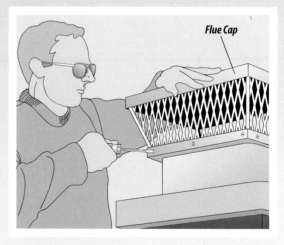

Rainwater and little critters can damage the inside of your chimney. Keep them out with a flue cap.

Prepare to work safely on the roof (pages 262–265).

Measure the flue, and buy a cap that will fit; there are only a few standard sizes.

To install, simply slide the cap over the flue, make sure it is reasonably level, and tighten the setscrews.

Insulation & Weatherproofing

Contents

INTRODUCTION

Many homeowners lose serious amounts of money because their heated or air-conditioned air is allowed to escape to the outside. Often, time and money spent insulating and weather-stripping will pay big dividends down the road. And a tight house is a more comfortable house, with evenly distributed heat and few drafts.

Evaluating Your Needs and Options

Focus your efforts where they will do the greatest good. For instance, adding a door sweep (page 309) can reduce drafts dramatically, but having a contractor blow insulation into your walls will cost thousands and may not make much of a difference in heat loss.

Start with the Obvious

Inspect your house's exterior for gaps around windows and doors, cracked or damaged siding, and any other places where outside air gets in. Renail loose trim boards, and repair the siding where needed (pages 284–295). Stuff a large gap with fiberglass insulation, then cover it up with a siding or trim board. Fill gaps that are ⅛ inch wide or narrower with caulk.

Test for Leaks

Conduct a simple test. On a day when your heat or air conditioning is running, carefully feel the air around windows and doors; you may be surprised at how much air is coming in. You may need to simply caulk the exterior trim. Before doing so, however, pry off an exterior trim board, and see if the cavity behind it is filled with insulation. If not, insulate it, renail the trim, and caulk the joint.

If your home is still drafty after these simple measures, see page 311 for more sophisticated tests and for tips on hiring a pro.

Insulating and Venting

HOW AN ATTIC IS VENTED

Attic venting is a crucial part of a home's heating and cooling systems. An poorly ventilated attic can result in problems all year 'round, even if it is insulated from the rest of the house. Summer temperatures in an unventilated attic can reach 150°F, keeping the rest of the house hot long after sundown and putting a heavy and expensive load on air conditioners. In winter, enough heat can accumulate in an attic to melt snow on the roof. The resulting water could run down the roof and freeze at the eaves, creating "ice dams" that can damage your home's structure.

A steady flow of air through the attic, let in by soffit vents and expelled through roof vents, solves both problems at once—removing hot air in summer and keeping attic air cold and dry in winter.

Venting Requirements

For every 300 square feet of roofing area, you typically need 1 square foot of vent opening—ideally, evenly divided between eave and roof vents. If the vents are heavily screened to keep out critters, the requirements can triple.

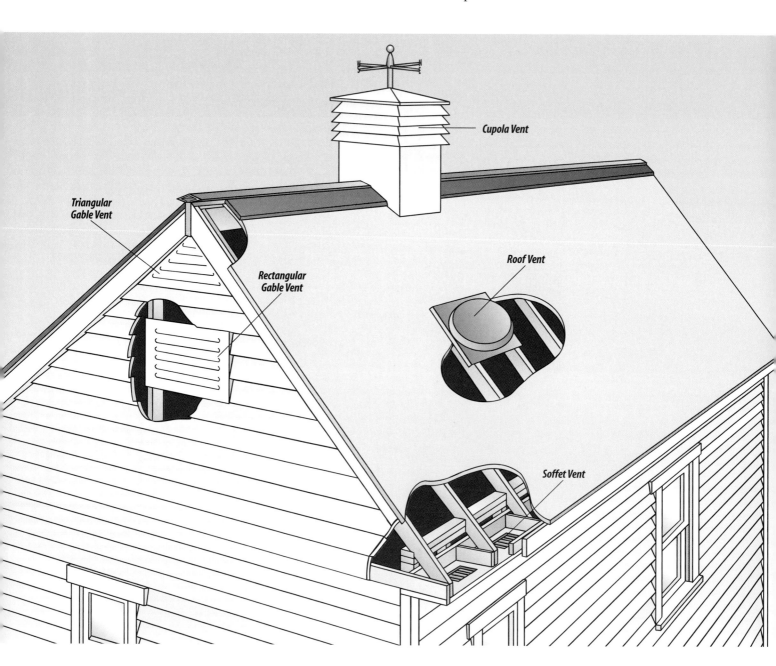

Cupola Vent

Triangular Gable Vent

Rectangular Gable Vent

Roof Vent

Soffet Vent

A Range of Vents

No one house would have all the vents shown on the opposite page, but this illustration shows typical locations of vents. Soffit vents fit into the panels, or soffits, that run along the underside of the eaves. They are available in separate units or long strips (below left), or the soffit itself may be fully vented (below right). Gable vents are installed in a gable wall near the roof peak. Roof vents are set into the roof between rafters. Cupola and ridge vents are set into the roof at its highest point.

Maintaining Good Ventilation

If your home does not have adequate venting, call in a professional to evaluate your needs and install vents.

It is important that any eave vents (soffit vents) be unobstructed. From the inside of your attic, check to see that they are not covered up with insulation. If they are, move the insulation away and perhaps wedge in boards to keep the insulation from creeping back over the vents.

BEFORE YOU START

Take a peek in your attic to see whether it is insulated. If there are floorboards, you may have to peek under them. The insulation, whether in rolls or loose, should be fluffy and nearly as thick as the joists. If not, you would probably save money over time if you were to add attic insulation (pages 300–301).

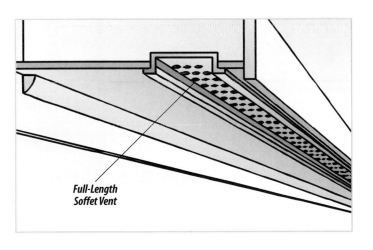

Full-Length Soffet Vent

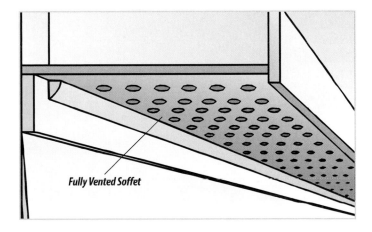

Fully Vented Soffet

Insulating an Attic "Floor"

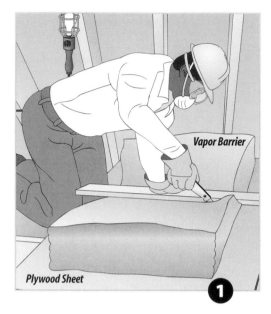

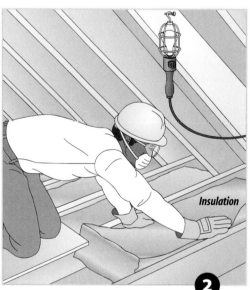

1. Cutting the batts or blankets

- Provide yourself with a large working surface so you can roll out long sections of insulation for measuring.

- Wear long-sleeved clothing, gloves, goggles, and a dust mask to protect yourself from flying fiberglass particles. Provide as much ventilation as possible.

- With the vapor barrier facing up, lay the insulation on a flat, firm surface, such as a sheet of plywood. Compress the material by holding a straight board along the cutting line, then slice through it with a utility knife (left).

2. Insulating between joists

- Start each row of insulation at one eave, pushing the batt or blanket between the joists with its vapor barrier facing down (below left). Do not jam the insulation against the eaves if you have eave vents—this will block the airflow.

- Once you reach the middle of the attic, finish the row from the opposite eave, butting the ends of the insulation tightly together.

- Cut the insulation to fit snugly around obstacles, like pipes, and slide it under wires. For any electrical fixture not marked "IC" (Insulation-Contact Rated), build a plywood box around the fixture to separate it from the insulation by at least 3 inches.

- Wrap chimneys with heavy-duty aluminum foil, fastening and sealing the foil with caulk rated for contact with chimneys.

3. Adding extra insulation

- If you want to provide a base for new flooring, cut 2×4 supports long enough to span from the attic floor to 1 inch above the new insulation. With 3-inch screws, fasten them at 2-foot intervals to one side of every other joist.

- Top the existing layer of insulation with batts or blankets without vapor barriers, laying them perpendicular to the joists (right).

Insulating an Attic's Walls and Ceiling

1. Insulating the ceiling

Insulate an attic's walls and ceiling only if you want the attic itself to stay warm or cool.

- Cut lengths of insulation to fit between the collar ties; place them vapor-barrier down, and staple the flanges along the sides of the insulation to the bottom edges of the ties at 6-inch intervals.

- In the same manner, fasten insulation to the rafters from the collar ties down to the floor (left).

- At the junction of the collar tie and rafter, seal the seam between lengths of insulation with duct tape, creating a continuous vapor barrier.

2. Insulating a knee wall

- With the vapor barrier facing the finished room, fit batts or blankets between the studs of knee walls and end walls (right). Staple the flanges of the insulation to the studs every 6 inches.

Insulating an Unheated Crawl Space or Basement

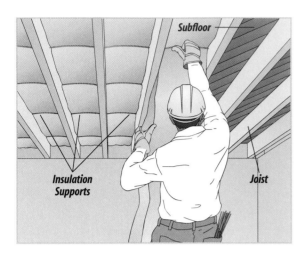

Using wire insulation supports

The point of this procedure is to keep the floor above warm, rather than to insulate the basement or crawl space.

- Push batt or blanket insulation, with the vapor barrier facing up, into the spaces between the floor joists. Make sure the pieces fit snugly, with the vapor barrier lightly touching the subfloor.

- Every 16 inches, slide an insulation support (a thin rod) in place between joists, flexing it toward the insulation and exerting slight pressure (left).

Wraps for Ducts

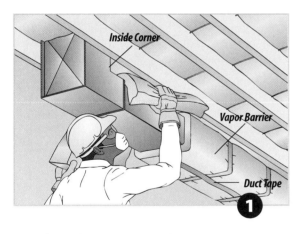

1. Covering the sides of a duct

- Wrap an insulation blanket around the duct, then mark and cut the blanket to length. Use this piece as a template to cut the other sections.

- Install the pieces of insulation, vapor barrier facing out, and seal the seams along the bottom and between the sections with professional-grade duct tape.

- Once you've covered most of the horizontal section, cut and apply a narrow strip of insulation to the inside corner where the duct rises to the floor above.

2. Trimming the end pieces

- Cut a last section to cover the bottom and sides of the rest of the duct and extend beyond the end by one-half the duct width.

- Tape the section to the duct, then make a T-shaped cut in the bottom, creating two flaps.

- Cut off the portion of the flaps that extend below the bottom of the duct (right).

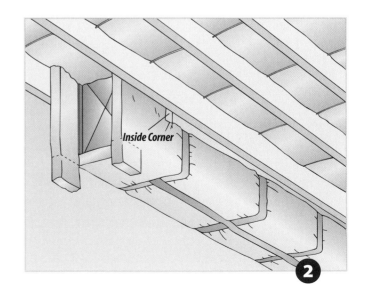

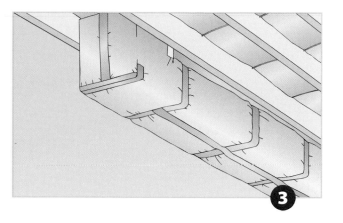

3. Sealing the end of the duct

- Fold the flaps of insulation over the end of the duct, trimming them or adding new material so that the ends butt together.

- Tape the flaps together securely (left).

- If the insulation hangs below head level, protect it from damage by covering it with 15-pound building paper stapled to the joists on either side.

Insulating a Recessed Duct

Stapling insulation to the joists

- To insulate a duct nestled between joists, cut blanket sections long enough to wrap around the bottom of the duct and to cover the edges of the joists.

- Push about 1 inch of insulation back from the ends of each section, leaving the vapor barrier intact.

- Wrap the insulation around the duct with the vapor barrier facing out, and staple the ends to the joists (right).

- Extend the last section of insulation beyond the end of the duct by the thickness of the insulation. Fit a piece of insulation over the end of the duct, and seal all the seams with duct tape.

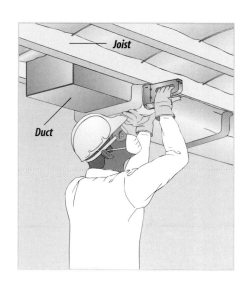

Installing Protective Pipe Sleeves

Attaching foam-rubber insulators

- Prepare the pipes by cleaning them, scraping off any rust with a wire brush.

- Cut to length pieces of foam-rubber pipe insulation that fit the diameter of the pipe.

- Open the slit in each tube, and slip the insulation over the pipe (right).

- At joints, cut a V-shaped wedge at the end of one piece and matching notches in the other two pieces, resulting in a Y-shaped intersection of the three pieces of insulation.

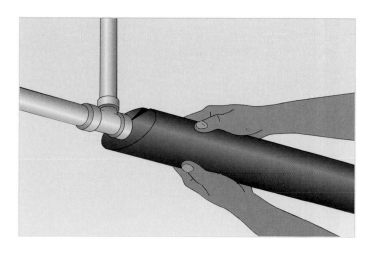

Weatherproofing

HOW THEY WORK

Choosing the Right Caulk and Weatherstripping

Carefully match weatherstripping to its job. The illustrations (below and right) show some of the more common products, all available at hardware stores and home centers.

All contacting surfaces of windows and doors are candidates for weatherstripping. However, if a window is in good shape, it may seal tightly enough not to need weatherstripping.

One way to find out where you need weatherstripping: On a windy day, hold a lighted match near a window and then near a door; the flame will waver and perhaps go out wherever outside air is infiltrating your house.

Self-adhesive foam strip and plastic V-strip are, in a sense, easy to install: Just peel off the paper backing and stick it on. But if the piece needs to be placed precisely, things get pretty tricky, because once stuck, they cannot be adjusted without compromising the adhesive.

Rigid jamb weatherstripping and door sweeps take a little more time to install but are the most user-friendly, because you can easily adjust their position both as you install them and after they are in place.

Applying Caulk

Choose caulk that will both stick and last. Latex-only caulk adheres well but wears out quickly; silicone caulk lasts forever but often comes loose from surfaces that were not perfectly clean and dry when it was applied. Silicone-fortified latex caulk is usually the best choice for both inside and outside.

Wherever you have a joint that does not open or slide, use caulk to seal it. Spend a couple of hours with a caulk gun, hunting for gaps on the outside of your house—where the siding meets window or door trim, around a hose spigot, and at the bottom of the siding, for example. Then move inside; see pages 306–307 for directions.

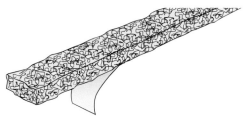

OPEN-CELL FOAM STRIP

Application: *A compressible seal for the closing side of a doorstop, the bottom rail of double-hung windows, and other places with fairly even gaps.*

Installation: *Self-adhesive; you may need to add staples for better adhesion.*

Durability: *Wears out quickly and deforms easily. Check and replace regularly.*

TUBULAR GASKET

Application: *A compressible seal for irregular gaps along door- and window stops, and on the bottom rail of double-hung windows.*

Installation: *Sometimes self-adhesive, but usually requires nails or staples. Ugly because it is bulky, but less noticeable if installed on the exterior side.*

Durability: *Long-lasting as long as it is not pulled off. May wear out quickly on sliding surfaces.*

V-STRIP

Application: *A seal for sliding as well as closing doors and windows.*

Installation: *Metal V-strip is nailed in place. Plastic V-strip is self-adhesive.*

Durability: *Long-lasting, but the plastic version may pull off and need to be replaced (it cannot be stapled).*

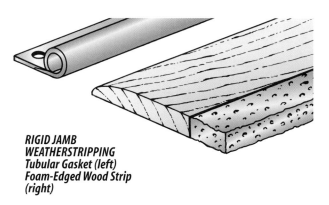

RIGID JAMB WEATHERSTRIPPING
Tubular Gasket (left)
Foam-Edged Wood Strip (right)

Application: *A compressible seal for hinged doors and windows.*

Installation: *Screwed or nailed into a door or window jamb.*

Durability: *Long-lasting.*

Choose and install weatherstripping carefully. Remove all traces of old caulk or weatherstripping with a utility knife or paint scraper. Remove old adhesive with rubbing alcohol or mineral spirits. Sand all surfaces smooth.

Where possible, hold the weatherstripping piece in place and mark it for cutting, rather than measuring with a tape measure. Cut metal pieces with a hacksaw or tin snips; use a miter box for wood pieces.

COMPLETE THRESHOLD

Application: *A sliding seal for the bottom of an exterior door when replacing a threshold.*

Installation: *Screwed to the doorsill through the metal plate. Door needs to be trimmed to fit fairly precisely.*

Durability: *Long-lasting. Has a replaceable rubber insert.*

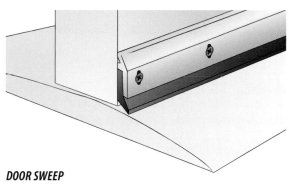

DOOR SWEEP

Application: *A sliding seal for gaps at the bottom of an exterior door.*

Installation: *Screwed to door bottom inside. Easy to adjust and does not require door to be trimmed precisely.*

Durability: *Moderately long-lasting, depending on how much rubbing it must do. Easily replaced.*

Caulking Minor Gaps

1. Preparing the caulk

- Cut off the tip of a tube of silicone or water-based acrylic caulk with a utility knife (left) so its opening is slightly smaller than the width of the crack. Some people prefer to cut the tip at a steep angle, while others like working with a tip that is cut nearly straight.

- If the caulk tube is not all plastic, you may have to break a foil seal at the base of the tip by inserting a long nail or a piece of stiff wire.

Foam Spray for Large Gaps

Use foam to fill gaps wider than ¼ inch, as long as you do not care about the finished appearance of the joint. If you feel a lot of air coming in from around a piece of molding, there may be a large gap behind the molding. Pull the piece off, and fill it with foam.

Some types of foam spray expand more than others after they have been sprayed. Experiment on scrap pieces before you start applying the spray.

Open the window for ventilation, and put on rubber gloves and safety goggles. Attach the applicator tube to the nozzle of the can, shake it, and turn it to a 45-degree angle.

Insert the tip into the gap (right) and press the nozzle. Fill no more than half the depth of the gap; the foam will expand to fill it. Release the trigger 5 inches before the end of the gap, but continue to move the applicator to the end.

Foam

2. Applying caulk around trim

- Although caulking behind the trim is the best way to stop air leakage, caulking around it saves you from removing the trim.

- Clean the outer edge of the trim with mild soap solution, rinse, and dry.

- For a more finished-looking bead of caulk, stick masking tape in straight lines to one or both sides of the future caulk bead.

- With a caulking gun, lay a continuous bead between the trim and the wall (left).

- You may simply apply a bead of caulk and then leave it alone, or smooth it out (Step 3).

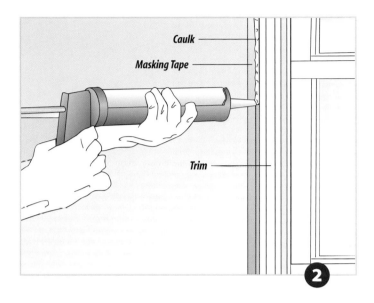

3. Smoothing the caulk (optional)

- Let the caulk dry until it is no longer tacky but has not yet formed a skin.

- Then, wearing rubber gloves, gently slide an ice cube over the center of the bead of caulk (right) to make a smooth, slightly concave surface.

- Alternatively, smooth the caulk using a bare or gloved finger moistened with a soap-and-water solution (or mineral spirits if you are using nonlatex silicone caulk) (inset).

- If you applied masking tape, pull it off. Cut away excess caulk with a sharp utility knife.

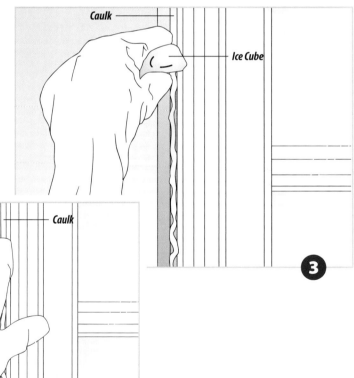

Weatherstripping Wood Windows and Doors

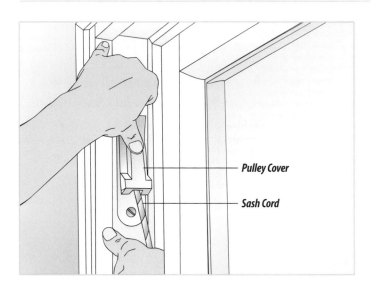

Pulley Cover

Sash Cord

Weatherstripping around pulley covers

Seal air leaks around a pulley with a self-adhesive pulley cover.

- Clean around the pulley with alcohol, then apply the self-adhesive gasket to the back of the pulley cover, leaving the backing paper undisturbed.

- Position the cover over the pulley, and snap the sash cord into the opening in the bottom of the cover (left).

- Outline the cover with a pencil. Then peel off the backing and press the cover against the sash channel.

Adding a foam strip to the bottom of a sash

- Remove loose paint and old weatherstripping or caulk from both the bottom of the sash and the bottom of the window frame with a paint scraper.

- Wash the surface with a soap-and-water solution. Rinse and dry it, then wipe it with a cloth dampened with alcohol.

- To install the foam strip, start at one end and slowly peel off the paper backing as you press the strip in place (right).

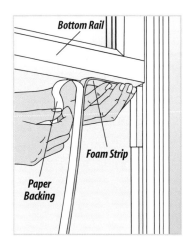

Bottom Rail

Foam Strip

Paper Backing

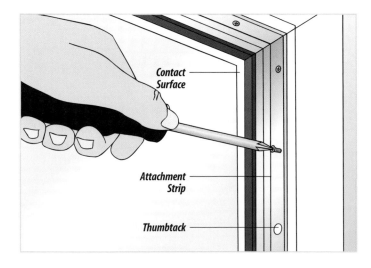

Contact Surface

Attachment Strip

Thumbtack

Installing rigid jamb weatherstripping

- With a hacksaw or tin snips, cut a strip to match the height of the door jamb.

- Close the door, and position the piece so it is fairly tight against the door—so it will seal but not make closing the door difficult.

- Holding it in place, drive the nails or screws that came with the weatherstripping into the centers of the holes so you will be able to adjust it outward or inward.

- Do the same for the other side of the jamb, and then the top.

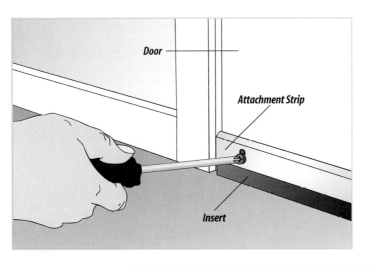

Adding a door sweep

To block a gap between the door and the threshold, install a door sweep with a replaceable rubber insert. Cut it to size with a hacksaw or tin snips.

- Close the door and place the door sweep against the interior bottom edge of the door. Be sure that the flexible insert covers the gap entirely but does not fit so tightly that it will make the door difficult to close.

- Drill pilot holes, and then fasten the sweep with screws (left).

Installing V-strips

Here we show how to install metal V-strips. To install a plastic V-strip, just remove the paper backing and stick it in place.

- Prepare the surface as for foam weatherstripping (opposite page).

- To place a V-strip in a sash channel (right), cut the piece 2 inches longer than the opening. Raise the lower sash, position the strips in the lower sash channel, and snake the strips up between the raised sash and the jamb. Then nail it into place.

- To put a V-strip on the bottom rail of a sash, cut it to length and position it, with the V opening downward, and nail it in place (inset).

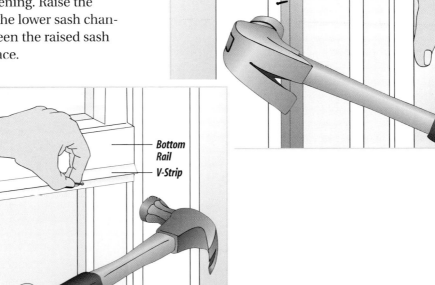

Resealing Metal Windows and Doors

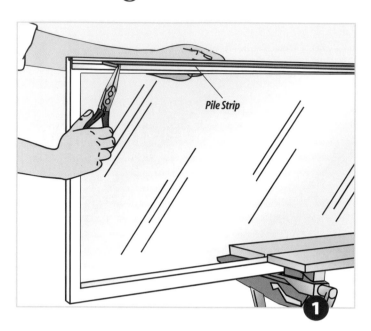

1. Removing a factory-installed pile strip

Most metal windows come with factory-installed pile strips.

- To replace a matted or worn strip, start by removing the sash from its tracks.

- Check both ends of the pile strip for two tiny metal tabs that may be securing it. Bend them up gently with a screwdriver.

- With long-nose pliers, grasp the strip and pull it out of its channel (left).

- Take the strip to a window repair specialist for an exact replacement.

2. Replacing the pile strip

- Clean the pile strip channel with an old toothbrush.

- Cut the new strip with scissors to the length of the channel.

- Feed a thick pile strip back into its channel from one end (right). To install a thin pile strip, place it over the channel, and snap the strip into the channel with the concave end of a splining tool.

- Bend the metal tabs back over the ends of the strip, and replace the sash in its track in the frame.

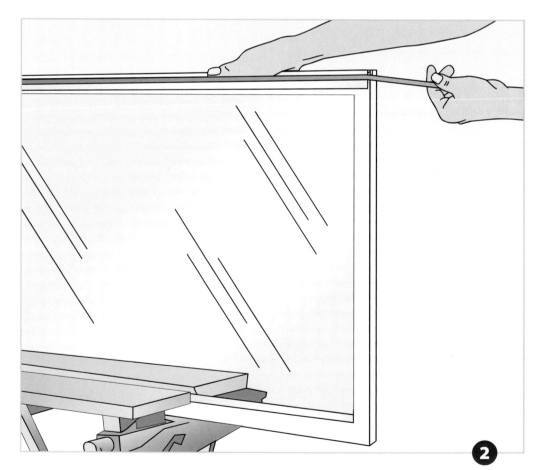

Measuring for Drafts and Insulation with a Thermometer

Air drafts are usually too subtle to be felt. On a cold day with your heat cranked up, or on a hot day with the air conditioning running, use a thermometer to test for drafts and insufficient insulation.

To test for drafts, measure the temperature in different parts of a room, placing the thermometer at the same height for each location. If you find differences of more than a few degrees, you have drafts than need to be corrected. Usually, the source of the draft will be evident—for instance, if you get a variant reading near a window.

To test your insulation, first place a thermometer on the floor, then on the ceiling directly above. If the air near the ceiling is more than 10 degrees warmer than the air near the floor, the room is poorly insulated.

Checking Your Insulation

Look at your roof at various times during the winter. If snow melts there sooner than on other homes with similar slopes, then you are losing more heat through your roof than they are, and you could use some attic insulation.

If you have an unheated crawl space, its walls do not need to be insulated, but the floor above it should be. A heated basement will lose heat if its walls are not insulated.

It's harder to tell whether your walls are insulated. If a wall feels very cold or very hot, it is probably under-insulated or not insulated at all. If the wall feels colder or hotter as you move up along the wall, you may have loose insulation that has settled over the years; blowing in some more will save in heating costs, though it may cost too much to actually save you money. In some homes, only some of the walls are insulated, while others are unprotected. Shut off power to an electrical outlet on an exterior wall (page 88), and remove the cover plate. With a flashlight, peer into the side of the electrical box and check for insulation.

Getting Professional Opinions

A professional insulation contractor can do a more scientific study and will be aware of problems typical in your area. Call one in for an evaluation, and be prepared to pay for it so that you don't feel obligated to hire him or her to do work afterwards.

A pro should be able to tell you which needs are greatest, and can estimate the "payback" for various installations. For example, adding attic insulation may pay for itself within a few years, while replacing a furnace with a more efficient model may take more than 15 years to pay back.

Professionals can blow loose insulation into walls, a job that is very difficult for a do-it-yourselfer. They may leave behind holes that need to be plugged. Insulating an attic requires no special skills or equipment, but it is difficult work, and the fiberglass may irritate your skin and eyes.

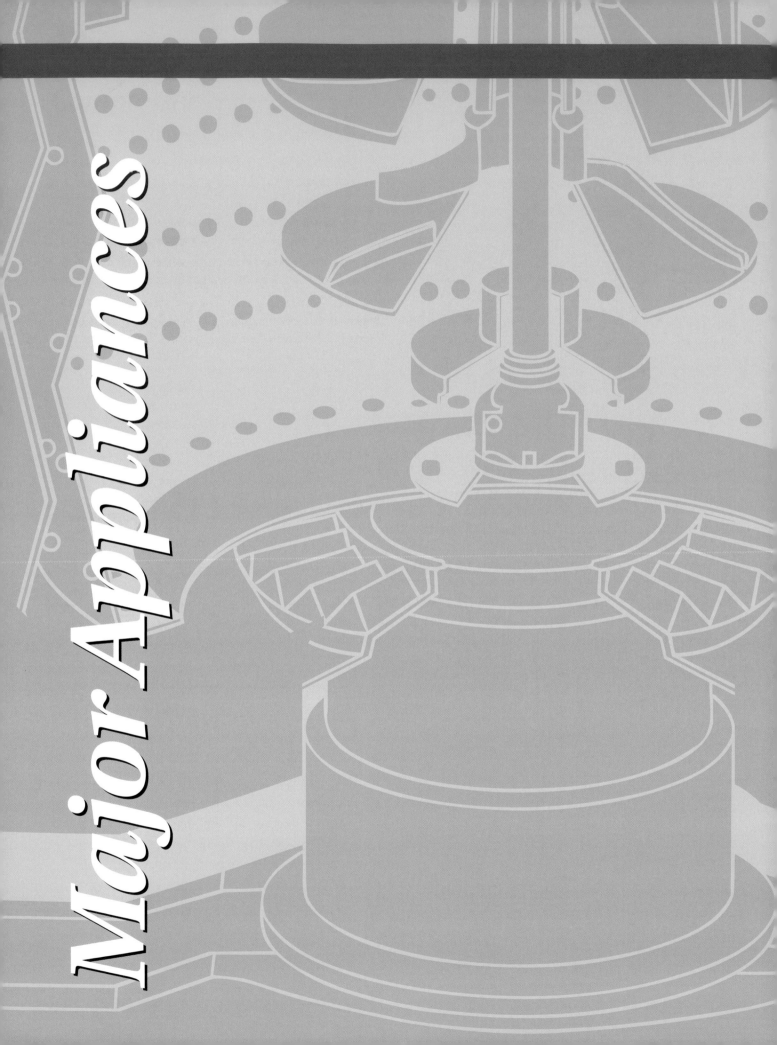

Major Appliances

Contents

INTRODUCTION

Not many homeowners attempt to repair a refrigerator or other large appliance, and not because of laziness. Often parts are so expensive that it makes more sense to buy a new machine than to make a repair. And with so many brands out there, you need special manuals and lots of experience for many repairs. But many other repairs cost little, require no special skills, and can extend the life of an appliance for years. This chapter concentrates on those repairs.

Regular Maintenance

Thorough cleaning can have a surprising impact on an appliance's efficiency and longevity. Many parts that lie just out of sight—filters, drains, coils, and mechanisms—work a lot better and last longer when they are not covered with scum or dust. The manual that came with an appliance should discuss these cleaning operations.

Test, Then Get Advice

Because there are so many models and makes in circulation, we sometimes give directions only for testing, and not for replacing, a part.

Once you have performed a test and determined that a part needs to be replaced, find out how much the part will cost. Find a reliable salesperson at an appliance parts source and seek out advice. Is the machine worth the money for the part and the trouble to install it?

If you decide to make a repair, get all the information you'll need. Some parts have helpful and complete instructions on the packaging; some do not. If one salesperson is not helpful, talk to another, or go to another store.

Refrigerators

HOW THEY WORK

The illustration below shows a typical two-door, frost-free refrigerator with floor-level condenser coils.

Refrigerators work by means of a sealed cooling system. A compressor pumps liquid refrigerant under high pressure through a narrow capillary tube into the evaporator coils. There, liquid quickly expands into a gas,

absorbing heat from inside the refrigerator to cool it. Next, pressure from the compressor forces the gas into the condenser coils, which dissipate the heat to the air outside the refrigerator. Now a liquid, the refrigerant passes again into the evaporator coils, as the cycle of heating and cooling continues.

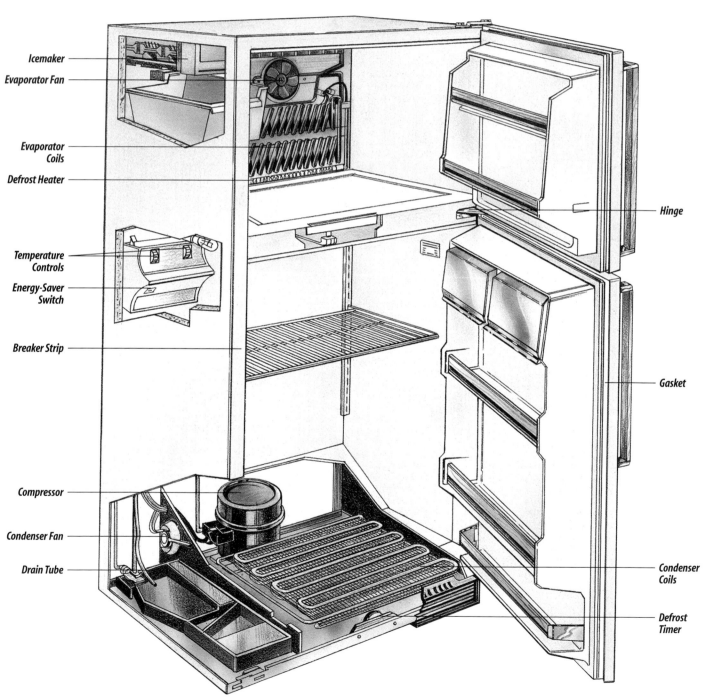

Icemaker

Evaporator Fan

Evaporator Coils

Defrost Heater

Temperature Controls

Energy-Saver Switch

Breaker Strip

Compressor

Condenser Fan

Drain Tube

Hinge

Gasket

Condenser Coils

Defrost Timer

BEFORE YOU START

A refrigerator that is properly maintained should last at least 15 years.

Keep the Machine Clean

Clean the interior and exterior regularly, paying special attention to the coils and the drain tubes. If the coils are clean, the refrigerator will work more efficiently. Immediately clean up any spills inside the refrigerator, because these can lead to clogged drain tubes, odor, and ice buildup.

Refrigerators and freezers are most efficient when they are about three-quarters full. If needed, fill plastic soda bottles or milk jugs with water and place them in the refrigerator to compensate for excess empty space.

Solving Problems

With common tools, you can diagnose and repair poorly sealed doors and gaskets, the door switch, the evaporator fan, the defrosting system, and the controls. Repairs to the cooling system require special skills and equipment and must be handled by a professional.

Never attempt to work on a refrigerator that is plugged in.

Refrigerators and very heavy. Never tilt a refrigerator without a helper or two.

When to Buy a New Refrigerator

A new refrigerator may be much more energy-efficient than your old one, so that you can actually save money by buying a refrigerator that is more pleasant to use. Check efficiency labels on a new model, and ask a salesperson to help you figure how much it can lower your electric bill.

A new refrigerator of the same outside dimensions may also give you 1 or 2 additional cubic feet of storage space, since newer insulation is thinner.

Troubleshooting

If your refrigerator doesn't run and the light doesn't work

- Check that the refrigerator is plugged in and that the plug or cord is not damaged
- Check the circuit breaker that controls the refrigerator outlet **88–89**

If your refrigerator doesn't run but the light works

- Clean the condenser coils **317**
- Check the temperature **322**
- Test the temperature control ... **322–323**
- Test the evaporator fan **324–325**
- Service the compressor **328–329**
- Test the defrost timer **326**
- Test the compressor relay **328**
- Test the overload protector **329**
- Service the condenser fan and motor **326–327**

If your refrigerator starts and stops rapidly

- Clean the condenser coils **317**
- Service the compressor **328**
- Test the compressor relay **328**
- Test the overload protector **329**
- Service the condenser fan and motor **326–327**

If your refrigerator runs constantly

- Defrost the refrigerator
- Clean the condenser coils **317**
- Check the door seal **318**
- Replace the door gasket **319**
- Service the condenser fan and motor **326–327**

If your refrigerator is not cold enough

- Check the temperature **322**
- Test the temperature control ... **322–323**
- Clean the condenser coils **317**
- Check the door seal **318**
- Replace the door gasket **319**
- Test the door switch **321**
- Test the evaporator fan **324–325**
- Test the defrost heater and timer **325–326**
- Call for service if you suspect a refrigerant leak

If your refrigerator does not defrost automatically

- Clean the drain tube

Ice buildup in the drain pan or water in the bottom of the refrigerator

- Service the defrost heater or timer **325–326**

If the interior light does not work

- Replace the bulb and test the switch **321**

If your refrigerator runs noisily

- Adjust the leveling feet to level the refrigerator
- Reposition the drain pan
- Check the evaporator fan **324–325**
- Replace the compressor mountings **327**

Condenser Coils

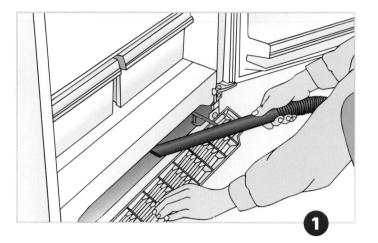

1. Floor-level coils

An accumulation of dirt and dust prevents condenser coils from dissipating heat, making the refrigerator cool poorly, run constantly, or even stop completely if the compressor overheats. Clean floor-level coils twice a year—more often if you have pets.

- To clean the coils, unplug the refrigerator and remove the grille cover. Use a vacuum cleaner with a wand attachment to suck out dust and pet hair (left).

2. Rear-mounted coils

- Clean rear-mounted coils yearly.

- Unplug the refrigerator and move it away from the wall to access the coils. Vacuum the coils, or clean them with a stiff brush (left).

- If they are especially dirty or greasy, wash the coils with warm, soapy water and a stiff brush. Take care not to drip water on other parts of the refrigerator.

Maintenance Tips

Never hammer at ice buildup or attempt to pry it away with a sharp tool. You'll risk puncturing the evaporator coils. Instead, melt ice with a hair dryer, or place pans of hot water in each compartment. Have rags on hand to soak up the overflow from the drain pan.

If there's a power outage, food will keep in a closed refrigerator for 24 to 36 hours. Keep the door closed as much as possible. If food must be removed, put it in a bathtub covered with newspaper and ice or a cooler.

If the refrigerator isn't running and the light is out, first check the power cord. It can be damaged if the refrigerator's weight is shifted onto it.

A refrigerator should sit level from side to side and front to back for a tight door seal. Use a carpenter's level to evaluate, and adjust the refrigerator's feet if necessary.

Door Seal

Examining the gasket

Open the door and place a dollar bill against the breaker strip (left). Close the door. Slowly pull the bill out. If the gasket seals properly, you will feel tension as you pull. Repeat this test all around the door.

Feel the gasket for brittleness, and inspect it carefully for gaps or cracks. Replace a defective gasket.

Sagging doors

1. The upper and lower hinges

Any of three hinges can be adjusted to fix a sagging upper or lower door.

- To adjust the upper hinge on a top-mounted freezer door, pry off the hinge bolt cover, if present. Loosen the bolt with a wrench or a nut driver (inset). Realign the door, and tighten the bolt.

- To slightly adjust the refrigerator door, loosen the bolt on the lower hinge with a wrench (right). Lift or push the refrigerator door square with the refrigerator cabinet, and retighten the bolt.

- If the adjustment doesn't hold, check to see whether the hinge cam is worn. Replace it if needed.

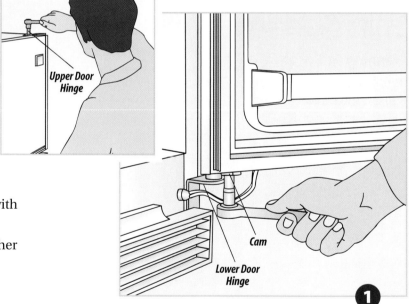

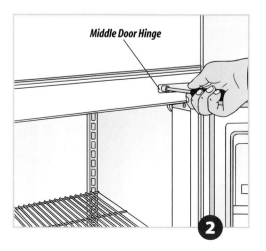

2. The middle hinge

- Access the middle hinge between the door and the face of the refrigerator cabinet.

- To adjust it, loosen the bolts with a wrench or nut driver. Shift the hinge in or out to realign. Tighten the bolts (left).

- If the door still doesn't seal properly, realign the door panels to correct warping (opposite page).

Warped Doors

Aligning door panels

A warped or misaligned door panel will result in a poor seal.

- Open the door. Locate the retaining strip that holds the gasket in place. Loosen, but do not remove, the screws along all four sides of the panel (right).

- Grasp the outer door panel at the top and side, and twist it opposite to the warp.

- Hold the door in this position and have a helper partially retighten the screws. Close the door and check to see whether the warp has been corrected. If the door seals properly, have your helper tighten the screws while you hold it in place.

- Avoid placing heavy items on the door shelves. If the warping continues, replace the door.

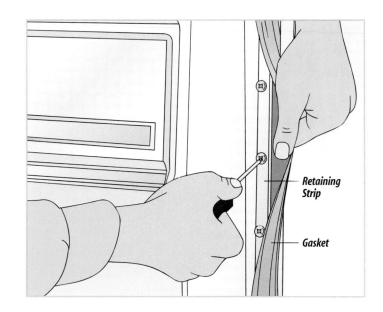

Retaining Strip

Gasket

Door Gaskets

1. Removing the old gasket

- Pull back the gasket to expose the retaining strip, and loosen the screws that hold it in place (above, right). If it is merely clamped to the door by the retaining strip, pull the gasket free (near right).

- If the screws pass through the gasket, remove the screws and gasket along the top, and one-third of the way down both sides of the door (far right).

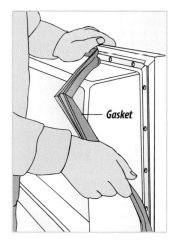

Gasket

Retaining Strip

1

2. Attaching a new gasket

- Have a helper hold the door steady to prevent warping.

- Starting at an upper corner, insert the gasket flange behind the retaining strip. If screws pass through the gasket, fasten the gasket to the top of the door and along the top-third of the sides (left). Then attach the middle third, followed by the lowest third and the bottom of the door.

- Partially tighten the screws as you go. Once the gasket is in place, tighten all of the screws securely, starting in the lower corners and working in and up.

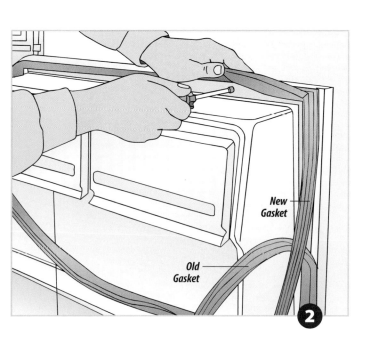

New Gasket

Old Gasket

2

Breaker Strips

Breaker Strip

Hot Towel

1. Softening a breaker strip

A damaged breaker strip allows moisture to enter the insulation between the inner and outer walls of the refrigerator. Inspect the breaker strips around the inner frame for any warps, cracks, or splits. To replace a damaged strip, first unplug the refrigerator.

• The breaker strip is brittle when cold. To prevent snapping it during removal, soften the strip by pressing a hot, wet towel along its entire length (left).

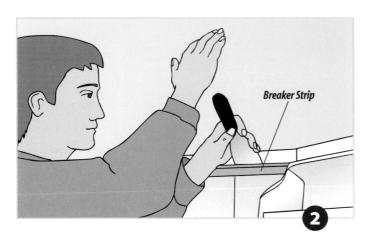

Breaker Strip

2. Releasing the strip

• Using a putty knife, pry the breaker strip away from the cabinet (left). Be careful not to damage the foam insulation behind the breaker strip.

• If the insulation is wet or ice-clogged, or if it has an unpleasant odor, leave it uncovered for a few hours to dry, or dry it with a hair dryer set on LOW.

• Snap an identical replacement in place.

Removing Other Types of Breaker Strips

Breaker strips are installed differently from model to model. Some are attached with sealant: Cut through sealant with a utility knife. Replace the strip and reseal the corners with a sealant that's rated safe for use with food appliances.

The most difficult breakers to remove run the full length of the appliance, from the bottom of the refrigerator to the top of the freezer, and are held in place by the center console: Remove the screws that hold the console in place. Gently pull the console forward (right) and rest it in the freezer without disconnecting the wires. Replace the breaker strip and reinstall the center console.

Door Switch

1. Removing the door switch

In most refrigerators, a single switch controls the interior light. If the light doesn't work, first replace the bulb. If the new bulb doesn't glow, remove and test the switch. If you think the light is on when the door is closed, press the switch by hand. If the light stays on, remove and test the switch.

• Unplug the refrigerator and pry out the switch with a putty knife (right). Pad the knife with masking tape to avoid scratching the breaker strip.

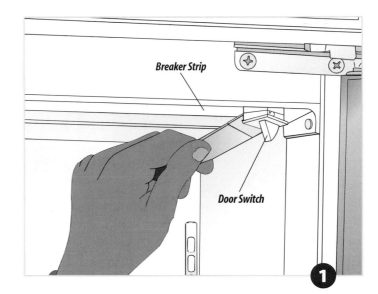

Breaker Strip

Door Switch

2. Disconnecting the switch

• Pull the switch out far enough to expose an inch or two of the wiring. The switch will have either two or four terminals; if it has four terminals, it is a combination fan and light switch.

• Remove the push-on connectors (right), and label the wires for reassembly.

• Replace the connectors if the existing ones are burned or corroded.

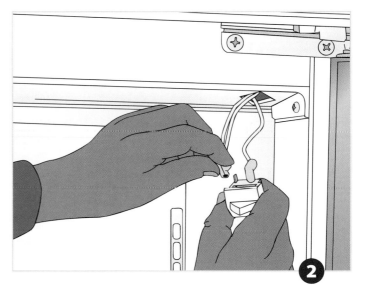

3. Testing the switch

• Set a multitester to RX1 (page 96).

• If the switch has two terminals, clip the probe to one terminal and touch the second probe to the other terminal (right). If the meter indicates continuity with the switch button out, and an open circuit with the button in, the switch is good.

• If the switch fails any test, replace it.

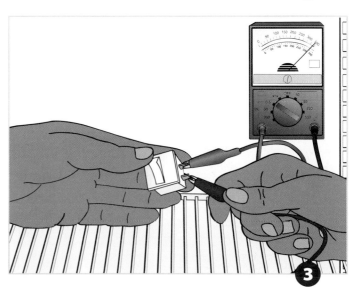

Temperature Controls

1. Checking temperatures

The ideal temperature for a refrigerator is between 38° and 40°F. For the freezer compartment the ideal temperature is between 0° and 8°F.

- To test, place a cup of water in the refrigerator and leave it for 2 hours (left); leave a cup of cooking oil in the freezer. Place a cooking thermometer in each liquid and wait 3 minutes.

- Adjust the temperature controls as needed. If a problem persists, test the temperature control.

2. Removing the control console

- Unplug the refrigerator. Unscrew and remove the console that houses the temperature control and the energy-saver switch (right).

- Let the console hang by its wiring; the freezer vent control will remain attached to the refrigerator wall.

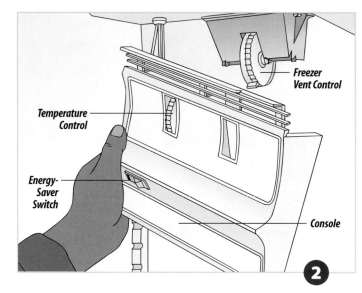

3. Checking the freezer control

- Unscrew the freezer vent control from the refrigerator wall.

- Use a hair dryer set on low to melt any ice from the freezer vent control. Remove any food residue.

- Reach up into the freezer channel, where the freezer control fits, and check for obstructions. Reinstall the freezer vent control.

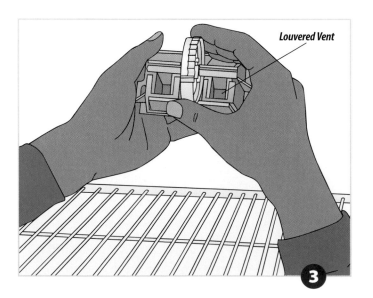

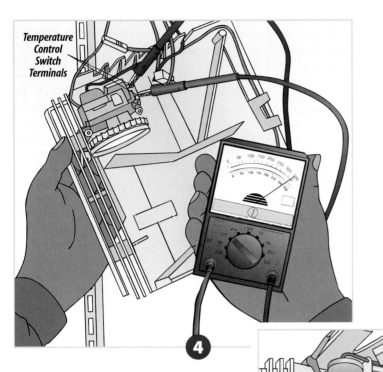

Temperature Control Switch Terminals

4. Testing the energy-saver switch and temperature control

- Remove the push-on connector and the ground wires from the temperature control terminals (left).

- Set a multitester to test for continuity (page 96). With the temperature control turned to its coldest setting, the tester should read 0 ohms. With the control turned off, it should read infinity.

- If the control does not pass this test, replace it (Step 5).

- Remove the push-on connector on the energy-saver switch (if there is one) and test the switch for continuity (inset). Place a probe on each terminal; the tester should show continuity when the switch is on.

- If the test indicates that the switch is faulty, pull it off the console, snap on an exact replacement, and reattach the push-on connector.

Energy-Saver Switch

5. Replacing the temperature control

- Note the position of the temperature control's capillary line in the console. The new one must be installed the same way.

- Pull out the old control and snap in an exact replacement, threading the capillary line into place in the console (right).

- Remount the console on the refrigerator wall; recheck the temperature (opposite page).

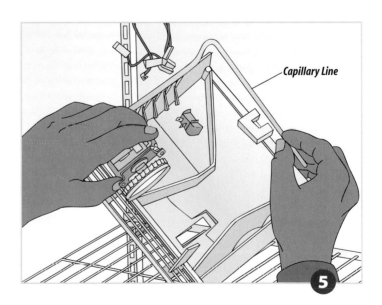

Capillary Line

Evaporator Fan

1. Accessing the evaporator cover

The evaporator coils are part of the sealed refrigeration system and should be serviced by professionals only. But the evaporator fan and the defrost heater—usually located in the rear wall of a top-mounted freezer, behind the evaporator cover—are easy to test and replace.

- Unplug the refrigerator. Remove any obstructions that prevent access to the rear wall of the freezer, including shelves and icemaker, if present.

- Remove the screws from the vent plate, as well as any brackets that may secure the back wall of the freezer.

- Pull off the back wall of the freezer compartment to expose the evaporator coils, the evaporator fan, and the defrost heater (right).

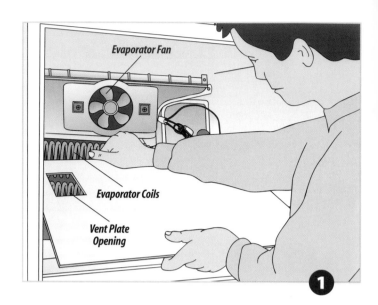

2. Freeing the fan assembly

- Remove any screws that attach the evaporator fan housing.

- Lift the fan assembly a few inches and disconnect the wires (left). Use long-nose pliers if you cannot pull the connectors off with your fingers.

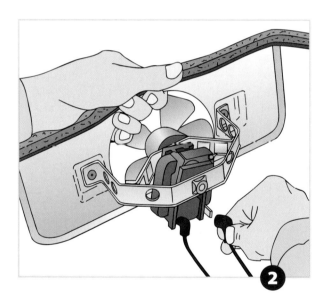

3. Checking the fan blade

- If the blade is bent, cracked, or badly scratched, pull off the retainer at the center, pull the blade off the motor shaft, and slide on a new blade. Be sure to orient the angle of the blade fins in the same direction as the old blade. Replace the retainer.

- Hold the fan horizontally in one hand, then spin the blade to check for binding in the motor (right).

- Replace the motor if the blade does not spin freely (Step 4).

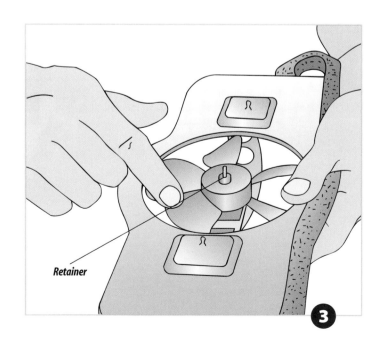

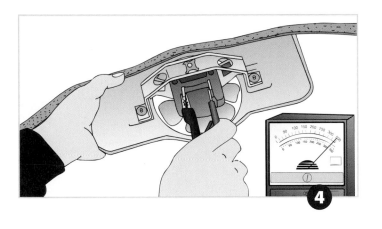

4. Testing the motor

- Set a multitester to RX1 (page 96). Touch a probe to each motor terminal (left). The meter should show continuity; if not, replace the motor.

- To remove the motor, first remove the fan blade. Unscrew the smaller bracket at the front of the motor, and remove the motor from the housing.

- Install the new motor and replace the bracket and fan blade. Take care not to reverse the blade.

Defrost Heater

Testing a defrost heater

The defrost heater element may be enclosed in a glass tube hidden beneath a metal shield mounted under the evaporator coils (right). Or, it may be wrapped in aluminum foil (below right), or it may be an exposed metal rod (below left). Test all elements the same way.

- Unplug the refrigerator. Remove the evaporator cover (opposite page).

- Pull the wire connectors from the terminals at each end of the defrost heater.

- Set a multitester to RX1 and attach a probe to each defrost heater terminal to test for continuity (page 96).

- If the test indicates that the circuit is open—infinite resistance—replace the defrost heater.

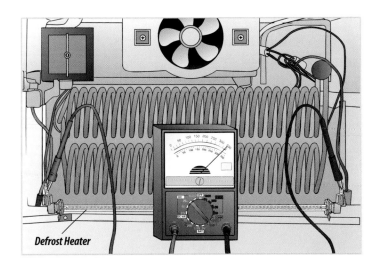

Defrost Heater

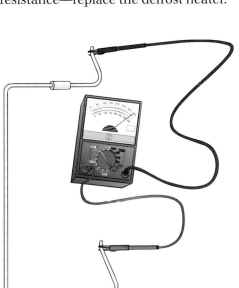

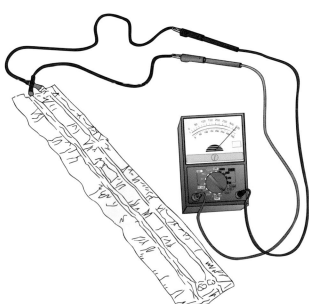

Defrost Timer

1. Removing the defrost timer

The defrost timer is usually located behind the front grille of the refrigerator. But it may also be located in the compressor compartment in the back of the refrigerator, or behind a cover plate inside the refrigerator.

- Unplug the refrigerator and remove the front grille (right). Unscrew the timer from its mounting plate and slide it out.

- Gently wiggle the defrost timer out of the plug connecting it to the refrigerator (inset). The plug is polarized so that you cannot reconnect the defrost timer incorrectly.

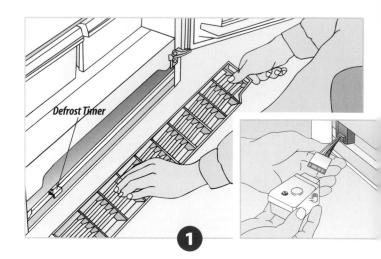

2. Testing the timer

- The common terminal of the timer is usually connected to the white wire of the harness plug; if the terminals are numbered, it is number 3.

- Set the multitester to RX1 (page 96). Attach one probe to the common terminal and touch the other probe to each of the three other terminals (right). Two of these terminal pairs should have full continuity, while the third should have no continuity.

- Turn the defrost timer switch clockwise until you hear a click (inset). Test the timer again. Two of the terminal pairs should show continuity, while one— not the same pair as before—should not.

- Replace the timer if it fails either test.

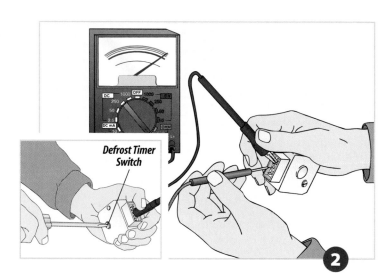

Condenser Fan

1. Inspecting the condenser fan

- Unplug the refrigerator and pull it away from the wall. Remove the access panel, if any.

- Clean the fan blade and turn it to see whether the blade rotates freely (right).

- To replace a damaged blade, unscrew the nut that holds it to the motor, then pull it off. Install a new fan blade, replacing any washers, and tighten the nut.

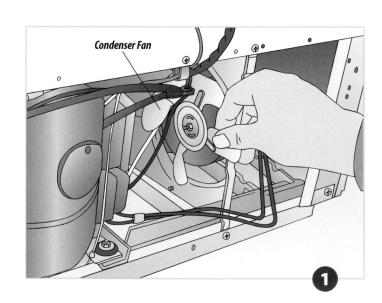

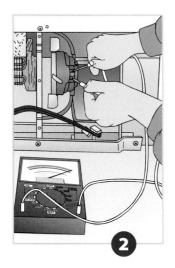

2. Testing the fan motor

- Disconnect the wires to the fan motor. Set the multitester to RX10 (page 96) and touch one probe to each terminal (left).

- The multitester needle should move to the medium range of the scale, indicating partial resistance. A reading of 0 or infinity means the motor is faulty and should be replaced.

- Set the multitester to RX1000 and touch one probe to the motor terminals and the other to any unpainted metal on the refrigerator. If the multitester needle moves at all, the motor is grounded and should be replaced.

Compressor Mountings

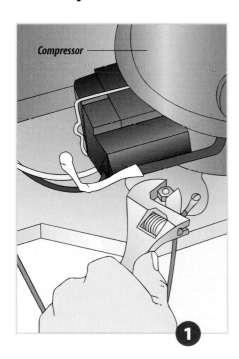

Compressor

1. Loosening the mountings

If its compressor vibrates too much, a refrigerator may run noisily. Compressors rest on shock absorbers that are designed to dampen the vibrations.

- To check the mountings, pull the refrigerator away from the wall and unplug it. Remove the rear access panel (if any) and unscrew the nut securing one foot of the compressor (left).

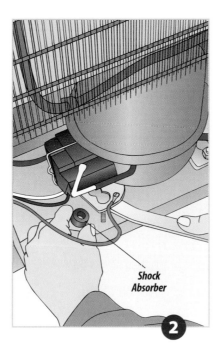

Shock Absorber

2. Removing the mountings

- Using a flat pry bar, lift the compressor foot just enough to lift out the mounting beneath it (left).

- Slip a new mounting in place and lower the compressor foot. Retighten the nut.

- Do this for all the mountings. Remove and replace the mountings one at a time.

Compressor

1. Removing the compressor relay

The terminal cover protects the relay, overload protector, and capacitor. It looks like a small box mounted on the compressor cover.

• Release the wire retaining clip that holds the cover in place. Slip off the cover and the clip.

• Pull the relay straight off the compressor without turning it (right). Remove the wire from the side terminal.

CAUTION: *If your compressor has a capacitor, it must be discharged before repair. You can make a capacitor-discharging tool yourself (page 192) and discharge the capacitor (see page 163).*

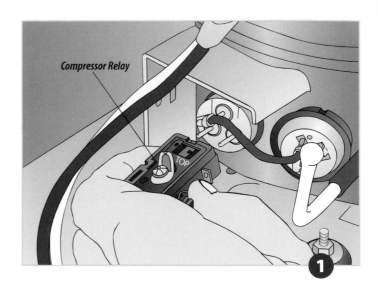

Compressor Relay

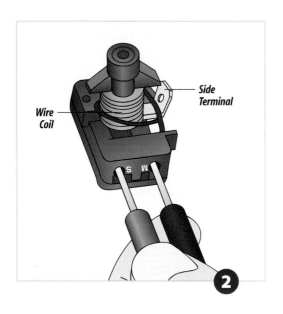

Wire Coil

Side Terminal

2. Testing the compressor relay

• If the relay has exposed wire coil, test it for continuity. If there is no visible coil, the relay is solid-state and cannot be tested for continuity. Skip this step and call for service if you determine that the relay needs to be tested.

• Set the multitester to RX1 (page 96). With the relay upside down (left), slip the probes into terminals S and M. The needle should show continuity. Remove the probe from M and place it on terminal L. The needle should move to 0. Remove the probe from S and place it in M; the needle should not move.

• Turn the relay over and listen for a click as the magnetic switch inside the relay engages. Perform the same tests. You should get the opposite results: no continuity between terminals S and M, and S and L; continuity between M and L. Replace the relay if it fails any of these tests.

3. Removing the overload protector

• With a screwdriver, gently pry open the circular spring clip that secures the overload protector to the compressor.

• Snap out the protector (right), and remove the wire connectors from the terminals.

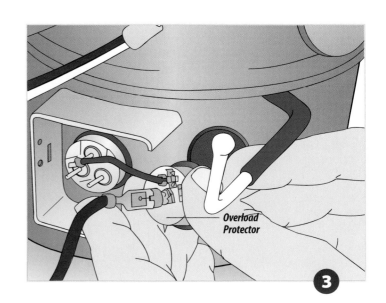

Overload Protector

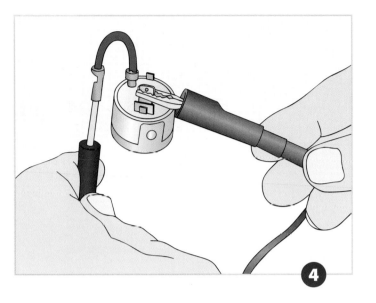

4. Testing the overload protector

- Set the multitester to RX1 to test for continuity. Touch a probe to each overload connector terminal (left). The needle should swing to 0, showing full continuity.

- If it fails this test, replace the overload protector by reattaching the push-on connector to the new overload protector. Clip it in place, and replace the terminal cover.

- If the overload protector passes this test, test the compressor (Step 5).

5. Testing the compressor motor

- Set a multitester to RX1 and test each of the three terminal pins against the others for continuity (right). Each pair should show full continuity (page 96).

- If any pair of terminals fails this test, the compressor motor is faulty; call for service.

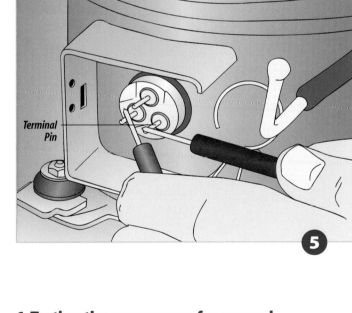

Terminal Pin

6. Testing the compressor for ground

- Set the multitester to RX1 and place one probe against the metal housing of the compressor (left). Scrape off a little paint to ensure contact with bare metal. Test each compressor terminal.

- If any of the three terminals shows continuity with the housing, the compressor is grounded. Call for service.

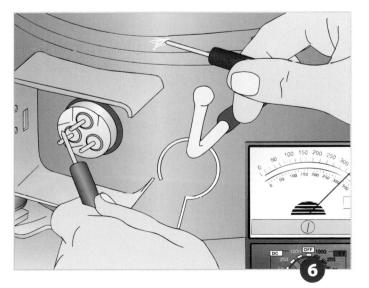

Ranges

HOW THEY WORK

Electric and gas ranges come in a variety of styles—freestanding, slide-in, cooktop, double oven, or wall oven—but all operate in the same way.

Electric Ranges

The illustration below shows a freestanding, four-burner range with commonly found features. An electric range operates on a 240/120-volt circuit—240 volts for the heating elements and 120 volts for the clock, light, and other accessories.

The heating elements are activated by electrical switches, which regulate the current reaching the elements to control burner heat. A thermostat senses and regulates oven temperature.

Gas Ranges

Some gas ranges have a pilot light that stays lit all the time. When control knobs are turned on, the pilot light ignites

the gas flowing to the surface and oven burners. Newer models have spark igniters or an electrically heated coil, called a glow bar or glow plug, to ignite the gas on demand. Igniters are wired to an ignition nodule on the back of the range; it produces the high voltage required for sparking.

Air shutters control the mix of air and gas flowing to the burners. A thermostat regulates oven temperature by turning the gas supply on and off.

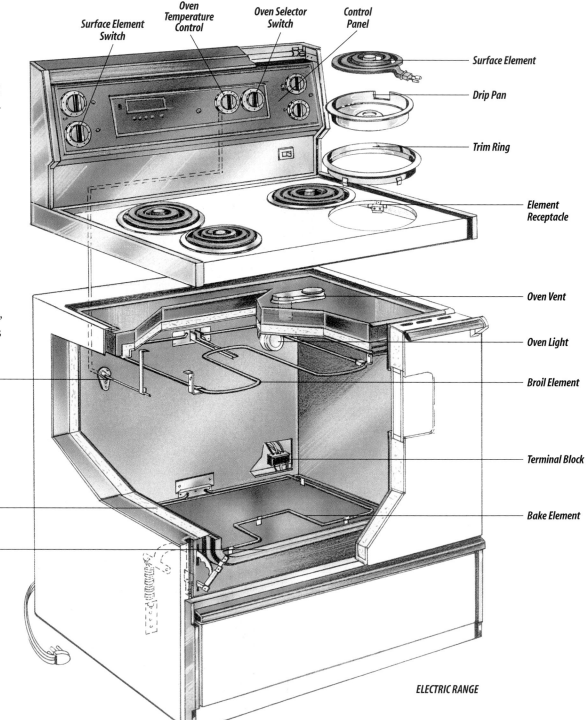

Surface Element Switch

Oven Temperature Control

Oven Selector Switch

Control Panel

Surface Element

Drip Pan

Trim Ring

Element Receptacle

Oven Vent

Oven Light

Broil Element

Terminal Block

Bake Element

Capillary Tube

Insulation

Oven Gasket

ELECTRIC RANGE

BEFORE YOU START

Keep any type of range you own clean. This is the most effective way of preventing problems with the internal components.

Don't use foil to line the drip pans under the burners or the oven element; it can short the electrical connections. Using the burners without drip pans can also harm the wiring. Never wash the gasket of a self-cleaning oven.

Before working on any oven, make sure that the appliance is unplugged and that the gas is turned off to the appliance. Any repairs involving the gas supply lines should be handled by a professional.

Make sure you know how to shut off the gas, or turn off power to the range at the service panel (page 88).

The parts on your range may look different from those we show, but in most cases the same instructions for testing and replacing apply.

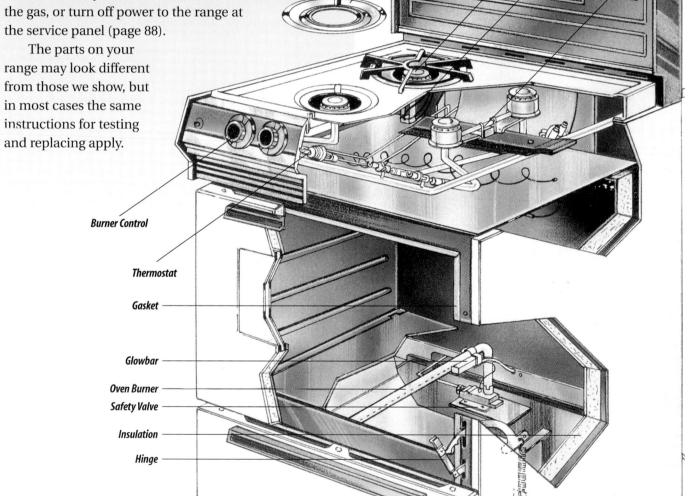

Burner Grate

Drip Pan

Internal Plug

Surface Burner

Igniter

Burner Control

Thermostat

Gasket

Glowbar

Oven Burner

Safety Valve

Insulation

Hinge

GAS RANGE

Troubleshooting

Oven Light

Replacing a bulb and testing a light switch

- To replace a bulb, pull down the wire protector or unscrew the glass shield (inset). Replace with an appliance bulb of the same size and wattage. If the bulb doesn't light, check the switch.

- If the oven has a door-operated light switch, follow the same test procedures as for a refrigerator light switch (page 321).

- Disconnect the power to the range (page 88) and open the control panel (page 336). Set a multitester to RX1 (page 96). Remove one wire from the switch and connect one probe to each terminal (right).

- Flip the switch on. The multitester should show continuity. If it fails this test, replace the switch.

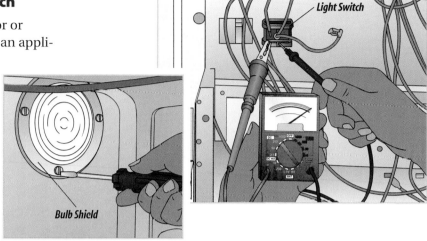

Light Switch

Bulb Shield

- To replace the switch, pull the switch out through the front of the range and install an exact replacement.

Oven Door

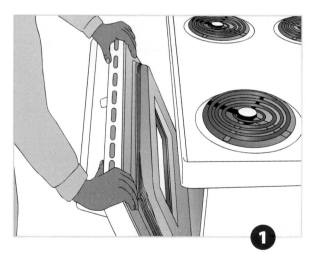

1

1. Adjusting the fit

- If the door is not straight, open the door and loosen the screws securing the inner panel. Hold the door at the top. Gently twist it from side to side to straighten it and seat it securely on its hinges (left). Shift the door only slightly if it has a glass front or window.

- Partially tighten the door screws. Do not overtighten—the porcelain can chip.

- To check the seal, insert a dollar bill between the seal and the top corners of the oven. The seal should tightly grip the bill.

2. Replacing cabinet-mounted springs

- Remove the door, and pull out the lower storage drawer. If you can't find the springs, remove the side panel and see whether you can access them. If not, call for service.

- Wearing safety goggles, unhook and replace the springs (right). Replace both springs even if only one is broken.

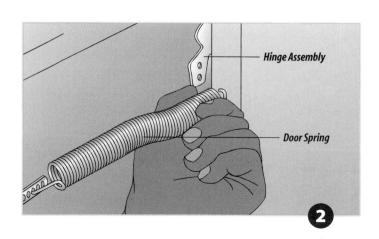

Hinge Assembly

Door Spring

2

Oven Selector Switch

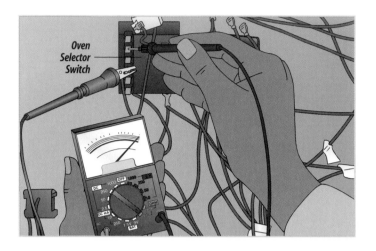

Testing and replacing the switch

The oven selector switch controls the BAKE, BROIL, TIMED BAKE, and CLEAN functions.

- To test, disconnect power to the range (page 88) and open the control panel (page 336). Set a multitester to RX1 (page 96). Disconnect one wire from each pair of terminals being tested, and check for continuity in each position (left).

- To replace the switch, remove screws from the front of the control panel and pull the switch out the back. Label and disconnect the wires. Replace with a switch made by the same manufacturer.

Clamped Oven Gaskets

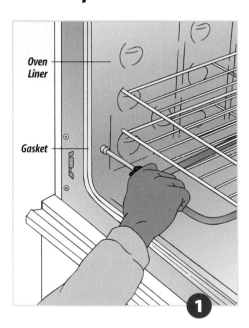

1. Gaining access to a clamped gasket

The gasket in some ovens is simply clipped to the cabinet; just pull it out.

- For the clamped type, remove the door and check for any screws or clips holding the oven liner in place. Remove the screws (left).

- If there are no screws inside the oven, disconnect power to the range (page 88) and pull it away from the wall. Locate the oven liner bolts that protrude from the back of the range, and loosen them about ¼ inch. If you cannot find the bolts, call for service.

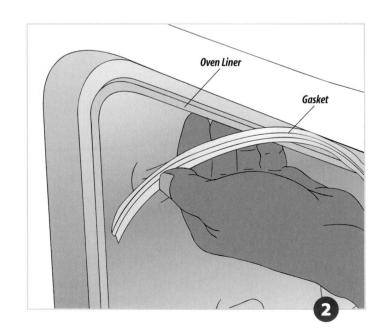

2. Removing and replacing a clamped gasket

- Partially pull out the oven liner by rocking it back and forth. Disengage the gasket from between the liner and cabinet (right).

- Position the lip of a new gasket behind the rim of the oven liner.

- Push the oven liner back into place, and replace the screws or tighten the bolts in the back of the oven.

Door-Mounted Gaskets

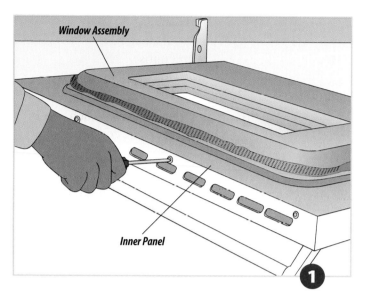

Window Assembly

Inner Panel

❶

1. Separating the door panels

On self-cleaning ovens, the gasket is held between the panels of the oven door and can be replaced only by taking apart the door.

- Unscrew the door-hinge arms and take off the door. Remove the screws on the inner panel and along the outside edges of the door (left). On some models, you have to remove the door handle as well.

- If tabs on the outer panel fit into slots in the inner panel, gently pry them apart with a screwdriver. Starting at the top, lift off the inner panel and window assembly.

2. Removing a door window

- Remove the screws that hold the window assembly to the panel (right). To reach the window on some models you must first remove a metal window shield and a layer of insulation.

- Lift off the window assembly to reveal the gasket attachment.

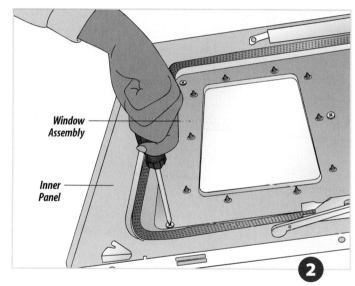

Window Assembly

Inner Panel

❷

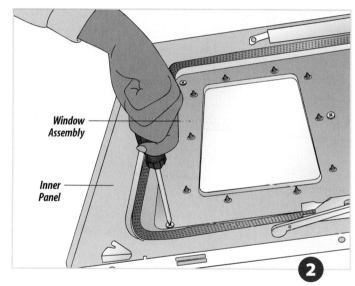

Insulation

Gasket

Bracket

❸

3. Replacing the gasket

- Locate the gasket between the window assembly and the inner door panel. Unscrew any clips that hold the gasket in place, and slip out the gasket.

- Position the new gasket with the small bead, or edge, against the panel edge; then hook the two gasket ends to the bracket (left). Loosely screw the window assembly and the door panel together.

- To adjust a loose-fitting gasket, use your fingers or the tip of a plastic scraper to wedge the excess between the door panel and the window assembly. Starting at the top of the door, push the gasket in, tightening the screws as you go.

- Screw the inner and outer door panels back together, and reinstall the door on the oven, tightening the screws securely. If necessary, adjust the fit of the oven door (page 333).

Access to the Controls (Electric)

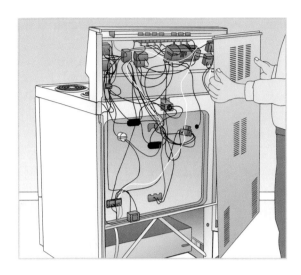

Removing the back of a freestanding range

- Unplug the range or disconnect power (page 88). Pull the range away from the wall.

- Support the back panel with a free hand or knee, then remove the screws from around the panel's edges to expose the wiring and controls.

- Some ranges have a single panel (left); others have a lower panel covering the terminal block where the power cord is attached, and one or more panels covering the wires and controls.

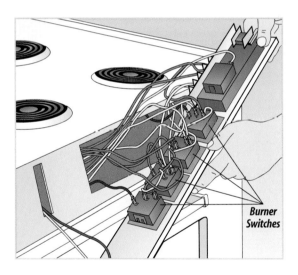

Burner Switches

Detaching front-mounted controls

- Disconnect power to the range (page 88). Remove the screws at each end of the control panel. The panel may also be held in place by a spring clip.

- Tilt the panel forward to expose the controls and wiring (left).

Removing the control panel from a wall oven

- Disconnect the power (page 88), then remove the screws at each end of the control panel. You may have to remove the screws from the inside of a recessed wall oven.

- Ease the panel forward (left), and rest it on the door or an oven rack.

- If the control panel is hinged at the bottom, simply open it toward you. In a double wall oven, if the upper oven has a built-in range hood above, release the latch pin under the hood to free the panel.

Plug-In Electric Burners

1. Checking a plug-in element

Most electric ranges have sheathed coil elements that plug into receptacles within the burner openings. Test both the element and receptacle if an element does not heat.

- Disconnect power to the range (page 88), then grasp the element, and push its terminals securely into the receptacle. If the problem persists, raise the edge of the element about 1 inch and pull it out (right).

- Inspect the coils for burns or holes. Replace the element if it is damaged. Buff corroded terminals with fine steel wool. Test the element by plugging it into a working receptacle on the range. Restore power and turn on the element. If it does not heat, replace it.

- If it heats in another receptacle, check the receptacle from which you unplugged the element (Step 3).

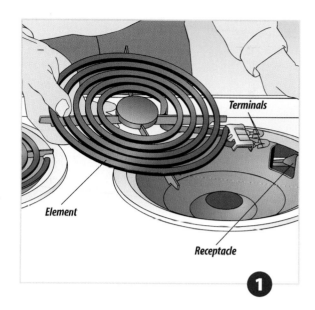

2. Clipping a tester probe to the burner switch

- Disconnect power to the range (page 88). Trace the wires from the burner's receptacle to the two corresponding terminals on the burner switch (usually marked H1 and H2).

- Set a multitester to RX1 (page 96) and clip one probe to one of the corresponding terminals on the burner switch (left).

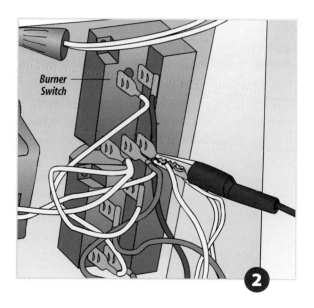

3. Testing the receptacle

- Unscrew the receptacle with a screwdriver or nut driver.

- Touch the other probe to each of the receptacle contacts in turn (right). Only one contact should show continuity.

- Repeat the test with a probe clipped on the second switch terminal. The other receptacle contact should show continuity.

- Replace the receptacle if it fails either test: Cut the wires to the receptacle and splice the new receptacle's leads to the wires using a porcelain wire cap.

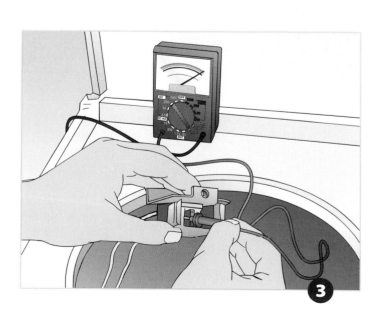

Wired Electric Burners

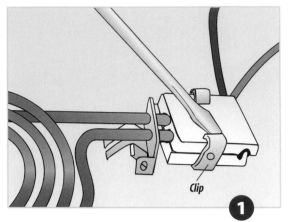

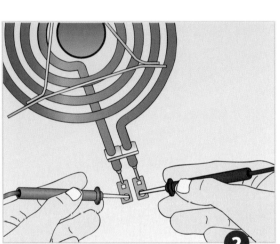

1. Disconnecting a wired element

The burners on some ranges are connected directly to the burner switch wires. The connection is protected by a glass or ceramic block.

- Turn off the power (page 88) or unplug the range. Remove the drip pan and unscrew the element and block from the range.

- Using a screwdriver, pry off the clips joining the two halves of the block (left). Tighten any loose connections, and test. Replace the element if the terminals are burned or corroded.

2. Testing the terminals

- Label and then detach the wires from the element.

- Set a multitester to RX1 (page 96) and touch one probe to each terminal (left). The meter should show continuity. If the element has several terminals, half of them are joined to form a common terminal. Touch one probe to this terminal and the other to each terminal in turn. The multitester should always show continuity.

- Test for a ground by clipping one probe to the sheathing and touching each terminal; the tester needle should not move. Replace the element if it fails any test.

Electric Burner Switches

Testing switch continuity

Power-supply wires are attached to terminals L1 and L2, or N1 and N2. Wires leading to the element are marked H1 and H2, or are simply numbered.

- Disconnect power to the range (page 88), and gain access to the range controls and switches (page 336).

- Disconnect one wire from each pair of terminals corresponding to the suspect burner. Turn the switch for the suspect burner to the ON position.

- Set a multitester to RX1 and test for continuity (right) between L1 and H1 and L2 and H2 (page 96). Replace the switch if there is no continuity.

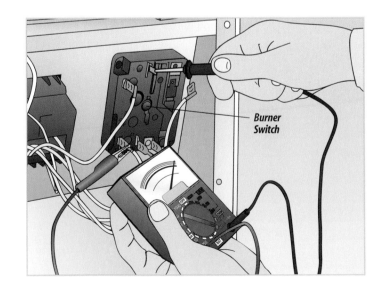

Burner Switch

Electric Oven Elements

1. Unmounting oven elements

BAKE and BROIL elements are tested and replaced in the same way. Lift out the oven door for easy access.

- Turn off the power to the range (page 88), or unplug it. Remove the screws or nuts that fasten the element to the back of the oven (right).

- If the capillary tube (page 340) obstructs the element, unclip it from its support, taking care not to bend it.

  CAUTION: *In self-cleaning ovens, the capillary tube contains a caustic fluid. Wear rubber gloves and handle it gently.*

- Unscrew any support brackets. Pull the element forward to expose wiring.

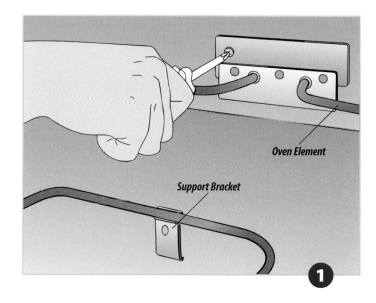

Oven Element

Support Bracket

2. Disconnecting the element

- Label the wires, and unscrew or unplug them from the element terminals (right). Don't bend the terminals, and watch that the wires don't fall back through the opening. Remove the element from the oven.

- Check the wire terminals for burns or damage. Cut them off and replace them if necessary, using crimp-on terminals (inset).

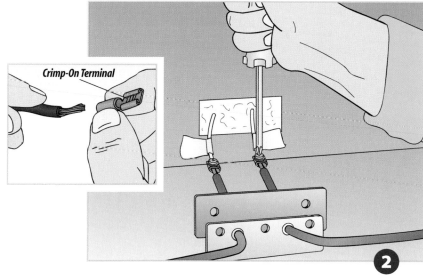

Crimp-On Terminal

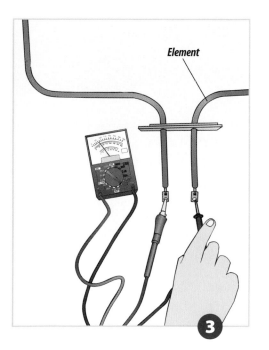

Element

3. Testing and replacing the element

- Set a multitester to RX1 (page 96) and touch probes to each of the terminals (left). The meter should show continuity.

- Test for ground with one probe on a terminal and the other on the element. The needle shouldn't move.

- If an element fails either test, replace it with an element of the same size, shape, and wattage.

Calibrating Oven Temperature (Electric Range)

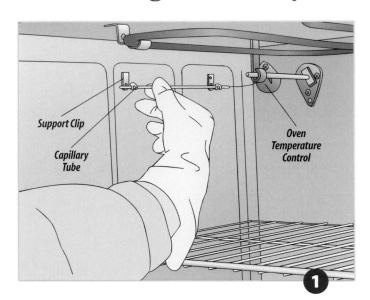

Support Clip

Capillary
Tube

Oven
Temperature
Control

1. Checking the capillary tube

If the oven gets moist from condensation, remove and clean the vent and duct (see the illustration on page 330).

- A capillary tube senses the temperature and activates the oven temperature control. If the tube touches the oven wall, reposition it on its support clips (left).

- If it is damaged, replace the tube and temperature control switch with exact replacements.

  CAUTION: *In self-cleaning ovens, the capillary tube contains caustic chemicals. Wear rubber gloves and avoid bending the tube.*

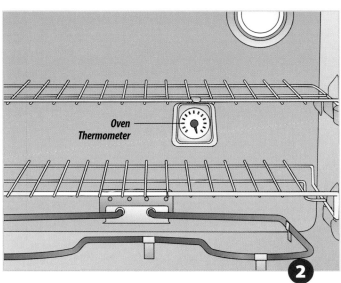

Oven
Thermometer

2. Testing oven temperature

- Place a thermometer in the oven, and set the temperature control to 350°F (left). Wait 20 minutes. Check the temperature four times over the next 40 minutes and calculate the average.

- If the result is off by less than 25°F, then the control is normal. If it is off by 25° to 50°, recalibrate the temperature control (Step 3). Replace the control if the temperature is off by 50° or more.

Calibration Ring

3. Calibrating oven temperature

Some ovens have a calibration ring on the back of the temperature-control knob. On others, temperature adjustments are made with a screw inside the control-knob shaft.

- Pull off the oven control knob. If the knob has a ring with marks indicating DECREASE and INCREASE (left), loosen the screws and turn the knob to move the ring in the appropriate direction. Retighten the screws.

- If there is no ring, hold the control shaft still with adjustable pliers. Insert a thin screwdriver, and chip away the factory seal. Then turn the inside screw clockwise to raise the temperature or counterclockwise to lower it. A ⅛ turn adjusts the temperature about 25°F.

Oven Temperature Controls (Electric Range)

1. Testing the temperature control

- Turn off the power (page 88) or unplug the range, and open the control panel (page 336). If any of the terminals appear discolored or burned, replace the temperature control.

- If the control has more than two terminals, identify which terminals to test, using the diagram located on the rear panel or inside the storage drawer or control panel.

- Set a multitester to RX1 (page 96). Disconnect one wire from the terminals being tested, and clip on tester probes (right). Set the oven temperature dial to 300°F.

- Replace the control if the meter doesn't indicate continuity (Step 3).

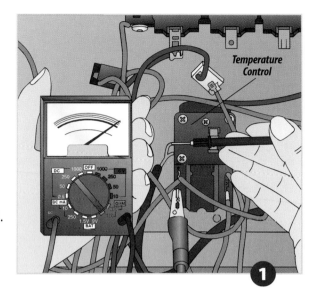

Temperature Control

2. Removing the capillary tube

- Unclip the tube from its supports in the oven (opposite page) and push it through the rear wall (right). You may need to loosen the screw that secures the baffle and slide it aside.

- From the back of the range, pull the tube completely out of the oven (inset).

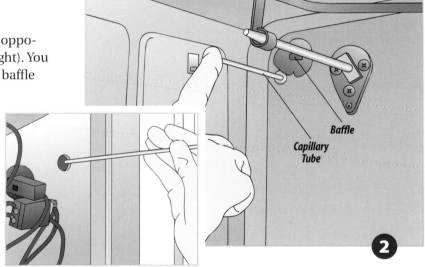

Baffle

Capillary Tube

3. Removing and replacing the temperature control

- Unscrew the two temperature control screws in the front, and remove the control from the back of the range (right).

- Label and disconnect the wires; replace any burned wire connectors (page 339).

- Connect the new control and screw it in place. Gently push the capillary tube through the back and into the oven, then clip it to its supports.

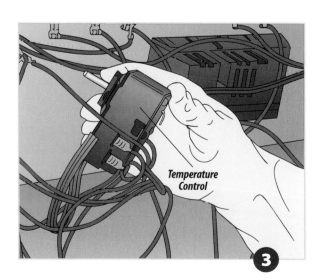

Temperature Control

Access to a Gas Range

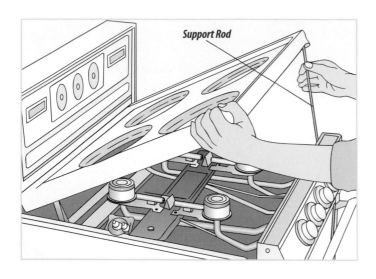

Support Rod

Opening the cooktop

In gas ranges with electrical components—clocks, lights, spark igniters—an internal harness plug connects the power cord to the internal wiring. Unplug this assembly to disconnect the range (next step).

- Remove the burner grates. Grasp the front edge of the cooktop and lift it up. Prop the cooktop open with the support rod located inside the range hood (left).

- On some ranges you can completely remove the cooktop by lifting it up and then pulling it out toward you.

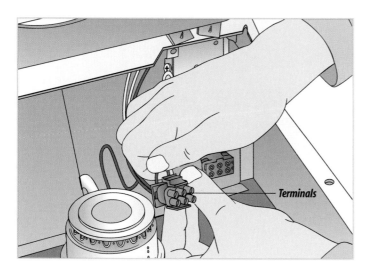

Terminals

Inspecting and replacing the internal range plug

- Disconnect the plug (usually at the right rear of the range).

- Examine the plug terminals (left). Straighten bent terminals, if possible.

- If the terminals are burned, replace the plug. Label the wires. Splice on a replacement plug using heat-resistant porcelain wire caps. Reconnect the plug.

- If the electrical components still don't work, call for service.

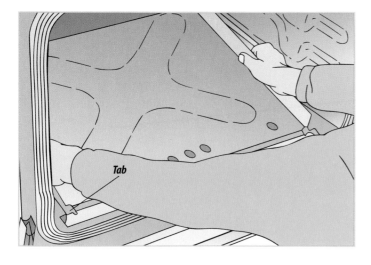

Tab

Removing the oven bottom

- On many ranges you can simply lift out the oven bottom. Others require that you slide forward the small locking tabs at the front or rear of the oven bottom (left). Remove any screws holding the oven bottom in place.

- To remove the baffle beneath the oven bottom, take out the wing nuts or screws holding it in place; lift it up and out.

Surface Burner Pilots

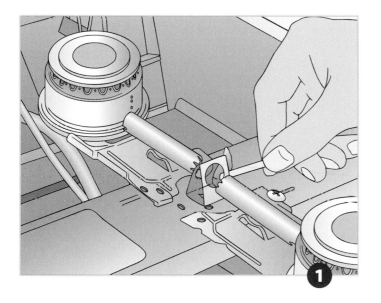

1. Relighting the pilot

Pilot lights that blow out often may be set too high or too low, or the pilot-burner may be clogged, hindering gas flow.

- Turn off all the range controls and prop open the cooktop (opposite page).
- Place a lighted match near the opening of the pilot, located midway between the two burners (left). Clean or adjust the pilot if it does not stay lit (Step 2).

    CAUTION: *If the pilot light has been out for awhile, or if you detect a gas odor, ventilate the room and call for service.*

2. Cleaning the pilot

- Remove the metal shield (if necessary) by pressing its tabs on either side.
- Insert a sewing needle in the pilot opening and move it up and down to remove any obstructions.
- Clean an oven burner pilot the same way.

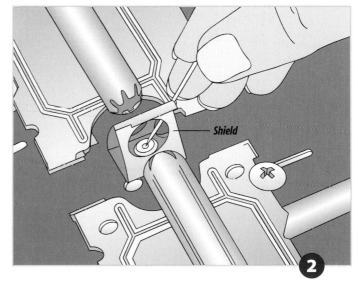

Shield

3. Adjusting the pilot height

- Turn the burner controls to OFF and prop open the cooktop (opposite page).
- Locate the pilot adjustment screw on the side of the pilot, or on the pilot gas line near the manifold at the front of the range, or behind the burner control knob.
- Turn the screw counterclockwise to increase the size of the pilot (left). The flame should be a sharp, blue cone, ¼ to ⅜ inch high.

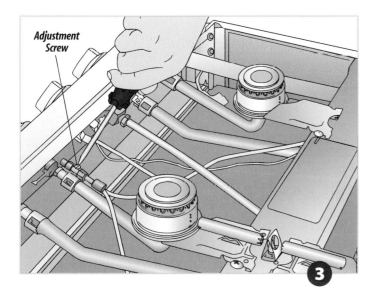

Adjustment Screw

Turning Off the Gas Supply

If you suspect a leak at any gas appliance, first turn off the gas. If there's a valve on the gas supply pipe, turn the handle perpendicular to the pipe to shut off the gas (below). If the appliance supply doesn't have a shutoff, turn off the gas at the meter in the same way. The gas meter may be on the outside of the house, or in the basement. If the gas smell does not dissipate, open some windows, leave the house, and call the gas company.

APPLIANCE VALVE

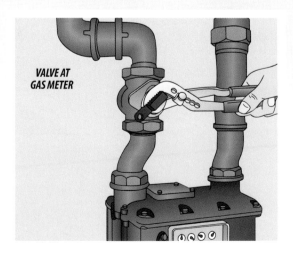

VALVE AT GAS METER

Analyzing the Flame

Insufficient Air
If a flame does not get enough air, it will be weak, without sharp blue cones. The flame may be red, yellow, or yellow tipped and may leave soot deposits on pots and pans.

Excessive Air
Too much air may make it difficult to get the flame lit. When it is lit, the flame is unsteady and makes a blowing noise.

Correct Air Adjustment
A properly adjusted flame burns steadily, quietly, and uniformly. The cones of the flame are blue and are sharply defined—about ½ to ¾ inch in length.

Surface Burners

1. Cleaning burner ports

If a burner will not light, raise the cooktop (page 342) and check that the pilot light or spark igniter is working (pages 343, 346). A shutter or sleeve on the burner tube controls the air-gas mix (Step 3).

- Check that the burner is properly seated. The flash tube must line up with the burner ports and with the pilot or spark igniter.

- Use a needle to clean the burner ports opposite the flash tube (right).

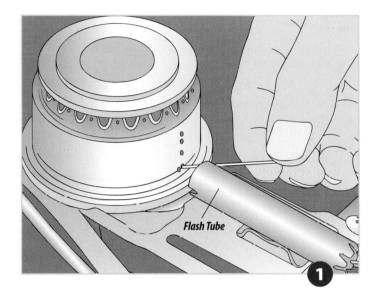

Flash Tube

2. Removing a surface burner

- Prop open the cooktop (page 342). Lift the burner from its support, then pull it backward off the burner valve (right). On some older ranges, only the top ring of the burner comes off.

- Wash the burner in hot, soapy water, and scrub the portholes with a brush. Clean out the flame openings with a needle. Let the burner dry thoroughly.

- Slip the burner back onto its supply valve, and rest it securely on its support.

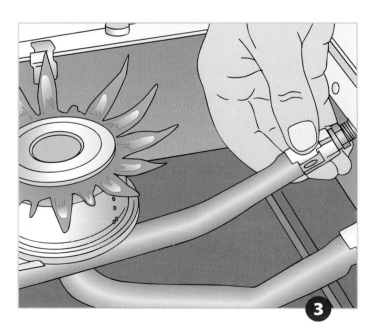

Burner Valve

3. Adjusting a surface burner air shutter

- Turn all of the controls to OFF, then raise the cooktop (page 342).

- Locate the air shutter. If it has a setscrew holding it in place, loosen it.

- Turn the burner on as high as it will go. Twist or slide the shutter open (right) until the flame shows symptoms of excessive air (opposite page). On models with an air-mixing chamber, loosen the retaining screw, slide the plate to adjust the air intake, then retighten the screw.

- Slowly close the shutter until the flame assumes the correct size and color. Turn off the burner, tighten the shutter screw, and replace the cooktop.

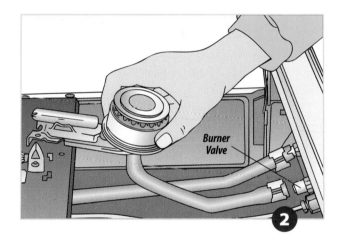

Surface Burner Spark Igniters

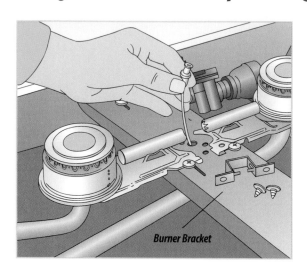

Burner Bracket

Checking and replacing the igniter

If there is no spark when you turn on a burner, turn on the other burner served by the same igniter. If the igniter sparks, the first burner control is faulty; call for service. If neither control activates the spark, unscrew the bracket, pull up the igniter (left), and clean it with a rag. Retest. If it still doesn't work, the igniter or ignition control module needs replacement.

- To replace an igniter, trace its cable to a terminal on the ignition control module at the back of the range (page 343). Remove the cover, disconnect the cable, and replace with a duplicate.

Oven Pilot

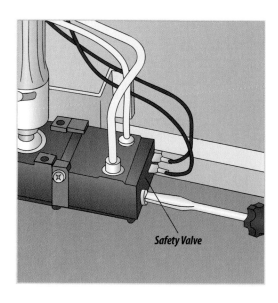

Safety Valve

Lighting and adjusting an oven pilot (safety valve)

- To relight an oven pilot, turn all controls to OFF, open the doors, and wait for gas to dissipate. Remove the broiler drawer, if any. Place a lighted match near the tip of the pilot on the burner assembly.

- If a burner does not light within two minutes of turning on the oven, adjust the pilot.

- If your range has a safety valve at the rear of the oven, find a slotted screw near the pilot gas line. If there is no adjustment screw, it has a thermostat (next step).

- If the pilot will not light, turn the screw slightly counterclockwise (left), then light the pilot. Continue to turn in tiny increments until the pilot has a blue flame.

- If the burner doesn't light within a couple of minutes, the safety valve needs replacing. Call for service.

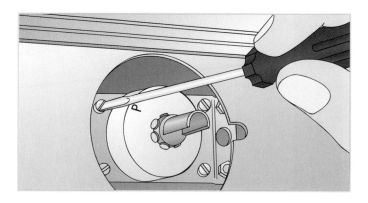

Adjusting the pilot (thermostat)

- Pull off the oven control knob and locate the oven-pilot adjustment screw (sometimes marked P or PILOT) on the front of the thermostat (left). Sometimes you'll find more than one adjustment screw for regulating other pilots within the range. If you can't find the screw at the front of the thermostat, raise the cooktop and inspect the back of the thermostat near the oven-pilot gas line.

- Adjust the pilot to a tight, blue flame. If the screw has no effect, the thermostat may be defective; call for service.

Oven Burner

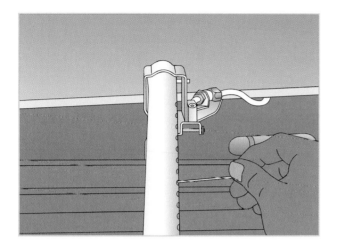

Cleaning an oven burner

Poor baking results or an odor of gas when the oven is turned on may be due to an uneven flame produced by a clogged burner.

- Turn all the range controls to OFF. Open the oven door and remove the oven bottom and baffle (page 342).

- Turn on the oven and observe the burner. If the flame is not continuous along the length of the burner, some flame ports may be clogged.

- Turn off the oven control and wait for the burner to cool. With a needle, clear each port in the burner (left).

Adjusting the oven flame

- Turn all of the range controls to OFF. Open the oven door and remove the oven bottom and baffle (page 342).

- Turn on the oven and observe the flame. A ragged, hissing flame shows that there is too much air (near right). A yellow orange flame indicates too little air. If the flame needs adjusting, turn off the oven and let it cool.

- Find the air shutter at the base of the oven burner, just above the safety valve. Some older ranges have an air-mixing chamber with a sliding plate that controls the size of the air opening.

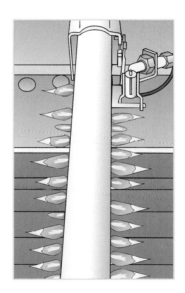
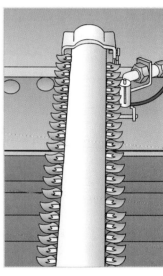

- Loosen the setscrew that locks the shutter or plate, and adjust the opening to increase or decrease the amount of air mixing with the gas (left). Then turn the oven on again.

- Repeat this process until you have adjusted the burner to produce a steady, blue, 1-inch flame with a distinct core about ½ inch long (above right). When the flame is at its best, turn off the oven and tighten the setscrew.

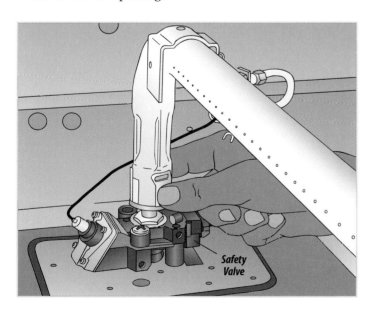

Safety Valve

Oven Spark Igniter (Gas Range)

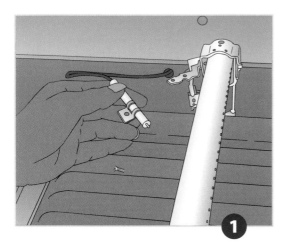

1. Checking the igniter

The igniter is connected to the ignition control module.

- Turn all of the range controls to OFF. Open the oven and remove the oven bottom and baffle (page 342).

- Unscrew the igniter from its mounting bracket and inspect it for cracks or other flaws (left). Replace it if it is damaged.

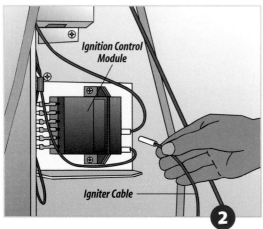

2. Replacing the igniter

- Follow the cable to the ignition control module and unscrew the cover.

- Thread the cable of a new igniter as described on page 346.

- Seat the new igniter to the bracket with its electrode ¼ inch from the pilot. Connect the cable to the module (left).

Don't Use Steel Wool to Clean Burners

Cleaning your oven and burners with steel wool pads may seem like a good way to remove heavy grease and cooking messes. But steel wool leaves behind small amounts of metal that can short out the spark from your electronic ignition, preventing ignition of the burners. Clean spills and heavy residue with a mildly abrasive cleaner and a pot-scrubbing sponge that has an abrasive pad on one side.

You can also purchase a steel wool substitute, available in 8- by 4-inch pads.

Oven Glowbar Igniter (Gas Range)

1. Testing the fuse

- In some gas ranges an electrically heated glowbar ignites the oven burner.

- Raise the oven cooktop and disconnect the internal range plug (page 342). Remove the oven bottom and baffle, and locate the fuse near the safety valve.

- Set a multitester to RX1 (page 96) and disconnect one of the wires to the fuse. Touch one probe to each end of the fuse (right). The meter should show continuity. If it doesn't, replace the fuse.

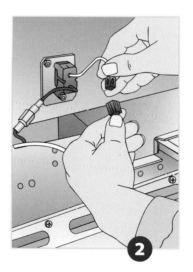

2. Checking the glowbar

- Turn on the thermostat; if the indicator light doesn't come on, call for service.

- Turn off the power to the range (page 88). Unscrew the cover plate over the glowbar wiring at the back of the range and disconnect the plugs (right), or find the glowbar beneath the oven baffle.

- Set a multitester to RX1 and touch a probe to each glowbar terminal. Replace the glowbar if it does not show continuity.

- If the glowbar has continuity, the safety valve may be faulty; call for service.

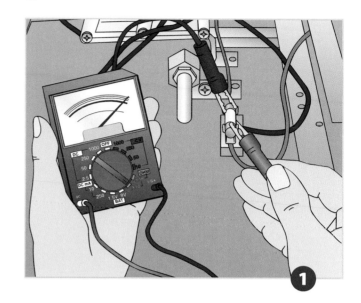

3. Replacing the glowbar

- Unscrew the glowbar from the burner support bracket and the oven wall. Pull the glowbar free of the terminal block (right).

- Mount a new glowbar in the burner support bracket at the back of the range. Reconnect its plugs at the back of the range and replace the metal cover.

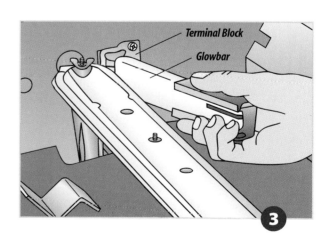

Terminal Block

Glowbar

Dishwashers

HOW THEY WORK

A dishwasher allows a preset amount of water through the water inlet into the tub. The detergent dispenser releases detergent in stages to clean the dishes. A heating element warms the detergent-and-water solution, and a pump channels the water to spray arms that disperse the water in a spray action, cleaning the dishes.

(Some dishwashers have upper and lower spraying arms; others have a single arm.) When the wash cycle is complete, clear water—or water mixed with a rinsing agent—is pumped and sprayed to rinse off the detergent. The heating element is also used to dry dishes.

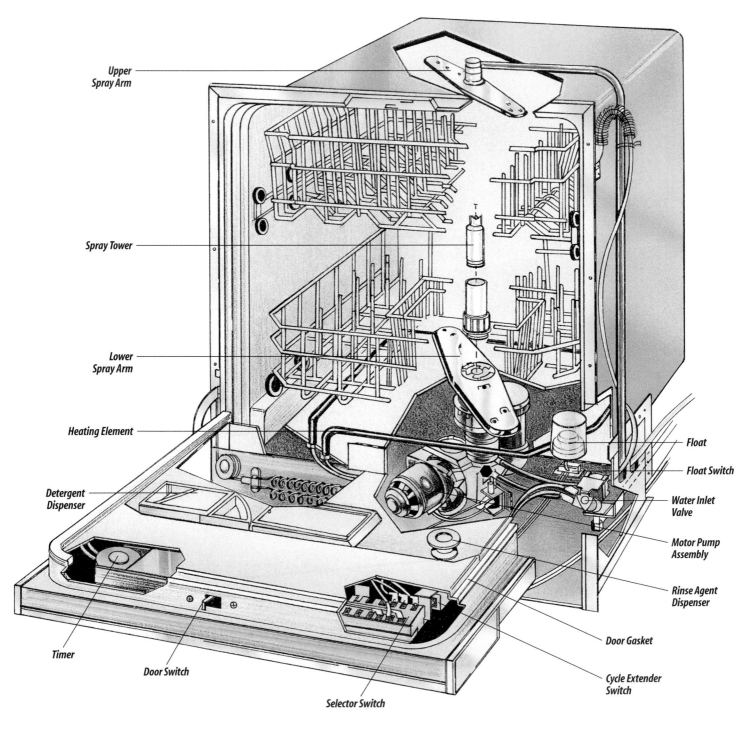

Upper Spray Arm

Spray Tower

Lower Spray Arm

Heating Element

Detergent Dispenser

Timer

Door Switch

Selector Switch

Float

Float Switch

Water Inlet Valve

Motor Pump Assembly

Rinse Agent Dispenser

Door Gasket

Cycle Extender Switch

BEFORE YOU START

Built-in dishwashers are installed under countertops with permanent wiring and plumbing connections. Portable models have a rubber coupler that connects to the sink faucet and a drain tube that runs through the sink drain; power is supplied through a regular 120-volt plug.

Helping Dishwashers Do Their Best

You know your dishwasher is not working properly when it doesn't clean the dishes. Check the owner's manual to make sure you are loading the dishwasher properly. If water in your area is high in minerals, try using more detergent. Make sure the dishwasher is getting enough water from the supply line. In older homes, the water pressure may not be strong enough to allow the dishwasher to run effectively.

Most other problems can be blamed on the internal electrical components in the dishwasher, many of which you can fix. Older dishwashers commonly have seals and rubber parts that wear out.

TIPS

- Make sure the power is off to the dishwasher before attempting to make repairs (page 88). Locate the water supply shutoff and turn the water off before beginning repairs.

- Most repairs to a built-in dishwasher can be made without removing it from under the countertop. The key parts are accessible through the front panels.

If you have dirty or spotted dishes
- Check loading recommendations
- Test the selector switch **353**
- Test the timer motor **354**
- Inspect the dispensers **355**
- Clean the spray arm **356**
- Test the water temperature **357**

If your dishwasher doesn't fill with water
- Check the water pressure **357**

If your dishwasher drains during the fill
- Check the water supply
- Check door latch and door switch . . . **354**
- Inspect and clean the spray arm **356**
- Inspect the float and float switch **358**
- Test the water inlet valve solenoid . . . **357**

If the water doesn't shut off
- Test the drain valve **359**

If the motor doesn't run
- Test the timer motor **354**
- Inspect the float and float switch **358**
- Service the water inlet valve **357**

If the motor hums but doesn't run
- Test the timer motor **354**
- Check door latch and door switch . . . **354**
- Test the motor **359**

If you have poor water drainage
- Test the timer motor **354**
- Inspect drain hose and spray arm . . . **356**
- Test the drain valve solenoid **359**

If your dishwasher leaks around the door
- Use recommended detergent only
- Adjust door latch, service door springs, or replace door gasket . . . **354–355**

If your dishwasher leaks from bottom
- Inspect drain hose and spray arm . . . **356**
- Check the water inlet connection . . . **357**

If your dishwasher doesn't turn off
- Test the cycle extender switch **353**
- Test the timer motor **354**

Access to the Controls

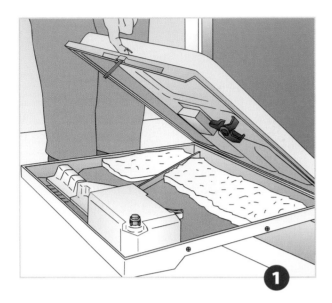

1. Removing the door panel

You will need to disassemble the door in order to service the selector switch, cycle extender switch, door switch, and timer.

- Unplug the dishwasher or turn off power at the service panel (page 88). Take out any retaining screws on the interior door and on the front of the control panel.

- Lift the interior door panel and set it aside to expose the rear of the control panel (left).

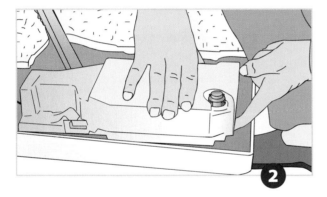

2. Accessing the control panel

- Take off any control panel covers you find. To do so, remove the plastic clips that secure the cover to the door. Lift the control panel cover to expose the control panel components (left).

3. Removing the lower panel

Many components can be reached only after the lower panel is removed.

- Turn off power to the dishwasher (page 88). Remove the retaining screws and free the panel by either pulling it down or lifting it off its hooks.

- The illustration at right shows the array of components found behind the lower panel of a typical dishwasher.

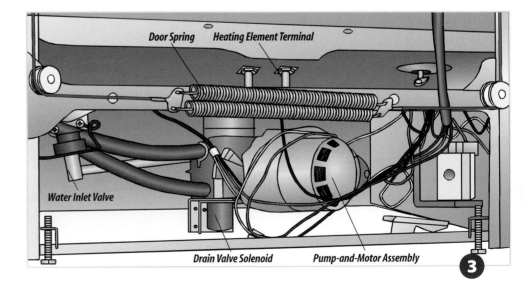

Door Spring   Heating Element Terminal

Water Inlet Valve

Drain Valve Solenoid   Pump-and-Motor Assembly

Connections

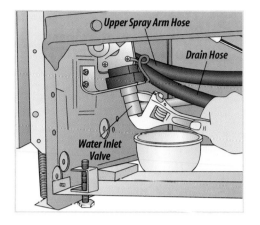

Disconnecting water lines

- Turn off the water and power to the dishwasher at their sources (pages 21, 88). Find the water inlet valve and place a bowl or bucket beneath it.

- With a wrench or pliers, unscrew the compression fittings on the water supply line from the water inlet valve (left). Disconnect the drain hose from the sink drain.

Selector Switch

Testing for continuity

- Turn off power to the dishwasher (page 88) and expose the control panel (opposite page).

- Set a multitester to RX1 (page 96) and disconnect the wires from one pair of terminals. Touch a probe to each switch terminal of the pair (right). The meter should show continuity when the related switch button is pressed.

- Test each pair of terminals on the switch, removing and replacing wires as you go. Replace the entire unit if any pair fails, swapping wires to the new switch one by one to ensure correct connections.

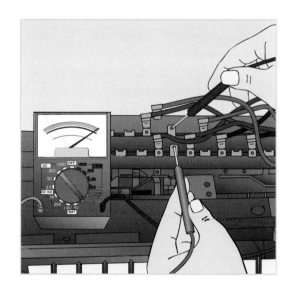

Cycle Extender Switch

Testing the switch

- Turn off power to the dishwasher (page 88) and expose the control panel (opposite page). Label and disconnect the wires from their positions on the switch, which is located adjacent to the timer motor.

- Set a multitester to RX1 (page 96). Test terminals H2 and L2 (right) for continuity. Set a multitester to RX1000 to test terminals H2 and H1 for resistance of about 5,400 ohms. Replace the switch if it fails either test.

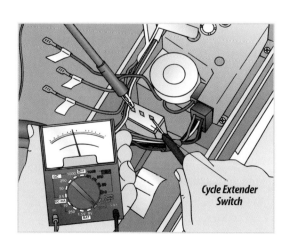

Cycle Extender Switch

Timer Motor

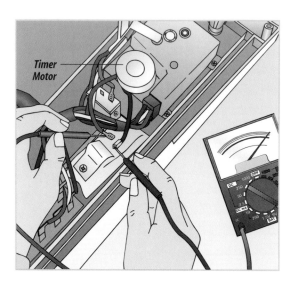

Timer Motor

Testing the motor

- Turn power off to the dishwasher (page 88) and expose the control panel (page 352). Disconnect the motor wires from the cycle extender switch.

- Set a multitester to RX1000 (page 88), and probe the motor wire terminals (left). Replace the timer if the resistance is not about 3,300 ohms.

Door Latch and Switch

Testing the door latch

- To adjust the door latch, loosen the retaining bolts with a nut driver, slide the latch in or out, and tighten the bolts (right).

- If the door latch closes securely and the machine will not run, test the switch (next step).

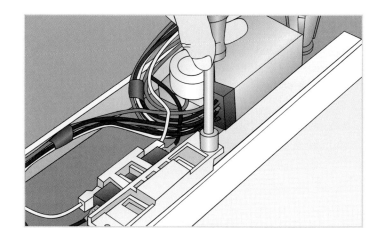

Testing and replacing the door switch

- Turn off the power to the dishwasher (page 88). Set a multitester to RX1 (page 96) and test the switch for continuity (right).

- The meter should indicate continuity with the switch button pushed in, and an open circuit when it's out. Replace the switch if your test results are different.

- To replace the switch, remove the door switch retaining bolts (previous step) and remove the switch assembly. Install a new door switch and reconnect the switch wires.

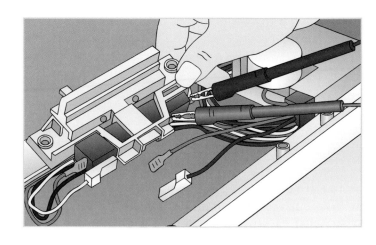

Door Springs and Cables

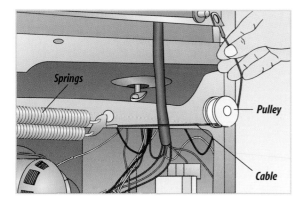

Springs

Pulley

Cable

Inspecting the spring, cable, and pulley assembly

If the door falls to a horizontal position when opened, examine the spring, pulley, and cable assembly.

- Turn off power to the machine (page 88) and remove the lower panel (page 352). Inspect the cables and springs. Always replace damaged springs and cables in pairs to ensure proper tension.
- Grasp a damaged cable (or spring) with your hand and remove it from its hook. Close and lock the door. Reroute a new cable around the pulley (left), secure it to the door assembly, and reinstall the lower panel.

Door Gaskets

Replacing the door gasket

- Open the dishwasher door and remove the dish racks. If the gasket is supple and not cracked, adjust the door latch (opposite page). Otherwise, replace the gasket.
- Pry out the old gasket with a screwdriver and remove it (right).
- Lubricate the new gasket with water only (don't use soapy water), and slide it into place. Using your thumb or the handle of a screwdriver, press the center of the gasket into the top center of the door. Continue around the door, pressing it into place a few inches at a time in each direction.

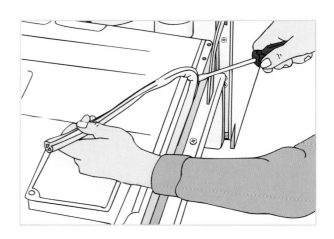

Detergent and Rinse Agent Dispensers

Inspecting the dispenser mechanisms

Caked-on detergent or rinse agent residue can clog dispenser mechanisms. O-rings can become hard or frayed with age. Clean away all caked-on soap. Check the O-rings on the covers; replace them if they are damaged.

- Remove the interior door panel (page 352). For a spring-and-lever mechanism (right), release the plastic tabs and remove the rinse agent dispenser. Check the spring-and-lever mechanism for stuck or broken parts. Replace any part that is damaged.
- To test an electronically operated dispenser, set a multitester to RX1 and test for continuity (page 96). If the circuit is open, unscrew the terminal assembly and replace it.

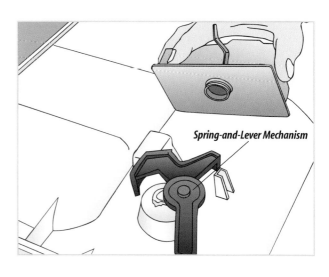

Spring-and-Lever Mechanism

Drain Hose

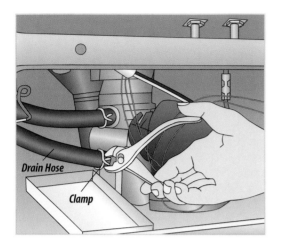

Drain Hose

Clamp

Replacing the hose

- Turn off power to the dishwasher (page 88) and remove the lower panel (page 352). Check that the clamp is secure and straighten any kinks by hand.

- To replace a broken or hopelessly kinked hose, use pliers to squeeze the spring clamp at the pump (left), and pull off the hose. Use a shallow pan to catch any drips.

- Disconnect the hose at the kitchen sink drain or faucet coupler. Cut and position the new hose carefully, so it won't kink, and reconnect it at both ends with new clamps.

Spray Arms

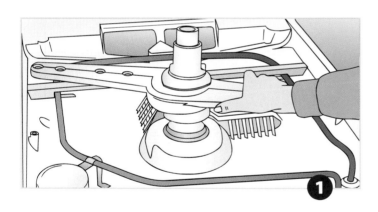

1. Checking arm movement

- Turn off power to the dishwasher (page 88) and slide out the lower dish rack. Rotate the spray arm to see whether it moves freely (left). The ends of the arm should also move up and down slightly. Repeat this test on the upper spray arm, if present.

- Also pull upward on the spray tower to see that the telescoping parts move easily. If not, replace the tower.

- Replace the arm if it doesn't spin freely, or if it has been damaged.

2. Removing the spray arm

- Unscrew the spray tower clockwise (it has reverse threads) by hand, and remove it (inset).

- Unscrew the bolt (if any) in the center of the spray arm (right). Lift out the spray arm and its washers, keeping them in order.

- Clean the holes in the spray arm or replace it if damaged. Reuse the old washers if the new spray arm does not come with new ones. Remount the spray arm and spray tower.

Spray Tower

Heating Element

Testing the heating element

- During the first cycle, open the door and measure water temperature with a candy thermometer. If it is below 140°F, test the element.

- Turn off power to the dishwasher (page 88) and remove the lower panel (page 352).

- Set a multitester to RX1 (page 96), disconnect one of the wires from the element, and touch one probe to each terminal (right). Look for a reading different from 0 or infinity.

- Place one probe on a terminal and the other on the element's metal sheath, and check for ground. Replace the element if it fails either test.

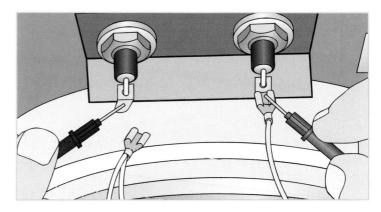

Water Pressure

Measuring the water level

Water flows into a dishwasher in a timed cycle. If the water pressure is too low, the tub will not fill enough for thorough cleaning.

- Turn on the dishwasher, and stop it midway through the first cycle. Open the door and let the steam clear.

- Stand a ruler on the sump (right). If the water level does not reach the ⅜-inch mark on the ruler, avoid using water elsewhere in the house when running the dishwasher.

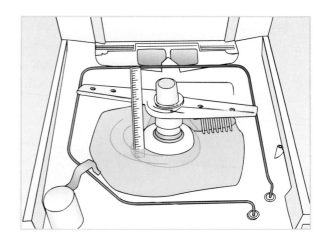

Water Inlet Valve

Checking for continuity

- Remove the lower panel (page 352). Make sure the incoming water line and the hose that connects the inlet valve to the tub are securely fastened.

- Remove the wires from the inlet valve terminals. Set a multitester to RX1 (page 96). Touch a probe to each terminal (right); a good valve will show some resistance. Remove and replace the valve if the meter reads infinity.

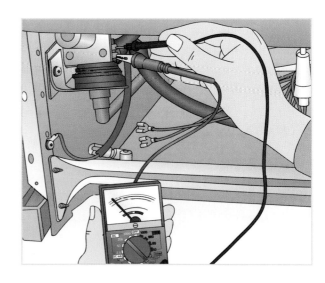

Float Switch

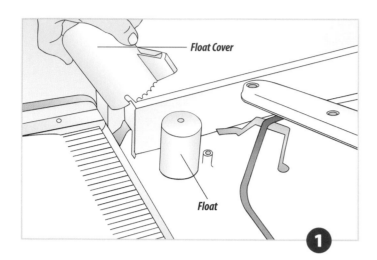

Float Cover

Float

1

1. Inspecting the float

- Turn off the power to the dishwasher (page 88), open the door, and remove the lower rack.

- Remove the float cover (left) and jiggle the float up and down to see whether it moves freely. Pull off the float, and clear any obstructions. If this does not solve the problem, test the float switch (Step 2).

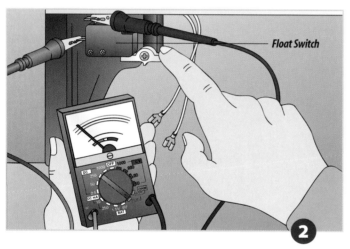

Float Switch

2

2. Testing the float switch

- Remove the lower panel (page 352). Find the switch directly below the float, and detach the wires from its terminals.

- Set a multitester to RX1 and clip a probe to each terminal (page 96). Pull down on the lever to put the switch in the ON position. A faulty switch will show no continuity (left); replace it.

Drain Valve

1. Checking the gate arm mechanism

Only dishwashers with nonreversible motors have a drain valve.

- Turn off power to the dishwasher (page 88) and remove the lower panel (page 352). Count the number of wires attached to the motor. A motor with two or three wires is nonreversible; a motor with four wires is reversible and has no drain valve.

- Move the gate arm mechanism by hand (right); it should move freely up and down. Inspect both springs and replace them if they are missing or broken.

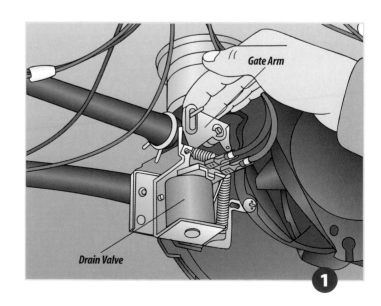

Gate Arm

Drain Valve

1

2. Testing the drain valve solenoid

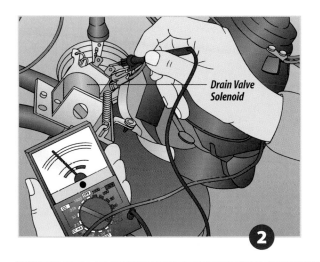

- Disconnect the wires from the drain valve solenoid. Set a multitester to RX1 (page 96). Clip a probe to each terminal on the solenoid and check for about 40 ohms of resistance (left).

- If the tester reads infinity, indicating an open circuit, replace the solenoid. Label the wires, detach the springs, and remove the screws. Install an exact replacement.

Drain Valve Solenoid

Pump and Motor Assembly

1. Inspecting the motor

- Turn off the power to the dishwasher (page 88), and remove the lower panel (page 352).

- Try to turn the motor fan blades by hand (right). Use a screwdriver if you can't reach in with a finger. If they don't move freely, look for obstructions or call for service.

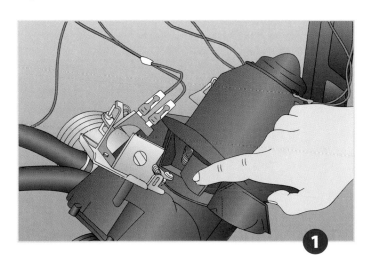

2. Testing the motor

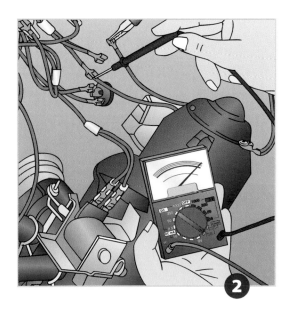

- Snap off any protective brackets, and disconnect the motor wires from their terminals. Set a multitester to RX1 (page 96), and attach a probe to each motor wire terminal (left). The motor should show about 2 ohms of resistance.

- If the test indicates full continuity (the needle swings to 0), test for a ground: Place one probe on the bare metal housing of the motor and the other probe on each terminal in turn. The needle should not move. If the motor fails either test, call for service.

Clothes Washers

HOW THEY WORK

Knobs on a washing machine's control panel send wash-cycle instructions to a timer and electrically operated inlet valves. The wash cycle begins by filling the washtub with hot, cold, or warm water that also permeates the spin drum. The agitator in the middle of the tub churns back and forth to clean the clothes. The spin cycle spins to extract water from the clothes, and a pump channels the soiled water into the drain.

In a direct-drive clothes washer (below left), the motor connects to the agitator and spin drum by means of bearings and gears. In a belt-drive washer (below right), the power to the motor is transferred to the agitator and spin drum by a belt-and-pulley system.

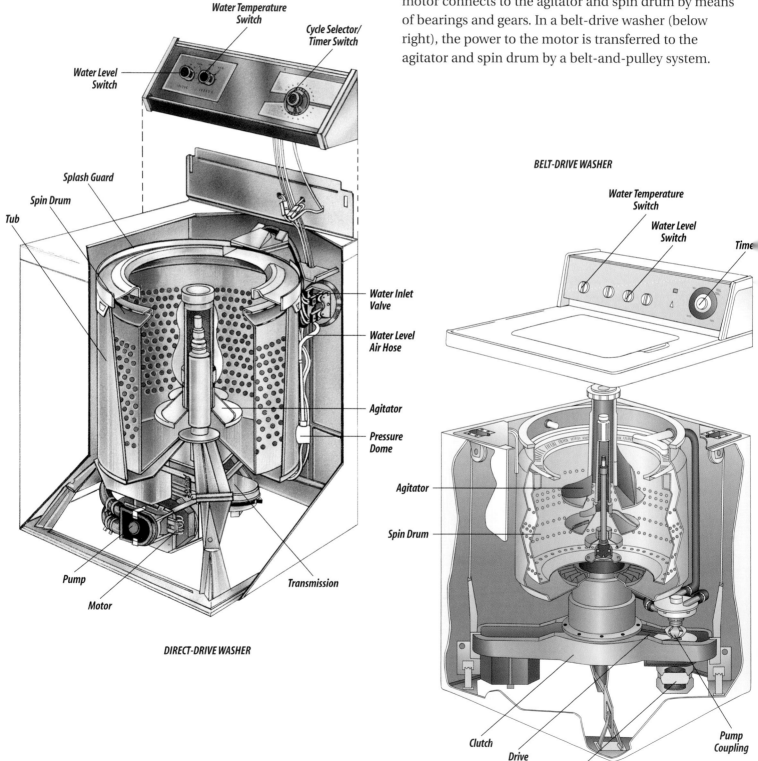

Water Temperature Switch

Cycle Selector/ Timer Switch

Water Level Switch

Splash Guard

Spin Drum

Tub

Water Inlet Valve

Water Level Air Hose

Agitator

Pressure Dome

Pump

Motor

Transmission

DIRECT-DRIVE WASHER

BELT-DRIVE WASHER

Water Temperature Switch

Water Level Switch

Time

Agitator

Spin Drum

Clutch

Drive Belt

Motor

Pump Coupling

BEFORE YOU START

Most repairs to your clothes washer can be made yourself with simple tools and a logical approach to troubleshooting.

How Machines Differ

Differences in housing designs mean different ways to get to the switches, timers, valves, and other internal parts. And some switch and pump designs differ from one model to the next.

In many cases, access and parts are much the same for belt- and direct-drive washers. We'll tell you when they differ.

TIPS

It is usually best to replace a faulty motor or transmission rather than to attempt repairs. When in doubt, call for service.

Access to Direct-Drive Washers

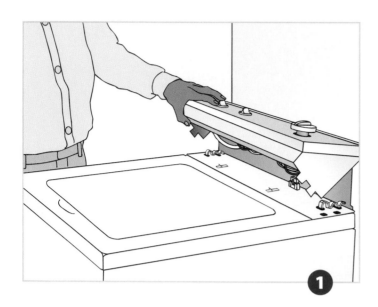

1. Tipping back the control console

- Unplug the washer. Remove the retaining screws from the bottom corners of the console. The screws may be covered by an adhesive trim strip. Some washers may have screws on the top or back of the console.

- Flip the console backwards (left) to expose the timer, the timer motor, the water level switch, the water temperature switch, and the selector switch.

2. Removing the cabinet clips

- With a screwdriver, pry off the two retaining clips on each side of the washer. To do so, stick the screwdriver into the clip opening and rest it in a U-shaped trough (right). Then push the screwdriver handle toward the rear to dislodge the clip.

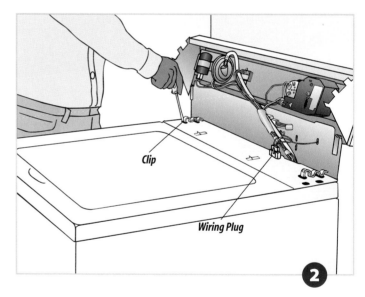

Clip

Wiring Plug

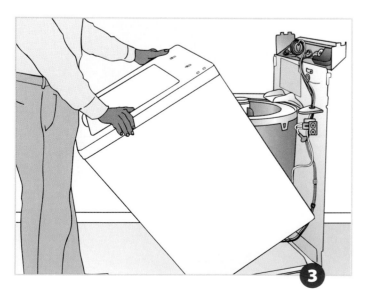

3. Pulling the housing forward

- Pull out the plug for the lid-switch wiring harness (Step 2) to disconnect the control console from the washer housing. If necessary, use a screwdriver to help loosen the clasp that secures the plug.

- Tilt the housing forward at a 45° angle to disengage the tabs securing the washer to the frame (left).

- Maintaining a 45° angle, pull the housing straight out and set it aside.

- To reinstall the housing when repairs are complete, hook the front edge under the front bottom rail, then lower the housing onto the side rails. Snap the tabs into cutouts in the housing.

Access to Belt-Drive Washers

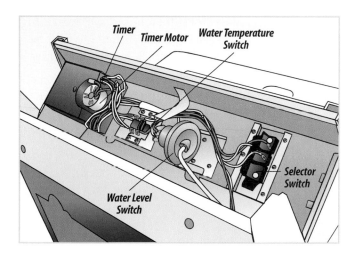

Access through the control panel

- Remove the screws from the corners of the control console.

- Tilt the console forward—the console (left) is shown from the rear—to expose the timer and its motor, as well as the water temperature, water level, and cycle selector switches.

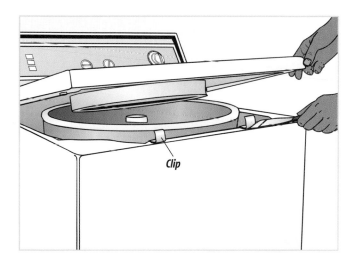

Access through the top

- Wrap the end of a putty knife with tape. Slip it between the top and the cabinet, then push inward to release the two spring clips securing the top of the washer. On some belt-drive washers, the spring clips are located at the front (left). Others have spring clips on the sides.

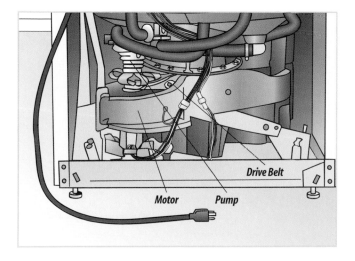

Access through the back panel

On belt-drive washers, you can usually expose the motor, pump, water inlet valve, and drive belt by removing the back panel (left).

- Unplug the washer and disconnect the hoses from the water supply. Pull the washer away from the wall.

- With a nut driver, take out the screws that secure the back panel. Remove the panel and set it aside.

Water Level Switch Assembly

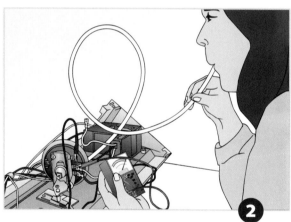

Water Level Switch

Air Hose

Pressure Dome

1

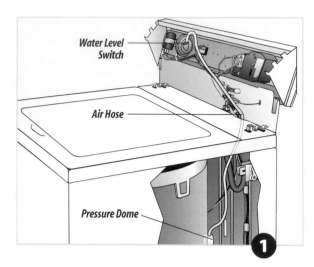

2

1. Inspecting the air hose and air pressure dome

• Unplug the washer and access the control console (page 362 or 363). Remove the top or housing, as needed.

• Inspect the water level air hose for wear, and straighten any kinks. Look for signs of water leakage on or around the hose and air pressure dome (left). Check that all air hose connections are airtight.

• Replace the pressure dome if cracked or if the seal between it and the tub is broken.

2. Testing a water level switch

• Label and remove the three wires from the water level switch and push them aside. Set a multitester to RX1 (page 96).

• Pull the air hose off the switch and attach a shorter tube of the same diameter. Gently blow into the tube (left). Listen for a click as the switch trips to the FULL position.

• Continue blowing and test all three pairings of the switch terminals. Two pairs should show continuity, and one pair should show resistance. Note the results.

• Stop blowing and retest the switch. The terminal pair that showed resistance earlier should show continuity, and those that showed continuity should show resistance. Replace the switch if the results differ.

Timers

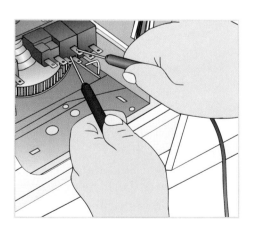

Testing timer switches (belt-drive)

• Unplug the washer and open the control console (page 363). Release the plastic tab and lift off the timer switch cover. Use the wiring diagram on the washer and timer chart below to identify the switch functions. Label and disconnect the wires, omitted here for clarity.

• Turn the selector knob to the malfunctioning cycle. Set a multitester to RX1 and touch probes to the corresponding terminals (left). If the readings differ from those in the chart below, the switch is faulty; call for service.

	SWITCHES					
	1	2	3	3B	4	4B
Control Knob Position	Motor	Special Function	Main Power	Bypass	Wash	Spin
Off	Open	**See**	Open	Open	Open	Open
Wash	Open	**Timer**	Closed	Open	Closed	Open
Spin	Open	**Chart**	Closed	Closed	Open	Closed

Checking the motor (direct-drive)

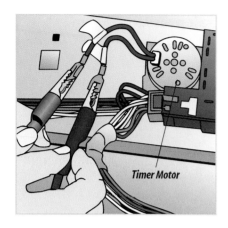

Timer Motor

- Unplug the washer and open the console (page 362). Label and remove the wires leading to the timer motor.

- Set a multitester to RX100 (page 96) and clip a probe to each terminal (left). Look for a resistance reading of 2,000 to 3,000 ohms. Replace the timer motor if the result differs.

Water Temperature Switch

Testing the switch

The water temperature switch may be either push-button or rotary. Both are tested the same way.

- Unplug the washer and remove the control console (page 362 or 363). Check the wiring diagram on the washer for the markings used on the terminals that control the inoperable setting. Label and disconnect the wires from the terminals.

- Set a multitester to RX1 and set the switch to the inoperative setting (page 96). Touch probes to terminals (right). The tester reading should indicate continuity. If not, replace the switch.

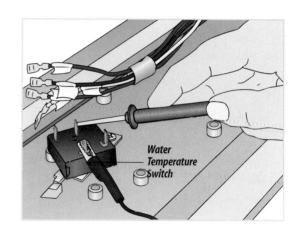

Water Temperature Switch

Lid Switch

Testing the switch

The lid switch turns off the washer when you open the lid.

- Unplug the washer and remove the housing or top (page 362 or 363). Unplug the switch wiring harness (right). Set a multitester to RX1 and touch a probe to each switch terminal (page 96). The meter should point to 0 with the switch button pressed, and infinity with the button out.

- Replace the switch if you obtain different test results. On most washers, mounting screws are located in the recess under the lid. On others, the harness receptacle is held in place by two spring clips; pry them off with a screwdriver.

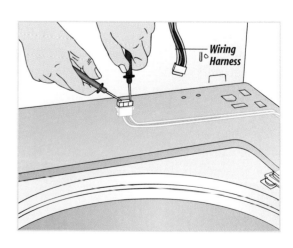

Wiring Harness

Agitator and Tub

1. Removing the agitator cap

If the washer twists clothing excessively, disassemble and inspect the agitator assembly. It is also necessary to remove the agitator to inspect the tub for leaks.

- Lift out the softener dispenser, if any, from the center of the agitator cap. Using a screwdriver, pry off the cap (right).

- Washers that have a softener dispenser in the agitator have a shield with a watertight O-ring covering the agitator bolt. Replace the O-ring and shield if they are worn.

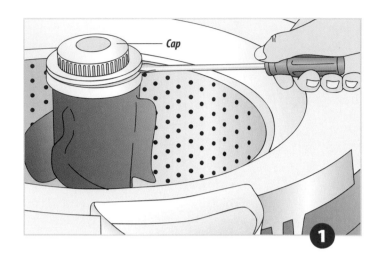

2. Removing the agitator bolt

- Using a socket wrench and an extension, remove the bolt securing the agitator (left).

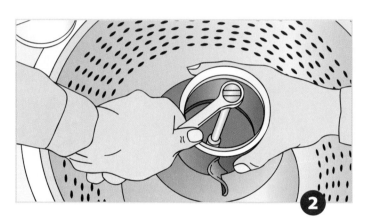

3. Lifting out the agitator

If the agitator dogs are worn, the agitator will move in only one direction, twisting clothes and cleaning less effectively.

- To remove the spin drum for tub inspection, first lift out the agitator top, then remove the bottom (right).

- Pull out the clutch assembly from the agitator top and inspect the dogs (inset). If they are worn, remove them and snap new dogs into place.

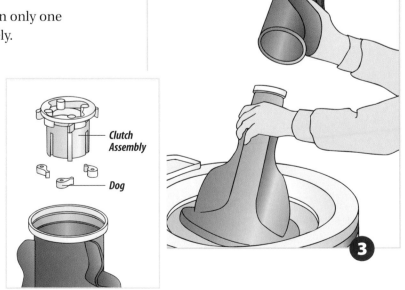

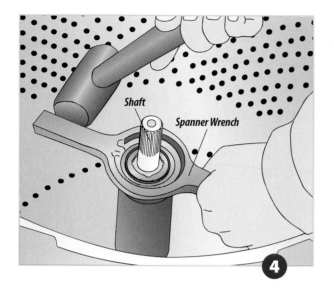

4. Dislodging the spanner nut

- If you have a spanner wrench, place it over the nut encircling the transmission shaft. Strike the wrench with a hammer or rubber mallet to loosen the nut (left). (Take care not to damage the spin basket's porcelain finish.) If you don't have a spanner wrench, tap the nut with a piece of scrap wood.

- After freeing the nut, remove it by hand.

5. Removing the splash guard

- Using your fingers, release the plastic tabs securing the splash guard to the tub. Don't pry these with a sharp tool, or you will mar the finish and may snap the tabs.

- Lift off the splash guard (right) and set it aside.

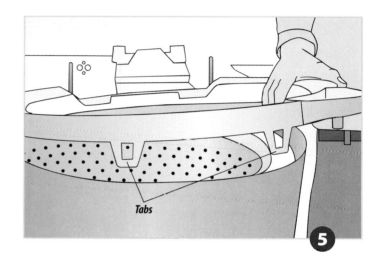

6. Removing the spin drum

Damage to the tub is often caused by contact with the spin drum when the load is imbalanced.

- Gently rock the spin drum back and forth, then turn it a half-rotation. Gently rock the drum again to break any soap deposits that could cause it to stick.

- Lift the spin drum straight up out of the tub (left). Inspect the inside of the tub for signs of rubbing or cracks, and call for service if you find any.

Water Inlet Valve

Testing the valve solenoids

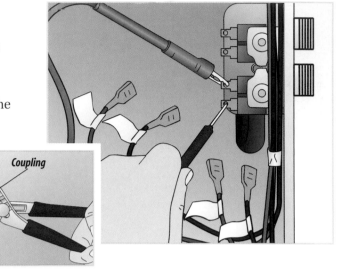

- Unplug the washer and shut off the water supply. Loosen the couplings with pliers (inset) and remove the hoses. Check the filter screen inside each valve port. If the screen is more than half clogged, replace the valve.

- To test the valve solenoids, label and remove the wires from the solenoid terminals. Set a multitester to RX1 (page 96) and touch a probe to each pair of terminals in turn (right). The meter should indicate between 100 and 1,000 ohms of resistance on each pair. Replace the valve if the test result differs.

Coupling

Direct-Drive Pump

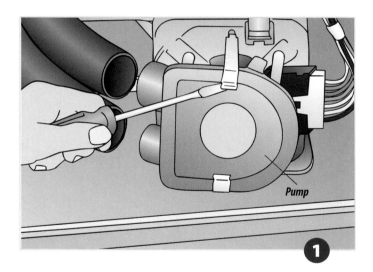

Pump

1

1. Unsnapping the clips

- Unplug the washer, turn off the water supply, and remove the housing (page 363). Loosen the hose clamps with pliers, slide them over, and pull the hoses from the pump inlet and outlet. Be sure to label the hoses for reinstallation.

- Use a screwdriver to pry off the clips that secure the pump to the motor (left).

2. Removing the pump

- Pull off the pump (right). Examine it for damage, and remove small parts of clothing that may be blocking its path.

- If it is damaged, or if it continues to leak after you reinstall it, replace it. (When reattaching the pump, be sure to connect the inlet hose and outlet hose to the correct port.)

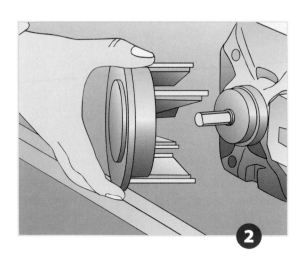

2

Direct-Drive Motor

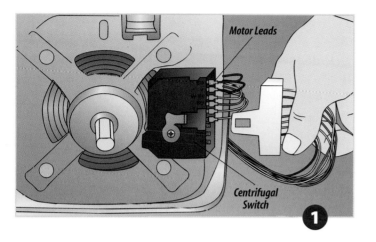

1. Disconnecting the centrifugal switch

- Unplug the washer. Remove the harness plug attached to the centrifugal switch (left).

- Label and remove the motor leads (wires) from the centrifugal switch.

- Remove the mounting screw connecting the centrifugal switch to the motor.

2. Testing the centrifugal switch

- Set a multitester to RX1 (page 96). Press the switch lever in (right). The multitester should show continuity between R to BK and OR to BU. With one probe on R, test all other terminals; none should show continuity.

- Release the switch. The multitester should now show continuity between OR and V. There should be no continuity between the other terminals. Replace the switch if you obtain different results.

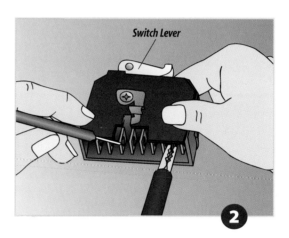

3. Testing the motor

- Set a multitester to RX1 (right). The following wire combinations should show continuity: white to blue, white to black/white, white to violet, and yellow to black.

- The following wire combinations should not show continuity: white to yellow, and white to black.

- Replace the motor if you obtain different results.

(CONTINUED)

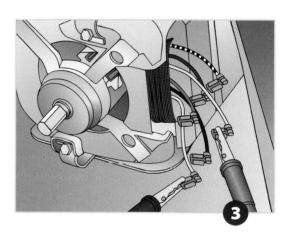

Direct-Drive Motor—continued

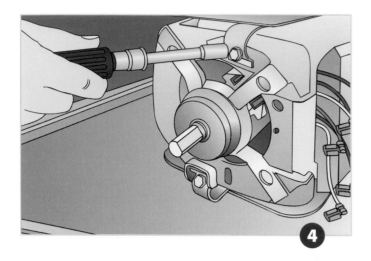

4. Removing the motor

- With a nut driver, unscrew the bolts holding the retaining clips in place (left). Use a screwdriver to pry out the clips securing the motor. Some motors are secured by bolts only.

- Slide out the motor. Install an exact replacement.

Direct-Drive Transmission and Clutch

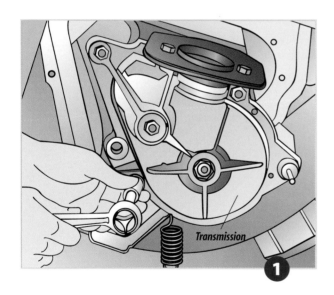

Transmission

1. Unbolting the transmission

If the spin drum doesn't spin or the agitator does not agitate, inspect the transmission.

- Unplug the washer and turn off the water supply. Remove the agitator, spin drum, and tub (pages 366–367). Disconnect and remove the pump and motor (Step 4 above).

- With a helper, lay the washer on its back to expose the transmission from the bottom side. Use a socket wrench to remove the mounting bolts (left).

2. Removing the transmission and drive shaft

- Pull out the transmission (right); the drive shaft will also pull free. With a socket wrench, remove the nuts securing the motor mounting plate.

- Take the transmission to a professional for inspection. It is usually wiser to replace rather than repair a transmission.

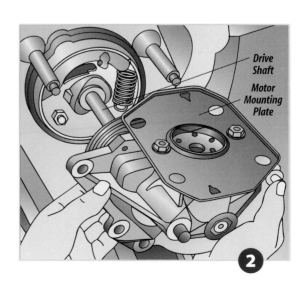

Drive Shaft

Motor Mounting Plate

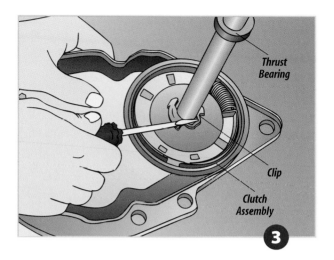

3. Removing the clutch

If the spin drum won't stop spinning, you may need to replace the clutch.

- Pull the thrust bearing off of the drive shaft.

- With a screwdriver, pry off the retaining clip securing the clutch assembly (left). Holding the shaft vertical to prevent spillage of transmission lubricant, slide the clutch off the shaft. Reverse the steps for reassembly.

Drive Belt

1. Removing the drive belt

- Unplug the washer and remove the back panel (page 363). Unscrew the clamps above and below the pump coupling, and remove the coupling (right).

- With a socket wrench and extension, loosen the motor mounting nuts on the mounting plate to release tension on the belt.

- As you pry off the belt, reach under the tub and turn the transmission pulley. Remove the belt from the clutch pulley, and pull the belt out of the machine.

2. Installing a new drive belt

- Fit the new belt around the transmission pulley and hold it there while you loop it around the clutch pulley (right). If the belt is tight, rotate the transmission pulley with your hand and shift the motor slightly toward the right.

- Reinstall the coupling and tighten the clamps.

- Push the belt with your thumb; if you can deflect it more than ½ inch, pull the motor toward you to take out the slack, then tighten the motor mounting nuts.

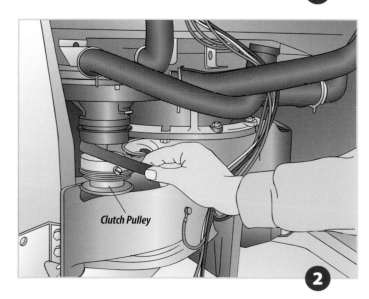

Clothes Dryers

HOW THEY WORK

Gas and electric dryers differ from each other mainly in the source of heat; all other parts are much the same.

All dryers combine air, heat, and motion to remove moisture from clothes. A motor turns a drive belt that revolves a drum, which tumbles wet garments to keep them separated. A blower, also powered by the motor, forces air past a heating element or gas flame and into the drum. The warm airflow draws lint and moisture from the clothes through a lint screen and out the exhaust duct. Electrical switches, thermostats, and a timer regulate the temperature, drying time, and other cycle variations.

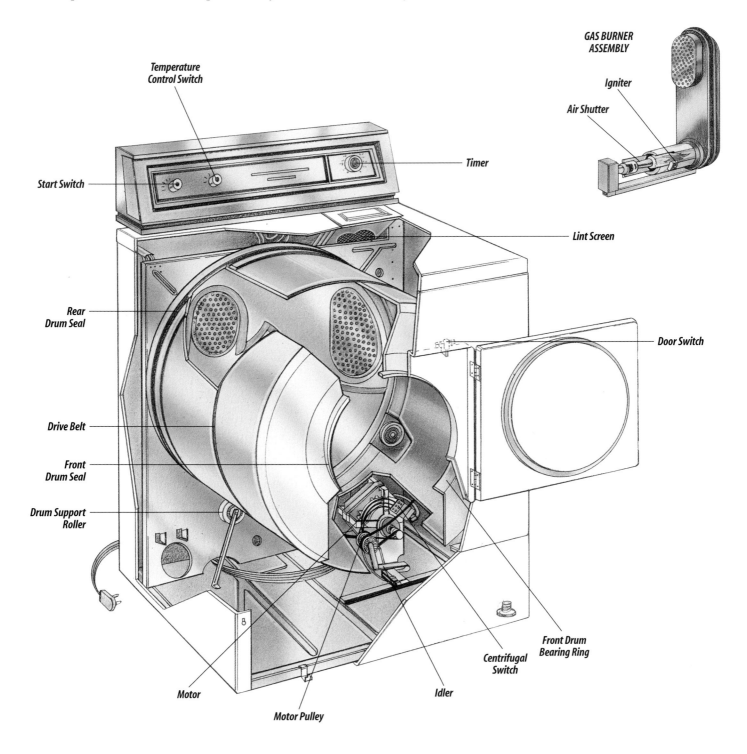

GAS BURNER ASSEMBLY

Igniter

Air Shutter

Temperature Control Switch

Timer

Start Switch

Lint Screen

Rear Drum Seal

Door Switch

Drive Belt

Front Drum Seal

Drum Support Roller

Front Drum Bearing Ring

Centrifugal Switch

Motor

Motor Pulley

Idler

BEFORE YOU START

Diagnosing heating-element problems in an electric dryer is something you can do. But when heat fails in a gas dryer, there is little you can do aside from adjusting the air shutter to obtain the optimum mix of air and gas. Call for service if you have other problems with your gas dryer.

Except for the heat source, dryers are simple machines and remarkably alike. Procedures for repairing one model generally apply to all others as well.

A Gremlin in Your Dryer

The enemy of all dryers is lint. It is pervasive and can coat the moving parts. Even if you clean the filter after every load, lint eventually accumulates around moving parts and in the exhaust duct, forcing the dryer to work harder. Once a year, unplug the dryer, remove the housing, and vacuum the inside.

TIPS

- If your electric dryer runs but doesn't heat, check the main service panel. Your dryer's circuit breaker is a pair, so one may be on and the other tripped.

- If you have a gas dryer, call a technician or the gas company before attempting to move the dryer.

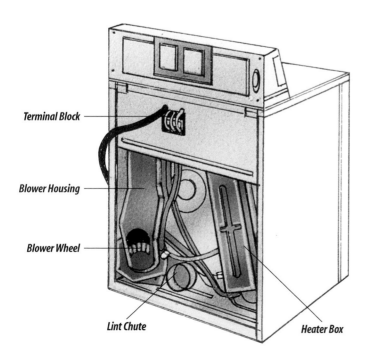

Terminal Block

Blower Housing

Blower Wheel

Lint Chute

Heater Box

If your dryer doesn't run at all

- Check that the dryer is plugged in and check for a blown fuse or tripped circuit breaker
- Inspect the power cord
- Test the door switch **377**
- Test the start switch **376**
- Test the timer and timer motor **376**
- Motor may be malfunctioning—call for service

If the motor runs, but dryer doesn't heat

- Check that the dryer is plugged in and check for a blown fuse or tripped circuit breaker
- Test the temperature selector switch, the timer, and the timer motor **376**
- Test the thermostats **377**
- Test the centrifugal switch **377**
- Replace the heating element **379**

If the motor runs but drum doesn't turn

- Check the drive belt and the idler . . . **378**
- Call for service on the drum

If your dryer runs when the door is open

- Test the door switch **377**

If your dryer will not turn off

- If the room is too cool, the dryer will not work properly
- Test the timer and timer motor **376**
- Test the heating element **379**
- Test the thermostats **377**

If the drying temperature is too hot

- Clean the lint screen
- Clean or unkink the exhaust duct and vent
- Test the thermostats **377**
- Replace the heating element **379**

If your dryer is excessively noisy

- Adjust the leveling feet so the dryer is level
- Tighten any loose screws on the dryer housing and rear panel
- Check the drive belt **378**
- Check the idler **378**

Access to the Controls

1. Freeing the control console

- Unplug the dryer or turn off power to the dryer at the main service panel (page 88).

- Unscrew the console at each end. Some models have screws at the bottom front of the console. Others have screws at the top or sides of the console. In some models, you have to peel back a decorative strip to get at the screws (right).

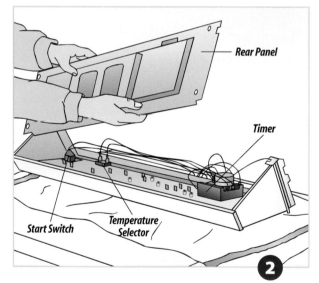

2. Exposing the connections

- Spread a towel on top of the dryer to protect its finish. Lay the console cover facedown on the towel (right).

- If the console has a rear panel, unscrew it to expose the start switch, temperature selector, circuit diagram, and timer.

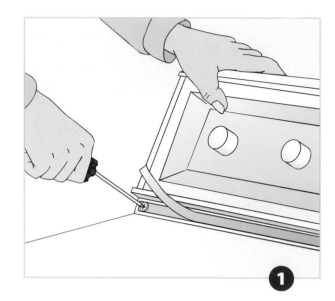

Rear Panel

Timer

Temperature Selector

Start Switch

3. Unlatching the catches

To access the drum, you must remove the top cover of the dryer.

- Unplug the dryer. On an electric dryer with a top-mounted lint screen, pull out the screen and remove the two screws at the front edge of the screen slot.

- Wrap a putty knife with tape, and push it under the top to disengage the hidden clips that hold the top in place (right).

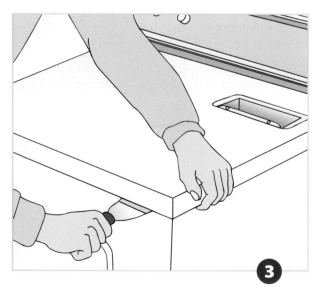

4. Unfastening the rear panel

- Unplug the dryer and disconnect the exhaust duct. Move the dryer away from the wall to expose the rear panel.

- Remove the screws around the panel edges (right), and take the panel off. Some models have more than one panel; remove each as needed.

- If you have a gas dryer that must be disconnected from the gas supply in order to move it, see page 344 for shutting off the gas. Disconnect the gas line, using a pair of channel-joint pliers, only after you are sure the gas is off.

5. Removing the toe panel

- Unplug the dryer and remove any retaining screws.

- Insert a taped putty knife near the center top of the toe panel. Push down and in against the hidden clip while pulling on a corner of the panel (right).

- Lift the panel off the two bottom brackets and remove it.

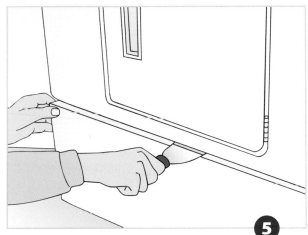

6. Unscrewing the front panel and corner screws

- Raise the top (Step 3) and remove the toe panel (Step 5). Loosen, but do not remove, the screws (if any) at the bottom front corners of the front panel (right).

- Support the drum with blocks of scrap wood so that it won't drop down when you remove the front panel.

- From the inside of the dryer housing, disconnect and label the wires leading to the door switch.

- Supporting the front panel with one hand, remove the screws at each inside corner (inset). Lift the panel off the lower screws or brackets.

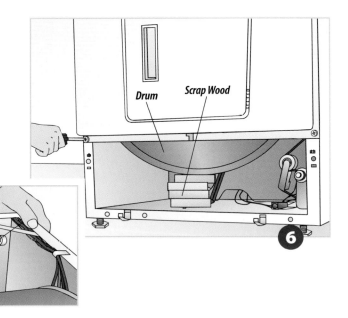

Drum Scrap Wood

Door Switch Wires

Start Switch

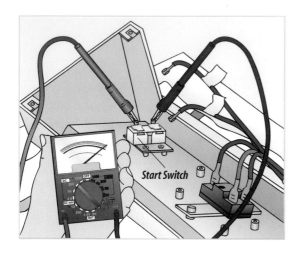

Start Switch

Checking for continuity

- Unplug the dryer and access the control console (page 374). Label and then disconnect the wires from the start switch terminals.

- To test a two-terminal switch (left), set a multitester to RX1 (page 96) and clip one probe to terminal CO (or R2) and the other to NO (or R1). The meter should indicate an open circuit before you press START, and continuity when you press it.

- To test a three-terminal switch, set a multitester to RX1 and clip one probe to terminal NC (or CT1) and the other to CO (or R1). The meter should indicate an open circuit when you press the START button, and continuity when you release it.

- If a switch fails a test, replace it.

Temperature Selector Switch

Testing the switch

Rotary and push-button switches are tested in the same way.

- Unplug the dryer. Free the control console and tilt it forward (page 374). Label and disconnect the wires from the temperature selector switch.

- Check the wiring diagram, located on the back of the dryer, to identify terminals regulating the inoperative cycle. (If you cannot read a wiring diagram, consult a professional who can.)

- Set the knob to the inoperative cycle. Set a multitester to RX1 and touch one probe to each terminal (right). Look for continuity.

- To replace a faulty switch, unscrew the old switch from the control console and install a new switch, transferring the wires.

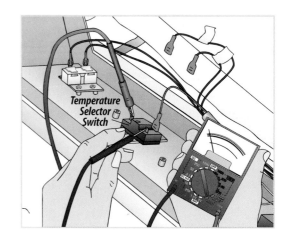

Temperature Selector Switch

Timer

Checking the motor

If you cannot read the dryer's wiring diagram, consult a professional who can.

- Unplug the dryer. Free the control console and tilt it forward (page 374). Disconnect the two wires leading to the timer motor. Set a multitester to RX1000 (page 96). Touch one probe to each lead on the motor wires (right). The tester should read 2,000 to 3,000 ohms of resistance. If you obtain a different result, replace the timer motor.

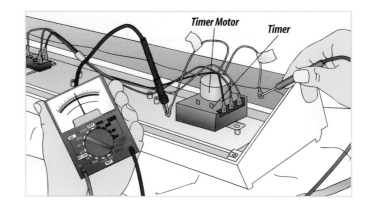

Timer Motor   Timer

Centrifugal Switch

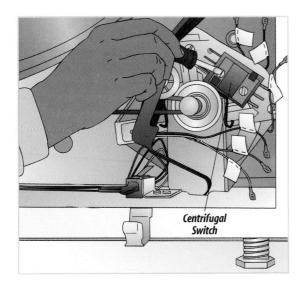

Centrifugal
Switch

Multiple continuity tests

The centrifugal switch is mounted on the motor. How you gain access to it depends on the model.

- Label and disconnect the wires leading to the centrifugal switch, and unscrew the switch from the motor (left).

- Set a multitester to RX1000 (page 96) and place the probes on terminals 1 and 2, then 5 and 6, then 5 and BK (or 3).

- Test with the switch button out, then in, checking for continuity and resistance. Replace the switch if the test results differ from those listed in the chart below.

Terminal Pairs	1–2	5–6	5–BK (3)
Out	Continuity	Continuity	Resistance
In	Resistance	Resistance	Continuity

Door Switch

Checking for continuity

- Raise the dryer top (page 374) and access the door switch, mounted near one of the front corners.

- Label and disconnect the wires from the terminals and set a multitester to RX1 (page 96). Touch a probe to each terminal that was connected to a wire (right); ignore the other terminals.

- When the door is closed, the meter should show continuity. When the door is open, the meter should indicate an open circuit. If results differ, replace the switch.

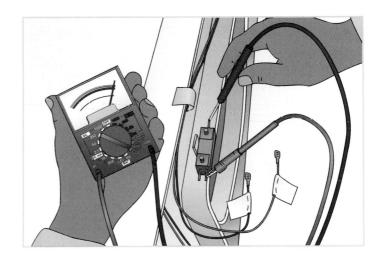

Thermostats and Fuses

Testing the switch inside

The safety fuse and thermostats are located on the blower housing and on the heater box. Test each the same way.

- Unplug the dryer. Label and disconnect the wires from the thermostats and the safety fuse.

- Set a multitester to RX1 (page 96) and touch a probe to each terminal (right). The meter should show continuity. If any thermostat or fuse fails this test, replace it.

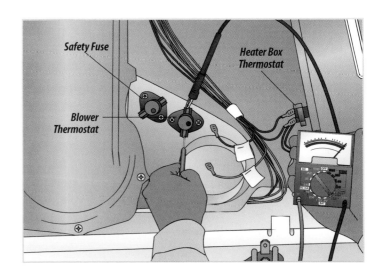

Safety Fuse

Heater Box
Thermostat

Blower
Thermostat

Drive Belt and Idler Pulley

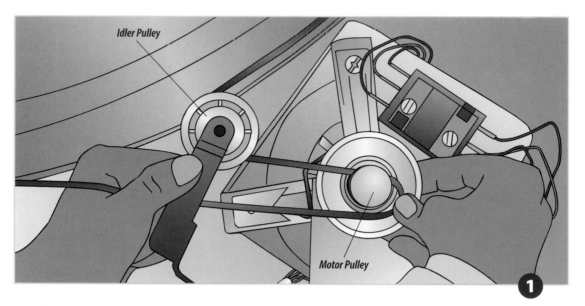

1. Disengaging the belt

To access the idler pulley, remove the top panel, or raise the top and remove the front panel (pages 374–375).

- Prop the dryer drum on a piece of wood. Push the idler pulley toward the motor pulley to slacken the drive belt, then disengage the belt (above).

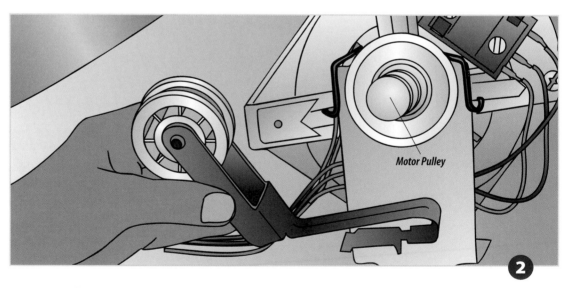

2. Removing the idler

- Inspect the idler bracket, pulley, and spring. One type of idler is held in place in the dryer floor by belt tension (above).

- Another type has a tension spring. Unhook the spring and replace it if it is worn or broken. This type of idler may have a replaceable pulley.

Electric Dryer Heating Elements

1. Checking resistance

- Unplug the dryer and remove the rear panel (page 375). Label and disconnect the wires to the heater terminals.

- Set a multitester to RX1 (page 96). If the heater has two terminals, touch one probe to each terminal (right). The meter should show 5 to 50 ohms.

- If the heater has three terminals, touch one probe to the middle terminal and the other probe to the outer terminals in turn. The meter should read 10 to 40 ohms in each case.

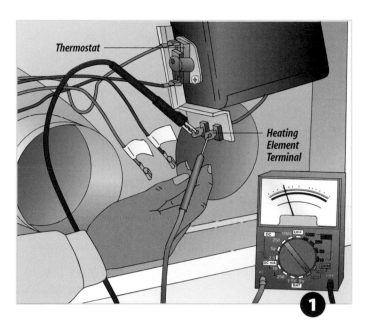

Thermostat

Heating Element Terminal

1

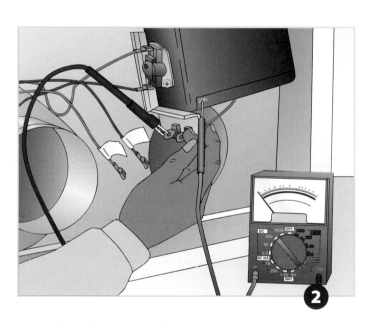

2

2. Testing for ground

- Set a multitester to RX1 and touch one probe to the heater box (above). Touch the other probe to each terminal in turn. The meter should not move.

- If the element fails this test or the test in Step 1, replace it.

Servicing Other Dryer Heat Sources

Some electric dryers have circular heating coils (below left). To replace them, flatten the small tabs with pliers, then pull the terminals through the block and remove the old coil. Stretch the new coil to the same length before installing it.

Gas dryer burners seldom fail. More often, problems occur in the electronic ignition or pilot assembly. Leave these repairs to a professional. But you can adjust the air shutter to admit more or less air: Loosen the thumbscrew and rotate the shutter until the flame is light blue (below right).

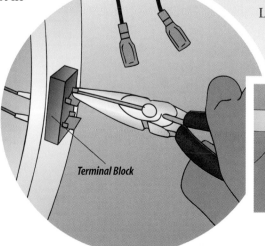

Terminal Block

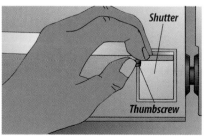

Shutter

Thumbscrew

Home Safety

Contents

INTRODUCTION

Homes today are more comfortable than they ever were. For the most part, they are also safer. We no longer cook over fireplaces that are apt to set the kitchen on fire. We don't drink from inadequate wells, and we have sturdy doors that keep out both the weather and intruders. But it still pays to think about what could happen. In an emergency, the payoff for planning ahead is enormous.

Fire is the single most dangerous threat to a home. Fortunately, it's a simple matter to reduce the risk and prepare yourself and your family. Knowledge is the key—take the time to learn a few simple facts about smoke detectors and how to install them. Plan escape routes in the event of a fire. Learn how to use a fire extinguisher. These simple steps save thousands of lives every day.

There are also invisible chemical threats to your home—radon, carbon monoxide gas, and lead contamination. Knowing how to detect them and how to get them out of your home will keep your family healthy and may save their lives.

And of course, you want to protect your home against intruders. Light the area well. Put locks on the windows, and deadbolts on the doors. To discourage intruders and warn your family, consider a home security system. All the safety and security devices discussed in these pages are available to you through most local home centers or hardware stores.

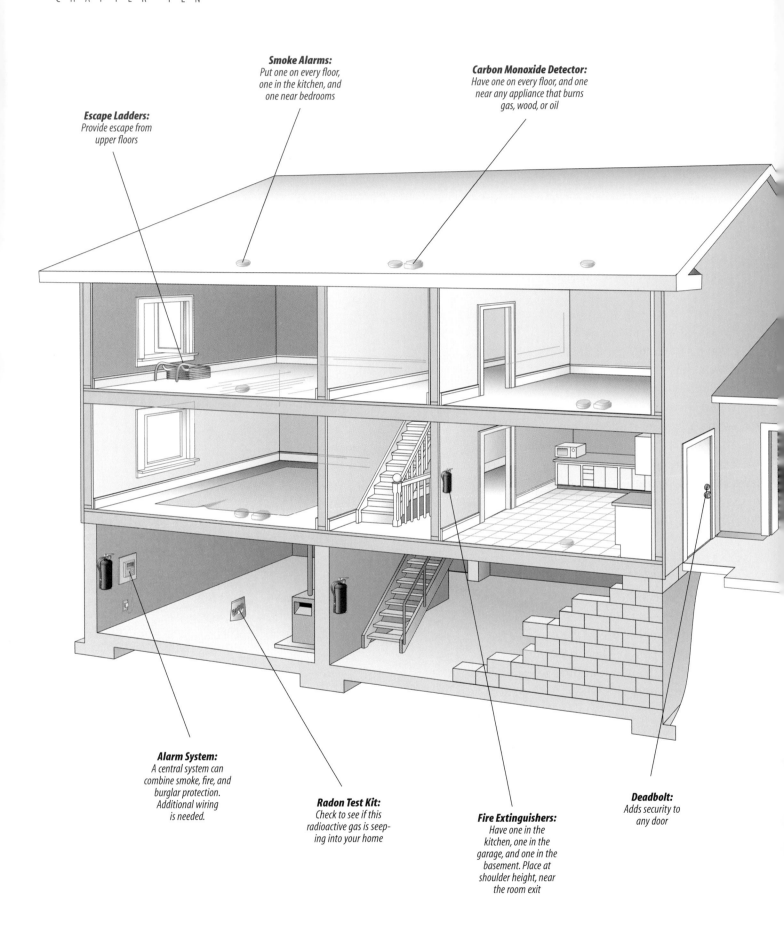

Escape Ladders:
Provide escape from
upper floors

Smoke Alarms:
Put one on every floor,
one in the kitchen, and
one near bedrooms

Carbon Monoxide Detector:
Have one on every floor, and one
near any appliance that burns
gas, wood, or oil

Alarm System:
A central system can
combine smoke, fire, and
burglar protection.
Additional wiring
is needed.

Radon Test Kit:
Check to see if this
radioactive gas is seep-
ing into your home

Fire Extinguishers:
Have one in the
kitchen, one in the
garage, and one in the
basement. Place at
shoulder height, near
the room exit

Deadbolt:
Adds security to
any door

Smoke Detectors

There are two types of smoke detectors, ionization and photoelectric. An ionization smoke detector contains a small amount of radioactive material and uses atomic particles to sense smoke. It's a clever device, but it's prone to false alarms. A photoelectric smoke detector "sees" smoke in the air, using a small beam of light. It is less prone to false alarms and does not contain radioactive material. Both types are approved for home use, although you may have slightly less trouble with the photoelectric variety.

Both types can be powered by batteries, or by "hard-wiring" them to the electric supply. If you hard-wire, make sure there is a battery in the detector to serve as a backup during a temporary loss of power. When hard-wiring smoke detectors, wire them so that when one smoke detector is activated, they all sound the alarm.

Most people don't hard-wire. Battery-powered smoke detectors are easier to install, and as long as you change the battery every six months, they are quite reliable. You can also purchase detectors that have a built-in emergency light that automatically comes on when the alarm is sounded. This can be a godsend in an emergency. When seconds count, you don't want to waste them searching for a light switch in the smoke.

Where to Put a Battery-Type Smoke Detector

As a rule of thumb, smoke detectors should be located on the ceiling or near the top of the wall in each story of the house. Upstairs, the detector should be installed on a wall or ceiling near the top of the stairs. Check to see whether you can hear this detector through closed bedroom doors. If not, install an additional detector close enough that you can hear it when the door is closed.

You should also have a smoke detector in the kitchen. To prevent false alarms, get a photoelectric detector. Better yet, get a combination ionization/photoelectric detector. It'll respond quickly in case of a real fire, but the ion detector has been made slightly less sensitive and is less likely to cause false alarms.

How you install a smoke detector depends on the detector you purchase—they all come with installation instructions. Screws alone will tear out plaster and drywall, so if you're mounting the unit in either of these, use the anchors that come with the alarm. (If there aren't any

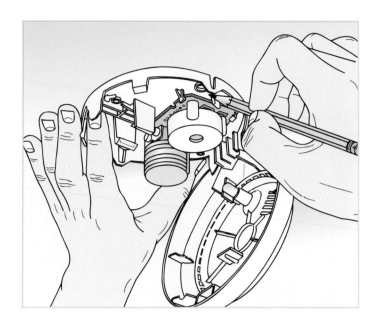

anchors with the alarm, take it to a hardware store or home center, and have someone help you get the right size and kind.)

Most alarms are simple to install:

- Open the unit. Using the back as a template, mark the wall or ceiling for the anchors and screws (above). (Anchors are not required when installing directly to a wood surface.)

- Wearing safety goggles, bore holes for the anchors using the appropriate size bit for the anchor. Put tape on the drill bit to mark the anchor length, and stop drilling when the tape brushes against the wall or ceiling.

- Tap the anchors in place with a hammer so they are flush with the wall or ceiling. Put a screw in one anchor, and drive it until the head protrudes only about $\frac{1}{8}$ inch.

- Hang the smoke detector by sliding the slot in the detector over and behind the screw you installed. This will hold the detector while you position it. Once you've positioned the detector, drive the remaining screw into the anchor. Tighten all of the screws.

- Install the battery, close the smoke detector cover, and test the detector.

(CONTINUED)

Smoke Detectors—continued

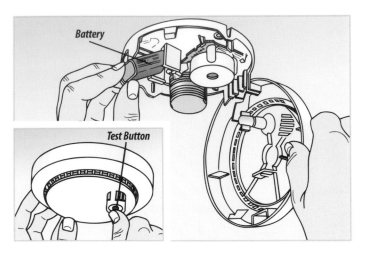

Battery

Test Button

Testing and Replacing Batteries

Smoke detectors should be tested weekly. To test a detector, press the test button (inset) or buy a can of smoke detector aerosol and spray it toward the vents. Replace the battery if the smoke detector does not sound when it is tested. Most smoke detectors emit chirping sounds when the battery is weak. If your detector is chirping, replace the battery immediately. If for any reason you are not sure whether or not your smoke detector is working properly, replace the detector with a new one.

Batteries should be replaced periodically, even if the detector is not chirping. The standard wisdom is to replace them in the spring and fall, when most people change from standard time to daylight savings time and back again. To replace a battery, open the smoke detector case and pull the old battery out (above). Be gentle when removing batteries so that you do not damage the detector. Replace the battery with an exact duplicate. The detector may sound when the new battery is installed to let you know it works. Close the cover and test the smoke detector.

Cleaning a smoke detector

Smoke detectors should be cleaned every six months, when you change the batteries. Dirt and debris can interfere with the detector's ability to detect smoke. They may also lead to false alarms. Keep the vents clear by using a brush head on a vacuum cleaner to gently clean the outside of the detector. You can also open the detector to clean the inside of the cover. After cleaning the detector, test it.

Testing for Radon Gas

Radon gas is produced by uranium decay deep in the ground. You cannot see it or smell it. It can migrate up through the soil and into your home through any crack or crevice under the house. Radon can also leach into a house through a well, if you have one. Exposure to radon can cause lung cancer and is the second leading cause of lung cancer in the United States, after smoking.

Testing for Radon Gas

If you suspect radon in your home, purchase a radon test kit at your local home center. Set up the test following the instructions provided. Generally speaking, they will call for you to place the detector on the lowest level of your house about 20 inches from the floor and 4 inches from any object. Avoid placing it near any heat source or in a draft. Mark the kit identification number, setup date, and setup location on the log sheet provided with the kit. When the test period ends, remove the kit and seal it in the storage packet provided with it. Record the retrieval date on the log sheet and return it with the storage packet to the manufacturer for analysis.

If test results show that you have an unacceptable level of radon in your home, test again. If the results are still high, you need to take steps to combat the radon.

Getting Rid of Radon

Some solutions are simple. Carefully seal any cracks or crevices in the foundation and around utility pipes. Seal any crack in concrete block (if applicable). If you have a dirt basement or crawl space, cover it with plastic at least 6 mils thick. Run the plastic up the basement or crawl space walls a couple of feet and secure it so that there are no gaps around the perimeter.

The Environmental Protection Agency, however, says that simple solutions usually aren't enough. Other solutions are more technical and require a trained technician. "Sub slab depressurization," one of the most important tools in removing radon, involves piping air from under the basement floor, and venting it into the air. To remove radon from a well, you have two options: a high-capacity activated-charcoal filter, or an aeration system on your well that forces the radon out by introducing oxygen into the water. Most states license radon contractors. Contact your state health department for information.

Dealing with Lead

Lead is a soft metal with a low melting point. It was once added to paint to make it more durable. Because it was easily worked, some pipes were made entirely of lead. And because of its low melting point, lead was a key ingredient in plumbing solder. As a result, lead is common in most older homes, where it can lead to lead poisoning. Symptoms of lead poisoning include loss of appetite, fatigue, insomnia, constipation or diarrhea, and joint and abdominal pain. Lead poisoning can cause brain damage and is especially a threat to young children.

Lead in the Water

Lead can leach from copper and brass pipe fittings where it was used in the solder to join pipe together. Lead in pipe solder was banned in 1986, and homes constructed after that should not contain lead solder. If you suspect lead in your water, contact your state health department and ask where you can have your water tested for lead content. They will point you to a lab in your area where you can send a sample. If they find contamination, arrange to have your entire plumbing system checked, and replace the pipes or joints containing lead.

To identify a lead pipe, poke it with a screwdriver. If it dents easily, it's lead. Hire a plumber to replace it.

Lead Paint

Lead was also used as an ingredient in paint until the 1970s, when it was outlawed. It is especially dangerous to small children who breathe in the dust from the deteriorating paint, or who may eat old, chipping paint. The simplest treatment, and a very effective one, is to paint over the lead paint with either latex or alkyd paint. This seals off the problem—and only lead paint that can be ingested or inhaled is dangerous.

Wherever paint is likely to chip off—such as on windows and doorways—scrape away the old paint and clean up before painting.

If you have concerns about exposed lead paint in your home, call a lead abatement contractor to have it tested.

Asbestos

Asbestos is a fire- and corrosion-resistant material that has been linked to certain types of cancers. It was banned in the 1970s but can still be found in old wall spackling, pipe insulation, floor and ceiling tiles, exterior siding, and roofing that were installed before the ban. If left undisturbed, asbestos may not be dangerous. If it's cut, flaking, or deteriorating, however, it releases dangerous particles into the air. If you live in a house built before 1970 and suspect that it contains asbestos, call a professional to inspect your home. You cannot clean up asbestos yourself without risk of exposure.

Fighting Fires

A fire extinguisher is an important piece of safety equipment, and no home should be without one. However, you must remember that the first thing to do in the event of a fire, no matter how small, is to call the fire department or 911. You may not be able to put out the fire with the extinguisher, and you don't want to find out when it's too late. Also, a fire that you think is out can rekindle or smolder and start again. Call the professionals first. Then, if you do manage to stop the blaze, wait for them to check it and give you the all clear.

TYPES OF FIRES

Fires come in all shapes and sizes. Each burns differently, and you have to fight each type differently. Combating a stove-top grease fire the same way you would fight a brush fire could prove disastrous. Use the following guidelines to fight each type of fire. Remember, if it looks dangerous, get out, and wait for the fire department.

Kitchen Fires

In case of an oven fire, close the oven door and turn the oven off. Oxygen feeds a fire, and closing the door deprives it of oxygen. This will usually extinguish the fire.

If a pan or skillet catches fire, cover it with a lid and turn off the heat. This deprives the fire of oxygen and smothers it. If a lid is not handy, pour dry salt or baking soda over the pan to extinguish the fire, being careful not to splash grease or cooking oils out of the pan. Never try to use flour or baking powder (rather than baking soda) to extinguish a fire—these substances may catch fire themselves. Don't ever use water on a grease (or electrical) fire. This can spread the fire. Your best bet is always to cut off the fire's oxygen by putting a lid on it, or by using dry, nonflammable substances.

Furniture Fires

Smother fires in fabric and upholstery by covering them with a thick blanket, a sheet, or a towel. If you can, wet the sheet or towel to keep it from catching fire, too. Once the fire is out, douse the fabric with water to prevent the fire from erupting again. Noxious fumes can be released by burning upholstery or mattresses, so ventilate the area after the fire is out. As soon as possible, carry or drag the fabric or upholstery out of the home and well away from it.

Clothing Fires

If your clothes catch fire, *stop, drop, and roll.* Running or even walking for help will fan the flames. Fall on the ground, and roll around to smother the flames. If you can reach a blanket, towel, or rug while rolling, wrap yourself in it to help cut off the supply of oxygen to the flames. Once the flames are out, stay covered up and get help. If someone else's clothes catch fire, force them to the ground and roll them. Try to cover them up with anything you can. Keep them covered until emergency help arrives. Never throw water on a person whose clothes are on fire—the steam that's produced when the water hits the flames could sear their lungs.

FIRE EXTINGUISHERS

Most home fires can be extinguished with portable fire extinguishers, allowing you fight the fire from a safe distance. There are three classes of fires and fire extinguishers:

- Class A fires are fed by solid fuel, like wood or paper.
- Class B fires are fed by liquids, such as gasoline or grease.
- Class C fires are live electrical fires.

You can buy a class ABC fire extinguisher, which will combat all three types of fires. Keep one extinguisher in your kitchen where you can reach it easily, and keep another one in the basement. Keep one within easy reach in the garage. Mount extinguishers in open view at shoulder level near an exit, away from the possible source of a fire. An extinguisher mounted next to the stove is useless if a stove fire keeps you from reaching it.

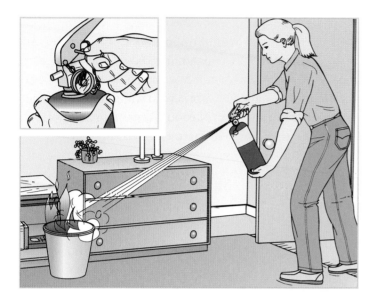

Using a Fire Extinguisher

In case of a fire, call the fire department first. Then take the fire extinguisher from the holder and set it on a solid surface. Remove the lock pin with one hand as you steady the extinguisher with the other (inset above). With one hand on the release trigger of the fire extinguisher and the other directing the nozzle, stand 6 to 10 feet from the fire with your back to an exit. Squeeze the trigger and spray the base of the fire with a side-to-side motion (above). Spray until the fire is completely extinguished. Watch carefully for any signs that the fire is still smoldering, keeping the extinguisher ready until help arrives. If the flames get out of control, or the extinguisher empties before you have put out the fire, leave the building immediately.

Make sure your fire extinguishers are recharged after any use. Check them every six months, or as directed, to be sure they have stayed charged.

FIRE ESCAPE LADDER

A portable ladder can help you escape from a second or third story in the event of a fire. The ladder below is typical. In case of fire, you hook it over the windowsill, and then drop the rungs and the supporting chain out the window. If the ladder snags on something, shake the chain to loosen the snag. If it persists, bring the rungs and chain back up, remove the snag, and lower the ladder again. Check that the hook is secure on the windowsill, and then carefully climb out. If smoke and fire block your path out the window or down the ladder, wait for help.

You can also install a permanent safety ladder that bolts to the floor below a window. This type of ladder stores in a box. In the event of a fire, you open the box and let the ladder out of the window. No need to worry about whether the ladder is properly hooked over the windowsill—just climb out and let the bolts hold the ladder as you descend.

Installing Deadbolt Locks

Increase the security of your exterior doors by installing deadbolt locks. When you lock the deadbolt, a metal rod slides from the door through the jamb, creating a lock that is almost impossible to disengage from the outside.

To install or replace a deadbolt, first take some measurements. If replacing the lock, measure the distance between the door edge and the keyhole (called the lock's backset). Get a lock with the same backset when you buy a replacement. If you are installing a new deadbolt, you have a choice of backsets. Common backset dimensions are 2⅜-inch and 2¾-inch. In addition to the backset, you'll need to know the thickness of your door. Most new locksets will fit 1⅜-inch- or 1¾-inch-thick doors.

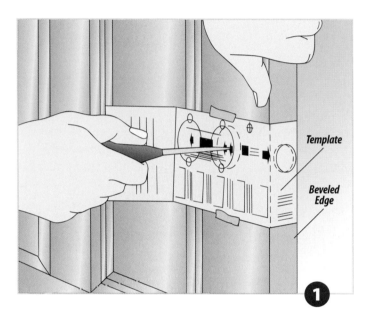

Template

Beveled Edge

1

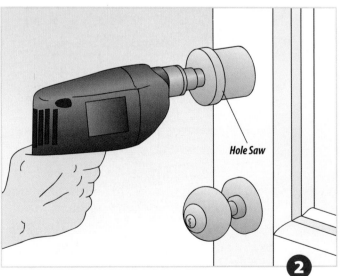

Hole Saw

2

1. Mark the holes for the cylinder and bolt

- Most locks come with instructions and a paper template to help you lay out the holes you'll need to drill. Read the instructions before you start.

- Position the paper template on the door, and tape it in place. Using an awl, mark the locations of the center of the holes. Mark both the door edge for the bolt and the door face for the cylinder assembly.

2. Drill the holes

- Wedge the door in place with shims at the bottom so it will hold steady while you drill. Check the directions for the size hole required, and put the appropriate hole saw in the drill. Center the hole saw over the mark and begin cutting slowly through the door. Check and recheck the drill from above and from the side to make sure you are drilling perpendicular to the door.

- As soon as the pilot bit on the hole saw protrudes from the opposite side of the door, stop drilling, move to the other side, and finish the hole from there. This will reduce tear-out and splintering.

3. Bore the bolt hole

- The bolt hole needs to be perpendicular to the edge of the door, so use a drill guide for this operation. Check the directions for the size of the hole. Using the proper size spade or Forstner bit, bore the bolt hole. As you finish drilling the hole, be careful to hold the drill steady to prevent excessive tear-out in the cylinder hole.

- Clean both holes of all debris. Insert the bolt assembly into the hole in the edge of the door. With the bolt assembly in place, mark the recess for the plate on the edge of the door, tracing around it with a utility knife. Score the wood inside the lines with a utility knife, and carefully pare away the wood with a chisel until the plate fits flush in the recess.

- Screw the bolt assembly in place. Test to make sure it works by slipping a screwdriver in the slot for the knob and turning the screwdriver.

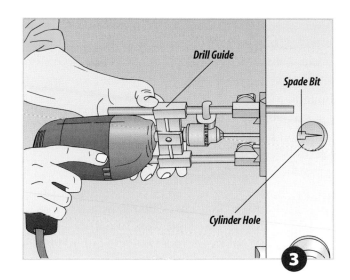

4. Install the cylinder

- Put the cylinder housing on the outside of the door.

- Put the retaining plate against the cylinder hole on the inside of the door, and screw it through the door into the back of the cylinder housing. Attach the knob.

- Check that the lock works with the door open before installing the strike plate.

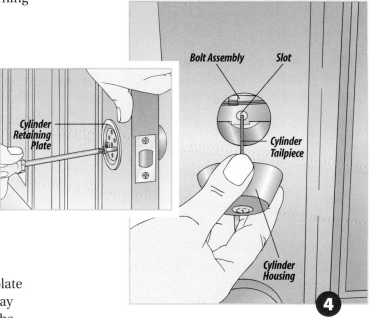

5. Bore the strike hole and attach the strike plate

- When you lock the deadbolt, it travels through a strike plate into a hole you've drilled in the doorjamb. The easiest way to lay out the hole is to rub some lipstick on the end of the deadbolt. Retract the bolt, close the door, and turn the key to force the bolt against the doorjamb.

- Position the strike plate over the resulting smudge on the jamb. Trace around the plate and the opening in it with utility knife. Drill the bolt hole in the jamb using the appropriate bit (⅛ inch larger than the bolt diameter in most cases).

- With a utility knife, score the wood inside the outline you made of the strike plate. Chip away the wood with a chisel to create a recess for the strike plate.

- Pre-drill for the screws that secure the strike plate. Most lock kits come with 3-inch screws that penetrate the stud behind the doorjamb. It will be difficult to drive these screws without drilling pilot holes.

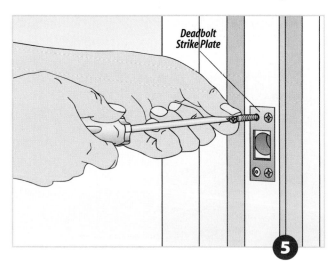

Alarm Systems

Alarm systems alert you and the police that someone is trying to break into your home. They are relatively inexpensive and easy to install. The simplest versions are battery-powered and self-contained. You can attach them to a door or window so that they sound when the door or window is opened.

Hard-Wired Alarm Systems

Some systems combine smoke and fire alarms with a burglar alarm. There is a central control unit, usually powered by the home electrical system, and a battery backup. These systems have a variety of sensors, including contacts on windows and doors, pressure-sensitive doormats, and ultrasonic or heat-sensitive motion detectors.

Planning for a Security System

When planning a security system, work from the outside in. Start with security lighting around the exterior of the home. Motion detector lights are easy to install and effectively discourage most would-be intruders. Next, plan to install simple alarms on windows and exterior doors that are accessible from the ground. Once you've secured the ground level, consider expanding the system to protect second- and third-story entrances against really determined burglars.

The Family Dog Is Your Best Defense

A family dog can be the best security system you can buy. You can train a dog to sound the alarm for any intrusion or threat. False alarms are easy to deal with if the dog is well trained—just tell the dog to stop barking. Without question, statistics prove that break-ins occur more often in homes without watchdogs.

Carbon Monoxide

Carbon monoxide is an odorless, invisible gas that can build up in a home and cause dizziness, nausea, and even death. It's usually the result of improperly burning wood, gas, or oil, or is the result of improperly venting the fumes. It is easily detected by a carbon monoxide detector.

Installing and Using a Carbon Monoxide Detector

Carbon monoxide detectors, like smoke detectors, can be battery-powered or hard-wired. (Some models simply plug into an existing outlet.) Install them on every floor of the home, especially in any room with an oil-, gas-, or wood-burning appliance. Place the detector somewhere between outlet level and 6 feet off of the ground, with no obstructions within a 3-foot radius. Do not put them within 15 feet of a furnace, gas stove, or other gas appliance. Test the detector once a month and replace the battery every six months. Replace the battery if the detector emits a chirping sound—this indicates that the battery is low. If your detector sounds the alarm, call the fire department immediately and evacuate the home.

Index

Time-Life Books is a division of Time Life Inc.

TIME LIFE INC.

Chairman and CEO	Jim Nelson
President and COO	Steven L. Janas

TIME-LIFE TRADE PUBLISHING

Vice President and Publisher	Neil Levin
Vice President of Content Development	Jennifer Pearce
Director of New Product Development	Carolyn Clark
Director of Marketing	Inger Forland
Director of Trade Sales	Dana Hobson
Director of Custom Publishing	John Lalor
Director of Special Markets	Robert Lombardi
Director of Design	Kate L. McConnell

HOME & GARDEN TELEVISION'S COMPLETE FIX-IT

Project Editor	Jennie Halfant
Technical Specialist	Monika Lynde
Production Manager	Carolyn Bounds
Quality Assurance	Jim King, Stacy L. Eddy

Designed by Gibson Design Associates, Charlottesville, Virginia
New illustrations by Michael J. Powers and Will Cypser.
Illustration adaptations by Mary Michaela Murray, Sara Dean, Jim Gibson,
Christine Orlando, Charles Peale, and Richard Rumble.

Heartwood Books Staff

Executive Editor	Jeff Day
Managing Editor	Steve Cory
Editor	Nick Engler
Writer	Adam Blake
Copy Editor	Barbara M. Webb
Indexer	Nan Badgett

Printed in the United States
10 9 8 7 6 5 4 3 2

TIME-LIFE is a trademark of Time Warner Inc. and affiliated companies.

Library of Congress Cataloging-in-Publication Data
Home & garden television's complete fix-it.
    p.   cm.
    Includes index.
        ISBN 0-7370-0315-4 (hardcover) — ISBN 0-7370-0316-2 (softcover : alk. paper)
    1. Dwellings—Maintenance and repair—Amateurs' manuals. 2. Household appliances—Maintenance and repair—Amateurs' manuals. I. Time-Life Books.
TH4817.3 .C623 2000
643'.7—dc21   00-044742

ISBN 0-7370-0315-4

Books produced by Time-Life Trade Publishing are available at a special bulk discount for promotional and premium use. Custom adaptations can also be created to meet your specific marketing goals. Call 1-800-323-5255.

> **NOTE**: Every effort has been taken to ensure that all information in this book is correct and compatible with national standards generally accepted at the time of publication. This book is not intended to replace manufacturers' instructions in the use of their tools or materials — always follow their safety guidelines. The authors and publishers disclaim any liability for loss, injury, or damage incurred as a consequence, directly or indirectly, of the use and application of the contents of this book.
>
> **You can find more great home improvement ideas at www.hgtv.com**